Making the GRADE

Everything Your 6th Grader Needs to Know

by
Carol Karton

BARRON'S

About the Author

Carol Karton began her career as a sixth-grade teacher in Illinois. For more than 20 years Carol has been creating middle-school math, science, social studies, and language arts programs closely correlated to state and national standards, including an award-winning spelling program. Carol holds a B.A. in English from the University of Michigan, an M.A. in English from Northwestern University, and an Illinois Teaching Certificate. Carol has been included in *Who's Who of American Women.*

All inquiries should be addressed to:
Barron's Educational Series, Inc.
250 Wireless Boulevard
Hauppauge, New York 11788
http://www.barronseduc.com

Library of Congress Catalog Card No. 2002043985

International Standard Book No. 0-7641-2483-8

Library of Congress Cataloging-in-Publication Data
Karton, Carol.
    Making the Grade: Everything Your 6th Grader Needs to Know / Carol Karton.
        p. cm.
    At head of title: Barron's
    Includes bibliographical references and index.
    ISBN 0-7641-2483-8 (alk. paper)
    1. Sixth grade (Education)—United States—Curricula—Handbooks,
manuals, etc. 2. Home schooling—United States—Curricula—Handbooks,
manuals, etc. 3. Curriculum planning—United States—Handbooks, manuals,
etc. I. Title: Barron's Making the Grade. Grade 6. II. Title.

LB15716th .K37 2003
372.19—dc21   2002043985

Printed in Hong Kong
9 8 7 6 5 4 3 2 1

Table of Contents

How to Use This Book vii

For Homeschoolers xi

Communicating Between Home and School xvii

Meet Your Sixth Grader xix

 1

Lesson 1.1   Reading Fiction 3

Lesson 1.2   Exploring Short Stories 13

Lesson 1.3   Investigating Oral Traditions of Folktales 23

Lesson 1.4   Exploring and Analyzing Biographies 31

Lesson 1.5   Reading and Writing Poetry 39

Lesson 1.6   Appreciating Drama 45

Lesson 1.7   Listening and Notetaking Effectively 55

Lesson 1.8   Researching and Reference Using
                 MLA Style 63

Lesson 1.9   Editing and Publishing 67

                 In Your Community 75

                 We Have Learned Checklist 76

MATH

. . . . 77

Lesson 2.1 Making Sense of Number Theory 79

Lesson 2.2 Using Fractions and Estimation 83

Lesson 2.3 Working with Decimals 91

Lesson 2.4 Using Percents 99

Lesson 2.5 Understanding and Using Ratios,
Proportions, and Probability 105

Lesson 2.6 Interpreting Data, Statistics, and Graphs 111

Lesson 2.7 Exploring Integers 119

Lesson 2.8 Learning About Measurements 125

Lesson 2.9 Understanding Perimeter, Area,
and Volume 133

Lesson 2.10 Comprehending Geometry and
Motion Geometry 139

In Your Community 149

We Have Learned Checklist 150

SCIENCE

. . . . 151

Lesson 3.1 Classifying Living Things 153

Lesson 3.2 Exploring the Plant Kingdom 161

Lesson 3.3 Exploring the World of Cells, Genetics,
and Microscopes 169

Lesson 3.4 Understanding Systems of the
Human Body 177

Lesson 3.5   Exploring Human Health and Growth 187

Lesson 3.6   Using the Scientific Method 191

Lesson 3.7   Exploring Earth's Living Systems 195

Lesson 3.8   Digging into Earth's Surface 201

Lesson 3.9   Exploring the Universe 207

Lesson 3.10 Understanding Energy 211

Lesson 3.11 Discovering Sound and Light 217

Lesson 3.12 Understanding Matter 221

   In Your Community 227

We Have Learned Checklist 228

SOCIAL STUDIES 229

Lesson 4.1   Exploring the Contributions of
Ancient Civilizations 231

Lesson 4.2   Discovering Ancient Egypt 237

Lesson 4.3   Exploring Asian and African Cultures 243

Lesson 4.4   Discovering Ancient Greece and Rome 249

Lesson 4.5   Investigating Feudal Europe in the
Middle Ages 255

Lesson 4.6   Investigating the Church and the Rise
of Monarchies   261

Lesson 4.7   Exploring the Beginnings of
Modern Society 265

Lesson 4.8   Investigating the Causes and Effects
of the Reformation 271

Lesson 4.9 Exploring the Seas, the Skies, and
the Mind 275

Lesson 4.10 Tuning In to the Industrial Revolution 281

Lesson 4.11 Understanding Contemporary Conflicts 287

In Your Community 293

We Have Learned Checklist 294

Assessment 295

Assessment Answers 335

Answers 341

Glossary 351

Venn Diagram 353

Comparison Chart 353

Web 354

Sequence Chain 354

Grid 355

Index 356

Credits 362

How to Use This Book

Welcome to the *Making the Grade* series! These seven books offer tools and strategies for hands-on, active learning at the kindergarten through sixth-grade levels. Each book presents real-world, engaging learning experiences in the core areas of language arts, math, science, and social studies at age-appropriate levels.

Who should use this book?

Whether you're a stay-at-home or working parent with children in school, a homeschooler who's taking control of your children's education, or a teacher who's looking for additional ideas to supplement classroom learning experiences, this book is for you.

- If you have children in school, *Making the Grade* can be used in conjunction with your child's curriculum because it offers real-world, hands-on activities that exercise the concepts and topics he or she is being taught in school.
- If you're a homeschooler who's taking control of your children's education, this series presents you with easy-to-access, engaging ways to interact with your child.
- If you're a teacher, this book also can be a source for additional activities.

This book is your passport to a whole new world, one that gives you enough support to be a successful "teacher" while encouraging independent learning with one child or shared learning among your children.

What is *Making the Grade*?

We're glad you asked! First, we'd like to tell you what it's not. It's not a textbook series. Rather, each book in the series delivers age-appropriate content in language arts, math, science, and social studies in an open-ended, flexible manner that incorporates the "real" world. You can use this book as a supplement to your core learning instruction or use it to get a jump start on the fundamentals.

Each subject section presents lessons comprised of both "teaching" pages and "student" pages. And each book in the *Making the Grade* series is perforated for flexible learning so that both you and your child can tear out the pages that you're working on and use one book together.

How do the lessons work?

The teaching and student pages work together. The lesson instruction and teaching ideas for each specific lesson appear first. Then activities that offer opportunities for your child to practice the specific skills and review the concepts being taught follow. Creativity and imagination abound! Throughout each lesson, hands-on activities are incorporated using concepts that are meaningful and relevant to kids' daily lives. The activities account for all kinds of learners—that is, visual, auditory, or kinesthetic learning. For more information on learning styles, see the Glossary on page 351.

Objective and Background

Each lesson opens with an objective that tells you exactly what the lesson is about. The background of the lesson follows, giving you the rationale behind the importance of the material being addressed. Each lesson is broken down for you so that you and your student can see how the skills and concepts taught are useful in everyday situations.

Materials and Vocabulary

Have you ever done a project and found out you're missing something when you get to the end? A list of materials is given up front so you'll know what you need before you begin. The lessons take into account that you have access to your local library, a computer and the Internet, writing instruments, a calculator, and a notebook and loose paper, so you won't find these listed. The materials are household items when possible so that even the most technical of science experiments can be done easily. The *Making the Grade* series paves the way for your learning experience whether you and your student are sitting side by side on the couch or in a classroom, at the library, or even on vacation!

Following the materials list, vocabulary words may be given offering clear, easy-to-understand definitions.

Let's Begin

Let's Begin is just that, "Let's Begin!" The instructional portion of the lesson opens with easy, user-friendly, numbered steps that guide you through the teaching of a particular lesson. Here you'll find opportunities to interact with your student and engage in discussions about what he or she is learning. There also are opportunities for your student to practice his or her critical-thinking skills to make the learning experience richer.

In the margins are interesting facts about what you're studying, time-savers, or helpful ideas.

Ways to Extend the Lesson

Every lesson concludes with ways to extend the lesson—teaching tips, such as hints, suggestions, or ideas, for you to use in teaching the lesson or a section of the lesson. Each lesson also ends with an opportunity for you to "check in" and assess how well your student has mastered the skill or grasped the concepts being taught in the lesson. The For Further Reading section lists books that you can use as additional references and support in teaching the lesson. It also offers your student more opportunities to practice a skill or a chance to look deeper into the content.

Student Learning Pages

Student Learning Pages immediately follow the teaching pages in each lesson. These pages offer fun opportunities to practice the skills and concepts being taught. And there are places where your student gets to choose what to do next and take ownership of his or her learning!

Visual Aids

Throughout the book, you'll see references to the Venn Diagram, Comparison Chart, Web, Sequence Chain, and Grid found in the back of the book. Many lessons incorporate these graphic organizers, or visual methods of organizing information, into the learning. If one is used in a lesson, it will be listed in the materials so that prior to the lesson you or your student can make a photocopy of it from the back of the book or you can have your student copy it into his or her notebook. See the Glossary for more information on graphic organizers.

What about field trips or learning outside the classroom?

One very unique feature of the *Making the Grade* series is the In Your Community activities at the end of each subject section. These activities describe ways to explore your community, taking advantage of your local or regional culture, industry, and environment while incorporating the skills learned in the lessons. For example, you can have your student help out at a farmer's market or with a local environmental group. These unique activities can supplement your ability to provide support for subjects. The activities give your student life experiences upon which he or she can build and expand the canvas upon which he or she learns.

These pages are identified in the Table of Contents so that you can read them first as a way to frame your student's learning.

How do I know if my student is learning the necessary skills?

Although each lesson offers an opportunity for on-the-spot assessment, a formalized assessment section is located in the back of this book. You'll find a combination of multiple-choice and open-ended questions testing your student on the skills, concepts, and topics covered.

Also, at the end of every subject section is a We Have Learned checklist. This checklist provides a way for you and your student to summarize what you've accomplished. It lists specific concepts, and there is additional space for you and your student to write in other topics you've covered.

Does this book come with answers?

Yes. Answers are provided in the back of the book for both the lessons and assessment.

What if this book uses a homeschooling or educational term I'm not familiar with?

In addition to the vocabulary words listed in the lessons, a two-page Glossary is provided in the back of the book. Occasionally terms will surface that may need further explanation in order for the learning experience to flourish. In the Glossary, you'll find terms explained simply to help you give your student a rewarding learning experience free from confusion.

Will this book help me find resources within the schools for homeschoolers?

In Communicating Between Home and School, there are suggestions for how to take advantage of the opportunities and resources offered by your local schools and how these benefits can enhance your homeschooling learning experiences.

I'm new to homeschooling. How can I find out about state regulations, curriculum, and other resources?

In For Homeschoolers at the beginning of the book, you'll find information about national and state legislation, resources for curriculum and materials, and other references. Also included is a comprehensive list of online resources for everything from homeschooling organizations to military homeschooling to homeschooling supplies.

How can I use this book if my student attends a public or private school?

Making the Grade fits into any child's educational experience—whether he or she is being taught at home or in a traditional school setting.

For Homeschoolers

Teaching children at home isn't a new phenomenon. But it's gaining in popularity as caregivers decide to take a more active role in the education of their children. And despite prejudices that still exist, homeschoolers regularly succeed in college, the workplace, and in society.

Whether you're new to homeschooling or have been educating your children at home for quite some time, you've probably found that the homeschooling path can be riddled with detours and unhelpful information. This book hopes to minimize those detours by offering information on state regulations, homeschooling approaches and curriculum, and other resources to keep you on the path toward a rewarding learning experience.

Regulations

There never has been a federal law prohibiting parents from homeschooling their children. A homeschooler isn't required to have a teaching degree, nor is he or she required to teach children in a specific location. Nonetheless, each state has its own set of regulations, educational requirements, and guidelines for those who homeschool.

Some states and areas of the United States have stricter regulations than others. Alabama; Alaska; Arizona; California; Delaware; Guam; Idaho; Illinois; Indiana; Kansas; Kentucky; Michigan; Mississippi; Missouri; Montana; Nebraska; New Jersey; New Mexico; Oklahoma; Puerto Rico; Texas; Virgin Islands; Washington, D.C; Wisconsin; and Wyoming are considered to have a low level of regulation. Maine, Massachusetts, Minnesota, Nevada, New York, North Dakota, Pennsylvania, Rhode Island, Utah, Vermont, Washington, and West Virginia are considered to have a high level of regulation. The remaining states and areas not mentioned are considered to have a moderate level of homeschooling regulation.

But what do low, moderate, and high regulation mean? These classifications indicate the level of regulation that a particular state can enforce upon someone who has chosen to teach a child at home. Within each of these levels, there also are varying rules and laws.

These regulations begin with how to enter the world of homeschooling. Some states, such as New Jersey, don't require parents to notify the school of their intent to teach their children at home, yet a letter of intent often is submitted out of courtesy. New Jersey's regulations note that all children of compulsory school age must be in an instructional program equivalent to that provided in the public schools. In Texas, another state that's considered to have a low level of regulation, parents don't have to notify anyone of their intent to homeschool their children. Texas homeschools are considered private schools and aren't subject to state regulation.

States with moderate levels of regulation often require letters of intent to homeschool be submitted, as well as regular logs of instruction be kept, and other guidelines be followed. Florida, for example, requires that parents send a letter of intent to their local superintendent. Florida homeschoolers also have to log schoolwork and have the child annually evaluated using one of the methods of evaluation.

Other "moderate" states ask different requirements of their homeschoolers. In South Carolina, parents who are intending to homeschool their children must have either a high school diploma or have passed the GED (general educational development) test. Parents have three choices when it comes to homeschooling in this state: (1) they can maintain instruction under the supervision of their local school district, which would vary by district, (2) they can homeschool under the direction of the South Carolina Association of Independent Home Schools (SCAIHS), which would require them to pay annual dues, have their child tested annually, and have their curriculum reviewed, or (3) they must be accountable to one of the state homeschooling associations.

States that are considered to have a high level of homeschooling regulation often require parents who teach their children at home to follow guidelines throughout the school year. Pennsylvania has a strict policy for homeschoolers, and requires parents to submit a notarized affidavit of intent to homeschool, along with medical records and learning objectives for certain subjects. Note that the school only has the authority to say whether the required documentation was submitted, not to determine whether the homeschooling plan of instruction is acceptable or unacceptable. The parents also must keep records of instruction and of attendance during the year. At the end of the school year, the child must be evaluated by either a certified teacher or a licensed psychologist, a portfolio of schoolwork needs to be submitted, and in certain grades the child must take a standardized test. Also, parents who plan to teach their children at home must have a high school education. Pennsylvania does offer another homeschooling option, however. Parents can have children homeschooled by a tutor who is a certified teacher, in which case the parents only need to submit the tutor's credentials and criminal record.

Parents intending to homeschool their children in New York, another state considered to have a high level of regulation, must file a letter indicating their intentions and submit an IHIP (Individualized Home Instruction Plan). As in Pennsylvania, the school doesn't have the authority to determine the acceptability of the IHIP, only whether information was submitted as outlined by the state. The parents also must submit quarterly reports during the year and engage the child in at least 900 hours of instruction for grades K–6. At the end of each school year, the homeschooled child must be assessed, which can mean taking a standardized assessment test in some years and having the parents provide a narrative of assessment in others. In Minnesota, another state that has a high level of regulation, parents must submit the names and birth dates of the children they plan to homeschool annually. The parents also must have a bachelor's degree, or else they will have to submit quarterly report cards to the school. Parents also must provide supporting documentation about the subject matter that is being taught, although the information needed may vary from school district to school district. In addition, homeschooled children in this state must be tested annually, but the school doesn't need to see the test results.

No matter what level of regulation your state has, there are ways to operate your homeschool with success. Here are a few tips as you negotiate the homeschooling waters:

- Be aware of what is a requirement and what isn't; you don't have to send extra forms and documentation if it's not required. Even if some schools ask for or prefer to see certain things, you don't have to comply if it's not legally required!

- All of these laws, rules, and regulations may seem like more trouble than they're worth. The Home School Legal Defense Association (HSLDA) can help in outlining your state's requirements; go to the association's Web site at *http://www.hslda.org*. For even more information on your state's laws and related references, see the Homeschooling Online Resources that follow. This Web site can help you find information on your specific state, and may be able to direct you to local homeschooling groups.

- Veteran homeschoolers in your area can be a fountain of practical knowledge about the laws.

Homeschooling Military Families

Frequently moving from location to location can be exhausting for families with one or more parent in the military. If you have school-age children, it can be even more complicated. Schools across states and U.S. schools in other countries often don't follow the same curriculum, and states often can have varying curriculum requirements for each grade.

The Department of Defense Dependent Schools (DoDDS) is responsible for the military educational system. There are three educational options for military families:

1. attend school with other military children
2. if in a foreign country, attend the local school in which the native language is spoken, although this option may require approval
3. homeschool

Homeschooling can provide consistency for families that have to relocate often. The move itself, along with the new culture your family will be exposed to, is a learning experience that can be incorporated into the curriculum. Note that military families that homeschool must abide by the laws of the area in which they reside, which may be different from where they claim residency for tax purposes. If your relocation takes your family abroad, one downside is the lack of curriculum resources available on short notice. Nonetheless, military homeschoolers may be able to use resources offered at base schools.

Approaches and Curriculum

If you're reading this book, you've probably already heard of many different approaches and methods to homeschooling, which is sometimes referred to as *unschooling* (see the Glossary for more information). It's important that you choose one approach or method that works best for you—there's no right or wrong way to homeschool!

The curriculum and materials that are used vary from person to person, but there are organizations that offer books, support, and materials to homeschoolers. Many homeschoolers find that a combination of methods often works best. That's why *Making the Grade* was created!

Support Groups and Organizations

Homeschooling has become more popular, and the United States boasts a number of nationally recognized homeschooling organizations. Also, nearly every state has its own homeschooling organization to provide information on regulations in addition to other support. Many religious and ethnic groups also have their own homeschooling organizations.

Homeschooling Online Resources

These are some of the online resources available for homeschoolers. You also can check your phone book for local organizations and resources.

National Organizations

Alliance for Parental Involvement in Education
http://croton.com/allpie/

Alternative Education Resource Organization (AERO)
http://www.edrev.org/links.htm

American Homeschool Association (AHA)
http://www.americanhomeschoolassociation.org/

Home School Foundation
http://www.homeschoolfoundation.org

National Coalition of Alternative Community Schools
http://www.ncacs.org/

National Home Education Network (NHEN)
http://www.nhen.org/

National Home Education Research Institute (NHERI)
http://www.nheri.org

National Homeschooling Association (NHA)
http://www.n-h-a.org

Homeschooling and the Law

Advocates for the Rights of Homeschoolers (ARH)
http://www.geocities.com/arhfriends/

Home School Legal Defense Association (HSLDA)
http://www.hslda.org

Children with Special Needs

Children with Disabilities
http://www.childrenwithdisabilities.ncjrs.org/

Institutes for the Achievement of Human Potential (IAHP)
http://www.iahp.org/

National Challenged Homeschoolers Associated Network (NATHHAN)
http://www.nathhan.com/

Military Homeschooling

Department of Defense Dependent Schools/Education Activity (DoDDS)
http://www.odedodea.edu/

Books, Supplies, Curriculum

Elijah Company
http://www.elijahco.com/

Federal Resources for Educational Excellence
http://www.ed.gov/free/

Home Schooling Homework
http://www.dailyhomework.org/

Home School Products
http://www.homeschooldiscount.com/

Homeschooler's Curriculum Swap
http://theswap.com/

HomeSchoolingSupply.com
http://www.homeschoolingsupply.com/

General Homeschooling Resources

Family Unschoolers Network
http://www.unschooling.org

Home Education Magazine
http://www.home-ed-magazine.com/

Homeschool Central
http://homeschoolcentral.com

Homeschool Internet Yellow Pages
http://www.homeschoolyellowpages.com/

Homeschool World
http://www.home-school.com/

Homeschool.com
http://www.homeschool.com/

HSAdvisor.com
http://www.hsadvisor.com/

Unschooling.com
http://www.unschooling.com/

Waldorf Without Walls
http://www.waldorfwithoutwalls.com/

Communicating Between Home and School

For homeschoolers, often there is limited contact with the schools beyond that which is required by the state. Yet a quick glance at your local schools will reveal opportunities, resources, and benefits that can offer you a flexibility to homeschooling and a supplement to your child's total learning experience.

Special Needs

If you have a child with special needs, such as dyslexia or ADHD (attention deficit hyperactivity disorder), taking advantage of the programs and services your public school provides can expand your support system and give you some relief in working with your child. In many instances, the easy access and little or no cost of these services makes this a viable option for homeschoolers.

Depending on your child's diagnosed needs, some school districts may offer full services and programs, while some may only provide consultations. Some school districts' special education departments have established parent support networks that you also may be able to participate in as a homeschooler. States and school districts vary in terms of what homeschoolers are allowed to participate in, so check with your local school administrator and then check with your state's regulations to verify your eligibility.

Two organizations, the Home School Legal Defense Association (HSLDA) and the National Challenged Homeschoolers Association Network (NATHHAN), offer a wide range of information and assistance on services and programs available for special needs children. Check them out on the Internet at *http://www.hslda.org* and *http://www.nathhan.com*. Your local homeschooling group—especially veteran homeschoolers—will have practical information you can use.

Additionally, some homeschooling parents combine the resources of a school with those offered by a private organization to maximize support.

Gifted Children

If your child is considered gifted, your local public school may have programs available for students who require additional intellectual attention. Check with your local school administrator and your state's regulations first. In addition to providing information on special needs children, HSLDA and NATHHAN offer resources for parents of gifted children.

Don't be afraid to check out the colleges in your area, too. Many times colleges, especially community colleges, offer classes or onetime workshops that might be of interest to your child. Check with your local schools to see how you can take advantage of these opportunities.

Extracurricular Activities

Locations of other homeschooling families in the area, schedules, and different homeschooling approaches can make creating clubs specifically for homeschoolers challenging. Nonetheless, extracurricular activities at your local schools can give your child opportunities for peer interaction, and can help him or her develop new skills and interests that homeschooling situations can't always provide. For example, if your child has shown an interest in music and wants to play in a band, many communities don't have youth bands or orchestras (or if they do, the child must play at a certain level). In a school setting, your child might be able to play in the school band at his or her own level. Sometimes taking music lessons from a school's band leader is also an option.

Other extracurricular activities, such as Girl Scouts and Boy Scouts (or if your child is older, a language club or an academic club, such as one for math, science, or debate), might offer additional opportunities for your homeschooler to interact with his or her peers and have a worthwhile learning experience at the same time. These types of groups often need parent volunteers as leaders, which can provide you with additional interaction with the school. If your homeschooled child is interested in extracurricular athletics, towns might not offer community-based athletics at a competitive level, so participating in school sports may be an option to consider, especially for your older child.

Your school also might have other resources that are suited to your needs. For example, the school library may be a better place than your community library to go to for the materials you need. Many schools also have certain times of the week or season when the gymnasium is open to the community for use. And some schools even host special seasonal activities for students during holiday breaks. Contact your local school district before participating.

Returning to School

If you plan on having your child return to school, taking advantage of the programs and opportunities offered can help ease the transition back into the classroom. Your child will already experience a sense of familiarity with his or her surroundings and peers, which can help smooth the transition to a different structure of learning.

Meet Your Sixth Grader

The often-challenging temperament of a child in the sixth-grade year is rooted in his or her inner struggle with two opposing forces: a fiery urge toward independence and an ongoing desire for stability, structure, and support. At times your sixth grader may seem like a walking contradiction. What he or she says and means aren't the same. "Leave me alone!" translates to "I need more privacy but don't go far in case I need you."

Preadolescent children can mature at wildly different rates. But while every child's physical, emotional, social, and intellectual development occurs in unique phases, basic developmental characteristics for a sixth grader do exist. There is no foolproof way to parent or teach children as they enter adolescence; however, a solid understanding about child development can help you promote your child's well-being and maintain your sanity.

Witness Awakening Independence

Between the ages of 11 and 12 and a half, many children go through a stage of inner uncertainty as they begin their profound and formidable transformation to adulthood. Cycles of child development often show a cyclical pattern of stability and turbulence. Since your sixth grader's changeability probably follows a previously steady period, it may seem like you're the one falling apart. You might begin to examine your parenting practices to figure out where things went wrong. Despite what you learn about past practices, what matters most is what you choose to do now. Most sixth graders have no idea how their behavior might affect other people, but you'll notice their changes and recognize the inner discomfort associated with physical and psychic growing pains. You're still the one best able to guide and support him or her through this stage.

As part of his or her awakening independence, a sixth grader begins to see teachers and parents as fallible human beings, and may constantly argue and contradict. Nonetheless, he or she is still very much in need of loving interaction and attention. This interaction might be found in recreational activities, outings, and celebrations with family and friends. Many of the lesson activities or In Your Community activities provide opportunities for your sixth grader to interact with adults in the family and neighborhood.

Your child may complain about having to participate in family activities, but most children in this age group, when asked by an outside adult, express a love of family life. Other adults probably will enjoy your sixth grader more than you sometimes do. In fact, you may find that your child has three different personalities depending on whether he or she is with parents, friends, or adults outside the immediate family. You can accept this and even arrange opportunities for your sixth grader to spend time with other relatives, such as aunts and uncles.

Keep Cool in Conflict

As your sixth grader struggles for independence, you may find that you're often the object of his or her antagonism. Be careful not to personalize his or her behavior as it most likely will have little to do with you directly. The harshest criticisms of a sixth grader are often directed toward his or her main adult caregiver (most often the mother), who is the most important person to a child in early development. You may feel hurt or angry by your child's insensitivity, but keep your cool and stay poised. It's okay to bow out of verbal power struggles before they escalate.

Daily conflict is natural and expected as your student goes through this rite of passage, redefining his or her relationship to authority and learning independence. If your child doesn't feel he or she is being heard, he or she will be more likely to tune you out when you begin to offer advice or input. Allow your child to express opinions even when they differ from yours. Getting your sixth grader's input on family vacation decisions, planning celebrations, or choosing gifts for relatives are examples. If you're afraid that this will threaten your parental control, remember that it doesn't prevent you from setting limits and enforcing necessary rules. If your child knows you're listening, he or she is more likely to listen to you and mind what you're saying.

Choose Your Battles

Part of the conflict you may experience stems from your sixth grader testing new waters related to self-awareness, responsibilities, and relationships. Try to let the smaller things go, knowing that you'll need to compromise more now than when your child was younger. Find areas in which you can give your child breathing room to explore and express himself or herself. You may choose to practice leniency in the areas of clothing choice or how a bedroom is decorated and kept up, two very personal areas for expression and self-discovery. This can be accomplished while still holding a healthy standard concerning self-respect and basic hygiene.

Your child is coming into his or her powers of logical, independent thought. Respect for his or her intelligence and ability to make good decisions will improve your rapport. Being open to negotiation about important rules, such as curfew or bedtime, may help the both of you come to a satisfactory agreement. Instead of imposing an arbitrary or traditional bedtime, one idea might be to sit down together and agree on an hour he or she can accept that still provides him or her with appropriate rest.

There are other areas, nonetheless, in which you will probably need to hold firm, such as the schedule for completing household chores and lesson assignments. Holding your sixth grader accountable for completing these types of tasks will help him or her learn responsibility. Stand your ground here. Your sixth grader still needs you to be the parent, not the friend. Even so, your sixth grader will be more open to compliance when he or she has had some say in the matter. Perhaps he or she can choose which chores to be responsible for or create a rotating schedule for more distasteful chores.

Similarly, your child has taken a step up in intellectual ability, and his or her lesson load will reflect this change. Having a specific time and area for completing lesson assignments is critical. Try setting up a special study area together. Be sure to make space for all of his or her supplies and reference materials.

Soothe Acute Self-Consciousness

Along with the growth of independence and change in self-awareness, your child is experiencing dramatic physical changes. Most children become supersensitive about their bodies at this age and develop appearance anxiety. Some girls begin menstruation and show physical signs of puberty, feeling the awkwardness of life in a body that is no longer completely childlike but not yet adult. For boys, there is an increased need to compete, be aggressive, and win. Puberty generally starts later for boys, but differences in maturity rates can make both faster and slower maturing boys self-conscious and subject to peer ridicule. Being sensitive to these intense physical and hormonal changes, and their social and emotional impact on your child, will help him or her feel understood and supported.

Give Praise and Encourage Interaction

In addition to all of these changes, friends become a primary focus as your sixth grader becomes increasingly sociable outside the family. He or she is learning about the importance of building relationships and wants human interaction. Though he or she may appear harsh and critical toward others, on the inside your sixth grader is extremely sensitive and vulnerable. Peer relationships, though highly valued, are prone to misunderstandings and arguments. He or she will feel a strong need to belong and may be devastated by the smallest criticism or slight.

There are ways to help your child through this transition. You can encourage him or her to participate in group activities, such as team sports, art or science clubs, or community youth organizations, in which he or she can interact and excel. Group interaction can balance and often facilitate academic learning. The activities in *Making the Grade* can be shared within the club or organizational setting as well. Your child also is seeking positive adult attention. Compliments, praise for a job well done, and kind words make an impact. Though it may be difficult, whenever possible try to let your child know you think he or she is just fine "as is."

Establish Routines and Structure

With so much inner change happening for a sixth grader, there is an increased need for structure. He or she may tend to be forgetful, daydream, and let his or her mind wander. Be patient and supportive and not shaming or demanding about absentminded behavior. If your child hasn't already, suggest that he or she begin to make checklists of important daily tasks to be accomplished. These might include study goals, morning and evening rituals, and self-care routines. Having a good breakfast every day is also very important at this stage and will help your sixth grader focus. In fact, because physical change and growth is happening so quickly, a sixth grader will need more food and perhaps eat more often throughout the day.

Recognize Changes in Intellect, Humor, and Personality

Of course, many positive changes are taking place. The mind of your sixth grader is evolving to embrace broader subjects. Thinking is less tied to concrete reality and becoming more flexible and open to abstract ideas. He or she is motivated to learn and develop new skills. Intellectual and analytical activities, such as chess or strategic card games, are positive. Your sixth grader will challenge and question ideas. Be open to engaging in healthy debates. Keep the debating lighthearted by taking turns debating the different sides of an issue.

In sixth grade, your child has begun to look for the deeper meaning or truth behind the facade. He or she may develop new concerns about matters in the outside world and interest in altruistic pursuits or activism. Anthropology, environmentalism, and wildlife conservation are popular with this age group. Ironically, the expansion of your child's mind plays a part in fueling his or her dissonance. He or she no longer yields to another point of view without a good reason. "Because I said so" is no longer a viable answer. Although trying for parents, this is the seed that later grows into creative, independent thought and leadership ability.

A sixth-grade child wants to be able to use new information in a meaningful and immediate way, and can become bored with material that doesn't seem to apply to real life. He or she becomes enamored with specific subjects, possibly to the neglect of others. It's feasible to keep up on basic skills while pursuing these specific interests in depth. The design of the *Making the Grade* series lends itself to just that sort of open-ended learning: branching out and exploring more deeply the areas that your child is drawn to.

These intellectual changes and your sixth grader's quick and lively thinking will create many opportunities for laughter. A sophisticated sense of humor is emerging and you may relate better to each other's jokes. He or she has a new appreciation for word play, political satire, and pointing out the ironies and inconsistencies in the world. This is a new skill, so be gentle if the humor gets off track or offends. It probably wasn't meant maliciously.

Your child's personality is evolving. Personal interests, such as popular music, friends, computers, and sports, are now obvious. Sixth graders become interested in exploring future career possibilities and may desire to visit a parent's workplace. Your sixth grader may need more one-on-one time with one or both parents or other adults that he or she is close with. Alone time with a parent or special adult on specially planned outings can help create a sense of connection that will stay with a child into adolescence and adulthood.

Embrace Your Own Sixth-Grade Self

If you reach a point when your child begins to seem like an alien who only resembles the son or daughter you once knew, it may be helpful to do an empathy exercise. You'll feel more strength of compassion when you appreciate the tremendous internal overhaul your child is going through. Take some time to remember what you were like at this age. How did you feel about yourself, your parents, your teachers, other authority figures? Look at photos of yourself at this age and call your parents, siblings, or old school friends and ask them for their memories of you. Listening to music from the time period also will help to bring back the emotions that were so strong for you.

Build a Solid Foundation

Share your passions and encourage your child to emerge into his or her own. Remember that this period is only one stage in your child's journey to adulthood. Your sixth grader may be changing but you still know his or her likes, dislikes, needs, and sensitivities better than anyone else. Despite everything else, sixth graders can be extremely humorous and display a fresh enthusiasm for life.

Promoting
Literacy

Promoting Literacy

Key Topics

Fiction
Pages 3–12

Short Stories
Pages 13–22

Folktales
Pages 23–30

Biographies
Pages 31–38

Poetry
Pages 39–44

Drama
Pages 45–54

Listening and Notetaking
Pages 55–62

Research and MLA Style
Pages 63–66

Editing and Publishing
Pages 67–74

Reading Fiction

*Although stories and characters in works of fiction are
invented, they often spring from experiences in the author's life.
Watch your own life for the seeds of a story.*

OBJECTIVE	BACKGROUND	MATERIALS
To help your student understand and apply various reading-analysis skills while exploring fiction	Your student will encounter fictional literature throughout his or her entire life. Noting details, making generalizations, and predicting outcomes are a few skills that will help your student better enjoy and comprehend fiction writing. In this lesson, your student will read a passage from Elizabeth George Speare's novel *The Sign of the Beaver* and practice his or her analysis skills with fiction.	■ Student Learning Pages 1.A–1.C ■ 1 copy Sequence Chain, page 354 ■ 1 pair scissors ■ tape or glue

VOCABULARY

PARAPHRASING retelling a story or passage in your own words

SYMBOLISM using an object to represent a person, a place, or an emotion

IMAGERY words and/or details used in a story to create a specific image

METAPHOR a comparison in which something is described using seemingly unrelated words

Let's Begin

1 **PREDICT AND INFER** Before your student reads the fictional piece, discuss what he or she thinks it will be about. Invite your student to look at the title. Ask your student to consider where the story might take place and if the tone will be serious or humorous.

2 **LOOK FOR CLUES** Remind your student to keep a notebook close by while reading the passage and to write down any words he or she doesn't recognize and their page number. Remind your student that he or she can use the context clues around the word to help understand its meaning.

3 **DISTRIBUTE AND READ** Distribute Student Learning Pages 1.A. Have your student read the passage from *The Sign of the Beaver*. Explain that **paraphrasing** is writing someone else's ideas in your own words. Ask your student to paraphrase the passage.

Tell your student that he or she will have five minutes to do this activity. Writing under time limitations is not only a skill that he or she will need throughout life, but it's also good college-preparatory work. When he or she is finished, review the work and discuss.

4   **GUIDE AND EXPLAIN** Make a copy of the Sequence Chain found on page 354. Have your student use the chart to list the order of events in the passage. When your student is finished, ask, *Are you interested in reading more of the novel?* Encourage your student to give details about his or her judgment of the writing.

5   **DISCUSS** Ask your student to give his or her perception of the characters in the passage. Ask, *Do you think you would want to be friends with Matt if you met him? Why? How do you feel about the father's character? Why?* Then have your student consider cause and effect. Ask, *Why does the family make the decision to split up?* [so that Matt and his father can build a cabin on their new property in Maine] *How might being alone affect Matt?* [possible answers: he might get lonely, scared, or hungry]

6   **DESCRIBE AND DISTRIBUTE** Author Elizabeth George Speare uses the literary devices of **symbolism, imagery,** and **metaphor** to reveal in detail the emotional experiences of Matt's character and the details of the setting. Review the meaning of each of these literary devices. Then have your student read the story to you out loud. Together, focus on finding examples of each device. Then distribute Student Learning Page 1.B.

Branching Out

FOR FURTHER READING

Nzingha: Warrior Queen of Matamba, by Pat C. McKissack (Scholastic, Inc., 2000).

Shakespeare's Scribe, by Gary L. Blackwood (Penguin Putnam Books for Young Readers, 2002).

Tuck Everlasting, by Natalie Babbitt (Farrar, Straus and Giroux, 2002).

TEACHING TIP

Join your student while he or she is silently reading. Showing your student that you enjoy sitting down with a good book creates a great example for him or her to follow!

CHECKING IN

Observe how your student responds to reading the passage from *The Sign of the Beaver.* Watch your student's eye movement. Is he or she able to concentrate on reading? If your student is having difficulty, explore the need for further vocabulary instruction or other problems with comprehension that may affect your student's ability to enjoy the passage.

Read Fiction

The Sign of the Beaver
by Elizabeth George Speare
Chapter 1

Matt stood at the edge of the clearing for some time after his
father had gone out of sight among the trees. There was just
a chance that his father might turn back, that perhaps he had
forgotten something or had some last word of advice. This
was one time Matt reckoned he wouldn't mind the advice, no
matter how many times he had heard it before. But finally he
had to admit that this was not going to happen. His father had
really gone. He was alone, with miles of wilderness stretching
on every side.

He turned and looked back at the log house. It was a fair
house, he thought; his mother would have no cause to be
ashamed of it. He had helped to build every inch of it. He had
helped to cut down the spruce trees and haul the logs and
square and notch them. He had stood at one end of every log
and raised it, one on top of the other, fitting the notched ends
together as snugly as though they had grown that way. He had
climbed the roof to fasten down the cedar splints with long
poles, and dragged up pine boughs to cover them. Behind the
cabin were the mounds of corn he had helped to plant, the
green blades already shooting up, and the pumpkin vines just
showing between the stumps of trees.

If only it were not so quiet. He had been alone before.
His father had often gone into the forest to hunt, for hours
on end. Even when he was there, he was not much of a talker.
Sometimes they had worked side by side through a whole
morning without his speaking a single word. But this silence
was different. It coiled around Matt and reached into his
stomach to settle there in a hard knot.

He knew it was high time his father was starting back. This
was part of the plan that the family had worked out together
in the long winter of 1768, sitting by lamplight around the pine

(CONTINUED) ▶

table back in Massachusetts. His father had spread out the surveyor's map and traced the boundaries of the land he had purchased in Maine territory. They would be the first settlers in a new township. In the spring, when the ice melted, Matt and his father would travel north. They would take passage on a ship to the settlement at the mouth of the Penobscot River. There they would find some man with a boat to take them up the river and then on up a smaller river that branched off from it, many days' distance from the settlement. Finally they would strike out on foot into the forest and claim their own plot of land. They would clear a patch of ground, build a cabin, and plant some corn. In the summer his father would go back to Massachusetts to fetch his mother and sister and the new baby, who would be born while they were gone. Matt would stay behind and guard the cabin and the corn patch.

It hadn't been quite so easy as it had sounded back in their house in Quincy. Matt had had to get used to going to sleep at night with every muscle in his body aching. But the log house was finished. It had only one room. Before winter they would add a loft for him and his sister to sleep in. Inside there were shelves along one wall and a sturdy puncheon table with two stools. One of these days, his father promised, he would cut out a window and fasten oiled paper to let in the light. Someday the paper would be replaced with real glass. Against the wall was a chimney of smaller logs, daubed and lined with clay from the creek. This too was a temporary structure. Over and over his father had warned Matt that it wasn't as safe as a stone chimney and that he had to watch out for flying sparks. He needn't fear. After all the work of building this house, Matt wasn't going to let it burn down about his ears.

"Six weeks," his father had said that morning. "Maybe seven. Hard to reckon exactly. With your ma and sister we'll have slow going, specially with the new little one.

"You may lose track of the weeks," he had added. "Easy thing to do when you're alone. Might be well to make notches on a stick, seven notches to a stick. When you get to the seventh stick you can start looking for us."

(CONTINUED) ▶

A silly thing to do, Matt thought, as though he couldn't count the weeks for himself. But he wouldn't argue about it, not on the last morning.

Then his father reached up to a chink in the log wall and took down the battered tin box that held his watch and his compass and a few silver coins. He took out the big silver watch.

"Every time you cut a notch," he said, "remember to wind this up at the same time."

Matt took the watch in his hand as gently as if it were a bird's egg. "You aim to leave it, Pa?" he asked.

"It belonged to your grandpa. Would've belonged to you anyhow sooner or later. Might as well be now."

"You mean—it's mine?"

"Aye, it's yourn. Be kind of company, hearing it tick."

The lump in Matt's throat felt as big as the watch. This was the finest thing his father had ever possessed.

"I'll take care of it," he managed finally.

"Aye. I knowed you would. Mind you don't wind it up too tight."

(CONTINUED)

Then, just before he left, his father had given him a second gift. Thinking of it, Matt walked back into the cabin and looked up at his father's rifle, hanging on two pegs over the door.

"I'll take your old blunderbuss with me," his father had said. "This one aims truer. But mind you, don't go banging away at everything that moves. Wait till you're dead sure. There's plenty of powder if you don't waste it."

It was the first sign he had given that he felt uneasy about leaving Matt here alone. Matt wished now that he could have said something to reassure his father, instead of standing there tongue-tied. But if he had the chance again, he knew he wouldn't do any better. They just weren't a family to put things into words.

He reached up and took down the rifle. It was lighter than his old matchlock, the one his father had carried away with him in exchange. This was a fine piece, the walnut stock as smooth and shining as his mother's silk dress. It was a mite long, but it had a good balance. With this gun he wouldn't need to waste powder. So it wouldn't hurt to take one shot right now, just to try the feel of it.

He knew his father always kept that rifle as clean as a new-polished spoon. But because he enjoyed handling it, Matt poked about in the touchhole with the metal pick. From the powder horn he shook a little of the black powder into the pan. Then he took one lead bullet out of the pouch, wrapped it in a patch of cloth, and rammed it into the barrel. As he worked, he whistled loudly into the stillness. It made the knot in his stomach loosen a little.

As he stepped into the woods, a bluejay screeched a warning. So it was some time before he spotted anything to shoot at. Presently he saw a red squirrel hunched on a branch, with its tail curled up behind its ears. He lifted the rifle and sighted along the barrel, minding his father's advice and waiting till he was dead sure.

The clean feel of the shot delighted him. It didn't set him back on his heels like his old matchlock. Still, he hadn't quite

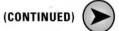

(CONTINUED)

Making the Grade: Everything Your 6th Grader Needs to Know

got the knack of it. He caught the flick of a tail as the squirrel scampered to an upper branch.

I could do better with my own gun, he thought. This rifle of his father's was going to take some getting used to.

Ruefully he trudged back to the cabin. For his noon meal he sat munching a bit of the johnnycake his father had baked that morning. Already he was beginning to realize that time was going to move slowly. A whole afternoon to go before he could cut that first notch.

Seven sticks. That would be August. He would have a birthday before August. He supposed his father had forgotten that, with so many things on his mind. By the time his family got here, he would be thirteen years old.

Create a Story Cube

Trace the box design onto a sheet of tracing paper. After reading the excerpt from *The Sign of the Beaver* by Elizabeth George Speare, fill in each square according to the numbered instructions. Be creative! Then cut the outside edges of the box, fold the paper, and use tape or glue to create a three-dimensional story cube!

1. Picture of the main character

2. Author of the book

3. Title of the book

4. Facts about the characters

5. Opinions about the characters

6. Your predictions for the book

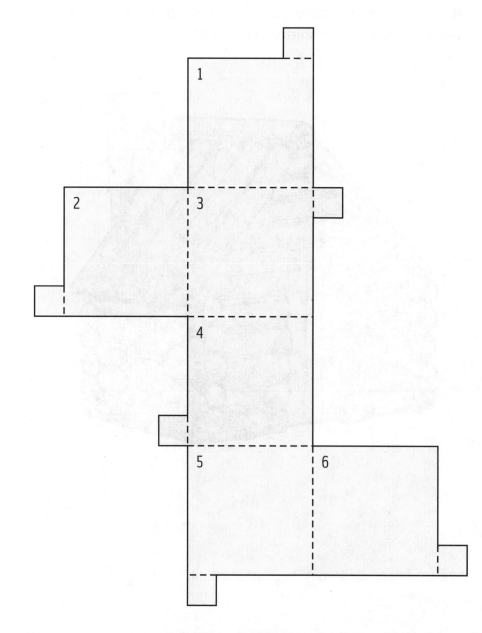

What's Next? You Decide!

PROMOTING LITERACY

1.C

Now it's your turn to choose what to do next in the lesson. Read the activities and decide which one you want to do—you may even want to try them both!

Write and Act a Future Scene

STEPS

So far you've read only a small part of the beginning of the novel *The Sign of the Beaver.* The characters in the story still have many experiences and adventures that await them. What do you think will happen to the characters? Here is your chance to decide!

❑ Write a script of an exciting scene from *The Sign of the Beaver.* Go live to that scene. What are the characters doing and saying?

❑ Share your script with an adult. Ask him or her for feedback.

❑ Invite friends to perform the scenes you've written.

❑ Get into costume and design a stage. What would each character wear? What props would you use? Here is a list of things to consider when organizing your future scene:

   ❑ costumes

   ❑ props

   ❑ lighting

   ❑ music

   ❑ stage/setting

   ❑ number of characters

Design a "Stained-Glass" Character Mobile

MATERIALS

❑ 1 wire hanger

❑ colored yarn

❑ construction paper

❑ tape

❑ 1 pair scissors

❑ glue

❑ markers or colored pencils

❑ colored tissue paper

STEPS

Using the characters from *The Sign of the Beaver* or characters from another fiction story of your choice, design a stained-glass character mobile.

❑ Draw each character—or just your favorites—on the construction paper.

❑ Color the figures with markers or colored pencils. Then cut out the figures.

❑ Cut the colored yarn into the lengths you want the images to hang from the hanger.

❑ Glue one end of the yarn to the paper and tie the other end to the hanger.

(CONTINUED)

❏ Cut the colored tissue paper into different shapes. Tape the pieces together to make one large, colorful piece.

❏ Wrap this large piece around the hanger (with the tape not showing) and tape it. You may have to make adjustments for the yarn.

❏ Then hang the hanger in a window that gets lots of sunlight. Now you have a stained-glass mobile!

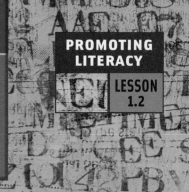

Exploring Short Stories

*A short story gives you all of the juiciness of a novel
while allowing you to finish it in one sitting.*

OBJECTIVE	BACKGROUND	MATERIALS
To have your student learn about the uniqueness of short stories while using strategies for understanding and comprehending literature	Folktales are traditional stories that have been passed down through a group of people over generations. These are often fictional short stories that tell something about the culture they belong to. In this lesson, your student will read and discuss an Iranian folktale. Then he or she will analyze it using several important comprehension skills.	■ Student Learning Pages 2.A–2.C ■ 1 copy Sequence Chain, page 354 ■ 12 index cards

VOCABULARY

NOVEL a long work of fiction

BANDIT a person who steals as a way of life

PORTER a person who carries things

SHAH a king in ancient Persia

CARAVAN a group of people traveling together through a difficult area

ONOMATOPOEIA a word that sounds like what it means

Let's Begin

1 **EXPLAIN AND REVEAL** Explain to your student that a short story is a piece of fiction that is shorter than a **novel** but that usually contains all of the elements in a novel. A short story can often be read in one sitting, which is why it is a popular type of literature. Reveal that short stories allow the reader to experience the entire story plot and all of the characters' actions at once. Ask your student to think of a short story that he or she has read lately. Ask, *What did you think about it?* Discuss.

2 **DISTRIBUTE** Distribute Student Learning Pages 2.A. Tell your student that he or she will be reading *The Shah Weaves a Rug*, which is a short story that is considered a folktale. Ask, *What do you think a folktale is?* [an often timeless tale with a universal theme, usually passed along orally through generations of a people] More information about folktales is given in Lesson 1.3.

Describe that the story the student will read has been handed down by the people of Iran for many years. On a map,

have your student locate the present-day country of Iran. This particular story reveals information about the daily life in Iran years ago, which was once called Persia. For more information about Persia, see Lesson 4.1. The story also gives information about the people who tell this story today.

3 **REVIEW AND READ** Before your student begins reading, review a few vocabulary words with your student, going over the definitions of **bandit, porter, shah,** and **caravan** given above. Then have your student read the short story. Help your student with any other words he or she encounters in the reading as needed.

4 **EXAMINE FACT AND OPINION** Together look at the first paragraph of the story and point out that it contains both facts and opinions. Give the student an example of a factual sentence and an opinion sentence. Remind him or her that a fact is something that is proven to be true, while an opinion is the unproven belief held by one or more people. Then ask the student to write three sentences of fact and three sentences of opinion. Evaluate your student's examples and help him or her adjust them if necessary. Then read the first paragraph from the story together, finding examples of fact and opinion in the reading. Discuss.

5 **EXPLORE GENERALIZATIONS** Explain to the student that generalizations are general statements about people or things. Tell your student that in the first paragraph the author makes generalizations about the good people of the land and the bad people of the land. Ask the student to reread the sentence beginning "Good people of that land . . ." Point out to the student that it's possible that not *all* good people loved the shah and not *all* bad people feared him; therefore, this statement is a generalization. Although it may be true of most people, it's not a fact that *all* people felt this way. Invite the student to look for details in the story to make a generalization about one or more of the following topics:

- The intelligence of bandits
- The attitude of the shah toward the people of his country
- The queen's attitude toward the shah

Then discuss.

6 **INTERPRET LITERARY DEVICES** Explain to the student that authors often use literary devices to help the reader envision the situation in the story. A literary device is something that the author does, such as using particular words, to make the story more vivid and interesting. Continue reading the story through the paragraph beginning "Clang!" Ask the student to reread the paragraph without the word *clang,* which is the kind of word that might be found in a comic book. Help him or her see that although the meaning doesn't change, it's more difficult for the reader to picture what is happening. Explain that the formation of a word from the sound that it makes is called **onomatopoeia.** Ask, *What are other onomatopoeias?* [crack, smash, sizzle, zip]

7   **FORM PREDICTIONS FROM DETAILS** Explain to your student that a reader can often predict what will happen next in a story using details in the story along with personal knowledge. For example, when the shah followed the holy man and the listeners, one could predict that the listeners and the shah would be captured.

      The prediction would be based on details from the story: people in the city are missing, the listeners are under a spell, the people are being led away from the city. Personal knowledge may also help the prediction. Continue reading with the student until he or she reaches the part of the story where the shah begins making the rug. Stop and ask the student to copy the chart below into his or her notebook, making it large enough for him or her to write in each of the boxes. Then have your student complete the chart to predict what might happen. Help the student find details in the story and also use personal knowledge to support his or her prediction. Guide as necessary.

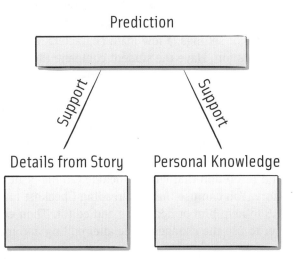

8   **REVEAL INFERENCES** Have your student continue reading until the queen sees the rug. Reveal to the student that authors don't always tell the reader exactly what's happening. It's up to the reader to infer, or draw conclusions, about what's happening. Help the student make inferences about what message the shah might have woven into the rug. Then have him or her predict what the queen will do in response to the message. Continue reading to find out if the inference and prediction was correct.

9   **EXPLAIN AND DISTRIBUTE** After completing the story, explain to the student that the order of events in the story is very important. In order to study the sequence of events, it's helpful to use a Sequence Chain. Make a copy of the Sequence Chain found on page 354. Have the student fill in the main story events in the boxes. Then ask the student to draw and label the events that he or she feels are the beginning, middle, and end events of the story. Help the student see that the turning point is the event in the story where the problem begins to be resolved.

10 **EXPLORE CAUSE AND EFFECT** Relate to the student that a cause is an event that makes something happen and an effect is the event that happens as a result of the cause. Give a few examples of cause and effect in everyday life. For example, if the cause is "My alarm didn't go off in the morning," the effect might be, "I woke up late." Ask, *What are some causes and effects that you can think of?*

Explain that there are many cause-and-effect relationships in this story. Create cause-and-effect index cards to be completed by the student. On the front of the index cards, write these effects:

- The queen allowed the strangers to come into the palace.
- The bandit did not see the shah's soldiers following him.

Have the student write the cause of each effect on the back of each card. Then have the student look in the story for more examples and create a few cards of his or her own.

11 **DISTRIBUTE AND COMPLETE** Distribute Student Learning Page 2.B. Explain to the student that short stories include a setting or settings, a few main characters, a problem, and a resolution. Have the student complete the worksheet. Then discuss.

12 **CREATE** Invite the student to look at the story components listed on Student Learning Pages 2.A (setting, characters, plot) and use them as a beginning point for the creation of his or her own short story. Have him or her list the setting, characters, problem, and resolution that will be included in his or her original short story. You can use the Proofreading Checklist found in Lesson 1.9 to help him or her revise and edit it. Then encourage him or her to use the changes made after editing and make a final copy.

Branching Out

TEACHING TIP

Remind the student that it is important to have a small number of characters in a short story. Since the reader does not have much time to get to know the characters, it is best to have a few well-developed characters rather than a lot of vague ones.

CHECKING IN

Explain to the student that one way to check comprehension of what we read is to paraphrase, or reword or summarize, it. Ask the student to paraphrase the shah's solution to the problem he faced. Ask, *What did he do to free himself and the other captives?* Have the student write the paraphrased version of the story in his or her notebook.

ENRICH THE EXPERIENCE

If the student comes to words that he or she does not know in the story, help him or her use context clues to infer the meaning of the word.

FOR FURTHER READING

Animal Stories by Young Writers, William Rubel and Gerry Mandel, eds. (Tricycle Press, 2000).

More Ready-to-Tell Tales from Around the World, David Holt and Bill Mooney, eds. (August House Publishers, 2000).

Stories to Solve: Folktales from Around the World, by George Shannon (HarperCollins Juvenile Books, 2000).

Discover Short Stories

The Shah Weaves a Rug

The king of Persia was called a shah. Some shahs were good, and others were not so good. The shah in this story was the best ruler Persia had ever had. Good people of that land who obeyed its laws loved him, but the bad people who did not obey the laws of their land were afraid of this shah. This shah was clever, and his heart was big. Often he would hide by wearing the rags of a beggar. No one knew who he was when he slipped out of his palace to walk on the city streets and along the country roads. In this way, he could see for himself what was going on in the land.

There was a time when bad news was spread throughout the shah's city. Everyone whispered, "People are disappearing each night. No one knows what becomes of them." The word was brought to the ears of the shah. Day after day, the same report was made. Wives came to the palace seeking their husbands and husbands came whose wives could not be found.

"I must look into this mystery for myself," the shah decided. He put on the clothes of a farmer and went into the marketplace.

People were selling and buying. Above the noise of many voices was heard the sound of sweet singing. The clear tones of the song rang out like the bells of a temple.

Under the shade of a tree, men and women had gathered around a singer dressed as a holy man.

"What can this be?" The shah stopped to listen at the edge of the crowd. "Who is this holy man that has never been brought to sing for me in the palace?"

The singer began to move backward. Under the shade tree, he backed little by little into a street that led out of the city. But he kept on singing. It seemed that his listeners were under a spell, for they moved after him. He slowly led them on. Farther and farther they followed him until the houses of the city were left behind them.

"This is strange!" The shah could not explain what was happening. So he went along to find out what it all meant.

At last, the singer came to the courtyard of an ancient fort that was no longer used. And as if by magic, the great gates of the fort were opened wide. Still singing loud and clear, the holy man walked backward in through the gates with the listeners following him.

"These people are being held in a magic spell!" the shah said to himself. "I must follow this to the end." So he, too, followed the singer in through the iron gates.

(CONTINUED)

Student Learning Pages 2.A: Discover Short Stories　**17**

"Clang!" The great gates swung shut. Then a huge iron bar dropped across them. It was too late.

The song died. A crowd of strong men with fast-swinging clubs rushed out and began to attack the frightened listeners. Soon every man and woman was tied hand and foot, including the shah.

"What will you do with us?" the shah asked those who were dragging him into the fort.

"Sell you in the slave market in a neighboring land," he was told. "You are strong and well fed. You will bring a good price. As soon as the moon shows its face over the desert, our caravan will leave."

"So this answers the mystery of why so many have disappeared." It was all clear to the shah now. Then he spoke to the captors.

"But I will not bring you nearly as much money in the slave market as I could right here. There is a way I am worth very much more. Let me speak to your chief."

Well, the leader of the bandits was always greedy for more money. "Let him tell us about this money he promises," the leader shouted to the men who had tied the shah up.

"I am a skilled weaver, although I am dressed like a farmer," said the shah. The words were true. When the shah was only a boy, he had learned from the palace weavers how to make a carpet. He loved the bright colors of the silk and wool threads. No one could weave a more beautiful rug than he.

"My fingers make magic on the weaving looms. The rug I can make for you will be worth three times my price as a slave."

"Go bring a loom." The leader's greedy eyes were shining. "Let this weaver show us his magic. If he has lied, we can sell him in the slave market on our next trip."

Each day the bandits watched the shah working at the loom. The chief of the bandits was very pleased when he saw the bright colors woven into beautiful flowers and birds.

"How much should I ask for this rug?" he asked the shah, who was nearly finished.

"Five thousand gold coins."

"Five thousand! Who would pay so much?"

"The shah himself would pay it, but I am told he is away from the city just now. Take it to his queen. She also loves beautiful rugs. No doubt she will pay you that much."

"You speak intelligently," the head bandit said. "I will take the rug to the queen when you have finished."

The shah's fingers flew faster. He seemed to take special care with the pattern on the rug's end. The flowers and birds matched those in the rug's center. But there were also letters like those in old Persian writings. The bandits had never seen letters like these before. Such writing was known only to people of royal families. At last, the shah's rug was finished.

(CONTINUED)

"I myself will go with the porter to carry the rug to the palace," the chief bandit said. "I will give it to the queen. If you are right, Weaver, I will come back here with five thousand gold coins."

"Unroll the rug only under the eyes of the queen herself," the shah said. "Do not let the gatekeeper or the doorkeeper stop you."

"The shah is not here. The queen is broken-hearted. She will see no one." At first, the guards would not let the bandit and his porter into the courtyard.

"But I have a rich gift for the queen." The bandit would not go away. "She will be angry if you do not let us come in."

So the gatekeeper let them pass. They entered the queen's part of the palace. There a guard also stopped them.

"I will take your gift to the queen. And I will let you know if it pleases her." The doorkeeper was going to turn the strangers away when the voice of the queen came from behind her curtains.

"Let the strangers come in," she cried out. "I will look at his gift. It will take away from my heart the worry I feel because of my husband's absence."

So the curtains were put aside and the chief bandit bowed low for the queen. Her dark eyes looked curiously over the veil that hid the lower part of her face.

When the rug was spread out, a cry of joy came from her lips. This was a rug of great beauty, like those already in the palace.

Then the queen gave another cry—a cry of surprise. She bent down to examine the end of the rug. She read it like a book. Then she said, "This is a rich gift, O Stranger. I accept it with pleasure. How much is it?"

"Five thousand gold coins for you, my Queen." The bandit bowed very low. "For someone else it would be more than twice that amount."

"Ten thousand gold coins. I shall give you that sum because the rug pleases me very much." Calling one of her guards, she added, "I myself will go with this man to count the coins. You, Stranger, wait here until we return."

In this way, the queen had a chance to give secret orders to the palace guards.

"Into the pattern of that rug," she told them, "our shah has woven a message for me. He calls for help. This man who has brought me the rug holds him prisoner in an old fort outside the city walls. When these men leave, follow them. Give orders to fifty of our best warriors to follow you. Be sure that the gates of the fort do not close before you rescue the shah."

The chief bandit knew nothing of the message that the shah had woven into the border of the rug. Because he was so happy about the bags of gold, the bandit did not see the shah's soldiers following him.

When the chief bandit and the porter came back to the fort, they met the false holy man, who was singing. Another group of bewitched listeners was following him.

The chief bandit stopped to let them pass inside the iron gates. His cruel eyes

(CONTINUED) ▶

shone with satisfaction as he watched the last one go to his doom.

But before he could enter the courtyard, the fifty strong palace soldiers had fallen on him. Before the gate could swing shut, they had captured the bandits. The soldiers seized the false holy man with the sweet singing voice, and they tied up the chief bandit.

With their shining swords, the shah's men quickly took over the fort. They freed their shah and the people who had just fallen under the spell of the singer.

These men and women fell to their knees before the good shah, who had saved them from the slave market. With all the people of the city, they celebrated after the chief and his band were put to death.

"Blessed be weavers!" This saying was heard all over Persia. And from that day to this, this country has been famous for its beautiful rugs.

Study Story Structure and Characters

On the top half of the page, complete the chart about the story structure. Then choose one character from the story and list character traits, or characteristics, that he or she has and examples of those traits from the story.

Story Structure

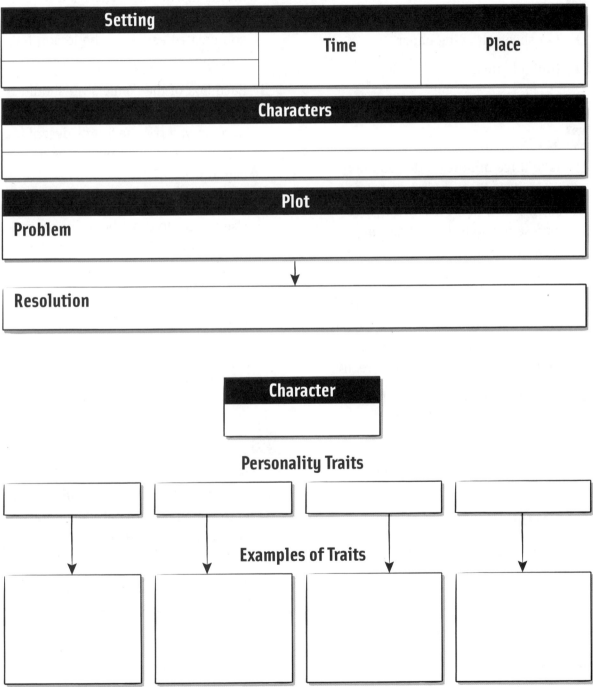

Setting		
	Time	**Place**

Characters

Plot
Problem

↓

Resolution

Character

Personality Traits

Examples of Traits

Student Learning Page 2.B: Study Story Structure and Characters

What's Next? You Decide!

Now it's your turn to choose what to do next in the lesson.
Read the activities and decide which one you want to do—
you may want to try them all!

Time Yourself and Illustrate Onomatopoeia

MATERIALS

- ❏ 3–5 sheets drawing paper
- ❏ 3-minute timer
- ❏ markers or crayons

STEPS

- ❏ Take three minutes to list as many onomatopoeic words as you can. (Remember, these are words that represent a sound, such as *clang, crash,* or *boom.*)

- ❏ When three minutes are up, look at your list. Choose three of the words to illustrate. Your illustration should include a situation in which that sound would be created. Be creative!

- ❏ Then ask others to guess what word you've drawn. Can they tell?

Create a Comic Strip

MATERIALS

- ❏ scratch paper
- ❏ 1 sheet drawing paper
- ❏ markers or colored pencils
- ❏ 1 black felt-tip marker
- ❏ 1 ruler

STEPS

- ❏ Create a comic strip illustrating the events in *The Shah Weaves a Rug.* Refer to the Sequence Chain that you created earlier in the lesson for guidance.

- ❏ Each box of the comic strip should represent one event in the story. If necessary, write the words describing the event below the picture as a caption.

- ❏ Sketch out drafts on scratch paper. Use a ruler to draw boxes or other shapes for your images—just like in newspaper comics. Use a marker to outline the shapes.

- ❏ Share your comic strip with others!

Become a Storyteller at Your Library

STEPS

Become a storyteller! Ask an adult to help you arrange to tell *The Shah Weaves a Rug* to young children at your library. Practice telling the story out loud to family and friends.

- ❏ What hand or other physical gestures would you use?

- ❏ Would you wear a costume?

On the day of the storytelling, get to the library early and be prepared!

Investigating Oral Traditions of Folktales

The spoken word of folktales is a powerful way to communicate lessons and stories of our lives.

OBJECTIVE	BACKGROUND	MATERIALS
To have your student explore and analyze folktales to learn the importance of oral tradition in storytelling	Folktales, along with myths and legends, are unique stories that are passed down through generations by spoken word. These stories are told aloud and often teach people lessons about life. There are many different types of folktales from all around the world. Every culture has a unique way of expressing traditions, beliefs, and values through this type of literature. In this lesson, your student will orally tell a story of his or her own and read a Japanese folktale.	■ Student Learning Pages 3.A ■ 1 copy Sequence Chain, page 354

VOCABULARY

FOLKTALES often timeless tales with a universal theme, usually passed along orally through generations of a people

IMAGERY words and/or details used in a story to create a specific image

SYMBOLS people, places, or things that represent something else

Let's Begin

1 **CONNECT TO EXPERIENCE** Explain to your student that **folktales** are stories about people and events that are passed down through spoken word. Explain that folktales are often stories told by people about people and their life experiences. They are frequently timeless and focus on a common theme. They also often teach an important lesson about life experience. Connect to your student's experience by choosing a tale that you know he or she is familiar with and have him or her read it aloud. You also can connect by asking him or her to think of a story he or she has heard or told about family and/or friends. Ask, *Why would you like to tell this story?*

2 **ORALLY DELIVER** Now have your student retell this story out loud. Before he or she begins, remind him or her to include physical gestures and facial expressions when telling the story

and to use a suitable volume and tone. Share that all of these elements make a story more meaningful.

3   **REVEAL** Reveal to your student that he or she just told his or her own folktale! Explain that folktales are a very unique type of literature. Tell your student that these types of stories began by being told out loud and were passed down through many generations and eventually written. Explain that folktales teach people important lessons about cultures, beliefs, values, and the actions and lives of human beings. Ask, *How can the story he or she just told teach people an important lesson?* Discuss.

4   **DISTRIBUTE AND EXPLAIN** Distribute Student Learning Page 3.A. Explain that your student is now going to read an ancient Japanese folktale called *A Frog's Gift,* as told by contemporary author and storyteller Rafe Martin. Mention that this tale addresses the importance of harmony and compassion, which is a theme that is often found in Japanese culture. Encourage your student to keep this in mind while reading this Japanese tale.

5   **MAKE PREDICTIONS AND INFERENCES** Before your student begins reading, have him or her look at the title of this tale. Ask your student to think about the words in the title and make predictions and inferences about what will happen in the story. Explain that we make predictions and inferences by making informed guesses about what will happen in the story based on what has already happened and what we know from our own life experience. This type of reading, called directed reading and thinking, will help your student understand and comprehend the meaning and purpose of the story and encourage your student to activate prior knowledge while reading. Ask, *Based on the title, what do you think the story is about?* Discuss. Then ask, *What title would you give your tale that you just told? Why?*

6   **READ AND EVALUATE** Now have your student read the story. As your student reads the story, encourage him or her to stop frequently and think about what has happened so far and what is going to happen next.

7   **EXAMINE AND SEQUENCE** When your student has finished reading, examine the details of the story with your student. Explain that understanding the sequence of events is crucial to the tale. Tell your student that it is important to understand how each event, decision, and interaction relates. Make a copy of the Sequence Chain found on page 354 and distribute to your student. Have him or her complete the chart, filling in the main events, decisions, and interactions of this tale. Discuss.

8   **UNDERSTAND CAUSE AND EFFECT** Explain that the events in the tale are based on cause-and-effect relationships. Cause-and-effect relationships occur when a person makes a decision or something happens, and, as a result, something else happens. Have your student make a list of cause-and-effect relationships that happen in this tale. Emphasize the idea that folktales can often teach us lessons about life. When we look at cause-and-effect relationships, we can see that choices and decisions can have either positive or negative effects. Ask, *What happened when the snakes began trying to sink the gourds and float the needles?* Then ask, *How did meeting the woman change the girl's life? What do you think would've happened if the gourds sank and the needles floated— do you think the girl would've met the woman?* Discuss.

9   **EVALUATE, GENERALIZE, AND CONCLUDE** Encourage your student to continuously evaluate and generalize what he or she is reading. Remind him or her that this should be ongoing throughout the reading process. Emphasize that generalizations, evaluations, and conclusions are based on specific details from the story and from our own life experiences. Ask, *What tricks would you have used to distract the snakes? Why?*

10   **EXPLORE AND IMAGINE** Explain that when an author uses specific words and details in a story to create a mental picture it is called **imagery.** The words and details help the reader create a specific image in his or her mind. Ask your student to find examples of imagery used in the tale. An example on page 29 is "'Come in, dear,' she croaked." The word *croaked* gives us the image of the frog and tells us that the woman may be related to the frog from the beginning of the story. Ask, *What do the examples of imagery you found mean?*

11   **EXPLORE THE SYMBOLS** Explain that the narrator of this tale also uses specific **symbols.** A symbol is a person, place, or thing that represents something else. For example, the frog in the story can be a symbol of someone who is peaceful and kind and who needs help in a bad situation. Ask, *What do people, places, and things symbolize in this tale?* Discuss. Then ask, *What are some symbols that he or she has seen lately that mean other things?* For example, a dove can mean peace and a skull and crossbones can mean poison. Have your student look around the house for symbols. Have him or her make a list of the symbols and their meanings.

Branching Out

TEACHING TIPS

❑   Help your student understand how to use context clues to help him or her understand vocabulary in a story. Explain that context clues are words or ideas in a sentence that help the reader understand an unfamiliar word. For example, in the sentence "And [the snakes] began to writhe and dance, turning and twisting in the dust," the meaning of the word *writhe* can be understood from the context clues *turning* and *twisting.*

If necessary, review the story again with your student and observe how he or she figures out the meaning of unfamiliar words by using context clues. Guide as necessary.

❑ Communities have different values, beliefs, and cultures. Have your student research the history of your community and find out about stories or folktales that may have come from the people in your community. Discuss these stories with older members of the community. Older generations always have stories to tell and would enjoy sharing them with people from younger generations!

❑ For a fun activity, invite friends and family to participate in a special folktale sharing with you at your home. Ask them to share stories out loud about other friends or family members. Explain that in ancient times this is how stories began and were passed down through generations. Share stories and discuss the life lesson people can learn from each story.

❑ Tape-record elders telling their favorite folktales.

❑ For another activity have your student create a talk show where he or she interviews each of the characters from *A Frog's Gift.* Have your student ask them specific questions about the events of the story and the lessons they learned. He or she also can ask them what they are doing now. Have your student write the questions and answers. Ask family members to role-play the interview in front of an audience.

CHECKING IN

Assess your student's understanding of folktales by having him or her search at the library or on the Internet for information on folktales from other cultures. Have him or her look for similarities and differences between the tales from around the world. Have him or her share the findings and make a list of common themes and/or life-experience lessons.

FOR FURTHER READING

Fearless Girls, Wise Women, and Beloved Sisters: Heroines in Folktales from Around the World, Kathleen Ragan, ed. (Norton, W. W. and Company, Inc., 2000).

Golden Tales: Myths, Legends, and Folktales from Latin America, by Lula Delaire (Scholastic, Inc., 2001).

Stories to Solve: Folktales from Around the World, by George Shannon; R. A. Katcher, ed. (HarperCollins Children's Books, 2000).

More Stories to Solve: Fifteen Folktales from Around the World, by George Shannon; Peter Sis, ill. (HarperCollins Children's Books, 2000).

Explore Oral Traditions of Folktales

A Frog's Gift
by Rafe Martin

Once a farmer walking along the road passed a field and saw a snake about to eat a frog. Without thinking he exclaimed, "Stop, Snake! Please let the frog go."

The snake turned toward him, its eyes glittering. "Why?" hissed the snake. "Will you take the frog's place?" And it opened its jaws wide and gave another long and horrible hiss.

"No," stammered the farmer, frozen with fear. "No. But I'll . . . I'll give you one of my daughters to marry." The snake's eyes glittered more brightly yet. "Done!" hissed the snake. And it closed its jaws with a snap.

At once the frog hopped into the water of the rice paddy and, *splash*, it was gone. The snake too glided quickly away. Ripples spread on the surface of the water, and as the farmer watched them fade, he began to wonder, with some dread, about what he had done.

When he reached home he went to his oldest daughter and said, "To free another creature I have promised a daughter to a snake. Will you go?"

"Never, Father!" she screamed. "How could you!"

He went to his second daughter. "I have offered one of my daughters to be a snake's bride. I saw a frog about to be eaten. This was the only way to save it—unless I let the snake devour me! Will you do it?"

"I won't!" shouted the second daughter. "Marry a snake! You must be mad!"

He went to his third and youngest daughter, but he didn't have much hope. "I have done a foolish thing," he said.

"What, Father?" his daughter asked.

"I saw a snake about to devour a frog," he answered, "and I felt so sorry for it that I found myself offering a daughter to save this frog. So, my daughter, will you marry the snake?"

(CONTINUED) ▶

"I will, Father," the third daughter answered. "It was a kind thing you did. But you must bring me one thousand gourds and one thousand needles before I will go."

"I will have them ready in the morning," the farmer promised. "And, Daughter, thank you."

The next morning the farmer went to town. He bought one thousand gourds and one thousand needles and hurried home.

Toward twilight the farmer and his daughters heard a drum beating. They looked down the road and saw a great host of armed men coming toward them. The torches they carried made their armor glitter and shine like scales. In the middle of this company of one thousand armed men rode a mighty warrior on horseback.

"I have come," said this handsome warrior in a low, hissing voice, "for the girl."

Weeping, the farmer packed the gourds and the needles. Then as the sun went down the poor girl set off with the great host of men into the blackness of the night.

They journeyed for several hours. They came at last to a great shining palace enclosed by a high wall of stone. The gates opened and the host passed within. But what was this? Once within the gates, the men turned into snakes. Their eyes glittered. Their scales shone. Their tongues flicked in and out. And they began to writhe and dance, turning and twisting in the dust. They seemed hungry and the girl began to fear that it was not a wedding but a feast to which she had been brought. And that she herself would be the meal. Then the Snake Lord said, "Sweet is this girl, sweeter than frogs!" and the others laughed and hissed.

Then the girl said, "I am ready for whatever may come. But before that I have one request. I must know your worth. I have a simple test. Sink one thousand gourds; float one thousand needles."

"That'sssssss eassssy," hissed the snakes. "Give us each a gourd and a needle and it will be done."

So the girl opened her pack and the snakes began trying to sink the gourds and float the needles. But gourds being

(CONTINUED)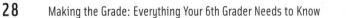

hollow and light can only float, and needles being solid iron will only sink.

The snakes were becoming exhausted—and furious—as their efforts failed. The chaos and the din grew louder and louder. In the midst of the confusion the girl ran. She opened the gate a crack, slipped through, and went running, running out into the darkness. In time she came to a little hut in the marshes. A fire was burning within. Exhausted, she knocked on the door. An old woman in a green robe with dark spots printed on it opened the door. She was small and squat but her wide eyes seemed kind. "Come in, dear," she croaked. "The smoke has made my voice hoarse, but you will be warm and safe here. Appearances are often deceptive. But I promise no harm shall come to you. Come in." The girl entered and the old woman closed the door tightly behind her.

"First eat," the old woman said in that strange, hoarse voice, "then we shall talk."

She brought the girl hot food and tea, rice, and many good things, and the girl ate and ate.

(CONTINUED)

"Tell me your troubles, dear. Perhaps I can help."

The girl told the old woman all that had happened. The old woman didn't seem scared or amazed at all. She just chuckled. "A thousand gourds to sink, a thousand needles to float. Oh, that's a good one. Yes, yes. That was good thinking indeed.

"Rest now, little daughter, and in the morning I'm sure I'll be able to help you find your way."

The girl was so tired she fell asleep almost at once. As she drifted off she heard frogs croaking melodiously from the marsh, and somehow it sounded beautiful.

In the morning the old woman prepared fresh tea. Then she told the girl, "I have thought about you a lot, my dear. And I have made inquiries on your behalf. My friends have told me that the lord of all this land is looking for a bride. You are beautiful, kind, and openhearted. I am sure it is you he seeks. I have a new kimono for you. It is fine, is it not?" And she held up a light green kimono beautifully made and splashed handsomely with the greens and yellows of the rice fields. It was indeed a beautiful thing. "Put this on and we shall go to the town."

When they arrived at the town, hundreds of girls were already waiting by the castle. The old woman led the girl to the end of the line. The steward came along, looking at each girl. "Maybe," he would say. Or, "No." When he got to the old woman and the girl, he smiled. "This is the one," he announced. "I'm sure of it. You may all go home. This girl shall be our dear lord's bride."

The old woman smiled a great *wide* smile. She blinked her large round eyes. She bowed. "Good-bye, dear child," she croaked. Then she turned and walked away with a hop to her step.

The girl was married to the great lord. They lived happily. Her father and sisters came to live nearby and were astonished that she who had been promised to a snake should have made such a good match in the end.

But she had, after all, saved the life of a frog. "And that might," said the girl, "have had quite a lot to do with it."

Exploring and
Analyzing Biographies

Biographies not only offer a glimpse into the life of someone else but also provide an opportunity for self-reflection on your own life.

OBJECTIVE	BACKGROUND	MATERIALS
To have your student explore the rich world of biographies	While some readers enjoy getting lost in the imaginary world of fiction, many others also enjoy reading about the actual lives and experiences of others. In this lesson, your student will read, explore, and learn the nature of biographies.	■ Student Learning Pages 4.A–4.C ■ age-appropriate and reading-level-appropriate biographies

VOCABULARY

BIOGRAPHY a true story of a person's life as told by another person

AUTOBIOGRAPHY a true story of a person's life as told by that person

LISTLESS having no energy or interest

METHODICALLY to do something with an order or arrangement

KNICKERBOCKERS loose-fitting pants that stop at the knee

MONOTONOUS having no variety

CHANTS words repeated again and again

DESPISED extremely disliked

RUSES tricks

DEVICE a tool or instrument

Let's Begin

1 **EXPLAIN** Explain to your student that a **biography** is nonfiction and describes a real person's life. A biography is a true story written about a person's life that is told by another person. Then explain to your student that an **autobiography** is a true story of a person's life as told by that person. Review with your student biographies and autobiographies he or she has read. Ask what he or she liked and disliked about them.

2 **REVIEW VOCABULARY** Distribute Student Learning Pages 4.A, which contain an excerpt from the biography entitled *Albert*

A TIME-SAVER

Your local librarian will be able to help you locate several biographies that are appropriate for your student.

PROMOTING LITERACY

LESSON 1.4

Einstein and the Theory of Relativity by Robert Cwiklik. Read aloud the last eight vocabulary words. Ask your student what he or she thinks each of the vocabulary words means. Help him or her find the words in the passage. After reading the sentences that contain the vocabulary words, ask your student to define the words again. Ask what clues within the sentences surrounding the words helped him or her define them. Discuss.

3 **DISTRIBUTE AND PREVIEW** Now, before reading the passage, distribute Student Learning Page 4.B. Invite your student to look over some strategies for reading biographies. Using these strategies will help your student note the details found in biographies, which can help make the learning experience richer. Now have your student read the passage.

4 **EVALUATE AND CONCLUDE** Encourage your student to continuously evaluate and generalize what he or she is reading. Remind him or her that this should be an ongoing process. Share that evaluating and concluding is more than just saying that something is good or bad. Discuss with your student his or her opinions about the book.

5 **EXTEND** Together with your student go to your library and ask for assistance in finding age-appropriate and reading-level-appropriate biographies and autobiographies. If more than one copy is available, check both of them out for you and your student to read together.

TAKE A BREAK

Give your student plenty of time to read and assess the passage. This also gives you time to prepare for the rest of the day's lessons! Alternatively, you could watch your student read and check such things as eye movement and fluency.

ENRICH THE EXPERIENCE

Reading along with your student shows that what he or she is doing is valuable and important.

Branching Out

TEACHING TIPS

- ❑ If your student shows interest, have him or her read the rest of the book, *Albert Einstein and the Theory of Relativity* by Robert Cwiklik.
- ❑ Develop your student's vocabulary by discussing synonyms, antonyms, and homophones. Invite the student to choose three words from the biography passage. Ask him or her to list a synonym and an antonym for each word. Next work with the student to brainstorm as many homophones as possible. Provide an example, such as *bear* and *bare,* to get the student started.

FOR FURTHER READING

Albert Einstein: Genius Behind the Theory of Relativity (Giants of Science), by Fiona MacDonald (Blackbirch Marketing, 2000).

Only Passing Through: The Story of Sojourner Truth, by Anne F. Rockwell and Gregory Christie, ill. (Knopf, 2000).

CHECKING IN

Assess your student's understanding of biographies and possible strategies for reading them by asking your student to create a poster that incorporates what has been learned in the lesson. Tell your student to make a poster that would help teach another student about the concepts studied.

Investigate and Enjoy Biographies

Albert Einstein and the Theory of Relativity
by Robert Cwiklik

On the morning of Albert's first day of school his mother was worried about him. He seemed so **listless** and unhappy. She watched him as he stood in the doorway getting ready to walk to school with his father.

Albert was moving very slowly. He took a long time tying his shiny, new school shoes, lacing them so tightly his mother thought they might never come off. He buttoned his new blazer sluggishly and **methodically.** Obviously, Pauline thought, he was in no hurry to get off to school. He seemed to think it was not a place he would enjoy.

On the walk to school Albert and his father came upon many fathers who were taking their sons and daughters to school. Hermann greeted all the people they met with a sunny smile and a hearty "Good morning." He knew almost everyone in the town, and had something to say to everyone. People must have thought it odd that this good-natured, outgoing man should be the father of shy Albert, who practically hid behind his father when someone passed by.

When Albert and his father arrived at the schoolhouse there was a crowd of little children in the playground outside. The little girls were huddled together in a corner, giggling, and admiring each other's new school dresses and skirts. The little boys were all wearing new blazers and **knickerbockers** to school, but that didn't stop them from running and playing games.

Albert said goodbye to his father and walked slowly onto the playground with the other children. Instead of joining the other boys in their games, he went and stood next to the schoolhouse with the girls.

(CONTINUED) ▶

Student Learning Pages 4.A: Investigate and Enjoy Biographies

When a couple of the boys raced over and asked Albert to join in their game of tag, Albert simply smiled and said, "No, thank you." He didn't enjoy playing sports and roughhousing. He had a different nature than most little boys; he preferred to stand by and observe things. The boys didn't say anything, but they did think it was a little strange that Albert was standing around with *girls* when he could be running and playing.

There was certainly no playing inside the classroom. The schools in Germany were very strict when Albert was a boy. The first thing that Albert's class learned was how to stand up all together when the teacher entered the room and respectfully say, "Good morning." The next thing they learned was not to sit down until the teacher said to, and then all were to sit down at the same time.

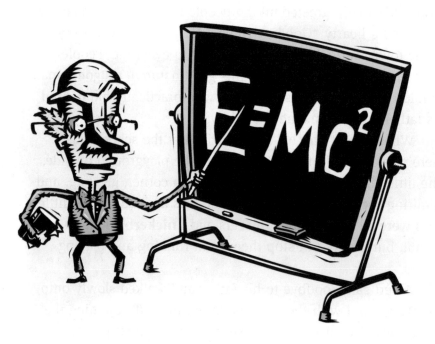

(CONTINUED)

There were many other such rules of the classroom that Albert and his fellow students learned. They also learned that a child who broke the rules received swift punishment. The classroom itself was as stern and harsh as the teaching. The benches the children sat on were made of hard wood. The backs of the benches were stiff and straight, and it was impossible to sit comfortably in them. They were designed to be uncomfortable so that students wouldn't relax too much in class. That would lead to daydreaming. Better for students to feel the bite of the hard wooden bench. Being uncomfortable kept the students alert and thinking clearly, or so the school officials thought.

Albert was very unhappy in school. He had been told by his parents that school was a place to learn about ideas and faraway places, so that one's outlook would be stretched and broadened. But Albert's school was not such a place, as even his idealistic and kind parents surely must have known. Knowledge and ideas were not discussed, but memorized and repeated in mindless, **monotonous chants,** over and over again.

After these boring rehearsals, the children had to repeat the things they learned on a test. Often they had not learned much beyond the skill of repeating the right things at the right times. And this skill they learned only to avoid the sting of the teacher's cane. Instead of broadening the mind, this kind of schooling made the spirit shrink and hide in boredom, and even fear.

Albert **despised** school. Sometimes he would pretend to be sick to be able to stay at home. But his mother and father, like most parents, were too clever to be fooled by such **ruses.**

Albert's parents understood how much he disliked going to school, but they had great respect for learning. They wanted their son to get an education, and they also felt that, given the chance, Albert might do well in his studies one day. After all, they thought, he possessed the one gift that is necessary for an education. He was curious about everything. He was always asking his parents and his uncle Jacob question after question about things that puzzled him.

One day, when Albert was really ill and had stayed home from school, Hermann returned from the shop with a present

(CONTINUED) ▶

Student Learning Pages 4.A: Investigate and Enjoy Biographies **35**

for his son. Wearing a wide smile that wrinkled the sides of his face, Hermann walked into Albert's room and up to the bed where his son lay huddled under blankets. Then he pulled his fist from behind his back and held it in front of Albert. When Hermann opened his hand, Albert saw in it a device that looked something like a watch. However, there were no numbers on its face, only four letters: *N, E, S* and *W.* There were no hands either, only a needle that jerked when the **device** was turned.

The instrument was a compass. A compass is used by travelers to help them determine in which direction they are traveling. Hermann explained to his wide-eyed son that the wonderful thing about a compass is that, no matter which way you turn it, the needle always points to the north. And, once you know which way the north is, it is easy to figure out which way south, east, and west are.

Albert suddenly did not seem to be sick at all. He was full of curiosity about the compass and he asked his father a great many questions about it. The main question on his mind was, how does the compass always know which way north is?

Explore Biographies

Read the strategies and the questions. Keep this nearby as you read and refer to it to answer the questions.

Before You Read

Preview

From what you know about Albert Einstein, what do you think a biography about him would include?

_____

Predict

From reading the book's title and the vocabulary words, what do you predict this passage will be about?

_____

While You Read

Generalize

Making generalizations about things while you read a biography can sometimes help you better understand the person's life. What generalizations can you come up with from reading this passage?

_____

Questions

As you read the passage, write any questions you may have along the way.

_____

After You Read

Evaluate

When you're finished reading the passage, think about and evaluate what you've just read. How do you feel about the book, the characters, the author's writing?

_____

Conclude

After evaluating the passage, what do you think will happen next? Is this a book you'd like to finish? Explain.

_____

What's Next? You Decide!

Now it's your turn to choose what to do next in the lesson.
Read the activities and decide which one you want to do.
You may want to try them both!

Make a Story Quilt

MATERIALS

- ❏ 1 biography
- ❏ 1 five-by-five-foot piece of fabric, such as an old sheet
- ❏ 1 tape measure
- ❏ 1 dark-colored fabric crayon or pencil
- ❏ fabric paint
- ❏ colored yarn
- ❏ 1 pair scissors
- ❏ glue

STEPS

- ❏ Choose a biography to read.

- ❏ As you're reading, think about scenes in the book, key aspects of the story, favorite characters, or a powerful word or phrase about a character. You can also think of words describing how you feel about the book.

- ❏ When you're finished reading, use the tape measure to divide the fabric into about 16 "quilt" squares by drawing a grid of squares on the material.

- ❏ Then think about what image or word you want to draw or write in each quilt square. Use the fabric crayon or pencil to sketch the image and then color it with the fabric paint. Be sure to ask an adult before you use the paint.

- ❏ Use yarn to connect the squares so that it resembles a quilt.

- ❏ Ask permission and hang your quilt on a wall.

Design a Business Card

MATERIALS

- ❏ 1 biography
- ❏ 1–2 sheets card-stock paper
- ❏ colored markers
- ❏ 1 pair scissors

STEPS

What would Madame Curie's or Thomas Jefferson's business card say? You get to decide!

- ❏ Choose a biography to read.

- ❏ Then design a business card for the person you just read about. You can use a computer or draw it on a piece of paper.

- ❏ Include all necessary information needed to inform people about the career or interests of the individual.

- ❏ Research the type of paper that was available during that time to see what paper your card would be printed on.

- ❏ Then think about what information your own business card might have on it—student, artist, musician, book reader, and so on. Design a business card for yourself!

Reading and Writing Poetry

Observe the world and the details in it and a poet will emerge out of necessity to share what has been seen, heard, felt, and tasted.

OBJECTIVE	BACKGROUND	MATERIALS
To have your student explore and understand poetry	Poems are popular throughout the world. With poetry, many ideas, feelings, and actions can be compacted into just a few short poetic lines. In this lesson, your student will explore strategies for analyzing poetry and be given opportunities for incorporating these strategies into his or her own writing.	■ Student Learning Pages 5.A–5.D ■ 1 copy Venn Diagram, page 353

VOCABULARY

RHYTHM how the words or syllables in the poem are emphasized

PERSONIFICATION when objects that are not human are given human qualities

SIMILE a comparison using *like* or *as* to compare two different things

METAPHOR a comparison in which something is described using seemingly unrelated words

RHYME when words end with the same sound

Let's Begin

1 **INTRODUCE** Begin this lesson by reading one of your favorite poems to your student. Then ask your student if there is a poem that he or she particularly likes. If so, ask him or her to share it. Ask, *Why is it your favorite?* Then reveal that together you will read two poems in this lesson and explore poetry's hidden treasures.

2 **SHARE** Share with your student that a good way to approach a poem is to read it aloud. Have your student read aloud the poem "October Saturday" on Student Learning Page 5.A.

3 **RESPOND** When your student is finished reading the poem, invite the student to share his or her initial responses to it. Invite your student to circle all the end punctuation marks in the poem. Share with your student that poets use end punctuation marks to help the reader know the **rhythm** of the poem. Ask your student to read the poem aloud again while pausing at each of the punctuation marks he or she has circled.

ENRICH THE EXPERIENCE

Many students are auditory learners and will learn how to read poetry more readily if they hear it out loud. If your student is struggling with pausing at punctuation marks, then model reading the poem for your student. Most likely you can find recordings of spoken poems at your local library for your student to listen to as well.

DID YOU KNOW?

Poems that do not have a regular rhythm are called free-verse poems.

4 **VISUALIZE** Ask your student to picture the images and comparisons the poem is trying to create. Focus your student by asking what the leaves do when the wind blows. [they rattle against each other, nervously chattering] Share with your student that this sentence is an example of the figurative language device called **personification**. Personification is when an author describes an object as if it had human qualities. Share with your student other examples of personification. [the city is hopping] Challenge your student to think of his or her own examples of personification.

5 **DIRECT** Share with your student the meanings of the words **simile** and **metaphor.** Like personification, these two ways of comparing people, places, and things help the reader see the ordinary in a new way. Ask your student to underline any examples he or she sees in the poem of simile or metaphor. If your student is having difficulty, direct your student to the first stanza of the poem.

Simile: "It [the scene of leaves] looks as if some giant's baby brother had tipped the box" [comparing the leaves to a big box of cornflakes tipped by a giant]

Metaphor: "All the leaves have turned to cornflakes." [comparing the leaves to cornflakes]

6 **DISTRIBUTE** Distribute Student Learning Page 5.B. Have your student read the poem silently and then aloud. Ask your student what he or she thought of it.

7 **COMPARE** Make a copy of the Venn Diagram found on page 353. Have your student use it and compare the rhythm and rhyme of the two poems in this lesson. Then direct your student to Student Learning Page 5.C. Share that he or she will complete a poetry log as he or she reflects on what was learned in today's lesson.

FOR FURTHER READING

My Kingdom for a Horse: An Anthology of Poems About Horses, by Betty Ann Schwartz (Henry Holt and Company, 2001).

The Paper Doorway: Funny Verse and Nothing Worse, by Dean R. Koontz (HarperCollins Juvenile Books, 2001).

The Random House Book of Poetry for Children, by Jack Prelutsky (Random House, 2000).

Branching Out

TEACHING TIP

Model for your student the process of reading poetry. Think aloud as you read the poems in this lesson. Saying things such as "I think the author could be saying this" and "I see an image of this" as you read will help your student understand how a poem can be interpreted.

CHECKING IN

Check if your student can generalize the skills learned in this lesson and apply them to other poems. Ask your student to select another poem and invite him or her to become the teacher. Have your student teach you about the literary devices used in the poem.

Discover Poetry

October Saturday
by Bobbi Katz

All the leaves have turned to cornflakes.
It looks as if some giant's baby brother
had tipped the box
and scattered them upon our lawn—
millions and millions of cornflakes—
crunching, crunching under our feet.
When the wind blows,
they rattle against each other,
nervously chattering.

We rake them into piles—
Dad and I.
Piles and piles of cornflakes!
A breakfast for a whole family of giants!
We do not talk much as we rake—
a word here—
a word there.
The leaves are never silent.

Inside the house my mother is packing
short sleeved shirts and faded bathing suits—
rubber clogs and flippers—
in a box marked SUMMER.

We are raking,
Dad and I.

Raking, raking.
The sky is blue, then orange, then gray.
My arms are tired.
I am dreaming of the box marked SUMMER.

Discover Poetry

The Poem That Got Away
by Felice Holman

There I was and in it came
Through the fogbank of my brain
From the fastness of my soul
Shining like a glowing coal—
The nearly perfect poem!

Oh, it may have needed just
An alteration here or there—
A little tuck, a little seam
to be exactly what I mean—
The really perfect poem.

I'll write it later on, I said,
The idea's clear and so's my head.
This pen I have is nearly dry.
What I'll do now is finish this pie,
Then on to the perfect poem!

With pen in hand quite full of ink
I try now to recall.
I've plenty of time in which to think
But the poem went down the kitchen sink
With the last of the perfect pie.

Write a Poetry Log

Choose one of the poems you've read today. Think about the poem, such as how it makes you feel, what images come to mind when you read it, what you think the poet wanted to say to the reader, and anything else. Write your thoughts in this poetry log. Then draw something related to the poem in the box. Have another person read the same poem and share with him or her some ideas from your poetry log.

Today's date: _____

I feel _____

_____

_____

_____

_____

_____

_____

_____

What's Next? You Decide!

Now it's your turn to choose what to do next in the lesson.
Read the activities and decide which one you want to do—
you may want to try them all!

Host a Poetry Reading

STEPS

Poetry readings are parties where people get together and orally share poetry they enjoy reading or have written themselves. Host one for people you know!

❏ Decide when you want to host your poetry reading.

❏ Make and distribute invitations announcing your big event. Invite friends, family, and neighbors to your poetry reading.

❏ Make sure you have a few poems selected and practiced that you can read at the poetry slam. Encourage guests to share a favorite poem of theirs that they have read or written.

❏ You may want to turn the event into a monthly activity!

Nominate a Poem of the Year

STEPS

❏ After reading several different poems, nominate one of the poems as the Poem of the Year.

❏ Write a nomination speech to read at the awards ceremony. The speech should include information about the poet and your understanding of the poem. Don't forget to share what literary techniques the poet used, such as similes, metaphors, or others.

❏ Give your speech to family and friends.

❏ Then design what the medal for Poem of the Year would look like!

Are You a Poet and Don't Know It?

STEPS

Have fun writing the silliest rhyming poem possible. Reading a Dr. Suess book such as *Green Eggs and Ham* or *Oh, the Places You'll Go!* may help you get started!

❏ Start by brainstorming as many words as you can that all rhyme. Remember, rhyme is when words end with the same sounds. You can use words with two or more syllables, such as *Billie* and *silly*, or you can use words with just one syllable, such as *me* and *tree*.

❏ Once you have your list, use the words to make a story within a rhyming poem.

❏ Finally, you may want to illustrate what the poem is about.

Appreciating Drama

Drama creates a connection between the written word and the audience; as the drama unfolds on a stage, the audience witnesses human experiences brought to life.

OBJECTIVE	BACKGROUND	MATERIALS
To read an excerpt from a play and apply reading and analyzing skills to the selection	Drama has been a popular type of literature for hundreds of years. Seeing a story performed has appealed to people of generations past and will appeal to generations to come. Plays allow us to understand the characters more completely than a simple story, and we can identify with the feelings and actions of the actors. Through dialogue and action, human experiences are brought to life for the audience. In this lesson, your student will read an excerpt from an age-suitable adaptation of William Shakespeare's *Romeo and Juliet* and then use it to explore characteristics of drama.	■ Student Learning Pages 6.A–6.C ■ 3 index cards

VOCABULARY

SIMILE a comparison using *like* or *as* to compare two different things

METAPHOR a comparison in which something is described using seemingly unrelated words

Let's Begin

1   **INTRODUCE THE GENRE** Explain that drama is a type of literature that is written in the form of a play to be acted out. There are many basic components that make up a play. Introduce the following components:

- Script—the written version of the play
- Cast—the group of actors who will take part in the play
- Setting—the time and place that the story occurred
- Monologue—a speech a character gives to the audience
- Dialogue—the conversation between actors
- Audience—the people watching the performance
- Stage—the place where the play is performed
- Stage directions—the words in parentheses or italics in a script that are not meant to be read but to be acted out by a performer

    Be sure that your student understands how the play is to be read and performed. Tell your student that the words that the actor or actress is meant to say are written after his or her

name, and stage directions are written in parentheses or italics. Then review with your student the components. Ask him or her to explain why each one is important. Discuss.

2 **DISTRIBUTE** Distribute Student Learning Page 6.A. With your student, act out part of the play for practice: begin with Romeo and end right before Capulet speaks. If there are only two of you, have the student play Romeo and you play the Servant and Tybalt. Then discuss why an author would choose to write in such a way. Help your student to see that drama is an effective form of writing because it allows people to relate to a character by seeing his or her words and actions performed. Ask the student for other ideas on why drama is an effective form of writing.

3 **SET THE STAGE** Explain to your student that the dramatic piece he or she will be reading is an excerpt from a version of William Shakespeare's *Romeo and Juliet.* Ask, *What do you know about Shakespeare?* Mention that Shakespeare lived in Elizabethan England, during the time of Queen Elizabeth's reign in the 1500s. Research with your student what daily life in Elizabethan England was like. Then explain that the setting of the story is a summer in Verona, an Italian city, where two families have a bitter conflict that goes back many years. In the midst of the violence, two teenagers, Romeo and Juliet, meet and fall in love. The Capulet family includes Juliet and her parents (Capulet and Lady Capulet), Juliet's childhood nurse, and Tybalt, Juliet's cousin. On the opposing side is the Montague family. In this excerpt, only Romeo and his servant Benvolio appear from the Montague side. Share that this excerpt takes place at a party that the Capulets are hosting; Romeo and Benvolio have come in disguise. Invite your student to predict what will happen when Romeo and Juliet learn of one another's identity.

4 **ACT IT OUT** Choose alternating parts for yourself and for your student. Read through the play once to get an idea of the plot. Ask your student to infer or predict some types of problems that may arise due to Romeo and Juliet's love for one another. Make a list of these problems. Ask, *What clues make you think that these problems may occur?*

5 **EXPLORE LITERARY DEVICES** Explain to your student that Shakespeare was a poet, and his plays often used imagery and descriptive language. This gave his stories a more romantic mood. Review the vocabulary words and define **simile** and **metaphor** for the student. Then direct your student's attention to the second line in the excerpt. In this paragraph, Romeo compares Juliet to a "brilliant ornament of the night" and a "rich jewel in an Ethiopian's ear." He claims that she stands out among the crowd "as a snow-white dove stands out among a troop of crows." These similes help the reader visualize and understand what Romeo is feeling. Help your student translate this paragraph into everyday, simple terms and compare the new paragraph with the version in the story.

6 **GENERALIZE** Relate to your student that a generalization is a general statement about people or things. Point out that Tybalt makes many generalizations about the Montague family. Ask your student to look back at Tybalt's scene and determine how he felt about Romeo. Then examine his reasons for feeling this way. Help your student see that generalizations are not always correct, as in this case—Romeo was not causing any trouble at the party.

7 **DISCUSS AND DISTRIBUTE** Remind your student that the story he or she just read is only an excerpt from a play. The entire play would contain an introduction, rising action, a climax or turning point, falling action, and a conclusion. Explain to your student that an introduction reveals background information and introduces characters; that conflict begins to grow during the rising action; that the climax or turning point sees the conflict come to a head and begins to be resolved; that the tension eases during the falling action and the story begins to wind down; and that the conclusion wraps up the conflict and the story. Ask your student to determine what part of the story he or she thinks this excerpt would fit into. Help him or her see that this excerpt would probably be part of the rising action, because Romeo and Juliet just met and their love has not been discovered by anyone yet. Distribute Student Learning Page 6.B. Encourage your student to summarize what he or she just read for the rising action and to use his or her imagination to create the other four parts of the story structure. Record them on the Student Page.

8 **EXAMINE** Direct your student's attention to the descriptions of characters in the story. Give him or her three index cards. On the top of each card, write one of the following names: Juliet, Romeo, and Tybalt. Then have your student write adjectives that someone in the story used to describe each person. In parentheses, write the person who described the character in such a way. For example, on Romeo's card, your student might write "lowlife (Tybalt)" and "gentleman (Capulet)." When this task is complete, invite the student to highlight similar words or synonyms in one color. Examine the words used to describe these characters, and notice the similarity between the descriptions of Romeo and Juliet and the contrast between Tybalt's and Capulet's description of Romeo. Use this as a springboard to discuss synonyms and antonyms.

9 **MODEL AND DEVELOP VOCABULARY** Remind your student that a reader will occasionally encounter unfamiliar words. When this happens, he or she can look up the word in a dictionary. However, it is often easier and faster to use context clues to form a definition of the word. Reread the following sentence with the student:

> How dare that lowlife come here, wearing a hideous mask to *mock* and make fun of our festivities?

Model the usage of context clues.

What does "mock" mean? It looks like it's something offensive to Tybalt, because he's unhappy with Romeo for doing it. And the word is followed by "and make fun of." I think that to mock something is to make fun of it.

As the student reads and discusses decisions that the characters in the story made or actions that they took, ask him or her to share opinions on whether the character acted as he or she would have and why.

Invite your student to practice this skill using the following sentences. Listen to his or her responses and help guide his or her thinking in the right direction.

He's a villain who's come here to be *spiteful* and to mock our occasion tonight.

I won't *endure* him being here!

10 **ASK AND DISCUSS** Ask your student if one can sometimes learn things about the characters that are not directly stated in the reading. Help your student see that by paying attention to details, he or she can learn more about the characters. For example, in the conversation between Tybalt and Capulet, we learn that Tybalt must respect and obey Capulet. Discuss some of the details that tell us that:

- Capulet calls himself the master.
- Tybalt feels "forced to be patient" but obeys anyway.

11 **CAUSE AND EFFECT** Explain that there is often a direct cause of events that occur in dramatic plays and stories. List the following effects for your student, and ask him or her to write the corresponding cause.

Juliet does not know who Romeo is.
Capulet allows Romeo to stay at the party.
Juliet becomes upset.
Tybalt does not start a fight with Romeo.

Invite your student to select one of the cause/effect relationships above and write a paragraph about what the effect would have been if the cause had not occurred. For example, if Romeo was not wearing a mask, what would have changed? Allow the student 10 minutes to write the paragraph.

12 **REVEAL** Reveal to your student that a good number of stories that were originally written as plays have been adapted to film. There are many film versions of Shakespeare's plays, including of *Romeo and Juliet*. You may wish to show your student one of them.

FOR FURTHER READING

Showtime: Over 75 Ways to Put On a Show, by Reg Bolton (DK Publishing, 1998).

Simply Shakespeare: Romeo and Juliet, Jenny Mueller, ed. (Barron's Educational Series, Inc., 2002).

William Shakespeare's Romeo and Juliet, by Bruce Coville (Dial Books, 1999).

Branching Out

TEACHING TIP

Remind your student that although an actor wouldn't read out loud the words in parentheses or italics (the stage directions), it's important that a reader is aware of these words.

CHECKING IN

Assess your student's understanding of the story line by having your student read the entire *Romeo and Juliet* play. Then have him or her review his or her answers on Student Learning Page 6.B.

Appreciate Drama

PROMOTING
LITERACY

6.A

Romeo and Juliet
by William Shakespeare

Act 1, Scene 5

Romeo [*spotting* **Juliet**] Who is the lady who is such an ornament
on the hand of that gentleman?

Servant I don't know, sir.

Romeo Oh, she shows the torches how to burn bright! She seems
to be a brilliant ornament of the night, like a rich jewel in an
Ethiopian's ear. Her beauty is too rich for everyday use, too
valuable for this earth. As a snow-white dove stands out
among a troop of crows, so does that lady stand out among
the crowd. When the dance is done, I'll watch where she goes,
and I'll make my rough hand blessed by touching hers. Did my
heart love before tonight? Then deny it, my eyes. For I've never
seen true beauty until this night.

Tybalt By the sound of his voice, I think this is a Montague. Get me
my sword, boy. How dare that lowlife come here, wearing a
hideous mask to mock and make fun of our festivities? Now by
my ancestors and my family's honor, I wouldn't call it a sin to
strike him dead!

Capulet Well hello, kinsman! What's making you so angry?

Tybalt Uncle, this is a Montague, our enemy. He's a villain who's
come here to be spiteful and to mock our occasion tonight!

Capulet Young Romeo, is it?

Tybalt That's him, that villain Romeo.

Capulet Calm down, gentle cousin. Let him alone. He's behaving
himself like a real gentleman. And to tell the truth, Verona
brags about him as a virtuous and well-behaved youth. I would
not be impolite to him in my house for all the wealth of this
town. So be patient, and ignore him. It's my wish.
If you respect it, you'll wear a pleasant face and stop this
scowling, which isn't a suitable expression for a feast.

Tybalt It's a suitable expression when such a villain is a guest.
I won't endure him being here!

(CONTINUED) ▶

Capulet He *shall* be endured! Who do you think you are, boy? I say he shall! [*Getting angry*] Well! Am I the master here or are you? Well now! You won't endure him! God save my soul, you'll cause a riot among my guests. You'll prance around boasting! You'll be the man!

Tybalt Why, uncle, it's shameful!

Capulet Well now, well! You're a smart-aleck boy. Is it shameful, indeed? This behavior may get you in trouble, I can tell you. You're going to cross me? Well, it's time— [*To his dancing guests*] Well done, my dears— [*To* **Tybalt**] You're a conceited, cocky young man! Go, or be quiet, or— [*To the* **Servants**] More light! More light!— [**To Tybalt**] For shame, I'll make sure you're quiet. [*To his guests*] Wonderful, my dears!

Tybalt [*to himself*] Being forced to be patient when he's so willfully angry makes me shake with anger. I'll go. This intrusion by Montague may seem all right now, but it will change to the bitterest feelings later.

[**Tybalt** *exits*]

Romeo [*taking* **Juliet's** *hand*] If I defile this holy shrine with my unworthy hand, then the gentler sin will be this: My lips, like two blushing pilgrims, stand ready to smooth that rough touch with a tender kiss.

Juliet Good pilgrim, you do your hand too much wrong. Your hand is showing pious devotion. The statues of saints have hands that pilgrims touch with their own hands. Placing a palm on the saint's palm is the holy pilgrim's kiss.

Romeo Don't saints have lips, and don't holy pilgrims have them too?

Juliet Yes, pilgrim. Lips that they must use in prayer.

Romeo Well then, dear saint, let lips do what hands do! They pray: "Grant me a kiss, or my faith may turn to despair."

Juliet Saints don't move, but they do grant prayers.

Romeo Then don't move, while I receive the benefit of my prayer. [**Romeo** *kisses* **Juliet**] So, the sin from my lips is washed away by your lips.

Juliet Then my lips have the sin that they've taken from yours.

Romeo Sin from my lips? How sweetly you tell me that I have sinned against you! Give me my sin back again. [*He kisses her again*]

(CONTINUED)

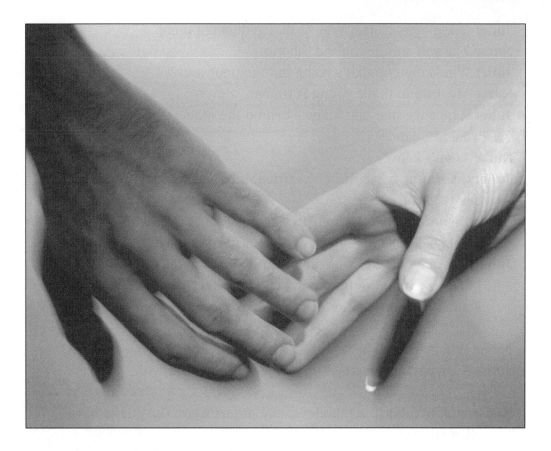

Juliet You kiss in a very proper way!

Nurse Madam, your mother wishes a word with you.

Romeo Who is her mother?

Nurse Well, young sir, her mother is the lady of the house. And she's a good lady, wise and virtuous. I nursed her daughter, to whom you were talking. I tell you, the man that can win her shall have some money.

Romeo Is she a Capulet? A terrible accounting! Now my life is in debt to my enemy.

Benvolio Come on, let's go. The best of the party is over.

Romeo Yes, I'm afraid so—which makes me more uneasy.

Capulet No, gentlemen, don't leave yet. We'll soon be serving some light refreshments. Is that so? Well, then, I thank you all. Thank you, good gentlemen. Good night. Bring more torches here. Come on then, let's go to bed. Well, servant, on my faith, it's getting late. I'm off to my rest.

[*Everyone exits but* **Juliet** *and the* **Nurse**]

(CONTINUED) ▶

Juliet Come here, Nurse. Who is that gentleman there?

Nurse The son and heir of old Tiberio.

Juliet Who's the one that's going out the door now?

Nurse My, I think that's young Petruchio.

Juliet Who's the one that follows behind the others, the one who wouldn't dance?

Nurse I don't know.

Juliet Go ask his name. If he's married, then my wedding bed will be my grave.

Nurse [*returning after asking*] His name is Romeo, and he's a Montague. He's the only son of your great enemy.

Juliet The only one I love is the son of the only one I hate. When I first saw him, I didn't know who he was. Now, too late, I know! What an ominous first love for me—that I must love a hated enemy!

Nurse What's this? What's this?

Juliet A rhyme I just learned from someone I danced with.

[**Juliet's** *mother calls her*]

Nurse In a minute! In a minute! Come on, let's go. The guests have all gone.

[**Juliet** *and the* **Nurse** *exit*]

Define Story Structure

Complete the chart using the information from the excerpt of *Romeo and Juliet* that you just read. What part of the story structure does the excerpt fit into? Then use your imagination and complete the rest of the chart. Be creative! Soon you'll find out if the story structure was as you had thought!

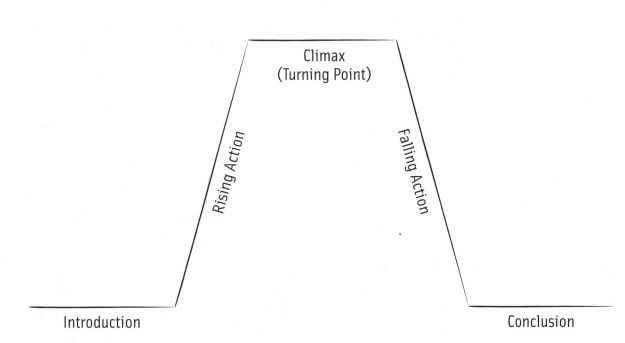

What's Next? You Decide!

Now it's your turn to choose what to do next in the lesson. Read the activities and decide which one you want to do—you may want to try them all!

Direct a Play

STEPS

❑ Gather enough friends and family to perform all of the characters in the excerpt from *Romeo and Juliet* that you read in this lesson.

❑ Be the director, giving instructions to the cast about how to act and speak.

❑ If possible, perform the play for a real audience! Think about what costumes, props, and other things you'd want to include.

Build Shakespeare's Theater

MATERIALS

❑ 1 shoebox

❑ construction paper

❑ about 12 plastic drinking straws

❑ glue

❑ 1 pair scissors

STEPS

Shakespeare performed his plays in the very famous Globe Theater, which is quite different from today's theaters. The Globe was more like an outdoor theater, with minimal decoration. Different parts of the theater and stage were called different things; for example, the roof was called the heavens, the area below the stage was called hell, and the general audience were called groundlings.

❑ Search the Internet for pictures of what the Globe looked like. Then, beginning with the shoebox as the main stage, begin building your own Globe Theater. Don't forget to make trapdoors and balconies.

❑ Search around the house for other supplies you may need—don't forget to ask permission before you use anything!

❑ When you're finished making the stage, cut out paper figures of the cast of *Romeo and Juliet;* glue them to straws and then put on your play!

Write a Present-Day Romeo and Juliet

STEPS

❑ When you understand the story line of *Romeo and Juliet,* write a present-day version of the play. Although this story was written hundreds of years ago, similar problems exist in our present society.

❑ Choose two groups of people who often conflict, and have one member from one group fall in love with a member from the other group.

Listening and Notetaking Effectively

*Paying attention to what you hear and read
will take you very far indeed.*

OBJECTIVE	BACKGROUND	MATERIALS
To have your student learn how to listen more effectively and to take efficient notes	One of the most crucial life skills that your student can master is the ability to listen. This goes hand in hand with learning how to effectively organize what he or she has read. In this lesson, your student will learn to listen and to take notes while reading nonfiction.	■ Student Learning Pages 7.A–7.C ■ 1 box cake mix ■ 1 newspaper or magazine article ■ 20 index cards

Let's Begin

1 **EXPLAIN** Explain that it's important to be an effective listener. Ask your student, *What could happen if someone didn't listen correctly?* [someone could add the wrong ingredients to a recipe, someone could go to the wrong meeting place, or worse, someone could get hurt]

2 **LISTEN AND MODEL** Have your student read the cake mix directions aloud to you. Model effective listening by repeating the major steps back to him or her. Did you miss anything? Then have him or her find directions to something else in the house, such as another box of food. Read the directions aloud to your student. Now have him or her tell you what the major steps are. If he or she misses any steps, review what would happen if those steps were omitted.

3 **PRACTICE LISTENING** Have your student select an article from a newspaper or magazine for you to read aloud—make sure the article isn't too long. Read this article aloud to your student and have him or her tell you what the article is about. Ask, *What is the article's main idea? Give some important details.* If your student is having trouble, read the article again, this time a bit more slowly. After each paragraph or two, discuss with your student what you've just read. Then, at the end of the article, review with your student the entire article. Then ask him or her to tell you about it in his or her own words.

4   **PROGRESS TO NOTETAKING** Mention that similar to listening, it's also important to remember what you're reading. One way to help you remember what you're reading is to take notes. Ask, *Why would someone take notes on what he or she is reading?* Guide your student into a conversation about how taking notes helps to organize the main ideas and details of what's being read.

5   **IDENTIFY** Have your student write in his or her notebook the terms *main idea* and *supporting details*. Ask what he or she thinks these terms mean. Relate that a main idea is the most important point of the passage. The supporting details are the other information that tells more about the main idea.

6   **DISTRIBUTE** Distribute Student Learning Pages 7.A. Reveal that often a heading can give the reader an indication as to the main idea of the section. Have your student read all of the headings in the passage.

7   **TAKE NOTES** Distribute the index cards to your student. Explain that using index cards to take notes is a handy way of organizing what you've read: one main idea can be used per index card.

8   **INTRODUCE** Before he or she begins, explain that when reading and taking notes, he or she might have to paraphrase, directly quote, or make generalizations about what he or she has just read.

    Paraphrase: A paraphrase is stating in your own words the information presented.

    Direct quote: If he or she is quoting the words exactly, he or she must put them in quotation marks and write the page number it was found on. For more information about accurately citing source material, see Lesson 1.8.

    Generalize: Then explain that throughout this passage your student will read a number of facts, and he or she will be making generalizations about them.

9   **PRACTICE** Now have your student read the passage and take notes on it using the index cards.

FOR FURTHER READING

Noteworthy: Listening and Notetaking Skills, by Phyllis L. Lim and William Smalzer (International Thompson Publishing Company, 2000).

Sport Success: Winning Women in Soccer, by Marlene Targ Brill (Barron's, 1999).

Branching Out

TEACHING TIP

Have your student read and take notes on the entire book *Sport Success: Winning Women in Soccer.* See For Further Reading.

CHECKING IN

Assess what your student has read by having him or her organize his or her index cards. Then have him or her write a few pages on what he or she has just read. Read the report together and discuss.

Read and Take Notes Effectively

Sport Success: Winning Women in Soccer
by Marlene Targ Brill

Almost every country enjoys some kind of soccer team.

Earliest Soccer

Games like soccer began more than 3,000 years ago. People throughout Asia played a team ball game with their feet. Chinese players kicked a ball of animal skin stuffed with hair and feathers through a net-covered goal. They called their game *tsu chu,* which meant kick ball. *Tsu chu* was played for the emperor's birthday and as part of his soldiers' training.

Similar kicking games existed among ancient peoples of Mexico and Central America. Remains from archeological digs showed figures hurling a rubber ball into a hoop. People played the game on a sunken court located near the main temple. The court's location gave kicking the ball a religious importance.

Roman Romp

Records offer little proof that these early games spread to other cultures. But historians know that ancient Greeks and Romans brought their games to the nations they conquered. Greeks invented a type of game where they used both hands and feet to move the ball across a field marked with lines. Romans adopted the Greek game, but they added a center line to the field and required players to shoot the ball over the other team's line. These adventures led to the English game of football.

English Football

At first, the English played this new game only on special days. Football games marked religious holidays or the coming of seasons.

Over the next few hundred years, the game moved from the fields into city streets. Sometimes, women played with the men. Other times, they held contests just with each other. As more people joined the fun, kicking balls started to get rowdy. By 1314, the game caused so much trouble that King Edward II issued the first of many bans on playing the game called football. The next king, Edward III, declared: "It is forbidden, on pain of imprisonment, to indulge in football."

Football Gets Serious—For Boys

Threats of prison never stopped the English from playing football. Instead, the game grew more popular throughout the country, at least for males. Women had an athletic change of heart. By the 1500s, most found the kicking game too rough to play.

(CONTINUED)

By the early 1800s, football had entered English boys' schools and colleges. Without any set rules, each school created its own game rules. But problems developed when schools played each other. In 1863, clubs and schools formed the Football Association to oversee the game nationwide. The association created the first national team and standard rules that all teams could follow.

Football Travels to Other Countries

Football spread around the world after the English Association was formed. Travelers to English colonies took their favorite game with them. Soon teams in other countries formed similar national associations. The problem was agreeing on a single set of rules. In 1904, men's football became an Olympic sport. That same year, representatives from seven European nations formed a world football governing board to devise international rules. They called the board the Federation Internationale de Football Association (International Federation of Association Football), or FIFA. Besides establishing rules, FIFA members created a world championship tournament just for football. The first World Cup games took place in 1930. Since then, winning the World Cup has become a football (soccer) team's greatest honor.

Soccer in America

Even with worldwide fame, soccer remained a hard sell in the United States. The game never seemed to catch on—with men or women. A U.S. soccer team participated in the 1904 Olympics, yet the nation took another ten years to form the U.S. Football Association, now the U.S. Soccer Federation, and join FIFA.

Women in the United States grappled with the U.S. tradition of not supporting the sport. They struggled against outdated views of women playing certain male-dominated games, which included soccer. Few people understood that modern girls and women had a strong desire to play soccer, too.

Quick-Kicking Women

During World War I, women worldwide replaced men who left their factory jobs to fight. In England, women got a taste of what men usually did during their off-work hours—play football. The Dick, Kerr Electric Company in Preston, England, formed one of the first women's football teams. One player suggested a match with another team as a way to raise money for wounded soldiers and their families. Their game attracted 10,000 curious viewers.

Women's games were so popular in England that matches continued after the war ended. In 1922, Dick, Kerr sent its well-known team on an American tour. The women assumed they would play other women's teams in Canada and the United States. But they discovered that Canada refused to let women play. In the eastern United States, they found only men's teams willing to play them. Unafraid, the women toured six states playing games with local men's teams. To everyone's surprise, the Dick, Kerr Ladies recorded an impressive 3 wins, 2 losses, and 2 ties.

(CONTINUED)

A Second Wave of Women's Soccer

During the 1960s, women around the world took to the soccer fields once again. German, Dutch, French, and English female athletes competed in more than twenty leagues. Eastern European governments encouraged women's teams at factories and schools. FIFA leaders noticed the changes. In 1969, they reversed their 67-year ban on women's matches.

In the United States, girls began playing soccer when their sisters overseas started. Many American girls joined soccer clubs during the 1960s and 1970s. High schools organized girls' teams. Still, there were few college soccer teams and no national teams for women.

In 1974, the American Ladies Soccer Organization began in Los Angeles. Similar clubs for women sprang up elsewhere in California and in the Northeast. None gained the kind of support that matched women's clubs overseas. Eventually, they died out. Soccer rarely received any attention from sports reporters. "In all the research I did, I didn't uncover anything about women," said Colin Jose, Soccer Hall of Fame historian. "It was bad for soccer men but worse for women."

Few girls had any idea that soccer was so famous worldwide. But they loved to play. Then, the landmark Title IX law for equal education was passed. Slowly, colleges added female soccer teams. Girls' high school and college soccer successes rarely made headlines, but they happened.

During the 1980s, female soccer players began to gain recognition. High school coaches named a yearly All-American team. The National College Athletic Association (NCAA), the ruling body for college sports, backed women's tournaments. In 1982, the NCAA began hosting national women's soccer championships every year. Soon more colleges boasted women's soccer programs. By 1997, 69 percent of colleges offered women's soccer.

At Last, a National Team

At first, women soccer athletes had nowhere to go after college graduation. A few left for Europe to play on women's teams. Others turned to different sports to keep in shape. They all hoped to play soccer on U.S. teams someday.

In 1985, soccer women got their chance. The Olympic Committee and U.S. Soccer Federation decided to host tryouts to select a women's national team. The women who made the team came from the ranks of clubs and college teams who played in the 1970s and early 1980s. The first year, the team never played in a tournament. They had no backers for ongoing training and no money to travel.

(CONTINUED)

By the second year, the team was ready for action. During their first tournament in Italy, the U.S. team lost three of four games and tied one. By 1986, the U.S. team beat Canada 2–0, winning its first international championship. That summer, they won two games in Italy before losing the trophy in the finals. These Americans were a young team. But they had a future.

First Women's World Championship
Soccer women wanted the same benefits as those given to their soccer brothers. Little changed, however, even after the announcement of the 1991 FIFA Women's World Cup in China. The U.S. women's team received no pay for training, as the men did, only rooms and meals. While they traveled, women washed their own laundry and cooked their own meals.

Women's soccer began to change after the United States beat Norway 2–1 in the first ever Women's World Cup. This was the first time that any U.S. team had ever won a world soccer title. The championship gave women a chance to shine on the world stage. Seventy-six thousand ticket holders watched the final game. Millions more stayed glued to live television broadcasts in almost fifty nations. Soccer fans everywhere, except the United States, applauded the winning team. Back home, only one reporter met the world champions when they got off the plane from China.

Some of this excitement reached people back home. A few players appeared on television shows and in magazine articles. As a result, thousands of young soccer lovers looked to the players as role models and decided to play soccer. In 1986, the Soccer Industry Council of America counted 85,173 high school girls playing soccer. Ten years later, the number had more than doubled to 209,287 players.

The Olympic Gold
The China games jolted world sports organizations into action. The 1993 Olympic Committee voted to include women's soccer in the 1996 games in Atlanta, Georgia.

For the first time, women's soccer grabbed the imagination of the U.S. sports fans. More than 76,000 fans filled the Atlanta stadium for the final game between the United States and Norway. This was the biggest crowd ever gathered to watch a women's soccer game. During the game, the United States fought to hold their 2–1 lead. When the final whistle blew, the U.S. women had won the gold— the first U.S. Olympic gold for soccer.

In 1994, the United System of Independent Soccer League (USISL) launched a women's professional soccer league. The league began with eight teams. After the Olympic win, numbers quickly grew to 32 teams in five divisions. From the beginning, games attracted large numbers of paying fans. Women's soccer was becoming big business.

The popularity of girl's soccer soared, too. In the United States, more than 7 million girls played soccer in 1998 alone. An expanding network of club teams for older girls prepared soccer players for college and national teams.

Listen Up or Lose the Hunt

Sometimes you can't always take notes, and you'll have to practice your listening skills. Have a scavenger hunt and test other people's ability to listen while having fun!

Ask about 1 to 5 other people to play, and gather about 5 to 10 items for them to find on the scavenger hunt. The hunt can be outside or inside, but don't forget to ask permission first about the items. Items can be a red shoe, a brown leaf, or whatever else you want! Then slowly say out loud a few times the items you want your players to find. Remind them that they can't take notes, so they must listen carefully as you name the items so they will remember them. Give them a time limit to find everything. When the time is up, have everyone gather together and see how many items each player found. Who found the most? Play again using different items.

List of Items

1. _____   6. _____

2. _____   7. _____

3. _____   8. _____

4. _____   9. _____

5. _____   10. _____

Player   Number of Items Found

1. _____   _____

2. _____   _____

3. _____   _____

4. _____   _____

5. _____   _____

What's Next? You Decide!

Now it's your turn to choose what to do next in the lesson. Read the activities and decide which one you want to do— you may want to try them all!

Get and Give Directions

STEPS

Have you or someone you know ever gotten lost while heading to a party, meeting, or event?

❑ Work with a partner. Your partner secretly chooses an activity that needs directions, such as how to turn on the computer, make a complicated dish, or build something.

❑ Your partner then reads the directions out loud while you listen and follow the directions exactly as they are given without writing anything down. Can you figure out what you're going to make or build or do?

❑ Then give directions to your partner. Can he or she figure it out?

Draw a Cartoon

MATERIALS

❑ scratch paper
❑ 1 sheet drawing paper
❑ 1 ruler
❑ colored pencils or crayons
❑ 1 black felt-tip marker

STEPS

Think about a humorous time when someone heard something wrong and it turned out to be a funny situation. For example, perhaps someone asked a friend to buy blue pegs and he or she came home with two eggs!

❑ Draw a newspaper comic showing this funny event. Remember, it has to be funny for everyone!

❑ Sketch out rough drafts on scratch paper. Use the ruler to draw boxes or other shapes for your images— just like in newspaper comics— or trace an object onto the paper for a shape. Then use the marker to outline the shapes.

❑ Make the final comic on a clean sheet of paper and use crayons or colored pencils to color your sketch.

❑ Share your comic with others.

Become a Reporter

STEPS

❑ Work with an adult and find a local community meeting that welcomes the public, such as a board meeting or organization's meeting.

❑ With an adult, attend that meeting and listen and take notes on what you hear, just like a news reporter.

❑ Then write a newspaper article about what happened at the meeting. Don't forget the five Ws and H: who, what, where, when, why, and how.

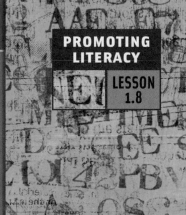

Researching and Reference Using MLA Style

Research is the key to discovering the events, experiences, and stories of our society, and writing is the way we communicate our important findings with the people of our world.

OBJECTIVE	BACKGROUND	MATERIALS
To teach your student how to effectively use research and reference materials and to cite them according to the MLA style	Learning how to accurately cite reference material is a crucial research skill that carries over to college and beyond. In this lesson, your student will learn the process of using different types of publications for research and using MLA style for citing documents. Then he or she will learn how to use research to write a news article.	■ Student Learning Pages 8.A–8.B ■ *MLA Style Manual*

VOCABULARY
MLA STYLE the style of the Modern Language Association of America is a common format for documenting sources used for research

Let's Begin

1 **CHOOSE A RESEARCH TOPIC** Explain that good research begins with choosing a specific topic that is interesting to the student. With your student, create a list of topics that he or she would like to learn more about and that would make a good newspaper article, such as current events. Then have your student choose a topic to write his or her article about.

2 **REVEAL AND EXPLORE** Work with your student to determine places and sources he or she can go to for information: library materials such as reference books, journals, periodicals, and other scholarly writing; and electronic sources such as the Internet. Then have your student find at least one newspaper article, one magazine article, one book, one reference book, and one Web site to use to gather information on the topic. Then have him or her take notes on the information.

3 **EXAMINE AND CITE** Explain that when we use published research for our own research and writing it is extremely

important to document the sources we use. Explain that the **MLA style** is a common format for citing material used for research. Examine the different types of publications your student used and explain that every type of publication has a specific MLA format that must be used to reference the material.

4 **FIND AND EXAMINE** With your student, locate a copy of the *MLA Style Manual* to find the specific formats for citing information. Explain that in a report often the sources that were used are found at the end of the report, usually in a bibliography.

5 **REVIEW AND DO** Review the *MLA Style Manual* and find the format used to cite the sources your student is using for his or her article. Choose one and walk your student through the citation. Then select a few types of publications around the house and have him or her cite them. When your student is finished, have him or her check his or her work using the *MLA Style Manual*. He or she also can find answers to questions about MLA style at http://www.mla.org. Here are a few basic examples.

   Book: Smith, Jennifer. *Research Made Easy.* New York: ABC Publishing, 2002.

   Magazine: Jones, Richard. "New Research Surprises Critics." *World News Magazine.* May 2002: 44–48.

   Newspaper: Hernandez, Juanita. "Government to Research Merits of New Plan." *The Daily Journal.* 9 Nov. 2002: B1.

   Web site: American Research Association. 21 May 2003. <http:www.ara.org> .

6 **LOOK FOR THE FIVE W'S AND H** Explain that a good article answers the five Ws and H: who, what, where, when, why, and how. Then distribute Student Learning Page 8.A.

7 **WRITE AND CITE** Now have your student write his or her article based on his or her research. Then have him or her cite the sources. Encourage your student to send his or her article to a local newspaper to see if it wants to publish it!

Branching Out

TEACHING TIP

Encourage your student to use detail and interesting words when he or she writes articles. Explain that a good article is both interesting and informative.

FOR FURTHER READING

MLA Style Manual, by Joseph Gibaldi (Modern Language Association of America, 1998).

CHECKING IN

Assess your student's understanding of citing research by having him or her write another article on another topic and properly cite the sources with little or no guidance.

Look for the Five Ws and H

Read a newspaper article and complete the chart by writing the
five Ws and H: who, what, where, when, why, and how.

Who?

What?

Where?

When?

Why?

How?

Student Learning Page 8.A: Look for the Five Ws and H

What's Next? You Decide!

Now it's your turn to choose what to do next in the lesson.
Read the activities and decide which one you want to do—
you may want to try them all!

Write a Family Newspaper

STEPS

❏ Create a family newspaper with stories about events and experiences of your family.

❏ Interview family members and research current events that affect them. Write stories about work, school, pets, sports, hobbies, and personal experiences. Focus on including the five Ws and H in each story.

❏ Type your articles and include illustrations or photographs. Publish and present the household news to your family. Don't forget to name your paper.

❏ You could even send the paper to friends and extended family members to update them on what's happening in your family.

❏ Be creative. Have fun. Use your research and writing skills!

Write a Newscast Script

STEPS

❏ Research a current event that is interesting to you. Use newspapers, magazines, and online resources to collect information.

❏ Then write a script for a newscast using what you know about how to write an accurate and interesting newspaper article. Present the facts, "interview" important people related to the story, and use pictures that help tell the story.

❏ Present your newscast to family and friends to inform them about this current event.

Navigate the Information Superhighway

MATERIALS

❏ drawing paper   ❏ colored pencils

STEPS

❏ Choose a topic to research.

❏ Use electronic resources to find information about this topic.

❏ Draw a road map showing the Web sites and electronic publications you researched and one fact about your topic.

❏ Show how one site can lead to another and to another and another. Connect each site by drawing a road (or information superhighway) and then representing each site along the research road by drawing a symbolic picture. Label each site using MLA style.

Editing and Publishing

A good piece of writing begins with a great idea, but if it's full of errors and not communicated effectively, the idea gets lost.

OBJECTIVE	BACKGROUND	MATERIALS
To teach your student to effectively follow the steps of the writing process and to edit and publish his or her work	Writing is a crucial form of communication that your student will use for the rest of his or her life. Learning how to edit and publish his or her work ensures that your student's message or idea will be communicated to the reader clearly and in a fashion that's suitable to the type of message. In this lesson, your student will write a personal narrative using the steps of the writing process and learn how to edit and revise his or her work. Then he or she will explore ways of publishing, or presenting, his or her writing and learn techniques for evaluating and improving.	■ Student Learning Pages 9.A–9.D ■ 1 copy Sequence Chain, page 354

Let's Begin

1 **CHOOSE A TOPIC** Explain that a successful piece of writing begins with a good idea that is well thought out. The first thing to do is to select a topic. Ask, *What do you want to write about? Do you want to tell a story, explain something, persuade someone, describe something?* Mention that the topic goes hand in hand with the type of writing you are doing.

2 **REVEAL** Reveal that there are four common types of writing:
- Persuasive writing
- Descriptive writing
- Explanatory writing
- Narrative writing

3 **EXPLAIN: PERSUASIVE WRITING** Explain that persuasive writing is writing that tries to convince the reader to do something, think something, or feel a certain way. Examples include advertisements and commercials. Tell your student to think of an advertisement or commercial that he or she recently read, saw, or heard. Ask, *What was the ad trying to make you do? Did it work?* Discuss.

4 **RELATE: DESCRIPTIVE WRITING** Relate that descriptive writing is writing that describes the way something smells, tastes, looks, sounds, or feels. Successful descriptions help the reader imagine the sight, sound, taste, or feeling of what you experienced. Read the two descriptions below out loud. Then ask, *Which do you think is a better description?*

> **Example 1:** The red flower
> **Example 2:** The tall, droopy flower with small red leaves
> Now have your student choose an object in the room and write a short description of it.

5 **EXPLAIN: EXPLANATORY WRITING** Mention that explanatory writing is writing that explains something, such as the steps of a process, how something works, who or what something is or was, or why or how something happens or happened. Ask your student, *What are some examples of explanatory writing?* [news article, directions] Then ask him or her to orally explain the steps of a process. Be careful not to prompt too much, but encourage him or her to thoughtfully identify the order of the steps.

6 **REVEAL: NARRATIVE WRITING** Reveal that narrative writing is writing that tells a story about someone or something. It's important in narrative writing to include the events that happened, details about the events, the outcome, and the reaction to the events. Explain to your student that he or she will write a personal narrative in this lesson. Ask, *What do you think a personal narrative is?* [see Step 7 for answer]

7 **ASK AND DISCUSS** Explain to your student that a personal narrative tells about the author's experience. It's written in the first person, the author, and is a true story that tells about a particular event or events that happened and how the author reacted to or feels about the experience. Ask your student to tell about something exciting that he or she has done recently, such as ride on a roller coaster. Specifically ask him or her to tell you two things: *what happened* and *what his or her reaction to it was.* Explain that when people talk about something that happened, they usually include how the event made them feel, such as happy, surprised, sad, and so on. Discuss.

8 **DISTRIBUTE** Distribute Student Learning Page 9.A. Have your student read the personal narrative. Then ask, *What happened in this essay?* [the writer went on a family vacation] *What was the writer's reaction to what happened?* [the writer enjoyed the vacation] Emphasize again that a well-written personal narrative tells what happened and the author's feelings about or reaction to what happened.

9 **CHOOSE AND IDENTIFY** Now have your student choose an experience that he or she has had. Ask, *What is the main idea?* Have him or her write the main idea in his or her notebook. This is the beginning of his or her personal narrative.

10 **ORGANIZE AND DISTRIBUTE** Now have your student make a time line of the events of the experience in his or her notebook. Encourage him or her to determine what happened first, second, third, and so on. Then make a copy of the Sequence Chain found on page 354 and distribute it to your student. Have him or her complete the chart, putting the events in chronological order. Review the time line and chart with your student. Are the events in the correct order? If not, discuss the order.

Suggest clue words that your student could use in his or her personal narrative that give the reader hints about what happens next. Ask your student to come up with some clue words. [then, next, after, first, second]

11 **EXAMINE** Look at each event with your student. Ask him or her to give you details about the events. Explain that details include sights, sounds, smells, tastes, and feelings. Details give the reader the opportunity to imagine what it was like to experience the events, and it can make the reading experience richer. Select one event from his or her experience. Ask, *What are some details you could include?* Have him or her write them in a notebook. Then give your student time to write details about each event in his or her narrative.

12 **WRITE** Now have him or her write his or her personal narrative. Remind him or her to review the time line, chart, and his or her notes. Be sure to give your student enough time to write.

A BRIGHT IDEA

Use this time to catch up on laundry, e-mails, and phone calls.

13 **DISTRIBUTE** When your student is finished, explain that not only does successful writing have to have good ideas, but it must be free of mistakes. Explain that part of the writing process is proofreading and then revising. Proofreading is checking for such things as misspelled words, incorrect punctuation, capitalization, and correct usage of words (e.g., *their* versus *there*). Revising is rewriting parts that have mistakes or are unclear based on what you have found while proofreading. Now distribute the Proofreading Checklist on Student Learning Page 9.B. Walk your student through the checklist.

14 **REWRITE** Now have your student revise and rewrite his or her personal narrative based on his or her notes on the Proofreading Checklist.

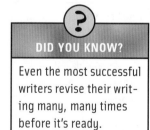

DID YOU KNOW?

Even the most successful writers revise their writing many, many times before it's ready.

15 **DISTRIBUTE AND REVIEW** Distribute Student Learning Page 9.C. Review with your student the scoring rubric. Explain that a scoring rubric is a way to assess, or grade, writing, which can be helpful for the writer to see how to make the writing better and where it might need improvement. Walk your student through each section of the rubric, explaining that for each area of evaluation the highest score is 3 and the lowest score is 1. Explain that the column for three points describes what features an effective personal narrative should contain.

16 **EVALUATE** Together with your student assess the sample personal narrative using the scoring rubric. Ask, *Does the personal narrative meet the goals for the assignment? Why or why not? In what ways might the personal narrative be improved?* Have your student take notes. Then discuss.

17 **READ ALOUD AND ASSESS** Have your student read aloud his or her personal narrative. Then, together use the scoring rubric to assess your student's personal narrative. Encourage your student to state which score he or she thinks should be given for each criterion and why. Discuss ways in which the personal narrative could be improved. Be sure that your student has the opportunity to express his or her ideas in a creative way! Have your student redraft the narrative as necessary.

18 **PUBLISH AND PRESENT** Now have your student think about his or her personal narrative and how he or she would like to share his or her writing with others. Explain that in addition to writing, he or she can communicate his or her experience in other ways. Ask, *How do you want to share your personal narrative? Who would you like to share it with?* Offer ideas such as he or she can make a collage that displays the narrative with photos and other items. Or he or she can turn it into a dramatic monologue or speech. Encourage your student to think of gestures or visual aids that could be used when telling the story. Help him or her think of ideas with the materials you have on hand.

Branching Out

FOR FURTHER READING

Craft Lessons: Teaching Writing K Through 8, by Ralph Fletcher and Joann Portalupi (Stenhouse Publishers, 1998).

Hands-On English, by Fran Santoro Hamilton (Portico Books, 1998).

Punctuation Power: Punctuation and How to Use It, by Marvin Terban (Scholastic Paperbacks, 2002).

TEACHING TIP

Remind your student that for a personal narrative, while it's important to describe the events in order, it's also important to tell the reader how you feel about the event and your reactions. Suggest to your student these words if you feel that he or she is struggling: *thrilled, amazed, delighted, upset, dejected, uplifted, confused,* and whatever else you can think of.

CHECKING IN

Assess your student's understanding of the writing process and the importance of editing and publishing his or her writing by reviewing the steps:

1. Choose a topic   **4.** Write a first draft   **7.** Publish and present

2. Organize and plan   **5.** Proofread and revise

3. Add details   **6.** Evaluate

Then have your student choose another type of writing from the examples given in Step 2 and write using the seven steps above. You may want to search the Internet ahead of time and find examples of those types of writings to use as models.

Read Personal Narrative Writing

My Favorite Vacation

My favorite vacation was last summer, when my family and I drove to the Black Hills of South Dakota. Overall, it was a great trip that my sister and brother and I really enjoyed.

The trip started on a Saturday morning. Our car was all packed and ready to go. We left early, at 5:00 a.m., and began the long drive from Chicago. We stopped several times throughout the day for lunch and dinner, but mostly we kept on driving. My dad really wanted to get there. After awhile I got really bored in the car, and I was feeling restless. I tried to sleep but couldn't. The ride seemed to last forever. I was so happy when we finally pulled into the campground in the Black Hills.

The first thing we did was set up our tents. As we were doing this, we heard a noise in the trees nearby. All of a sudden a large deer came running out of the woods and ran right past us! We were so surprised! It was a little scary but also very exciting.

The next day my sister and brother and I went for a swim in Lake Pactola. The water was sort of cold but we stayed in anyway. I floated on our inflatable raft and the others tried to knock me off of it. It was a blast! Later, my dad came in and we tried to knock him off the raft. This was also really fun. I just didn't like the rocky lake bottom, which hurt my feet.

The highlight of the vacation, though, was seeing Mount Rushmore. Mount Rushmore is a mountain that has the faces of four American presidents carved into the side of it. The presidents are George Washington, Thomas Jefferson, Abraham Lincoln, and Theodore Roosevelt. I was amazed. I couldn't believe how real the faces looked! It inspired me to make my own sculpture some day. It also made me feel proud to be an American.

We stayed in the Black Hills for five days, then drove back home. The drive didn't seem as difficult this time. When the vacation finally ended I was glad to be home. It was the best trip I ever took. I had a lot of fun.

Proofread Your Writing

Read the Proofreading Checklist. Check off each item as you complete it. You can use this checklist every time you write!

Proofreading Checklist

❏ My personal narrative has proper punctuation: commas, quotation marks, end punctuation.

Ways that I can improve this: _____

❏ Words are capitalized properly.

Ways that I can improve this: _____

❏ All words are spelled correctly.

Ways that I can improve this: _____

❏ Words are used correctly, such as *there, their,* and *they're; your* and *you're; it's* and *its; too, to,* and *two.*

Ways that I can improve this: _____

❏ I told the events in the order in which they took place.

Ways that I can improve this: _____

❏ I used clue words to help the reader understand the order of events.

Ways that I can improve this: _____

❏ I described my reactions and feelings to the events.

Ways that I can improve this: _____

❏ I used details to help the reader experience the events and make it interesting and more realistic.

Ways that I can improve this: _____

❏ My personal narrative is clearly written so that it is easy to understand.

Ways that I can improve this: _____

Evaluate Writing

Read the scoring rubric. Then answer the questions.

	3 Points	2 Points	1 Point	Score of Sample Personal Narrative	Score of My Personal Narrative
Events	Events are told in the correct order.	Some, but not all, events are told in the correct order.	Only a few events are told in the correct order.		
Reactions	Writer describes all of his or her reactions to the events.	Writer describes some, but not all, of his or her reactions to the events.	Writer describes only a few of his or her reactions to the events.		
Clear writing	Essay is clearly written. It is easy to understand.	Some parts of the essay are easy to understand but other parts are confusing.	Most of the essay is difficult to understand.		
Punctuation and spelling	Essay uses punctuation marks correctly and there are very few misspelled words.	Some sentences are properly punctuated but others are not. There are several mis-spelled words.	There are many incorrect punctuation marks and many misspelled words.		

1. What areas do you need to work on?

    _____

    _____

    _____

2. What can you do to improve your writing?

    _____

    _____

    _____

What's Next? You Decide!

Now it's your turn to choose what to do next in the lesson. Read the activities and decide which one you want to do—you may want to try them both!

Create an Advertisement

STEPS

❑ Choose one of your favorite items, such as a book, a game or toy, or a CD or cassette tape, and create an advertisement persuading people to buy your item.

❑ Decide who your audience is (kids your age who like to cook?) and what the best way is to communicate your message.

❑ Decide what advertisement to create. Should you make a TV or radio commercial—what channel and time of day should you run your ad? Should your ad go in a newspaper or magazine—which newspaper or magazine and in which section? What about advertising your item on the Internet or on a billboard?

❑ Once you have decided, figure out what materials you'll need (paper? cardboard? markers? tape recorder?). Get creative! What materials can you find around the house? Ask an adult to help you find supplies.

❑ Then present your commercial to someone. Does he or she want to buy your item?

Design a Comic About You

MATERIALS

❑ scratch paper
❑ 1 sheet drawing paper
❑ 1 ruler
❑ colored pencils or crayons
❑ 1 black felt-tip marker

STEPS

❑ Draw a newspaper comic that describes a time when you were very surprised. Remember that the events should be told in order, should include details, and should show your reaction to the experience, just like in a personal narrative writing.

❑ Think of what events occurred when you were surprised as well as the sights (including colors), sounds, smells, tastes, and emotions you experienced.

❑ Sketch out rough drafts on scratch paper. Use the ruler to draw boxes or other shapes for your images—just like in newspaper comics—or trace an object onto the paper for a shape. Then use the marker to outline the shapes.

❑ Make the final comic on a clean sheet of paper and use crayons or colored pencils to color your sketch.

❑ Share your comic with others.

In Your Community

To reinforce the skills and concepts taught in this section, try one or more of these activities!

Extra! Extra!

Journey to the offices where a local newspaper is created. Arrange for your student to speak with a reporter or editor. You also might visit a publishing house and have your student speak with the writers and editors there.

Local Folklore

Have your student research the folklore of your community. There may be folklore connected to the land or native people of your area. Have your student create a presentation. Then ask to have it displayed at your local library, community center, or town hall for others to view and learn from.

Storytelling

Contact a library, historical society, or literary society in your community to find out about local storytelling events. Some storytelling groups include "open mic" time, and your student may choose to tell a story of his or her own about your family's cultural heritage.

Bookstore Events

Attend a booksigning, poetry reading, or presentation by an author with your student at a local bookstore. While you're there, have your student familiarize himself or herself with the different literary genre sections in the store and relate them to the material he or she studied in the lessons.

A Book Club

Book clubs are becoming popular as more and more people are coming to know the pleasure and benefits of talking about the books they read. Start a parent/child bookclub in your community, or even just within your nuclear or extended family. Encourage nonjudgmental discussions and be open to a range of opinions. Some books may even have discussion guides published to accompany you in your group.

Community Biography

Ask your student to identify a senior member of the community whom he or she admires or respects. Arrange an introductory meeting with your student, the selected person, and yourself. Explain that you've been studying biographies and are interested in telling the stories of people in the community. Have your student prepare questions for a biographical interview and afterward write a short biography. Finally, have your student share the biography with the person and ask permission to submit it to a local newspaper.

We Have Learned

Use this checklist to summarize what you and your student
have accomplished in the Promoting Literacy section.

❏ **Fiction and Short Story**
❏ reading and analyzing fiction
❏ reading and analyzing short story
❏ writing fictional story with plot,
  characters, setting, dialogue
❏ characteristics of fiction
❏ characteristics of short story

❏ **Folktale and Oral Narrative**
❏ reading and analyzing folktale
❏ characteristics of folktale
❏ listening to oral narrative
❏ delivering oral narrative

❏ **Biography**
❏ reading and analyzing biography
❏ characteristics of biography
❏ before you read, while you read,
  after you read

❏ **Poetry**
❏ reading and analyzing poetry
❏ characteristics of poetry
❏ writing poetry

❏ **Drama**
❏ reading and analyzing drama
❏ characteristics of drama
❏ presenting drama to an audience

❏ **Listening and Notetaking**
❏ listening, understanding, analyzing,
  evaluating information

❏ comparing sources, comparing
  information
❏ procedure for notetaking

❏ **Research and MLA Style**
❏ comparing, categorizing, evaluating
  information
❏ finding main points, categorizing
❏ MLA style for sourcing documents
❏ writing news article

❏ **Editing and Publishing**
❏ fundamentals of effective writing
❏ editing, proofreading, revising
❏ explanatory, descriptive, narrative,
  persuasive writing
❏ publishing and presenting

We have also learned:

_____

_____

_____

_____

_____

_____

_____

Math

Math

Key Topics

Number Theory
Pages 79–82

Fractions
Pages 83–90

Decimals
Pages 91–98

Percents
Pages 99–104

Ratio, Probability, and Proportion
Pages 105–110

Data with Charts and Graphs
Pages 111–118

Integers
Pages 119–124

Measurement
Pages 125–138

Geometry
Pages 139–148

Making the Grade: Everything Your 6th Grader Needs to Know

Making Sense of Number Theory

Don't be intimidated by math—it can be simpler than you think.

OBJECTIVE	BACKGROUND	MATERIALS
To show your student how to use factorization in problem solving	Once your student gains a basic understanding of prime numbers and factorization, he or she will be able to grasp concepts such as greatest common factors and least common multiples. In this lesson, your student will learn these concepts and work through problems using fractions.	■ Student Learning Pages 1.A–1.B

Let's Begin

1 **MODEL** Explain that whole numbers can be divided into two types: prime numbers and composite numbers. A prime number is a whole number greater than 1 with exactly two factors (itself and 1). An example of a prime number is 13 because 1 and 13 are the only factors that equal 13. A composite number is a whole number greater than 1 with more than two factors. Twelve and 8 are examples of composite numbers, since each has several factors:

$$12 = 1 \times 12 \qquad 8 = 1 \times 8$$
$$2 \times 6 \qquad\qquad 2 \times 4$$
$$3 \times 4$$

2 **MODEL** Tell your student that the factors of composite numbers can be broken down into all prime numbers. This step, called prime factorization, can be accomplished like this:

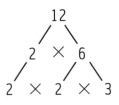

3 **MODEL GCF** Tell your student that he or she will be looking for the greatest common factor, or GCF (the biggest number by which

two or more numbers are divisible), of 27 and 36. One way to find the greatest common factor is to use prime factorization:

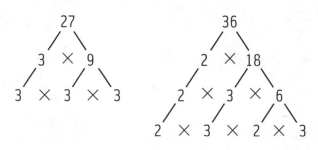

Then find the factors that are common to both and multiply them together. The GCF is 3 × 3, or 9.

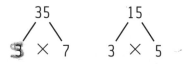

4   **MODEL LCM**   To solve this problem, show your student how to find the least common multiple, or LCM (the smallest number that is a multiple of two or more chosen numbers), of 35 and 15. One way to find the LCM is to use prime factorization:

$$\begin{array}{ccc} 35 & & 15 \\ \diagup \diagdown & & \diagup \diagdown \\ 3 \times 7 & & 3 \times 5 \end{array}$$

Use the prime factors to write the smallest product containing 35 and 15. Align common factors (if any):

$$\begin{array}{rl} 35 = & 5 \times 7 \\ 15 = 3 \times 5 & \\ \hline 3 \times 5 \times 7 = & 105 \text{ minutes} \end{array}$$

Write the products as shown, using each common factor only once.

5   **PRACTICE**   Have your student complete Student Learning Page 1.A for more practice.

Branching Out

TEACHING TIP

Have your student check his or her answers to be sure they make sense in the context of the problem.

CHECKING IN

As you assess your student's work, make sure he or she has a clear understanding of which approach to use to solve a problem.

FOR FURTHER READING

The Number Devil: A Mathematical Adventure, by Hans Magnus Enzensberger and Michael Henry Heim (Henry Holt and Company, 2000).

Teaching Mathematics: A Sourcebook of Aids, Activities, and Strategies (3rd Edition), by Max A. Sobel and Evan M. Maletsky (Allyn and Bacon, 1998).

Find Prime Factors and Greatest Common Factors

Write the prime factorization for each number in a pyramid shape. Use exponents in your answers where appropriate.

1. 46

4. 72

2. 60

5. 67

3. 27

6. 32

Find the greatest common factors (GCFs) for the following pairs of numbers. Then on a separate sheet of paper find the least common multiples.

7. 14, 30

9. 33, 63

8. 105, 50

10. 15, 18

What's Next? You Decide!

Now it's your turn to choose what to do next in the lesson.
Read the activities and decide which one you want to do—
you may want to try them both!

Measuring Up

MATERIALS

❑ 1 tape measure or yardstick

STEPS

❑ Using a tape measure or a yardstick, measure the height (in inches) of four family members or friends.

❑ Using these measurements, determine the greatest common factor of the measurements.

❑ What is the least common multiple? Are any of the measurements prime numbers?

Zero and One— Primes or Composites?

STEPS

❑ Think about what you know about prime and composite numbers and try to decide which category the numbers 0 and 1 fit into.

❑ Search the Internet and see if you can find out.

❑ Using the information you uncover, write a brief paragraph here describing what you've learned.

_____

_____

_____

_____

_____

_____

_____

_____

_____

_____

_____

_____

_____

_____

MATH

LESSON 2.2

Using Fractions and Estimation

Mmmm . . . $\frac{3}{4}$ of a sandwich—
I could eat that for lunch.
If it were only $\frac{4}{16}$ (a seemingly bigger number),
I'd barely be able to munch.

OBJECTIVE	BACKGROUND	MATERIALS
To show your student how to add, subtract, multiply, divide, and estimate fractions	When you and your student are sharing a pizza, following a recipe, measuring rooms, building models, or calculating time for activities, you constantly are working with fractions. In this lesson your student will apply basic addition, subtraction, multiplication, and division skills to fractions and mixed numbers.	■ Student Learning Pages 2.A–2.D ■ 12 index cards ■ 2 dice

VOCABULARY

EQUIVALENT FRACTIONS fractions with different numbers that have the same value
NUMERATOR in a fraction, the number above the bar
DENOMINATOR in a fraction, the number below the bar
IMPROPER FRACTION a fraction that is greater than or equal to 1
MIXED NUMBER the sum of a whole number and a fraction

Let's Begin

ADDITION AND SUBTRACTION

1 **DESIGN AND CREATE** Begin the lesson by making fraction strips. Fraction strips help your student relate **equivalent fractions.** Use index cards to label and measure fractions. Cut apart index cards to make strips: One whole strip equals 1. Work together to make fraction strips for thirds, fourths, sixths, eighths, and twelfths. Here is an example of fraction strips for thirds and twelfths.

Then have your student line up several fraction strips to demonstrate equivalent fractions such as $\frac{?}{6} = \frac{2}{3}$; $\frac{2}{8} = \frac{?}{4}$; $\frac{8}{12} = \frac{?}{3}$. [4; 1; 2] Ask your student to explain how to tell when two fractions are equivalent. [multiply or divide the **numerator** and **denominator** of one fraction by the same number to get the second fraction]

2 **DESCRIBE** Describe this scenario to your student: *You cut a pan of banana bread into 8 equal pieces. Your friends eat $\frac{5}{8}$ of it and you eat 2 pieces. What fraction of the banana bread was eaten? How much more banana bread was eaten by your friends than by you?* [$\frac{5}{8} + \frac{2}{8} = \frac{7}{8}$; $\frac{5}{8} - \frac{2}{8} = \frac{3}{8}$]

3 **ASK** Ask, *How would you solve this problem? What operations would you use?* Have your student solve the problems while you observe your student adding and then subtracting.

4 **EXPLAIN** Explain that in making the banana bread, the recipe called for $\frac{1}{3}$ cup shortening, $\frac{1}{2}$ cup sugar, and $1\frac{3}{4}$ cups flour. Ask, *How many cups of ingredients are there in total? How would you begin solving this problem?*

5 **MODEL AND WRITE** Work with your student to find equivalent fractions for the ingredients. Ask, *What is the common denominator?* [12] If necessary, have your student use fraction strips to make equivalent fractions before adding the ingredients. Ask, *What steps did you take to solve the problem?* [found common denominator, added fractions and whole number, changed **improper fraction** to **mixed number**; sum is $2\frac{7}{12}$]

6 **EXPLORE** Tell your student that you want to determine the total quantity of ingredients before you add the flour. Ask, *What is the sum of the shortening and sugar? What steps will you take to subtract the flour?* [subtract sum of shortening and sugar from total by finding common denominator, subtracting, and then simplifying fraction: $2\frac{7}{12} - 1\frac{3}{4} = \frac{9}{12} = \frac{3}{4}$]

7 **PRACTICE** Now distribute Student Learning Page 2.A for more practice.

MULTIPLICATION AND DIVISION

1 **DESCRIBE** Describe this scenario to your student: *You have a recipe that makes 4 servings, yet you need 6 servings. How much of each ingredient do you need additionally?* [multiply each ingredient by $1\frac{1}{2}$ to make 6 servings] Then relate: *A 4-serving recipe for vegetable soup calls for $\frac{3}{4}$ cups chopped onions and $2\frac{1}{2}$ cups string beans. How much of each ingredient is needed to make 6 servings?* [multiply each ingredient by $1\frac{1}{2}$]

2   **ASK** Ask, *How would you solve this problem? What operations would you use?* Have your student solve the problem while you observe your student. Go to Step 3.

3   **MODEL AND WRITE** Write the equations on a sheet of paper as shown and walk through each step showing how to multiply each ingredient by $1\frac{1}{2}$ and then simplify.

1. Write equations

   $$\frac{3}{4} \times 1\frac{1}{2} = ? \qquad 2\frac{1}{2} \times 1\frac{1}{2} = ?$$

2. Write mixed number as improper fraction

   $$1\frac{1}{2} = \frac{3}{2} = \frac{6}{4} \qquad 2\frac{1}{2} = \frac{5}{2} \qquad\qquad 1\frac{1}{2} = \frac{3}{2}$$

3. Multiply

   $$\frac{3}{4} \times \frac{6}{4} = \frac{18}{16} \qquad \frac{5}{2} \times \frac{3}{2} = \frac{15}{2}$$

4. Write fraction as mixed number

   $$\frac{18}{16} = 1\frac{2}{16} \qquad \frac{15}{2} = 7\frac{1}{2}$$

5. Simplify, if necessary

   $$1\frac{2}{16} = 1\frac{1}{8}$$

6. Solution

   $1\frac{1}{8}$ cups onions $7\frac{1}{2}$ cups string beans

4   **REVIEW** If you feel that your student needs additional review, have him or her convert the improper fractions into mixed numbers and the mixed numbers into improper fractions.

$$\frac{9}{4} = ? \quad (2\frac{1}{4}: \text{steps:} \quad 4\overline{)9} \;\; \begin{array}{r} 2 \\ \hline 9 \\ -\,8 \\ \hline 1 \end{array} = 2\frac{1}{4}$$

$\frac{16}{2} = ?$ (8: steps: $16 \div 2 = 8$)

$\frac{10}{3} = ?$ ($3\frac{1}{3}$: steps: $10 \div 3 = 3\frac{1}{3}$)

$3\frac{5}{8} = ?$ ($\frac{29}{4}$: steps: $8 \times 3 = 24$; $24 + 5 = 29$; $\frac{29}{4}$)

$1\frac{2}{9} = ?$ ($\frac{11}{9}$: steps: $9 \times 1 = 9$; $9 + 2 = 11$; $\frac{11}{9}$)

$4\frac{3}{5} = ?$ ($\frac{23}{5}$: steps: $5 \times 4 = 20$; $20 + 3 = 23$; $\frac{23}{5}$)

5   **EXPLAIN** Tell your student that sometimes you need to divide a recipe to make a smaller serving size. For example, if you have a recipe that makes 6 servings and you need 4 servings, you can divide each ingredient by $1\frac{1}{2}$ to make 4 servings. Describe: *A 6-serving recipe for vegetable soup calls for $1\frac{1}{4}$ cups chopped onions and $4\frac{1}{2}$ cups string beans. How much of each ingredient is needed to make 4 servings?* [divide each ingredient by $1\frac{1}{2}$]

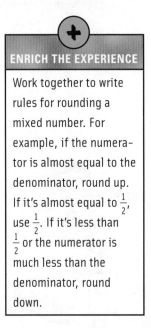
6 **ASK** Ask, *How would you solve this problem? What operations would you use?* Have your student solve the problem while you observe your student. Go to Step 7.

7 **MODEL AND WRITE** Write the equations on a sheet of paper and walk through each step showing how to divide each ingredient by $1\frac{1}{2}$.

1. Write equations
$$1\frac{1}{4} \div 1\frac{1}{2} = ? \qquad 4\frac{1}{2} \div 1\frac{1}{2} = ?$$

2. Write mixed number as improper fraction
$$1\frac{1}{4} = \frac{5}{4} \qquad\qquad 4\frac{1}{2} = \frac{5}{2}$$
$$1\frac{1}{2} = \frac{3}{2} = \frac{6}{4} \qquad 1\frac{1}{2} = \frac{3}{2}$$

3. Divide
$$\frac{5}{4} \div \frac{6}{4} = ? \qquad\qquad \frac{5}{2} \div \frac{3}{2} = ?$$

4. Rewrite as multiplication using the reciprocal of the divisor
$$\frac{5}{4} \times \frac{4}{6} = ? \qquad \frac{5}{2} \times \frac{2}{3} = ?$$

5. Cancel common factors
$$\frac{5}{\cancel{4}} \times \frac{\cancel{4}}{6} = \frac{5}{6} \qquad \frac{5}{\cancel{2}} \times \frac{\cancel{2}}{3} = \frac{5}{3}$$

6. Write fraction as mixed number
$$\frac{18}{16} = 1\frac{2}{16} \qquad\qquad \frac{5}{3} = 1\frac{1}{3}$$

7. Simplify
$$1\frac{2}{16} = 1\frac{1}{8}$$

8 **PRACTICE** Now go to Student Learning Page 2.B for practice.

Branching Out

TEACHING TIP

If your student enjoys cooking, then prepare a recipe that involves fractions. Allow your student to revise the recipe by calculating the amounts per serving.

CHECKING IN

Assess your student's ability by having your student read several recipes. Have him or her choose one or more recipes and double the recipe or cut the recipe in half.

Add and Subtract Fractions

Write equivalent fractions using fraction strips.

1. $\frac{6}{8}$ _____

2. $\frac{2}{3}$ _____

Write three fractions that are equivalent to $\frac{1}{5}$.

3. _____

4. _____

5. _____

Write the next three equivalent fractions. What is the pattern?

6. $\frac{2}{5}$, $\frac{4}{10}$, $\frac{6}{15}$, _____, _____, _____

Add or subtract. Write each answer in simplest form.

7. $\frac{3}{8} + \frac{2}{8} =$ _____

10. $10\frac{3}{4} - 5 =$ _____

8. $\frac{7}{12} + \frac{3}{12} =$ _____

11. $7\frac{1}{8} - 3\frac{5}{8} =$ _____

9. $4\frac{5}{8} + 2\frac{1}{4} =$ _____

12. $9 - \frac{3}{7} =$ _____

For more practice, on a separate sheet of paper subtract problems 7–9 and add problems 10–12.

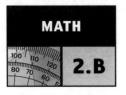

Multiply and Divide Fractions

Multiply. Write each answer in simplest form.

1. $\frac{2}{3} \times \frac{3}{5} =$ _____

2. $2\frac{3}{4} \times 1\frac{3}{5} =$ _____

3. $4 \times 2\frac{2}{9} =$ _____

4. $\frac{3}{7} \times 4\frac{5}{8} =$ _____

Divide. Write each answer in simplest form.

5. $\frac{1}{4} \div \frac{2}{3} =$ _____

6. $2\frac{3}{4} \div \frac{1}{2} =$ _____

7. $7\frac{1}{2} \div 2\frac{5}{8} =$ _____

8. $\frac{5}{8} \div \frac{3}{5} =$ _____

Multiply or divide.

9. A recipe for oatmeal cookies calls for 3 cups quick-cooking rolled oats to make 60 cookies. How many cups of the rolled oats are in one cookie?

   _____

10. If you wanted to make 100 cookies, how many cups of quick-cooking rolled oats will you need? Explain your answer.

    _____

11. The product of two fractions is $\frac{1}{8}$. The sum of the two fractions is $\frac{3}{4}$. Find two possible fractions.

    _____

Play Roll-Them Fractions

You and another player see who can get 10 points first. One player rolls two dice, one at a time. Both dice make a fraction. The first die is the numerator. The second die is the denominator. If the fraction is in simplest form, then the player gets two points. If the fraction isn't in simplest form, then the second player gets one point by writing the fraction in simplest form. Alternate play continues until a player gets 10 points. Keep track of points on this sheet.

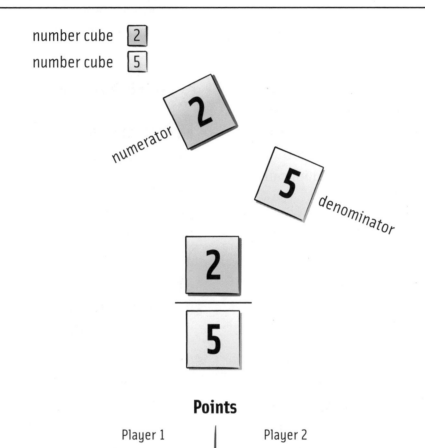

number cube 2
number cube 5

2   numerator

5   denominator

$$\frac{2}{5}$$

Points

Player 1	Player 2

What's Next? You Decide!

Now it's your turn to choose what to do next in the lesson. Read the activities and decide which one you want to do— you may want to try them both!

Play Equivalent Fractions

MATERIALS

❏ 44 index cards

STEPS

❏ Write the numbers 0 to 9 on two sets of index cards. On another set of cards write the symbols for addition, subtraction, multiplication, and division.

❏ One player shuffles the symbol cards while another player shuffles both sets of number cards together and places them in a stack.

❏ Both players receive 10 blank index cards. Player 1 draws four number cards and a symbol card, makes a fraction equation, and solves it on a blank index card on the game mat (for example, $\frac{3}{4} + \frac{2}{3}$). Here's an example:

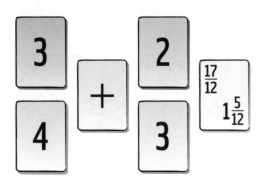

If the answer is correct, the player scores a point. If the answer is incorrect, Player 2 attempts to

answer the equation. If Player 2 has the correct answer, he or she receives two points. The first player to get 15 points wins.

Write a Recipe for Success

MATERIALS

❏ recipe books

❏ food advertisements in newspaper

STEPS

What recipe would you like to make?

❏ Look through recipe books to find a tasty recipe for hors d'oeuvres, a main course, a side dish, or a dessert.

❏ Then search your local newspaper for food advertisements and find items to buy for your recipe.

❏ Calculate the cost for the items and divide by the number of servings you'll be making. How much does each serving cost?

❏ In a notebook, write the recipe; below it, write your comments about it. Ask permission before making your dish.

MATH

LESSON 2.3

Working with Decimals

Use this lesson as a stepping stone to instruction about money, measurements, and quantities.

OBJECTIVE	BACKGROUND	MATERIALS
To show your student how to add, subtract, multiply, divide, and estimate decimals	Working with decimals is a lifelong skill that your student will use in all areas of life, whether it's using money, determining quantities, measuring, or working with such figures as athletic scores. In this lesson, your student will apply the addition, subtraction, multiplication, and division skills he or she already has to decimals.	■ Student Learning Pages 3.A–3.D ■ 1 copy Grid, page 355 ■ 1 die ■ 2 game pieces

Let's Begin

ADDITION AND SUBTRACTION

1 **DESCRIBE** Money is an easy way to apply real-world math, especially adding and subtracting decimals. Describe this scenario to your student: *Five items were purchased at the store for $15.64, $8.30, $19.99, $.25, and $12. What is the total cost of these items? What's the total cost if you returned the $15.64 item? What's the total cost if you returned the $12 item the next day?* [$56.18, $40.54, $28.54]

2 **ASK** Ask, *How would you solve this problem? What methods would you use?* [align the decimal points, add the five items, then subtract the returned items] Have your student attempt to solve the problem while you observe his or her method of doing so.

   If your student **solved the problem** correctly, ask, *What did you do to solve this problem?* Encourage your student to tell how he or she lined up the decimal points of the numbers before adding and then subtracting. Then skip Steps 3–6 and distribute Student Learning Page 3.A to give your student additional practice. If your student **didn't solve the problem** correctly, have him or her estimate the answer:

A BRIGHT IDEA

Use coins for game pieces.

15.64	→	16
8.30	→	8
19.99	→	20
.25	→	0
+ 12	→	+ 12
		56

Estimating shows where the decimal point would go in the answer. Then make estimates for the subtraction steps. Now have your student go to Step 3; check the estimates against the correct answers.

3 **MODEL AND WRITE** Make a copy of the Grid found on page 355. Write the five numbers on the Grid as shown. Be sure to align the decimal points! Explain to your student that the most important thing to remember when adding or subtracting decimals is lining up the decimals.

$$
\begin{array}{r}
15.64 \\
8.30 \\
19.99 \\
.25 \\
+\ 12. \\
\hline
\end{array}
$$

4 **MODEL** Show your student how to add zeros so that all of the numbers in the problem have the same number of places to the right and left of the decimal points. This makes it easier to add the columns of numbers. Then add the numbers and insert the decimal point.

$$
\begin{array}{r}
15.64 \\
\mathbf{0}8.30 \\
19.99 \\
\mathbf{00}.25 \\
+\ 12.\mathbf{00} \\
\hline
56.18
\end{array}
$$

5 **MODEL** Then have your student finish the problem by subtracting. Show him or her how the subtraction for this problem occurs in two steps:

STEP 1	**STEP 2**	
56.18	40.54	
− 15.64	− 12.00	(total from equation)
40.54	28.54	

Discuss how adding and subtracting decimals is different from adding and subtracting whole numbers.

6 **DISTRIBUTE** Distribute Student Learning Page 3.A and have your student complete the exercises.

MULTIPLICATION AND DIVISION

1 **DESCRIBE** Does your student complain about household chores? Describe this scenario to your student: *An 80-pound person mowing the lawn with a push mower uses about 2.63 calories per minute. If this person spends 15.5 minutes mowing the lawn on Saturday and 40.1 minutes on Sunday, how many calories does this person use each day mowing the lawn?* [40.765 Saturday, 105.463 Sunday]

Continue with: *If the person uses 118.35 calories mowing the lawn on Thursday and 315.6 calories on Friday, how many minutes does this person mow each day?* [45 Thursday, 120 Friday]

2 **ASK** Ask, *How would you solve this problem? What methods would you use?* [multiply calories per minute by number of minutes, then divide calories used by calories per minute] Have your student attempt to solve the problem while you observe his or her method of doing so.

If your student **solved the problem** correctly, ask, *What did you do to solve this problem?* Encourage your student to tell how he or she multiplied as usual and then counted the number of places to the right of the decimal points and inserted the decimal point in the answer; then he or she divided as usual and counted the number of places to the right of the decimal points and inserted the decimal point in the answer. Then distribute Student Learning Page 3.B to give your student additional practice.

If your student **didn't solve the problem** correctly, have him or her estimate the answer:

$$
\begin{array}{ccc}
2.63 & \longrightarrow & 3 \\
\times\ 15.5 & \longrightarrow & \times\ 16 \\
\hline
 & & 48
\end{array}
\qquad
\begin{array}{ccc}
2.63 & \longrightarrow & 3 \\
\times\ 40.1 & \longrightarrow & \times\ 40 \\
\hline
 & & 120
\end{array}
$$

Estimating shows where the decimal point would go in the answer. Next make estimates for the division steps. Now have your student go to Step 3; check the estimates against the correct answers.

3 **MODEL AND WRITE** Write the equations on a sheet of paper as shown and walk your student through each equation, showing how to multiply and divide as usual and inserting zeros as shown:

SATURDAY	SUNDAY	THURSDAY	FRIDAY
2.63	2.63	00045	001206
× 15.5	× 40.1	2.63)118.35	2.63)317.178
05315	000263		
13150	000000		
26300	105200		
40765	105463		

4 **MODEL** Then show how to count the places to the right of the decimals for multiplying and then for dividing:

2.**63**	2.**63**	00045	001206
× 15.**5**	× 40.**1**	2.**63**)118.35	2.**63**)317.178
05315	000263		
13150	000000		
26300	105200		
40765	105463		

5 **MODEL** Finally show where to place the decimal point:

2.**63**	2.**63**	00045.	00120.6
× 15.**5**	× 40.**1**	2.**63**)118.35	2.**63**)317.178
05315	000263		
13150	000000		
26300	105200		
40.765	105.463		

Discuss how placement of the decimal point can change the value of a number—show your student an old bank statement or checkbook register to open the discussion.

6 **DISTRIBUTE** Distribute Student Learning Page 3.B and have your student complete the exercises. Then distribute Student Learning Pages 3.C–3.D to your student. You may wish to play the game on Student Learning Page 3.C with him or her.

FOR FURTHER READING

The Grapes of Math: Mind Stretching Math Riddles, by Greg Tang (Scholastic Trade, 2001).

Math Phonics–Decimals: Quick Tips and Alternative Techniques for Math Mastery, by Marilyn B. Hein, Judy Mitchell, and Ron Wheeler (Teaching and Learning Company, 1999).

Math Skills Made Fun: Dazzling Math Line Designs, by Cindi Mitchell (Scholastic, Inc., 1999).

Branching Out

TEACHING TIPS

❏ You can have your student search the Internet and find the calories used per minute for chores other than mowing the lawn; then have him or her find the calories used for his or her favorite activities. Which uses more, the least favorite chore or the most favorite activity?

❏ The grocery store is filled with many opportunities to work with decimals—compare prices and quantities, use money, and explore measurements of different items.

CHECKING IN

Assess your student's ability by providing him or her with a list of prices of grocery items (use an actual receipt!). Have your student determine the total cost of the items. How much money would he or she have to pay if one item were subtracted from the total? Then have your student examine the costs of an item sold in different quantities. Have him or her determine the cost per the smallest unit of measure for each quantity.

Add and Subtract Decimals

Add and subtract.

1.   5.8
     + 1.08

2.   42.50
     − 13

3.   22.47
    + 14.03

4.   65.239
     − 45.01

5.   75.1
     + 2.411

6.   10.755
     − 1.12

7.   67
      23.45
     + 6.01

8.   99.14
      44.21
     − 23.88

9.   72.0
       .031
     + 2.9

For more practice, subtract the odd-numbered problems and add the even-numbered problems. Show your work.

Multiply and Divide Decimals

Multiply and divide.

1. 3.44
    × 1.7

2. 15)‾34.071‾

3. 22.67
    × 1.2

4. 2.2)‾46.42‾

5. 55.55
    × 2.3

6. 4.2)‾42‾

7. 11.11
    × .4

8. .011)‾121‾

9. 46.332
    × 44

For more practice, divide the odd-numbered problems and multiply the even-numbered problems. Show your work.

96   *Making the Grade: Everything Your 6th Grader Needs to Know*

Play Decimal Derby

Place your game pieces at start. Player 1 rolls the die and moves his or her game piece that number of spaces. Player 2 then makes an addition, subtraction, multiplication, or division decimal problem for Player 1 to solve using the numbers on that square. Solve the problem using paper and pencil. If the answer is correct, the player gets to stay on that square; if it's wrong, the player must go back to his or her previous position. The first player to reach finish wins. Check answers with a calculator.

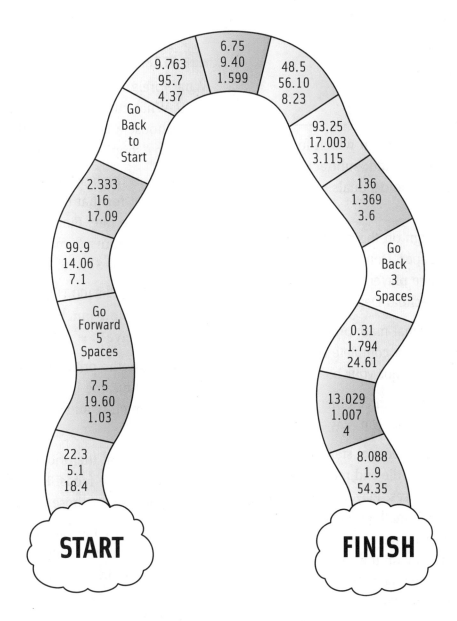

What's Next? You Decide!

Now it's your turn to choose what to do next in the lesson. Read the activities and decide which one you want to do— you may want to try them both!

Make Your Own Board Game

MATERIALS

❏ large piece cardboard, or 4 sheets paper taped together

❏ colored markers or crayons

❏ 4 game pieces

STEPS

Invent your own game in which four players will have to add, subtract, multiply, and divide decimals correctly to win!

❏ Draw a design on the cardboard or sheets of paper. Don't forget to decide where players start and finish. (Look at Decimal Derby for ideas.)

❏ Write in decimal math problems that the players must complete correctly to move ahead. Color your board game.

❏ Now find one to three other players— up to four people can play at once!

❏ Put the game pieces at start. The first player rolls the die and moves forward that many spaces. Player 1 must complete that math problem correctly. If he or she answers correctly, the player can stay on the space. If not, he or she must move back to the previous place. The player who reaches finish first wins the game!

Shop with Money from Another Country

MATERIALS

❏ 1 newspaper that lists international currency exchange rates

STEPS

What foreign country would you like to visit? What currency does that country use? Choose a country and then get ready to "shop" with its money.

❏ Look in the newspaper or on the Internet for that country's currency exchange rate. Find out how much of that country's money you could "buy" with $1 U.S.

❏ Now "buy" $100 U.S. of the foreign money. How much money would you receive?

❏ Suppose the price of a gallon of milk costs the same in both countries— how much would you pay in each country?

❏ Next look at the prices of some of your favorite foods. How much would pay for those in each country?

❏ Then follow the exchange rate of this country's money for at least two weeks. Make a chart and keep track of the daily rate. How does the rate change?

Using Percents

It's no coincidence that 100 cents is 100 percent of a dollar!

OBJECTIVE	BACKGROUND	MATERIALS
To show your student how to use fractions, percents, and decimals in real-world settings	In the real world, rarely a day goes by without the need to figure out sales tax or compute discounts. Your student will begin this section by converting percents, decimals, and fractions, then move on to problem solving using sales tax, discounts, and simple interest.	■ Student Learning Pages 4.A–4.B

VOCABULARY

PERCENT an expression of a ratio telling how many out of 100

CONVERTING changing

INTEREST money paid out or charged for the use of money or for borrowing money

PRINCIPAL money borrowed or placed in a bank account

RATE OF INTEREST the percent earned or charged on the principal

SIMPLE INTEREST interest that is paid only on the original principal

Let's Begin

1 **EXPLORE** Examine Student Learning Page 4.A with your student. Can he or she guess what it is? [a garden plan] Have your student note how many squares there are in the grid. [100] Show that the lettuce takes up 6 squares on the grid. Talk about how you can tell what **percent** of the garden space is devoted to lettuce. [6 out of 100 squares, or 6 hundredths, can be written as 6%]

2 **MODEL** Tell your student that 6% can also be written as a decimal—.06—or as a fraction—$\frac{6}{100}$. Reinforce the idea of **converting** percentages to decimals with your student using other vegetable rows; then pose the question, *What pattern do you see when you write a percent as a decimal?* [the decimal point moves two places to the left] Ask, *Do you think there is a pattern that would help us write decimals as percents? What do you think it is?* [move the decimal point two places to the right]

MATH

LESSON 2.4

3 **EXPLORE** Tell your student that a gardening magazine wants to feature a garden in an upcoming issue that has used $\frac{2}{5}$ of its total space for heirloom tomatoes. How can you determine if the garden in the plan is eligible? Have your student brainstorm ways to find out.

4 **MODEL** Show that one way is to write $\frac{2}{5}$ as a percent and then check that against the plan. Since $\frac{2}{5}$ means "2 divided by 5," divide the numerator by the denominator to get .40 (40%). Ask your student, *Does the garden plan use 40 spaces for heirloom tomatoes?* [no] *If this garden is not eligible, how could you change the plan to make it eligible?* [answers will vary]

Ask your student to think about how a percent might be written as a fraction. Remind him or her that for the magazine layout, 40%, or 40 spaces out of 100, were needed for tomatoes. By writing this as $\frac{40}{100}$, we can simplify the fraction to $\frac{2}{5}$ (by dividing both the numerator and denominator by 20). Ask your student to write a rule for changing percents to fractions [write the percent as the numerator and use 100 as the denominator, then simplify to its simplest form]

5 **PRACTICE** On Student Learning Page 4.A, have your student complete the table using information from the garden plan.

6 **EXPLORE** Explain that Wacko Wally's is having a huge sale with 20% off all rubber Spock ears, which normally cost $4.00 a pair. Ask your student to tell you some ways to determine the sale price of the ears.

7 **MODEL** Tell your student that the first step is to find how much money the discount will save you. An easy way to find the discount is to make an equation that will express how much is 20% of $4.00. (Tell your student that *of* is a word that can indicate multiplication.) The equation is:

$$20\% \times 4.00$$

or   .20 $\times$ 4   = .80 or 80 cents

Next, subtract the 80 cents from $4.00. The sale price is $3.20.

8 **PRACTICE** Give your student 12 index cards. Have him or her draw a picture of an object for sale on each of 4 cards, a percentage on each of 4 other cards, and a price on each of the remaining ones. Shuffle each set and have the student pick a card from each, determining the amount of discount and the new price of each item.

As with all math, your student should be encouraged to be sure that his or her answers are logical and make sense. A good way for your student to check his or her work is to have him or her estimate answers to problems in his or her head before putting a pen to paper. Have your student estimate the following problems mentally, being sure to round off numbers as necessary.

10% of 60 (.1 × 60 = 6)

15% of 20 (break 15% into 10% + 5%; 10% of 20 is 2; 5% of 20 is 1; 2 + 1 = 3)

25% of 400 (25% is the same as $\frac{1}{4}$, so 400 divided by 4 = 100)

20% of 492 (.20 × 500 [rounded up from 492] ≈ 100)

Practice this skill with your student, and he or she will see that sometimes, depending on the question being asked, an estimate is enough to solve the problem.

9 **EXPLORE** Talk about the concept of sales tax with your student. Express the idea that while discounts are subtracted from prices (always making the price lower), taxes are added to prices (making the price higher). Show a sales receipt with the sales tax on it. Ask, *What is the sales tax in our area?* [answers will vary] If your student doesn't know the local sales tax structure, have him or her call a local store to find out. Ask, *What tax does the store charge?*

Present the following scenario to your student: *You are shopping for mustache wax for your Uncle Felix. He has given you $5.00. At the store, you find the mustache wax with a price of $3.89. You know that the tax will be 7%. Will you have any money left over?* [yes]

10 **MODEL** Tell your student that the first thing to do is find out how much tax you'll need to pay. Set up the problem like this:

7% × 3.89

or   .07 × 3.89 (this is a good place to have your student practice estimating tax)

.07 × 3.89 = 27 cents in tax

Next, have the student add the sales tax to the price:

$3.89 + .27 = $4.16 is the total price

Have the student compare his or her estimate to the actual answer. Ask, *Could the question be answered using only the estimate?* Discuss.

11 **PRACTICE** Find some old store receipts and scratch out the tax amount and the final totals so they cannot be read. Have your student go through and figure out the taxes and totals for each receipt. Review the answers and discuss.

12 **EXPLORE** Talk about **interest** with your student. Explain that interest is additional money that a bank gives you for keeping your savings with them. The more money you have in your savings account and the longer you keep it there, the more money you will earn. The money in your savings account is often called the **principal.** If you know the **rate of interest** (the percent the bank promises to pay you on your principal), you can determine how much money you can earn.

13 **MODEL** Using the **simple interest** formula below, model how to find how much interest will be paid after 1 year if there is $100 in the bank and the rate of interest is 6.5%.

principal × rate of interest × time = interest
$100 × 6.5% × 1 year = interest
$100 × .065 × 1 year = $6.50 interest earned

Ask, *How much will the total balance in your savings account be after one year?* [$106.50] *How much will the total balance be if you have $50 and the interest is 7.25%?* [$53.75]

14 **PREDICT** Tell your student, *When you borrow money from the bank, you will need to pay interest to the bank for the loan.* Ask, *If you borrow $1,250 for 2 years at 8% interest, how can you determine how much interest you will owe?* [use the same formula used for collecting interest]

15 **PRACTICE** Have your student figure out the problem in Step 14 above.

$1,250 × 8% × 2 years = interest
$1,250 × .08 × 2 years = $200 interest owed

Ask, *How much will you repay in total?* [$1,450] *Why is it better to pay off a loan quickly?* [you pay less interest]

16 **PRACTICE** Have your student complete the activities on Student Learning Page 4.B.

Branching Out

TEACHING TIPS

☐ Your student should be aware that knowing how to compute discounts is an important skill. Collect some advertising supplements from your local newspaper and have your student determine exact prices for discounted goods. If regular prices are given alongside sale prices, have them determine the percentage of the discount.

☐ Help your student learn the important task of estimating the total cost of a purchase before approaching the cashier at a store. The next time you shop together, find out the grocery sales tax. Your student may be interested to learn that it is usually much less than regular sales tax. Ask your student to keep a running tally in his or her head of the items in your shopping cart. He or she may simplify the calculations by rounding up prices to the nearest dollar or half-dollar.

CHECKING IN

As you assess your student's progress, make sure he or she can describe the steps that are required in each computation (e.g., to change a fraction to a percent, divide the numerator by the denominator). It is important that your student understands and remembers the steps involved, as well as does the math correctly.

FOR FURTHER READING

Fractions and Decimals, by Lucille Caron and Philip M. St. Jacques (Enslow Publishers, Inc., 2000).

How to Work with Fractions, Decimals, and Percents, by Charles Shields (Teacher Created Materials, 2000).

Mental Math (Grades 4–8), by Richard Picirilli (Scholastic Prof. Book Div., 1999).

Convert Percents, Fractions, and Decimals

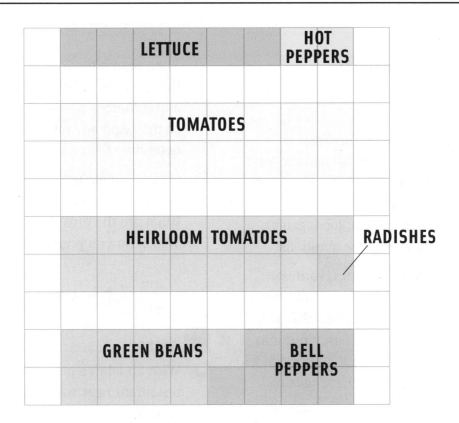

Complete the table using the information from the plan above.

	No. of squares out of 100	Percent	Decimal	Fraction
Lettuce	6	6%	.06	$\frac{3}{50}$
Bell peppers				
Hot peppers				
Tomatoes				
Heirloom tomatoes				
Green beans				
Radishes				

Student Learning Page 4.A: Convert Percents, Fractions, and Decimals

What's Next? You Decide!

Now it's your turn to choose what to do next in the lesson.
Read the activities and decide which one you want to do—
you may want to try them all!

Take a Poll!

STEPS

❏ You've been hired by *Hip Kids* magazine to write a questionnaire for the What Readers Think section. Your job is to think of a topic such as movies, sports, fashion, food, games, and so on and write the questions.

❏ Include questions about favorites, trends, likes, and dislikes. Make sure you write specific questions that will have answers you can easily put into groups. Have fun with it and design your questionnaire like a magazine page.

❏ Then distribute your questionnaire to friends and family members.

❏ Your next job is to tally the results and write a follow-up article. With your article, include charts or graphs showing percentages and fractions to reflect the questionnaire responses.

Go Shopping

STEPS

❏ Think of a book or CD you would like to purchase.

❏ With an adult's permission, find out the cost at a local store by visiting or calling. Determine the sales tax and the final cost of the item.

❏ Then search the Internet and locate the same item. Find out the price and if there is a sales tax or shipping charge. Add any other charges to determine the final cost.

❏ Which is cheaper—going to the store or purchasing from the Internet? What are the pros and cons of both? Which do you prefer?

Dine Out

STEPS

❏ With an adult's permission, visit a restaurant near your home or see if you can search the Internet for a copy of its menu.

❏ Invite your family to a virtual "dinner out." You will be their host and server.

❏ Have a pad of paper and a pen and go around the table writing down each person's dinner order. Then review the menu and write in the prices next to each food item.

❏ Next, total the bill and add the local sales tax.

❏ Finally, present the bill to your family and ask them to write in the amount of your tip. What percentage of the total bill did they leave you as a tip?

MATH | **LESSON 2.5**

Understanding and Using Ratios, Proportions, and Probability

Keep your eyes open for ratios, proportions, and probability—they are found everywhere!

OBJECTIVE	BACKGROUND	MATERIALS
To teach your student how to apply ratios, proportions, and probability to real-world situations	Whether your student is working with money, shapes, maps, scale models, scale drawings, or interpreting scores, he or she will be using ratios, proportions, and probability. Imagine calculating sports standings or adjusting room dimensions without knowing about proportions and probability. In this lesson, your student will apply multiplication and division skills to ratios, proportions, and probability.	■ Student Learning Pages 5.A–5.B ■ 10 dimes, 4 quarters, 1 $1 bill ■ 3 sheets red construction paper ■ 3 sheets yellow construction paper ■ 1 pair scissors ■ 1 local or state map ■ 2 number cubes labeled 1–6

VOCABULARY

RATIOS statements of comparisons of two quantities

PROPORTIONS equations showing that two ratios are equivalent

PROBABILITY the chance of an event happening

Let's Begin

RATIO AND PROPORTION

1 **RELATE** Mention to your student that money and shapes are tools that can be used to review and learn more about **ratios** and **proportions.** Place a $1 bill, dimes, and quarters on a table. Discuss with your student how quarters relate to 1 dollar. [4 quarters equal 1 dollar] Explain that this relationship shows a ratio. The ratio of quarters to 1 dollar is 4 to 1, 4:1, or $\frac{4}{1}$. Have your student reword the ratio so that 1 dollar equals 4 quarters. [1 to 4, 1:4, $\frac{1}{4}$]

2 **ASK** Ask, *What is the ratio of 1 dollar to dimes?* [1 to 10, 1:10, or $\frac{1}{10}$] Have your student show this relationship of 1 dollar to dimes with the money. Discuss.

3 **MAKE PROPORTIONS** To help your student understand ratios and proportions, use shapes to form concrete images to work with ratios and proportions. Work with your student to make 12 circles on red construction paper and 12 squares on yellow construction paper, all of equal size. Cut out the shapes. Describe this scenario for your student to model: Place 2 circles and 3 squares on a table. This is a ratio of 2 circles to 3 squares. It has a ratio of $\frac{2}{3}$. Have your student make another set in the same proportion and combine them, counting how many there are of each. Ask, *What is the number sentence?* [$\frac{2}{3} = \frac{4}{6}$] Continue with a third group of circles and squares. Ask, *What is the new proportion?* [$\frac{2}{3} = \frac{4}{6} = \frac{8}{12}$] Discuss with your student how the three ratios are proportions. Also, have your student make the connection that these groups are equivalent fractions.

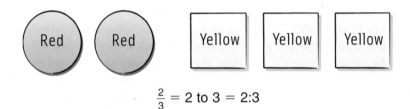

$$\frac{2}{3} = 2 \text{ to } 3 = 2{:}3$$

4 **EXPLAIN** Mention to your student that money and shapes are just one of many things that relate to ratios and proportions. Explain that scale drawings, maps, and scale models can also show ratios and proportions. Ask, *How is a map related to ratios and proportions?* [maps are scaled down to a certain percentage from the actual size; the size of the map is proportionate to the distances in real life, e.g., 1 inch on a map might equal 100 miles]

5 **EXPLORE** Use a local or state map and find the map scale. Ask, *What does the map scale tell you?* [the ratio of 1 inch to miles and meters] Ask, *How many miles does 1 inch equal?* Have your student use a ruler to calculate the distance from your city or town to the state's capital, to the largest city, and to the city or town nearest the northern border of your state.

6 **DISCUSS** Ask, *What is the ratio of miles to meters to your state's capital city? What is the ratio of miles to meters to the largest city? What distance represents 20 miles on the map? 50 miles? What distance represents 20 meters on the map? 50 meters?* Discuss.

7 **PRACTICE** Now distribute Student Learning Page 5.A for more practice with ratios and proportions.

PROBABILITY

1 **DISCUSS** Point out that ratios and proportions will help your student explore **probability**. Discuss examples of using probability in everyday life. [weather, board games, interpreting scores]

+

ENRICH THE EXPERIENCE

Have your student compare the forecasts of two meteorologists for one week. Who was right more often?

2   **ASK**   Ask, *What are the chances that the sun will shine this month?* [likely] *What are the chances that the sun will set in the west tonight?* [certain] *What is the chance that you will be driving the car today?* [unlikely] *What are the chances of tossing heads or tails on a coin?* [equally likely]

3   **EXPLAIN**   Mention that the questions you asked about the weather, driving the car, or tossing a coin involve probability. Ask your student why each of the scenarios in Step 2 have different probabilities. Discuss. Then have your student name and identify other examples of situations involving probability. (Examples: What are the chances it will snow in Florida today? What are the chances you will blink today?)

4   **MODEL**   Use a number cube labeled 1 to 6 to model the probability of rolling an odd number. Ask, *What are the odd numbers?* [1, 3, 5] Demonstrate how the odd numbers relate to the total number of rolls. [$\frac{3}{6}$ or $\frac{1}{2}$] Have your student in turn show how the probability of rolling an even number is the same as rolling an odd number. Provide time for your student to roll the number cubes several times and ask you probability questions.

5   **TAKE IT FURTHER**   To help your student learn about finding the probability of two or more events, make a letter cube using one of your number cubes. Work with your student to devise a letter code for the number cube (for example, 1 equals the letter *a*, 2 equals the letter *b*, 3 equals the letter *c*, and so on). Allow your student to roll one number cube and one letter cube.

	1	2	3	4	5	6
a						Roll 3
b			Roll 2			
c		Roll 1				
d				Roll 4		
e	Roll 5					
f			Roll 6			

6   **EXPLAIN AND MODEL**   Mention that to find the probability of two or more events you first find the probability of each event and then multiply to find the two probabilities. For example, rolling a 4 and the letter *c* has a probability of $\frac{1}{6}$ (rolling a 4) $\times \frac{1}{6}$ (rolling the letter *c*) $= \frac{1}{36}$, or 1 to 36. The probability would be the same for rolling a 2 and rolling the letter *e*. To find the probability for the two events, multiply $\frac{1}{36} \times \frac{1}{36}$, which equals $\frac{1}{1,296}$.

   Understanding and Using Ratios, Proportions, and Probability

7   **MODEL AND PRACTICE**   Use the number cubes to practice finding the probability of one and then two or more events. Set up a chart to record the results. Determine with your student how many times to roll the number cubes for one event and also for two events.

8   **PRACTICE**   Now distribute Student Learning Page 5.B for additional practice on probability.

Branching Out

TEACHING TIPS

❏   As your student rolls the number cubes, lead your student to predict that rolling a specific number, such as 2, is likely to happen but may not actually happen.

❏   Take ratios to the kitchen. Have your student help make a meal by following a recipe and determining the ratios of ingredients, such as the ratio of flour to water, basil to oregano, and so on. Then have him or her write a recipe for his or her favorite meal using ratios.

❏   On your next vacation find a sculpture or statue of someone that's greater than life size. Ask your child to add shoes, a book, or something to the statue—how big would the addition have to be?

CHECKING IN

Assess your student's ability by providing him or her with a brown bag and the cut-out shapes (circles and squares). Place the shapes in the bag and have your student choose shapes to name a ratio and a proportion, and then make a prediction about the probability of choosing two circles and two squares.

FOR FURTHER READING

Math Games for Middle School, by Mario George Salvadori (Chicago Review Press, 1998).

Percents and Ratios, by Lucille Caron (Enslow, 2000).

Work with Ratios and Proportions

Write each ratio three different ways.

1. 7 crayons to 10 pens

_____

_____

_____

2. 9 pens to 4 markers

_____

_____

_____

3. 20 pens to 5 pencils

_____

_____

_____

Write two equivalent ratios for each.

4. $\frac{7}{14}$

_____

_____

5. 12 to 15

_____

_____

6. 1:5

_____

_____

Use the definition of rate to solve each word problem.

> A **rate** is a ratio that compares two different
> units, such as speed, time, and money.

7. Mike and his dad travel by car at 55 miles per hour for 5 hours.

How many miles did they travel? _____

8. Sarah and her friends walked 30 miles. They averaged 15 minutes per mile.

How many hours did they walk? _____

9. A worker receives $90 for 6 hours of work. How much does the worker earn

in one hour? _____

10. Use what you know about rate to write and solve a problem of your own.

Show how you got your answer. _____

What's Next? You Decide!

Now it's your turn to choose what to do next in the lesson.
Read the activities and decide which one you want to do—
you may want to try them both!

Predict Probable Outcomes

MATERIALS

- ❏ 24 circle and square shapes
- ❏ 1 brown bag
- ❏ 1 recording sheet

STEPS

- ❏ Take the 12 circles and 12 squares you made earlier and place them in a bag.

- ❏ Make a recording sheet as shown.

Recording Sheet										
	1	2	3	4	5	6	7	8	9	10
Draws										
Circle										
Square										

- ❏ Make a prediction about how many times you will choose 3 circles and 4 squares if you choose 8 shapes each of 10 drawings. What is the probability of choosing those shapes?

- ❏ Choose the shapes from the bag and record your results. How close to your prediction were your actual selections?

- ❏ Then, with a partner, make new rules for the game. What is your prediction? How close were you to your actual selections?

Design a Model

MATERIALS

- ❏ 1–3 architectural magazines
- ❏ 1 inch/centimeter ruler
- ❏ 1 copy Grid, page 355

STEPS

What is your favorite room—your bedroom, the living room, the great room, a favorite hangout? You decide!

- ❏ Draw a scale model of your favorite room on a copy of the Grid found on page 355.

- ❏ Skim architectural magazines to get an idea of what a scale drawing looks like. Remember to add a scale to show equal ratios. Add the furniture and draw each piece to scale.

- ❏ When you finish, answer the following questions:
  - What are the actual dimensions of the room?
  - What is the scale for the drawing in fraction form?
  - Choose a furniture piece. How tall is it in the drawing?
  - What is the ratio of the scale drawing to the actual furniture piece?
  - What is the ratio of open floor space to floor space with stationary furniture on it?

Interpreting Data, Statistics, and Graphs

The way information is presented greatly affects the way it is received.

OBJECTIVE	BACKGROUND	MATERIALS
To teach your student to analyze data and make graphs	Whether you and your student are researching media products, talking about sports results, or comparing the latest fashions, you are collecting data and analyzing your results. This lesson will teach your student to organize data and statistics and present them clearly in various types of graphs.	<ul><li>Student Learning Pages 6.A–6.D</li><li>several issues of a local newspaper</li><li>2 number cubes or dice</li><li>1 copy Grid, page 355</li></ul>

VOCABULARY

AVERAGE another word for *mean* (see below)

RANGE the difference between the greatest and least numbers in a group

MEAN a number that is the sum of a group of numbers divided by the total number of items in the group

MEDIAN the middle number of a group of numbers arranged in order from least to greatest

MODE the number or numbers that are listed most often in a group of numbers

BAR GRAPH a graph that is useful for comparing the amounts for one set of data

DOUBLE BAR GRAPH a graph that is useful for comparing the amounts for two sets of data

LINE GRAPH a graph that is useful for showing how data changes over time

CIRCLE GRAPH a graph that shows data as parts of a circle and is labeled with functions, percents, or decimals

DATA information in the form of numbers

HISTOGRAM a type of graph that uses bars to show how frequently data occurs within equal intervals

INTERVALS sets of numbers between other numbers

PICTOGRAPH a graph that uses pictures or symbols to show data

Let's Begin

1 **DISCUSS** Talk about the pros and cons of receiving an allowance. Allow your student time to think about the advantages and disadvantages of allowances. Mention that the **average** allowances for children ages 7 to 12 are $4.10, $4.32, $5.52, $7.18, $7.92, and $9.58. Discuss ways that this information can be used. [organized in a chart or graph, used to make predictions]

2 **EXPLAIN AND CALCULATE** Explain that specific words are used to talk about data. Introduce and discuss the terms—*range, mean, median,* and *mode.* Ask, *What is the **range** of the allowances?* [$5.48] *What method did you use to find the range?* [subtract the least number from the greatest number] *If you wanted to find the **mean,** how would you do it?* [add all the allowances and divide by the number of allowances; $38.62 divided by 6; mean: $6.44]

3 **CONTINUE** Suggest that your student find the **median** and mode for the set of allowance data and explain what method he or she used to determine the answers. [median: $6.35; mode: no mode because no number is repeated or used twice]

4 **DISCUSS AND EXPLORE** Look through the local newspaper with your student for graphs, charts, or tables. Talk about other possible ways the charts in the newspaper could be presented. Explain that some types of graphs are better than others for presenting certain kinds of information.

For example, a **bar graph** is useful for comparing the amounts for one set of data or information, while a **double bar graph** is useful for comparing the amounts for two sets of data. When your student wants to show how data changes over time, a **line graph** is most helpful. A **circle graph** shows data as parts of a circle and labeled with fractions, percents, or decimals. Ask your student to identify examples of a bar graph, line graph, and circle graph. Have him or her paste or draw the examples into his or her notebook and label them.

5 **MODEL** Have your student create a graph using the average allowance data. Ask, *What is the best type of graph to show this data? Why?* [bar graph, because it shows the amount of allowances for children, ages 7 to 12] *How will you set up the data in a bar graph?* [list ages across and amounts on the side] *What will be the title of the bar graph?* [Average Allowances or Allowances for Kids Ages 7 to 12] *What will the bars represent?* [the amount of allowance for each age group] *What will be the intervals for the vertical scale?* [one-dollar intervals]

Average Allowances

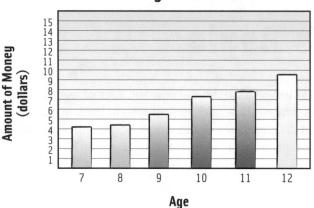

6 | **PRACTICE** Distribute Student Learning Page 6.A. Have your student complete the exercises before moving on to the next steps. Check his or her work and review.

7 | **PRESENT** Direct your student to copy on a sheet of paper the following data. The data shows the ages of the 43 U.S. presidents at the time of their inauguration.

> **Data:** 57, 61, 57, 57, 58, 57, 61, 54, 68, 51,
> 49, 64, 50, 48, 65, 52, 56, 46, 54, 49, 50,
> 47, 55, 55, 54, 42, 51, 56, 55, 51, 54, 51,
> 60, 62, 43, 55, 56, 61, 52, 69, 64, 46, 54.

8 | **MODEL AND WRITE** Explain that some topics involve many numbers, such as the list of numbers above. To organize this type of data, a **histogram** works well. Explain that a histogram is a type of bar graph that shows a grouping of data within equal **intervals**. The first step to creating a histogram is creating a frequency table. Direct your student to make a frequency table of the data. Give him or her the following headings for the table: age intervals, tally marks, and frequency of ages. Make sure the intervals are even, as shown below (five-year intervals). Have your student count the tally marks and record the frequency on the chart. Check his or her work against the table below.

DID YOU KNOW?

John F. Kennedy, the 35th president, was the youngest president elected to office, and Ronald Reagan, the 40th president, was the oldest president elected to office.

Age of U.S. Presidents When Inaugurated

Intervals	Tally Marks	Frequency
40 – 44	II	2
45 – 49	⊬⊬ I	6
50 – 54	⊬⊬ ⊬⊬ III	13
55 – 59	⊬⊬ ⊬⊬ II	12
60 – 64	⊬⊬ II	7
65 – 69	III	3
70 – 74		0

9 | **DIRECT AND MODEL** Tell your student that he or she can use the data from the frequency table to make a histogram. Prompt your student to give the graph a title, use the frequency numbers from the table as the scale for the side, and then draw a bar for each age interval. Check his or her work against the graph on the next page.

Interpreting Data, Statistics, and Graphs   **113**

Age of U.S. Presidents When Inaugurated

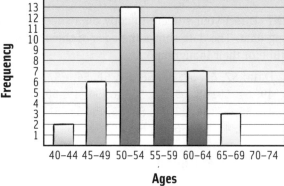

10 **ANALYZE** Work with your student to draw conclusions from the data in the histogram. Ask, *Which age group shows the most number of presidents inaugurated?* [ages 50–54] *Which age group shows the least number of presidents inaugurated?* [ages 70–74, 40–44]

11 **PRACTICE** Distribute Student Learning Page 6.B. Have your student complete the exercises. Check his or her work and review.

Branching Out

TEACHING TIP

As your student enters the ages into his or her frequency table, suggest that he or she use an *X* to cross off the ages that have been entered so that a number won't be left out or entered twice.

CHECKING IN

Assess your student's ability by having your student use resource books or newspapers to find data to graph. Observe your student as he or she determines the best way to display the data. Direct your student to provide a title for his or her chart and to write two questions about the data that can be answered using the information.

FOR FURTHER READING

Graphing, Statistics, and Probability: Inventive Exercises to Sharpen Skills and Raise Achievement, by Imogene Forte and Marjorie Frank (Incentive Publications, 2000).

Mastering Essential Math Skills, by Richard W. Fisher (Math Essentials, 1998).

Use Data and Graphs

Find the range, mean, median, and mode for each set of data.
Use a separate sheet of paper if you need more room for calculations.

	Range	Mean	Median	Mode
A. 5, 5, 5, 6, 7, 7, 7, 11				
B. 52, 68, 37, 48, 23, 72				

Use the circle graph to answer the following questions.

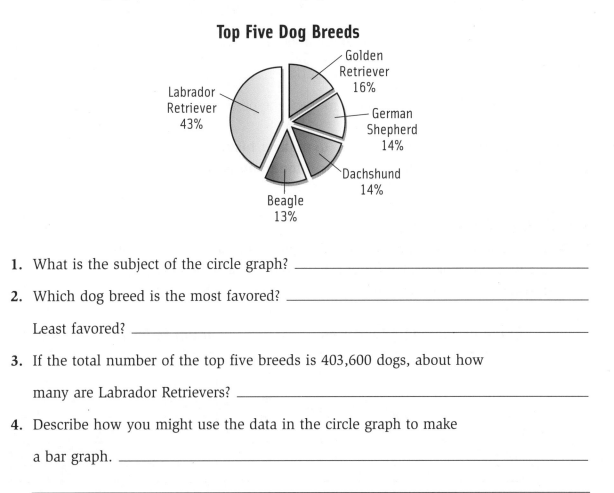

Top Five Dog Breeds

1. What is the subject of the circle graph? _____

2. Which dog breed is the most favored? _____

   Least favored? _____

3. If the total number of the top five breeds is 403,600 dogs, about how

   many are Labrador Retrievers? _____

4. Describe how you might use the data in the circle graph to make

   a bar graph. _____

Challenge Yourself!

Use resources such as local newspapers or Web sites to find data to use in a line graph. Remember, the purpose of a line graph is to show how data changes over time. Record your data and draw your line graph in your notebook.

Explore Frequency Table and Histogram

Use the data below to make a frequency table and answer the questions. Use five-year intervals, beginning with 45–49 for your table. Draw your table on a separate sheet of paper.

❑ This data represents the ages of U.S. presidents when they died.

❑ Of the 43 U.S. presidents, 6 are still living.

❑ 67, 90, 83, 85, 73, 80, 78, 79, 68, 71, 53, 65, 74, 64, 77, 56, 66, 63, 70, 49, 56, 71, 67, 71, 58, 60, 72, 67, 57, 60, 90, 63, 88, 78, 46, 64, 81

1. Which age group has the most tally marks? _____

2. Which age group has the least tally marks? _____

3. During which three age spans did most of the presidents die? _____

Use the data from the frequency table to make a histogram. Draw the histogram on a copy of the Grid found on page 355.

Challenge Yourself!

Look at the graphs below and answer the questions. Graphs can show the same data but look very different. Sometimes the scale of a graph is altered to create the appearance of a larger or smaller change in data.

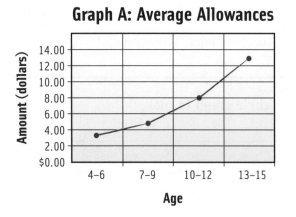

Graph A: Average Allowances

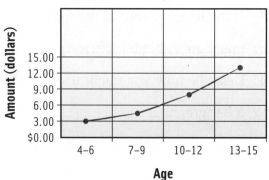

Graph B: Average Allowances

4. How do the graphs look alike? _____

5. Which graph is more useful? _____

Graph Your Research

❑ Use the library or Internet to research data for a graph. You may choose to research topics such as endangered vertebrates, heart rates for adults, populations of the 10 largest cities in the world, consumer prices for technology devices, kinds of music, and so on. Once you have decided on a topic and collected your data, find the range, mean, median, and mode of the data. Then write these values. _____

_____

❑ Next, organize your thoughts. Write a paragraph on the lines below that answers the following questions: Which type of graph would be appropriate for your data? Why? What will you title the graph? How will you arrange the data intervals? _____

_____

_____

_____

_____

❑ Create your graph on a separate sheet of paper. Then answer the following questions.

What does the data tell you? _____

_____

_____

What does the graph show? _____

_____

_____

Could there be a better way to display your data? Why? _____

_____

_____

❑ **Share what you have learned with an adult.**

What's Next? You Decide!

Now it's your turn to choose what to do next in the lesson. Read the activities and decide which one you want to do—you may want to try them both!

Create a Graph Book

MATERIALS

❑ business or financial sections of local newspapers or magazines

❑ 1 set markers or crayons

❑ several sheets drawing paper

STEPS

Create your own graph book!

❑ Use resources such as newspapers or magazines to find examples of a bar graph, a line graph, and a circle graph. If possible, try to find an example of a double bar graph and a double line graph.

❑ Label each type of graph, make a similar graph with real data from your research, and write two questions about the graph or data.

❑ Staple or tie the pages together and make a cover for your graph book.

❑ Share your book with a friend.

Make a Pictograph

MATERIALS

❑ several newspapers or magazines

❑ 1 set markers or crayons

❑ several pieces drawing paper

STEPS

A **pictograph** is a type of graph that uses pictures or symbols to show data. An example of one is shown below.

Number of Home Runs Hit by Baseball Players

Player A ⚾⚾⚾⚾⚾⚾

Player B ⚾⚾⚾⚾

Player C ⚾⚾⚾⚾⚾⚾⚾⚾⚾

KEY
Each ⚾ represents two home runs

❑ Use resources such as the Internet or newspapers and magazines to find data to represent in a pictograph. Examples of data include top-selling products, population numbers, or attendance at an event.

❑ Be sure to add a quantity key to show what your symbol represents. If you'd like, use a small rubber stamp for the symbol.

❑ Then show the same data in another type of graph. Which graph is the better choice to use for your set of data?

❑ Share your graphs with an adult.

Exploring Integers

Mathematics are a part of everyday life.

OBJECTIVE	BACKGROUND	MATERIALS
To teach your student how to add and subtract integers and to use integers in graphing coordinates	We use integers all the time, whether it's to calculate temperature changes, keep track of our money, calculate sports or science statistics, or chart geography. In this lesson, your student will write equations, graph coordinates, and apply other skills to working with integers.	■ Student Learning Pages 7.A–7.B

VOCABULARY

INTEGERS the counting numbers, negative and positive, including zero

EQUATIONS mathematical sentences that have an equal sign

POSITIVE greater than zero

NEGATIVE less than zero

COORDINATES a set of two numbers that indicate where a point is on a coordinate grid

ORDERED PAIR another term for coordinates

Let's Begin

1 **EXPLAIN** Tell your student that this lesson will be about **integers.** Use temperature as an example of how integers work. Ask, *If the temperature outside was –5°F at 7 A.M. and by 1 P.M. the temperature rose to 23°F, how many degrees did the temperature go up?* [28°F]

2 **DISCUSS** Discuss the different ways this problem could be solved. [make a number line to count the increase in temperature; subtract the low temperature from the high temperature] Have your student attempt to solve the problem while you observe his or her method. If your student solved the problem correctly, ask, *What did you do to solve the problem?* Encourage your student to explain what he or she did to arrive at the correct answer.

3 **EXPLAIN** Tell your student that a number line gives a visual example of how to add and subtract integers. Explain that integers are whole numbers—that is, counting numbers, including zero, and their opposites. Numbers greater than 0 are called **positive** integers, while numbers less than 0 are called **negative** integers.

DID YOU KNOW?

The South Pole, in Antarctica, has the coldest temperature on record at –96°F, while San Diego, California, has the warmest temperature on record at 111°F.

4   **MODEL** In his or her notebook, have your student use a ruler to make two number lines: one from −10 to +10 and the other from −10 to +25. Point out that a number line has arrows on each end. Explain that the arrows mean that the numbers continue and you can continue counting in either direction.

$$\xleftarrow{\quad} \underset{-10\ -9\ -8\ -7\ -6\ -5\ -4\ -3\ -2\ -1\ \ 0\ \ 1\ \ 2\ \ 3\ \ 4\ \ 5\ \ 6\ \ 7\ \ 8\ \ 9\ \ 10}{\big|\ \big|\ \big|\ \big|\ \big|\ \big|\ \big|\ \big|\ \big|\ \big|\ \big|\ \big|\ \big|\ \big|\ \big|\ \big|\ \big|\ \big|\ \big|\ \big|\ \big|} \xrightarrow{\quad}$$

5   **MODEL AND COUNT** Use the number line to illustrate the temperature problem counting from −5 to +23. Have your student place a finger on −5 and move to the right counting to +23. Ask, *What is the answer?* [28] Tell your student that to subtract he or she would move to the left on the number line. Have your student think of another word problem involving temperature and have him or her use the number line to solve it.

6   **MODEL AND COMPARE** Have your student use the −10 to +10 number line to compare and order integers. Direct your student to write the numbers +7, −3, +5, and −9 in his or her notebook. Have your student locate the numbers on the number line and order them from least to greatest and then from greatest to least. Ask, *Which is greater, +5 or −3? How do you know? Which is greater, −3 or −9? How do you know?* Observe your student as he or she uses the number line to locate the numbers and order them. Discuss.

7   **DISCUSS AND OBSERVE** Let your student know that there are some simple rules that help with adding and subtracting integers. You may want to have your student write these rules in his or her notebook for reference. Discuss each of the following:

Adding Integers:
- When adding integers, if both numbers are positive then the sum will be positive.
- If both numbers are negative then the sum will be negative.
- If one number is positive and another is negative, then the number that has the greater value will indicate whether the sum will be positive or negative.
- Adding a negative number is like subtracting a positive number.

Subtracting Integers:
- Subtracting a negative number is like adding a positive number. You can think of a negative sign as meaning "opposite." In subtraction, two negative signs cancel each other out.
- Subtracting a negative number from a positive number is the same as adding two positive numbers, so the answer will be positive.
- Subtracting a negative number from a negative number is the same as adding a positive number to a negative number, so the answer can be either positive or negative depending on which value is larger.

Now have your student copy these problems on the same sheet of paper with the number lines and ask him or her to solve each one.

$$+5 + +9 \qquad -6 + +5 \qquad +6 - -3$$

8   **CONNECT** Tell your student that he or she is going to work with **equations.** Return to the word problem about the temperature rising from the beginning of the lesson: *If the temperature outside was $-5°F$ at 7 A.M. and by 1 P.M. the temperature rose to $23°F$, how many degrees did the temperature go up?* [28°F] Have your student write the expression $+23 - -5$ in his or her notebook. Explain that adding an x to the expression makes it an equation. Each side of the equation $23 - -5 = x$ has the same value.

9   **EXPLORE** Use the following scenario to explore writing equations with integers: *The temperature at night was $-8°F$. By noon the following day the temperature was $10°F$. How many degrees did the temperature rise?* Ask, *What is the expression?* [$+10 - -8$] *How would you write this expression as an equation?* [$+10 - -8 = x$] *How would you solve the problem?* [since subtracting a negative number is the same as adding a positive number, add $10 + 8$] *What is the answer?* [18°F]

10   **APPLY** Have your student use the business section of your local newspaper to find the high and low prices of several stocks. Direct your student to list the prices and calculate the differences. Then suggest that your student write a word problem with positive and negative numbers and solve it using an equation. For example, a stock may have been at $15.81 one day and $14.35 the next. The problem might be to find by how much the stock price fell. [$15.81 - $14.35 = $1.46]

11   **PRACTICE** Distribute Student Learning Page 7.A. Have your student complete the exercises before moving on to the next section. Check his or her work and review together if necessary.

12   **EXPLORE AND RELATE** Have your student draw a coordinate grid like the one below, or make a photocopy for your student. Lead your student to make a connection between a number line and a coordinate grid. Point out that a coordinate grid is two number lines that cross at the number 0. The horizontal line is called the x-axis and the vertical line is called the y-axis.

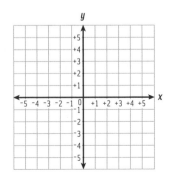

MATH

LESSON 2.7

13 **EXPLAIN** Point out that when naming a point on a coordinate grid, the *x*-axis is listed first, then the *y*-axis. On the coordinate grid, direct your student to point to the **coordinates** (3, 4). Observe your student as he or she finds the location. Continue this exercise until you feel your student is comfortable working with a coordinate grid.

14 **MODEL AND WRITE** Have your student mark the coordinate grid as you give the coordinates below. Ask, *If you connect the points of each **ordered pair,** what shape do the coordinates make?* [triangle]

- $x = 5, y = -3$
- $x = 0, y = 3$
- $x = -5, y = -3$

15 **WRITE** Have your student draw a square and a rectangle on the coordinate grid. Direct your student to write down the coordinates for the defining points of each shape.

16 **DISCUSS AND APPLY** Point out that maps and graphs that use coordinate grids are very common. On constellation maps of the stars, each constellation has specific coordinates. The world globe shows latitude and longitude. Each continent, ocean, and state has an ordered pair naming the exact location. Ask your student to use resource books or the Internet to find the latitude and longitude coordinates of your hometown and a place he or she would like to visit.

17 **PRACTICE** Distribute Student Learning Page 7.B. Have your student complete the exercises. Check his or her work and review.

FOR FURTHER READING

Homework Survival Guide: Math, by Teri Crawford Jones and Andrea Champlin, ill. (Troll Communications L.L.C., 1998).

Whole Numbers and Integers Grades 6–8: Inventive Exercises to Sharpen Skills and Raise Achievement, by Imogene Forte, Andrea Sukow, Marjorie Frank, and Terri Breeden (Incentive Publications, Inc., 1999).

Branching Out

TEACHING TIP

Mapping one or more star constellations on a coordinate grid will help reinforce using integers in real-world situations.

CHECKING IN

Assess your student's ability by asking him or her to solve this problem: *How can you solve the equation* a $- -5 = 18$? [rewrite the equation as an addition problem; solve for *a*; $a = 13$] Then have your student draw a number line and observe as he or she solves the problem.

Work with Integers and Number Lines

Write the corresponding integer for each point on the number line.

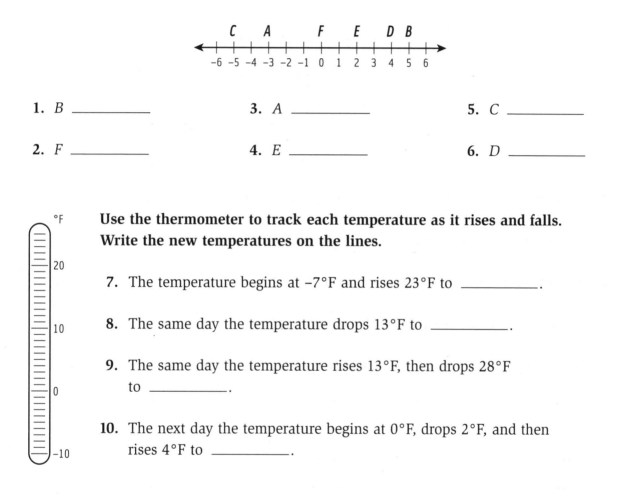

```
        C   A       F   E   D B
  ←─┼──┼──┼──┼──┼──┼──┼──┼──┼──┼──┼──┼──┼──→
   -6 -5 -4 -3 -2 -1  0  1  2  3  4  5  6
```

1. B _____

2. F _____

3. A _____

4. E _____

5. C _____

6. D _____

Use the thermometer to track each temperature as it rises and falls. Write the new temperatures on the lines.

7. The temperature begins at –7°F and rises 23°F to _____ .

8. The same day the temperature drops 13°F to _____ .

9. The same day the temperature rises 13°F, then drops 28°F to _____ .

10. The next day the temperature begins at 0°F, drops 2°F, and then rises 4°F to _____ .

Order these integers from least to greatest.

11. +6, −7, −3, +4, 0, +2, −5

_____

Circle T for *true* or F for *false* after each equation.

12. +7 − −3 = +4   T   F

13. +7 + −6 > +8 − +2   T   F

14. +2 − −4 < −4 − −2   T   F

Use Coordinate Grids

As you walk through the coordinate grid "neighborhood," use the grid map to mark your destinations. Your home at (0, 0) is your starting point for each trip. Each unit is one block. Read each sentence. Then answer the questions.

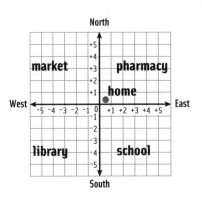

1. If you walk 2 blocks south and 3 blocks west, where will you be? _____

2. If you walk 3 blocks east and 4 blocks south, where will you be? _____

3. If you walk 1 block west and 2 blocks north, where will you be? _____

4. If you walk 4 blocks east and 4 blocks north, where will you be? _____

5. Write your own directions and label the coordinates on the neighborhood map.

_____

_____

_____

_____

_____

_____

_____

6. On a separate sheet of graph paper, mark the following coordinates and label them with the proper letter.

A. (−7, +3)	D. (+10, −6)
B. (+2, −3)	E. (−2, +9)
C. (+4, −10)	F. (−8, +8)

Learning About Measurements

It may be a small world . . . but it helps to know how to measure it.

OBJECTIVE	BACKGROUND	MATERIALS
To show your student how to calculate and convert measurements in the customary and metric systems	Most of the world measures in the metric system, which is based on the number 10. In the United States, we use a different measuring system but we also need to be able to "think metric." This lesson provides your student with practice in using measuring instruments, relating the different systems of measurement, and understanding time zones.	■ Student Learning Pages 8.A–8.D ■ 1 ruler, yardstick, or tape measure ■ 1 compass ■ 1 protractor ■ 1 map U.S. time zones

VOCABULARY

CUSTOMARY MEASURING SYSTEM the measurement system used in the United States that uses inches, feet, yards, and miles

METRIC MEASURING SYSTEM the measurement system used worldwide that uses measurements in units of 10

WEIGHT a measure of the gravitational force on an object

MASS the amount of material something contains

CAPACITY the maximum volume a container holds

Let's Begin

CUSTOMARY UNITS OF LENGTH

1 **EXPLAIN** Explain that in the United States we usually measure the dimensions of everyday objects in **customary measuring system** units—the familiar measurements of inches, feet, yards, and miles. Ask your student to copy this information into his or her notebook:

$$12 \text{ inches} = 1 \text{ foot}$$
$$36 \text{ inches} = 1 \text{ yard}$$
$$3 \text{ feet} = 1 \text{ yard}$$
$$5,280 \text{ feet} = 1 \text{ mile}$$
$$1,760 \text{ yards} = 1 \text{ mile}$$

Look at a ruler, a yardstick, or a tape measure with your student. Go over the conversion of 12 inches to a foot and 36 inches to a yard, as well as 3 feet to a yard. In the chart, point

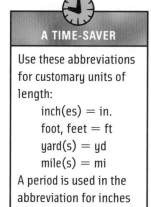

A TIME-SAVER

Use these abbreviations for customary units of length:

    inch(es) = in.
    foot, feet = ft
    yard(s) = yd
    mile(s) = mi

A period is used in the abbreviation for inches to avoid mistaking it for the word *in;* the same abbreviations are used for singular and plural.

out the number of yards in a mile and the number of feet in a mile. Ask, *How are they related?* [there are three times as many feet in a mile]

2 **ASK AND MODEL** Ask your student to solve the following problem: *A room is 12 feet long and 9 feet wide. What are its dimensions in inches?* [144 in. by 108 in.] *In yards?* [4 yd by 3 yd] Have your student try to solve the problem while you observe his or her method of doing so. Ask your student to explain his or her method of finding the answers and identify the part of the problem he or she did not understand or calculate correctly.

METRIC UNITS OF LENGTH

1 **EXPLORE AND DISCUSS** Have your student copy this information into his or her notebook:

$$1 \text{ meter} = 1 \text{ meter}$$
$$1 \text{ millimeter} = 0.001 \text{ meter}$$
$$1 \text{ centimeter} = 0.01 \text{ meter}$$
$$1 \text{ kilometer} = 1,000 \text{ meters}$$

Point out that in the **metric measuring system,** measurement units are multiples of 10. Ask, *If a centimeter is one hundredth of a meter, then how many centimeters are in a meter?* [100] *If a millimeter is one thousandth of a meter, how many millimeters are in a meter?* [1,000] *How many millimeters are in a centimeter?* [10] *How did you figure that out?* [divided 0.001 into 0.01 or 100 into 1,000] Explain that when you are converting to a smaller unit, use multiplication. When you are converting to a larger unit, use division.

2 **PRACTICE** Have your student calculate the following conversions. Discuss how your student arrived at his or her answers. Ask,
How many meters are in 8 kilometers? [8,000]
How many centimeters are in 8 kilometers? [800,000]
How many millimeters are in 8 kilometers? [8,000,000]
How many centimeters are in 8 millimeters? [0.8]
How many meters are in 8 millimeters? [0.008]
How many kilometers are in 8 millimeters? [0.000008]

CUSTOMARY UNITS OF WEIGHT

1 **EXPLAIN** Explain that customary **weight** is measured in ounces, pounds, and tons. Have your student copy the following weight conversions into his or her notebook: 16 ounces = 1 pound and 2,000 pounds = 1 ton. Ask, *How many ounces are there in a ton?* [32,000] If your student can't figure this out, have him or her refer to the proportion equation for converting feet to inches. Remind your student that division converts a smaller unit of weight to a larger one, and that multiplication converts a larger unit of weight to a smaller one.

A TIME-SAVER

Use these abbreviations for metric units of length:
millimeter(s) = mm
centimeter(s) = cm
meter(s) = m
kilometer(s) = km

ENRICH THE EXPERIENCE

The fractions of a meter use Latin prefixes: *centi-* is $\frac{1}{100}$ and *milli-* is $\frac{1}{1,000}$. Also, *deci-* is $\frac{1}{10}$. A decimeter is 10 centimeters, or $\frac{1}{10}$ of a meter. Multiples of a meter use prefixes originally from Greek: *kilo-* means 1,000. Also, a dekameter is 10 meters, and a hectometer is 100 meters. You can also see Latin prefixes used in the words *kilobyte,* *megabyte,* and *gigabyte.*

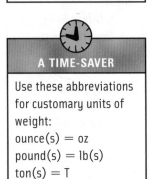

A TIME-SAVER

Use these abbreviations for customary units of weight:
ounce(s) = oz
pound(s) = lb(s)
ton(s) = T

2 **EXPLORE AND DISCUSS** With your student, look in magazines at pictures of rooms, building exteriors, and landscapes. Point to various objects and ask him or her which would be the most appropriate unit to use to measure the weight of each one.

Together take a walk around a room in your home. Ask him or her to tell you which unit would be best to measure various objects. Have him or her estimate how much each object weighs. Discuss.

METRIC UNITS OF MASS

1 **PREDICT AND DISCUSS** In the metric system, the basic unit of **mass** is the gram (g). Ask, *What would you predict 1,000 grams to be called? Why?* [kilogram; kilo- is the prefix for a thousand in the metric system] *What would you predict 0.001 grams to be called? Why?* [milligram; milli- is the prefix for one thousandth in the metric system] A metric ton is equal to 1,000 kilograms. Ask your student to create a conversion table for metric mass in his or her notebook that includes milligrams, grams, kilograms, and metric tons. Mention that the abbreviations for kilogram and milligram do not have periods. Have your student compute the number of grams in a metric ton (1 million) and the number of milligrams in a metric ton (1 billion).

2 **DISTRIBUTE AND PRACTICE** Distribute Student Learning Page 8.A. Have your student complete the problems and then check his or her work. Review any conversions he or she is having trouble with.

CUSTOMARY UNITS OF CAPACITY

1 **EXPLAIN AND EXPLORE** Explain that **capacity** refers to the maximum volume a container holds. The basic unit to measure capacity in the customary system is the cup. Have your student use a liquid measuring cup and water to measure the capacity of several kitchen cups, pots, and pitchers. Fill one pitcher with water and have your student practice pouring quantities of water from one container to the next.

2 **CHART** Now have your student copy this information into his or her notebook:

> 1 cup = 8 fluid ounces
> 1 pint = 2 cups
> 1 quart = 2 pints
> 1 gallon = 4 quarts

METRIC UNITS OF CAPACITY

1 **EXPLAIN AND MODEL** Explain that the basic metric unit to measure capacity is the liter, which is just a little larger than a quart. A kiloliter is 1,000 liters, and a milliliter is one thousandth of a liter. Show your student how to convert 6 kiloliters to liters

DID YOU KNOW?

In customary units, we speak of the weight of an object. In the metric system, we speak of the mass of an object. What's the difference? The mass of an object remains constant. Weight changes according to the pull of gravity. The weight of an object on Earth is greater than on the moon because Earth's gravity is greater. The mass of the object is the same in both places.

A TIME-SAVER

Use these abbreviations for metric units of mass:
milligram(s) = mg
gram(s) = g
kilogram(s) = kg
metric ton(s) = t

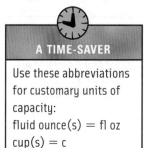

A TIME-SAVER

Use these abbreviations for customary units of capacity:
fluid ounce(s) = fl oz
cup(s) = c
pint(s) = pt
quart(s) = qt
gallon(s) = gal

(6 × 1,000 = 6,000 liters) and 6 liters to milliliters (6 × 1,000 = 6,000 milliliters). Then ask your student to calculate how many milliliters are in 6 kiloliters. [6 × 1,000 × 1,000 = 6,000,000 or 6 million milliliters]

2 **PRACTICE AND DISTRIBUTE** Distribute Student Learning Page 8.B. Check his or her work and review.

TIME ZONES

1 **EXPLAIN** Explain the idea of time zones to your student, reviewing Pacific time, mountain time, central time, and eastern time. Ask your student if he or she knows which time zone he or she lives in, and reveal the information if he or she doesn't know.

2 **DISTRIBUTE** Distribute Student Learning Page 8.C. Have your student practice finding the differences in time between various cities. Review your student's work and correct and assist as necessary.

Branching Out

TEACHING TIP

Your student may memorize the unit conversions quickly or may need to use the tables for reference. Work with your student at his or her own pace and use positive reinforcement. Creating flash cards is a good way to memorize new material.

CHECKING IN

You can assess how well your student understands the conversion of units by posing a conversion problem and asking him or her to explain the method or process needed to solve the problem, such as multiplying or dividing.

A TIME-SAVER

Use these abbreviations for metric units of capacity:
milliliter(s) = ml
liter(s) = l
kiloliter(s) = kl

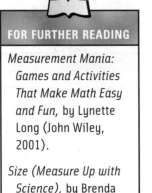

FOR FURTHER READING

Measurement Mania: Games and Activities That Make Math Easy and Fun, by Lynette Long (John Wiley, 2001).

Size (Measure Up with Science), by Brenda Walpole (Gareth Stevens, 1998).

Convert Length, Weight, and Mass

Complete the equations.

1. 30 in. = _____ ft _____ in.

2. 6 yd = _____ in.

3. 2 mi = _____ ft

4. 3 mi = _____ yd

5. 2,250 yd = _____ mi _____ yd

6. 96 ft = _____ in.

7. 30 m = _____ cm

8. 50 cm = _____ mm

9. 6 m = _____ mm

10. 2 km = _____ cm

11. 3 km = _____ mm

12. 96 mm = _____ m

13. 50 oz = _____ lb _____ oz

14. 50 T = _____ lb

15. 9 lb = _____ oz

16. 23 T = _____ lb

17. 9 oz = _____ lb

18. 1 T = _____ oz

19. 50 kg = _____ g

20. 23 t = _____ kg

21. 2,370 g = _____ mg

22. 1 t = _____ mg

23. 3,100 g = _____ kg

24. 3,100 g = _____ mg

Convert Customary and Metric Units and Capacity

Complete the equations.

1. 4 c = _____ fl oz

2. 16 c = _____ pt

3. 16 c = _____ qt

4. 16 c = _____ gal

5. 14 gal = _____ pt

6. 240 fl oz = _____ qt

7. 4 l = _____ ml

8. 90 ml = _____ l

9. 16 l = _____ kl

10. 14 kl = _____ ml

11. 33,000 ml = _____ kl

12. 240 l = _____ kl

Complete the charts using the conversions and what you've learned in the lesson. Read each row and write the equivalent measurements of the number that's given.

Metric Conversion Table
1 in. = 2.54 cm
1 mi = 1.61 km
1 qt = .95 l
1 oz = 28.35 g

c	pt	qt	gal	ml	l
		22			
		2			
20					

in.	ft	yd	mi	mm	cm	m	km
		9					
					30,000		
							2

Measure Time and Time Zones

Locate a map of the U.S. time zones. Read the map. Then answer the questions.

1. When it is 6:00 A.M. in Dallas, Texas, what time is it in Miami, Florida?

_____

2. When it is 4:25 A.M. in Honolulu, Hawaii, what time is it in Little Rock, Arkansas?

_____

3. When it is 2:20 A.M. in Pittsburgh, Pennsylvania, what time is it in Reno, Nevada?

_____

4. When it is 3:36 P.M. in Portland, Maine, what time is it in Portland, Oregon?

_____

5. When it is 5:50 P.M. in Omaha, Nebraska, what time is it in Scottsbluff, Nebraska?

_____

6. In summer, when it is 6:00 P.M. in Chicago, Illinois, what time is it
in Indianapolis, Indiana?

_____

7. In summer, when it is 5:09 A.M. in Phoenix, Arizona, what time is it
in San Diego, California?

_____

8. What is the time difference between Juneau, Alaska, and Tampa, Florida?

_____

9. What is the time difference between Honolulu, Hawaii, and Las Vegas, Nevada?

_____

10. What is the time difference between Boise, Idaho, and Mobile, Alabama?

_____

What's Next? You Decide!

Now it's your turn to choose what to do next in the lesson. Read the activities and decide which one you want to do—you may want to try them both!

Make Your Own Kind of Units

MATERIALS

❑ 1 copy Grid, page 355

❑ 1 ruler

STEPS

❑ Mark off the length of your foot on the blank side of a ruler.

❑ Think up a name for this new unit. You can name it after yourself, for example, *kyle* or *kayla.*

❑ Then divide it by 10 into smaller units. Think of a name for those as well, maybe *krunches.*

❑ Now choose a room in your home and draw an overhead floor plan of the room on a copy of the Grid found on page 355.

❑ Label the length and width in kaylas and krunches. Choose a scale for your floor plan, such as 1 square on the Grid = 5 krunches or 1 kayla.

❑ Next, measure the walls and windows and doors, and add in the furniture.

❑ After you're finished, convert the room measurements to customary units. Do you have to measure everything again? No! Create a conversion chart between your new measurement units and customary units.

Time to Take a Vacation?

MATERIALS

❑ 1 map world time zones

STEPS

❑ Suppose you're a tour guide planning trips for travelers. Ask about five different people where they'd like to go in the world and what time they'd like to arrive.

❑ Looking at the time zone map, figure out what time zones these people are located in.

❑ Then figure out what time zones the destinations are located in.

❑ Have an adult help you estimate the number of hours it would take to get to these destinations and backtrack and calculate what time the people would have to leave their time zone.

❑ Then ask them what time they'd like to return to their home state.

❑ Make a chart of departure times and arrival times just like at the airport, and post it for everyone to see.

Understanding Perimeter, Area, and Volume

Everything takes up space, and so everything has perimeter, area, and volume.

OBJECTIVE	BACKGROUND	MATERIALS
To show your student how to calculate the perimeter, area, and volume of various objects and to choose from among problem-solving methods	Perimeters, areas, and volumes have everyday applications to home and professional situations. In this lesson, your student will learn to find the length around and area of two-dimensional figures, and to find the total surface area and volume of three-dimensional objects or figures. Once your student is familiar with the formulas for finding these, the possibilities are endless!	■ Student Learning Pages 9.A–9.B ■ 1 ruler ■ 1 compass ■ 1 pair scissors ■ 1 length string

VOCABULARY

POLYGON   a two-dimensional figure bounded by straight lines

PERIMETER   the distance around a polygon

RECTANGLE   a figure that has two sets of equal sides and four right angles

AREA   the surface of a figure measured in square units

SQUARE   a special rectangle in which all four sides are equal

PARALLELOGRAM   a figure with two sets of equal sides and no right angles

QUADRILATERAL   a figure with four sides

TRIANGLE   a figure with three sides

CIRCLE   a figure in which every point is the same distance from the center

CIRCUMFERENCE   the distance around a circle

DIAMETER   the length of a line through the center of a circle

RADIUS   the length of a line from the center of a circle to any point on the circle

VOLUME   the amount of space a three-dimensional figure takes up

RECTANGULAR PRISM   a rectangle that has three dimensions, length, width, and height

Let's Begin

PERIMETER

1   **REVIEW AND EXPLAIN**   Distribute Student Learning Page 9.A. Review that a **polygon** is a two-dimensional figure bounded by straight lines. Its **perimeter** is the distance around it, or the sum

w = 20 ft

l = 50 ft

of the lengths of its sides. Ask, *How would you find the perimeter of a polygon whose sides are equal?* [add the length of one side the number of times equal to the number of sides, or multiply the length of one side by the number of sides] Have your student look at the diagram of a swimming pool in the shape of a **rectangle.** Explain that a rectangle has two sets of equal sides and four right angles.

The perimeter is the wall of the pool. Ask, *What is the perimeter of the pool?* [140 ft] *How would you express the perimeter of the rectangle in an equation if P stands for perimeter?* [P = l + w + l + w or 2l + 2w]

AREA

1 **EXPLORE AND DISCUSS** Have your student review the diagram of the swimming pool. Tell him or her that the **area** of the pool is the surface of the water enclosed by the perimeter. It is measured in square units (unit²). Using the letter *A* to stand for area, the area of the pool, and all other rectangles, can be expressed by the equation $A = lw$ (length × width). Ask, *What is the area of the swimming pool?* [20 × 50 = 1,000 ft²] Discuss that area is measured in square units: inches, feet, yards, miles. Ask your student to think of at least one example of an object that might be measured in each square unit.

2 **EXTEND** Your student can extend what he or she knows about the area of a rectangle to a **parallelogram.** Have him or her look at the diagram of the parallelogram. A rectangle is actually a special instance of a parallelogram. Each is a **quadrilateral** (a figure with four sides) and has two sets of equal sides, but a parallelogram has no right angles. Explain to your student that to calculate the area of a parallelogram, instead of length × width the equation is base × height, or $A = bh$. By moving the shaded **triangle** in the diagram from the left side to the right, your student can see how this formula works.

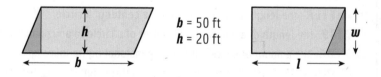

b = 50 ft
h = 20 ft

?

DID YOU KNOW?

A **square** is a special rectangle in which all four sides are equal. Using the formula $A = lw$, you can see that the area of a square is just the length of one side multiplied by itself ($A = s^2$).

3 **EXPLAIN AND DISCUSS** Have your student recognize that by drawing a diagonal line between two corners of a rectangle or parallelogram, two equal triangles are created. The area of a triangle is half the area of the larger figure, or $A = \frac{1}{2}bh$ or $\frac{bh}{2}$.

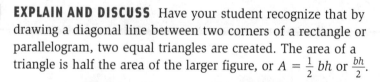

20 ft

50 ft

20 ft

50 ft

4   **PRACTICE**   Have your student complete Student Learning Page 9.A. Check his or her work and review.

5   **ELABORATE**   Ask your student to calculate the surface area of a rectangular box. Have him or her suppose that it is an old wooden chest used to store board games. Point out that this is a three-dimensional shape. Its dimensions are 36 in. by 24 in. by 18 in. Instruct your student to use a small paper or cardboard box as a model and break down the sides of the box until it lays flat (two-dimensional). Have your student draw a diagram of the broken-down chest in his or her notebook and label the dimensions of each square or rectangular section (see the diagram below). Ask your student to use his or her diagram and information from the lesson to calculate the total surface area. [total surface area = the sum of the areas of each section = 3,888 in.]

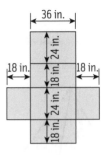

CIRCLES

1   **EXPLAIN AND DISCUSS**   Explain that just as you can find the distance around a polygon, you can also find the distance around a **circle.** This is called the **circumference.** Ask your student to make a paper model of a round hot tub with the scale 1 in. = 1 ft. Have him or her use a compass to draw a circle with an 8-inch **diameter** (or 4-inch **radius**), then cut it out. Remind your student that the diameter is a line from one point on a circle to another that passes through the circle's center, and that the radius is a line from the center of a circle to any point on the circle. Then direct him or her to cut a piece of string as long as the diameter and use it to measure the circumference. Ask, *How many times the diameter is the circumference?* [a little more than three times the circumference] Tell your student that the circumference of a circle is calculated using a constant called pi, a Greek letter that is written π. It equals approximately 3.14 or $\frac{22}{7}$. The formula for the circumference of a circle is $C = \pi d$ (C = circumference, d = diameter). Ask, *Since the radius of a circle equals half its diameter, how can this formula be written as a ratio to the radius?* [$2\pi r$]

radius = 4 ft
diameter = 8 ft

2   **DISTRIBUTE AND PRACTICE**   Distribute Student Learning Page 9.B. Have your student complete the section on the circumferences of circles.

3   **EXPLAIN**   Tell your student that the area of a circle (A) is found using the formula $A = \pi r^2$. Have him or her find the area of the hot tub in the diagram. [approximately 50 ft^2 = 3.14(4^2) = 3.14 × 16]

4   **PRACTICE**   Have your student complete the section on areas of circles on Student Learning Page 9.B. Review.

    Understanding Perimeter, Area, and Volume   **135**

VOLUME

1 **EXPLAIN AND PRACTICE** Explain that the amount of space that a three-dimensional figure takes up is called its **volume.** Have your student look at the diagram of the rectangular swimming pool. Have him or her suppose that the entire pool was 4 feet deep. A rectangle with three dimensions is called a **rectangular prism.** The volume of the swimming pool would be calculated by multiplying the length, width, and depth (or height): 50 ft $\times$ 20 ft $\times$ 4 ft = 4,000 cubic ft (ft^3). Have your student complete Student Learning Page 9.B. Check his or her work.

2 **APPLY** Point out that pyramids are triangular prisms and also have a volume. The equation for calculating the volume of a triangular prism is $V = hB/3$. In this equation, h = height and B = area of base or l^2 (length $\times$ length). Ask your student to make a drawing of a pyramid in his or her notebook with four equal sides and the following dimensions: h = 50 ft, l = 33 ft. Have him or her calculate the volume. [(33 $\times$ 33 $\times$ 50) $\div$ 3 = 18,150 ft^2]

3 **EXPAND** Referring to what he or she has already learned in the lesson, have your student create a formula for calculating the volume of a cylinder. Point out that the formula will follow the same concept as the rectangular and triangular prisms. Suggest that he or she use a straight-sided jar or water glass as a visual aid. Have your student write the equation in his or her notebook. [V = Bh; B = πr^2] Then have him or her calculate the volume of a cylinder that is 6 inches tall and 4 inches wide. Remind your student that the diameter (width) is two times the radius. [B = $\pi 2^2$ = 12.56; V = 12.56 $\times$ 6 = 75.36 in.^{2}]

Branching Out

TEACHING TIP

Have your student write a personal table of formulas for area and volume on an index card to keep for handy reference.

CHECKING IN

If your student gets the wrong answer to a problem, help him or her identify the reason by checking to see if a formula was applied incorrectly or if the error was in the calculation.

FOR FURTHER READING

Geometry and Measurements: Problem Solving, Communication, and Reasoning, by Carole Greens, Linda Schulman Dacey, and Rika Spungin (Dale Seymour Publications, 1999).

Homework Survival Guide: Math, by Teri Crawford Jones (Troll, 1998).

Janice VanCleave's Geometry for Every Kid: Easy Activities That Make Learning Geometry Fun (Science for Every Kid), by Janice VanCleave (John Wiley and Sons, 2001).

Calculate Perimeter and Area

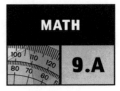

Find the perimeter of each of these figures.

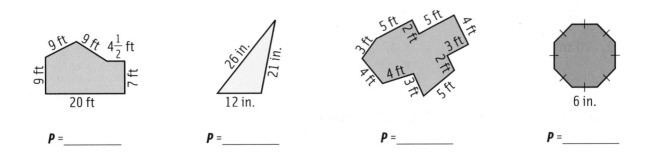

P = _____   P = _____   P = _____   P = _____

Find the area of each of these quadrilaterals.

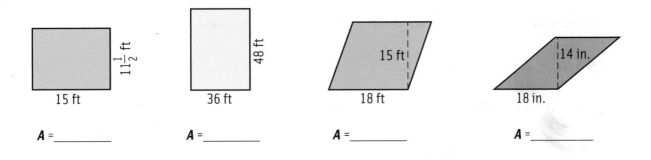

A = _____   A = _____   A = _____   A = _____

Find the area of each of these triangles.

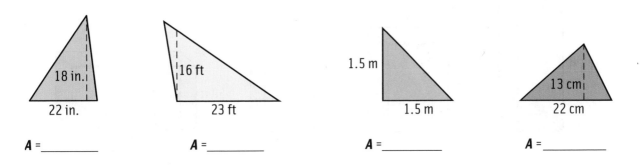

A = _____   A = _____   A = _____   A = _____

Calculate Circumference, Area, and Volume

Find the circumference of circles with these diameters.

1. 7 in. _____

2. 70 in. _____

3. 5 m _____

4. 29 m _____

5. 40 cm _____

6. 12 ft _____

Now find the area of each of the circles above.

7. _____

8. _____

9. _____

10. _____

11. _____

12. _____

Find the volume of rectangular prisms with these dimensions.

13. 23 in. × 29 in. × 12 in. _____

14. 20 cm × 12 cm × 9 cm _____

15. 14 m × 8.5 m × 8 m _____

16. 17 ft × 11 ft × 10 ft _____

Find the volume of these buildings.

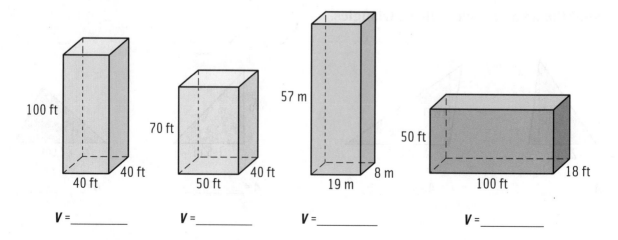

Comprehending Geometry and Motion Geometry

Geometry is far from abstract—you can see it throughout the natural world.

OBJECTIVE	BACKGROUND	MATERIALS
To show your student the properties of lines, angles, and circles, which form the basic components of many things around them	The word *geometry* literally means "the measurement of the earth." Examples of geometric concepts are all around you. Almost everywhere you look, lines form angles and shapes, and circles are parts of machines. In this lesson, your student will learn the basic terms of geometry and how to apply them to a variety of shapes that occur both in nature and in the manufactured world. He or she will also learn to work with shapes "on the move."	■ Student Learning Pages 10.A–10.F ■ 1 ruler ■ 1 compass ■ 1 protractor ■ 1 pair scissors

VOCABULARY

GEOMETRY the study of geometric figures

POINT that which marks an exact location

LINE SEGMENT a part of a line between two points

ANGLE the figure formed by two rays with the same endpoint

LINE a collection of points in a straight path extending endlessly in both directions

RAY a part of a line with one endpoint that extends endlessly in one direction

RIGHT ANGLE an angle of 90°

ACUTE ANGLE an angle of less than 90°

OBTUSE ANGLE an angle of more than 90° but less than 180°

STRAIGHT ANGLE an angle that equals 180°

CONGRUENT equal

PROTRACTOR a tool for measuring and constructing angles

Let's Begin

1 **EXPLORE AND DISCUSS** Begin this lesson on **geometry** by having your student look at a round clock that has two hands.
Ask, *For which of the terms in the chart can you find examples in the shapes of the clock?* [point—at the center; line segment—a hand; angle—the space between the hands] *What would you have to do to the clock to include the other terms?* [line—extend a hand endlessly in both directions; ray—extend

a hand endlessly in one direction] Have your student find examples of the six terms in the chart around the house and outside. Discuss.

Diagram	Read/Symbol	Description
• A	point A	A **point** marks an exact location.
A B	line AB; $\overleftrightarrow{AB}$	A **line** is a collection of points in a straight path extending endlessly in both directions.
A B	line segment AB; $\overline{AB}$	A **line segment** is part of a line between two points.
A B	ray AB; $\overrightarrow{AB}$	A **ray** is part of a line with one endpoint that extends endlessly in one direction.
B A C	angle BAC; $\angle BAC$	An **angle** is formed by two rays with the same endpoint, which is called a **vertex**.

2 **DISTRIBUTE AND OBSERVE** Distribute Student Learning Page 10.A. Have your student study the chart showing different kinds of lines, then find examples of each one inside or outside your house. Make sure your student understands that he or she won't find examples of true lines and that line segments will do. Ask your student to complete Student Learning Page 10.A. Review his or her work.

Diagram	Read/Symbol	Description
C M B A D	$\overleftrightarrow{AB}$ intersects $\overleftrightarrow{CD}$ at point M.	**Intersecting lines** meet at one point.
A B C D	$\overleftrightarrow{AB} \parallel \overleftrightarrow{CD}$; $\overleftrightarrow{AB}$ is parallel to $\overleftrightarrow{CD}$.	**Parallel lines** never intersect, although they are in the same plane.
C A D B	$\overleftrightarrow{AB} \perp \overleftrightarrow{CD}$; $\overleftrightarrow{AB}$ is perpendicular to $\overleftrightarrow{CD}$.	**Perpendicular lines** meet at right angles (such as those that form the corners of a square).
A D B C	$\overleftrightarrow{AB}$ and $\overleftrightarrow{CD}$ are skew lines.	**Skew lines** are in different planes. They do not intersect and are not parallel.

3 **EXPLORE AND DISCUSS** Distribute Student Learning Page 10.B. With your student, find a page in a book or an Internet site that shows how to measure and construct an angle with a protractor. Review with your student the definitions of the following angles: **right angle, acute angle, obtuse angle,** and **straight angle.** Then have your student write them in his or her notebook. Ask your student to complete Student Learning Page 10.B. Check his or her work.

4 **MORE PRACTICE** Have your student make an angle inspection of the house. Ask him or her to make a list of the kind and location of different angles.

5 **EXPLORE AND DISCUSS** Have your student look at the following table on classifying triangles. Then have your student use a pencil, paper, cardboard, **protractor,** and scissors to draw and cut out a triangle of each type. Ask, *What do you have to know to draw the sides of an equilateral triangle correctly?* [the angles are equal—all 60°]

?

DID YOU KNOW?

Angles are **congruent** if they have the same measure. Triangles are congruent if their sides and angles are congruent.

Classified by Sides		Classified by Angles	
5 in. 5 in. 5 in.	**Equilateral** All sides are of equal length.	(acute triangle)	**Acute** All angles are acute.
5 in. 5 in. 3 in.	**Isosceles** Two sides are of equal length.	(right triangle)	**Right** There is one right angle.
6 in. 4 in. 7 in.	**Scalene** All sides are of equal length.	(obtuse triangle)	**Obtuse** There is one obtuse angle.

?

DID YOU KNOW?

The sum of the angles in any triangle is 180°.

6 **EXPLAIN AND DESCRIBE** Distribute Student Learning Page 10.C. Remind your student that a quadrilateral is a polygon with four sides. Have your student write the names of the five types of quadrilaterals. Ask him or her to draw a picture of each and describe its defining characteristics, then complete Student Learning Page 10.C. Review his or her work. [trapezoid—one pair of parallel sides; parallelogram—two pairs of parallel sides; rhombus—parallelogram with congruent sides; rectangle— parallelogram with four right angles; square—rectangle with congruent sides]

7 **EXPLAIN AND DRAW** Explain that polygons are named by the number of sides they have. Have your student find the number of sides in a pentagon (5), hexagon (6), heptagon (7), octagon (8), nonagon (9), decagon (10), hendecagon (11), and dodecagon (12). Verify his or her results.

8 **DISTRIBUTE AND EXPLAIN** Distribute Student Learning Page 10.D. Tell your student that it is possible to move a figure without changing its size or shape. Designers of all kinds—from textile to industrial and beyond—use this principle when planning projects. It is easy to see in these diagrams of triangles that have been moved.

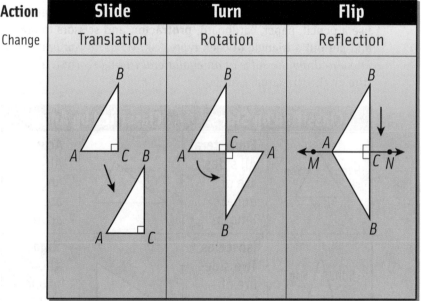

Action	Slide	Turn	Flip
Change	Translation	Rotation	Reflection

FOR FURTHER READING

How to Succeed in Geometry, by Charles Shields (Teacher Created Materials 2000).

Janice VanCleave's Geometry for Every Kid: Easy Activities That Make Learning Geometry Fun (Science for Every Kid), by Janice VanCleave (John Wiley and Sons, Inc., 2001).

Shape Up! by David A. Adler (Holiday House, 2000).

Branching Out

TEACHING TIP

If your student has difficulty memorizing geometry terms, you may want to make up flash cards to practice, alternating giving definitions for terms and terms for definitions. Also, you may want to put sticky notes around the house that illustrate various terms, such as *right angle, parallelogram,* and *intersecting lines.*

CHECKING IN

You can assess how well your student is doing with this material by how well he or she manipulates the compass and protractor in drawing lines and shapes.

Line Up

Place points on the diagram to create one of each of the figures. Label each point on the diagram with a different letter. Then write the name and symbol (if there is one) for each figure.

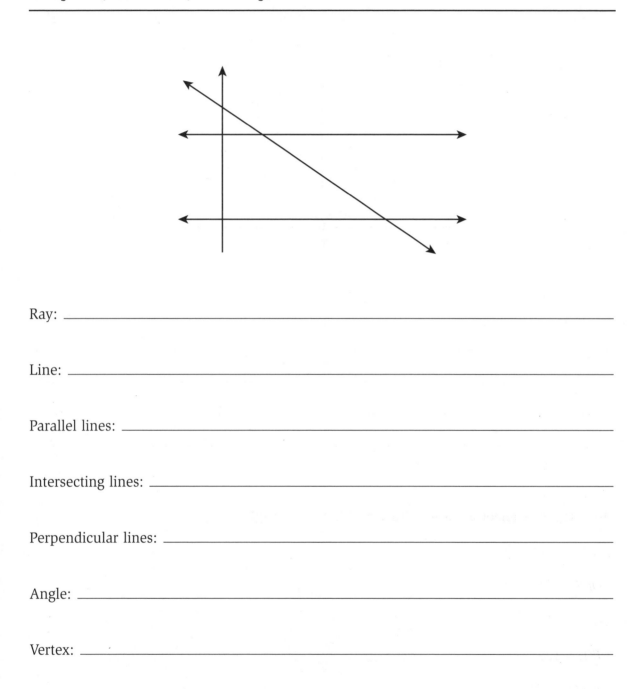

Ray: _____

Line: _____

Parallel lines: _____

Intersecting lines: _____

Perpendicular lines: _____

Angle: _____

Vertex: _____

Find Your Angle

Using the appropriate geometric symbols, list all the angles you can find in this diagram. (Hint: There are 10.) Measure each one and write its measurement. Then classify it as right, acute, obtuse, or straight.

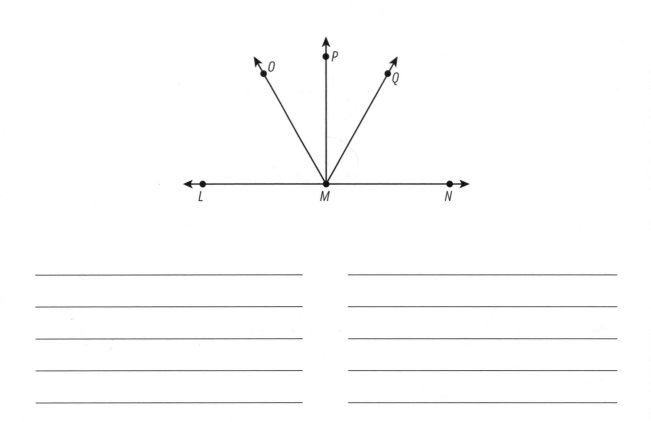

_____   _____

_____   _____

_____   _____

_____   _____

_____   _____

On a separate sheet of paper, draw and label the angles.

$\angle ABC = 45°$

$\angle DEF = 150°$

$\angle GHI = 75°$

$\angle JKL = 100°$

$\angle MNO = 20°$

$\angle PQR = 180°$

Fill in the Blank

Find the length of the unmarked angle or side in each of the quadrilaterals and write it into the diagram. Then write the name of each type of quadrilateral on the lines.

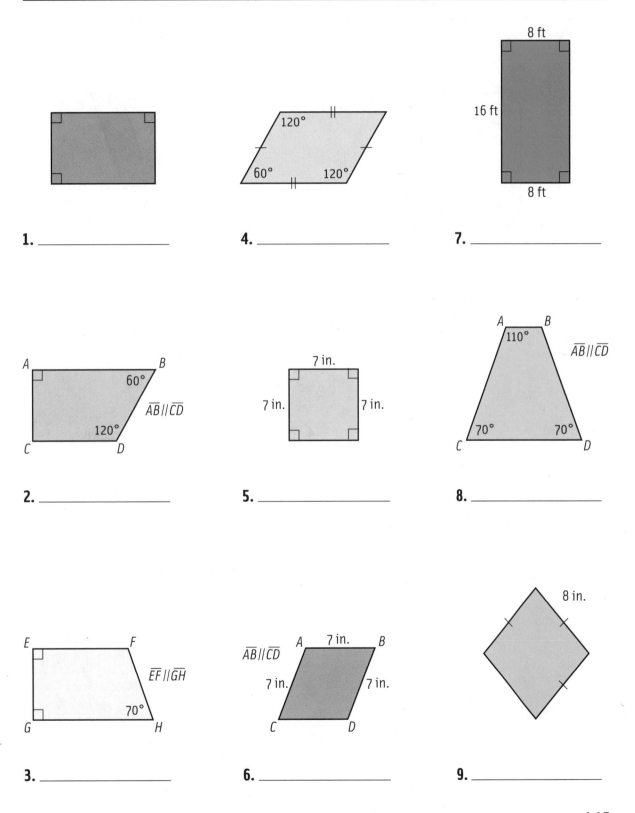

1. _____

4. _____

7. _____

2. _____

5. _____

8. _____

3. _____

6. _____

9. _____

Create Slides, Turns, and Flips

Follow the directions for moving each of the figures below and draw the new figure in the space provided.

1. Flip over line.

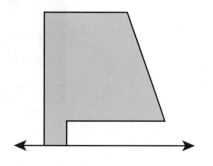

3. Flip over line.

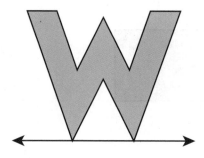

2. Turn 90°.

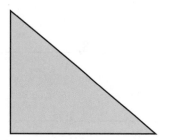

4. Draw a translation $1\frac{3}{4}$ inches down.

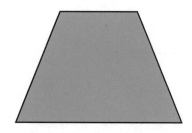

Be a Copycat

Follow the steps to construct congruent lines and figures without measuring.

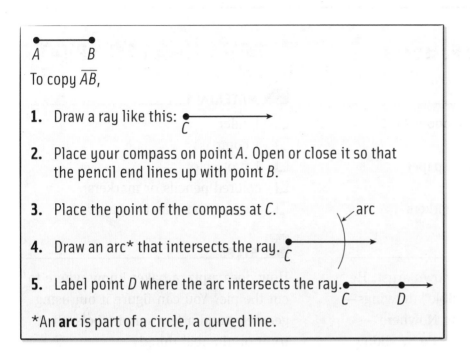

To copy $\overline{AB}$,

1. Draw a ray like this:

2. Place your compass on point *A*. Open or close it so that the pencil end lines up with point *B*.

3. Place the point of the compass at *C*.

4. Draw an arc* that intersects the ray.

5. Label point *D* where the arc intersects the ray.

*An **arc** is part of a circle, a curved line.

If you can copy one line, then you can copy an entire figure by copying one line at a time. Copy the lines and figures onto a separate sheet of paper using the method shown above. Use a protractor to measure the angles.

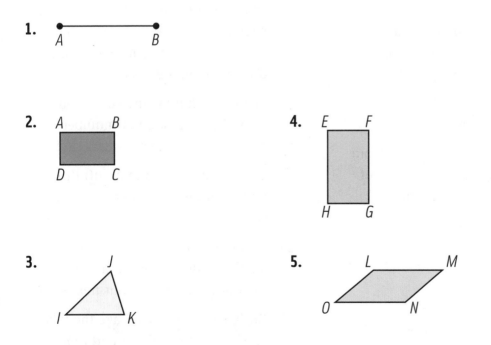

1.

2.

3.

4.

5.

What's Next? You Decide!

Now it's your turn to choose what to do next in the lesson. Read the activities and decide which one you want to do— you may want to try them both!

Find Life's Patterns

MATERIALS

❑ 1 book or Web site about M. C. Escher
❑ 1 sheet construction paper
❑ 1 ruler
❑ colored pencils or markers

STEPS

M. C. Escher is a well-known artist. He draws fanciful, "impossible" drawings— such as "The Stairway to Nowhere"— and elaborate patterns made by sliding, turning, and flipping shapes.

❑ Find some of Escher's drawings and study them for their geometry and artistry.

❑ Choose a shape and decide how you are going to repeat it by sliding, turning, and/or flipping until you have a design for a page.

❑ Draw it out first, then color it.

❑ When you are finished, mount your design on a slightly larger piece of construction paper as a frame.

Take a Piece of the Pi(e)

MATERIALS

❑ 1 ruler
❑ 1 compass
❑ 1 protractor
❑ colored pencils or markers
❑ 1 sheet construction paper

STEPS

How does a pizza baker know where to cut the pie? You can figure it out using geometry and a few simple tools, then try it on the real thing!

❑ Start by drawing a large circle on the paper. Put a dot at the midpoint.

❑ Then draw a radius (a line from the center to a point on the circumference) anywhere on the circle. Use this as your baseline to divide the pie into slices.

❑ Figure out how many slices you want. Then divide that number into 360° (the total degrees in a circle).

❑ Use a protractor to mark off the points on the circumference that correspond to the degrees in a slice.

❑ Join the point to the midpoint with another radius. Use the new radius as your baseline for your next slice.

❑ Fairly soon, you will have the whole "pie" laid out. Color it and draw your favorite toppings.

In Your Community

To reinforce the skills and concepts taught in this section,
try one or more of these activities!

Data from Your Community

Have your student research existing data or gather data of his or her own about a specific aspect of your community—such as the number of streetlights, population, or amount of water used per month—and create charts or graphs to illustrate the information. Then have him or her write an article and submit it to a local newspaper.

Hardware Math

Visit your local hardware store and have your student look at different types of wood, paint, and pipes. Call ahead and let the store personnel know you're coming. Then have them show your student how the hardware professionals take measurements, cut materials, and use machines for wood, paint, and pipes.

Weighing in at the Post Office

Explain to your student that the postage of a package or letter depends on its weight, size, and type of service. Go to the post office and get a chart that lists the different prices according to the various price factors. Have your student put a letter or package together to send to someone he or she knows. Ask him or her to estimate, based on the weight, size, and type of service, how much he or she believes it will cost to send.

Go to the post office together at a time when there isn't too much traffic and have the package weighed and posted. Encourage your student to ask the postal clerk any questions he or she has about how the scale works and how the scales have changed over time. If possible, arrange to have a tour of the post office.

Volunteer Cashier

Arrange for your student to help out handling money at a local farmer's market, a community or religious organization's rummage or bake sale, or other similar event. As customers purchase items, have him or her accept the money, count it, and give change, if necessary.

Favorite Areas

Have your student choose a favorite place in the community to measure. It could be a park, playground, recreational center, or garden. Explain that the length and perimeter can be easily measured using his or her personal foot length and carefully walking the length and width of the space. Then ask your student to draw a diagram showing length and width.

If the space is more like a circle, your student should measure the circumference, then calculate the radius. Have your student convert personal feet to customary feet and centimeters by using a measuring stick and then calculate the area of the space in yards and meters. The space probably won't be a perfect rectangle or circle, so point out that the area will be an estimate.

Tree-to-Car Ratio

Have your student find the tree-to-car ratio for a street in your town. Ask your student to collect data on (count) the number of trees and parked cars. If your town has many trees, you can decide only to count the trees along the median strips. Have him or her write the ratio in the lowest equivalent numbers and write a summary statement such as "today, on our block there are x trees for every y cars." Your student can also observe the ratio of cars to houses or people walking to people driving.

We Have Learned

Use this checklist to summarize what you and your student
have accomplished in the Math section.

❑ **Number Theory**
❑ greatest common factor, least common multiple
❑ prime numbers, fractions, decimals
❑ basic problem solving

❑ **Fractions, Decimals, and Whole Numbers**
❑ adding with like denominators, adding with unlike denominators
❑ dividing with like denominators, dividing with unlike denominators
❑ equations with fractions, equations with mixed numbers
❑ rounding, adding, subtracting
❑ multiplying decimals, dividing decimals

❑ **Percent and Ratio**
❑ estimating percents
❑ writing equations, solving percent problems
❑ computing discounts, computing sales tax
❑ understanding ratios, understanding proportions
❑ probability, rates, unit price

❑ **Data, Statistics, and Charting**
❑ creating histograms, creating bar charts, creating line graphs
❑ mean, median, mode, range
❑ interpreting charts, interpreting graphs

❑ **Integers**
❑ comparing integers, ordering integers
❑ solving equations with integers
❑ coordinate graphing

❑ **Measurement**
❑ customary units, metric units
❑ mass, volume, capacity
❑ measurement conversion, instruments of measurement
❑ perimeter of triangles, perimeter of quadrilaterals
❑ circumference of circles, area of circles
❑ area of triangles, area of quadrilaterals
❑ volume of prisms, volume of cylinders

❑ **Geometry**
❑ classifying lines, angles, circles, triangles, polygons
❑ measuring lines, angles, circles, triangles, polygons
❑ rotations, reflections
❑ constructing congruent geometric figures
❑ motion geometry

We have also learned:

_____

_____

_____

_____

Science

Science

Key Topics

Classification of Plants and Animals
Pages 153–168

Cells and Genetics
Pages 169–176

Human Body, Health, and Growth
Pages 177–190

Scientific Process
Pages 191–194

Earth's Surface and Ecosystems
Pages 195–206

Solar System
Pages 207–210

Physical Energy
Pages 211–216

Light and Sound
Pages 217–220

Chemical Properties of Matter
Pages 221–226

Classifying Living Things

*Who among us has never stopped to marvel at
the grand spectacle that is life on Earth?*

SCIENCE

LESSON
3.1

OBJECTIVE	BACKGROUND	MATERIALS
To help your student understand how animals are classified	Your student will surely find great wonder in the incredible array of animals that coexist with humans on Earth. In this lesson, your student will learn about the animal kingdom. He or she will study how biologists classify and conduct research about mammals, reptiles, amphibians, and fish. He or she will learn the characteristics of each animal group and be able to identify vertebrates and invertebrates, carnivores and herbivores, and warm- and cold-blooded animals. Your student also will research and come to understand the life processes and cycles of the animals.	■ Student Learning Pages 1.A–1.C ■ colored pencils, markers, or paints ■ 1 large posterboard or butcher paper ■ 1 copy Venn Diagram, page 353

VOCABULARY

KINGDOM ANIMALIA the kingdom used to classify living things that includes all animals

INVERTEBRATES a group of animals without backbones

VERTEBRATES a group of animals with backbones

CARNIVORES animals that eat meat

HERBIVORES animals that eat plants

WARM-BLOODED animals that maintain a constant body temperature regardless of the surroundings

COLD-BLOODED animals whose body temperature changes according to the surroundings

Let's Begin

1　**EXPLAIN** Explain that 9 or 10 million species of animals live on Earth. Tell your student that scientists use a system, or taxonomy, for naming and grouping living organisms. Within the system are seven groups or categories. Read the names of the groups from largest to smallest with your student:

- Kingdom
- Phylum
- Class
- Order
- Family
- Genus
- Species

Tell him or her that this lesson will focus on the animal kingdom, known by biologists as **kingdom Animalia.** Point out that this kingdom is the broadest of the groups in the system.

2 **DISCUSS AND REVEAL** Talk with your student to see what he or she currently knows about the animal kingdom. Ask, *What major groups of animals are you familiar with?* [mammals, reptiles, amphibians, fish] Ask your student to tell you what he or she knows about each group of animals. Then make a copy of the Venn Diagram found on page 353. Work with your student to create a Venn Diagram that shows things he or she already knows about mammals, reptiles, and amphibians. Discuss each of the groups. Explain that some well-known characteristics of mammals are that they feed their young with milk, are covered with hair, and have live births. Tell your student that well-known amphibians are frogs and toads, but that salamanders and newts belong in this group, too. They have moist skin and are hatched from eggs.

3 **DISTRIBUTE AND IDENTIFY** Distribute Student Learning Page 1.A. Have your student go to the library or search the Internet for information about the characteristics of mammals, reptiles, amphibians, and fish. Ask him or her to record names of animals that belong to each group and their distinguishing properties. Have your student identify several animals in each of the groups shown on Student Learning Page 1.A and write short descriptions of their properties.

4 **EXPLAIN** Explain that amphibians begin life inside eggs left in a well-protected place. They may be in water or a wet place, but can also be in a dry place. Point out that during the life cycle they may change from a water-breathing larva to a four-legged air-breathing adult, as in the case of a frog. Tell your student that mammals, reptiles, amphibians, and fish all have unique life cycles. Ask him or her to use the Internet or go to the library to find the stages in the life cycle for animals in each group and then make a booklet that illustrates the life cycle of one group. Your student can draw pictures to show the different stages or cut pictures from old magazines. Encourage your student to tell the life-cycle story to another family member using his or her booklet.

5 **RESEARCH AND DISTRIBUTE** Distribute Student Learning Page 1.B. Tell your student that another way of classifying animals is to put them in groups with and without backbones. Remind your student that animals without backbones are called **invertebrates.** Tell him or her that sponges, roundworms, insects, and spiders are examples of invertebrates. Point out that examples of **vertebrates** include dogs and humans. Have your student read and do research on vertebrates and invertebrates. Encourage him or her to create lists of each. Ask your student to learn about the animals' habitats, eating habits, how they reproduce, and if they are **warm-blooded** or **cold-blooded.**

DID YOU KNOW?

A Swedish botanist named Carolus Linnaeus is considered the father of the modern system of classifying groups of plants and animals. Learn more about him at http://www.plantex-plorers.com.

DID YOU KNOW?

The first vertebrate is thought to have been a conodont: a two-inch-long eel with a finned tail. It is believed to have lived in the seas 515 million years ago.

6 **RESEARCH AND SUMMARIZE** Explain to your student that animals of different groups may be carnivores (meat eaters) or herbivores (plant eaters). Direct him or her to research **carnivores** and **herbivores.** You can suggest the Electronic Zoo at http://www.netvet.wust/edu/e-zoo.htm as a resource. Encourage him or her to take notes and print illustrations. Ask your student to make a two-column chart to summarize his or her findings. Discuss the chart. Ask, *What physical properties can help you identify a carnivore? An herbivore?*

7 **GUIDE AND RESEARCH** Have your student find information about identifying warm- and cold-blooded animals. Guide your student to identify examples of each and to choose examples of each to learn more about. Ask, *What animals are warm-blooded?* [mammals] *What groups of animals are cold-blooded?* [fish, reptiles, amphibians] *Are you cold-blooded or warm-blooded?* [humans are warm-blooded]

8 **DESCRIBE AND ILLUSTRATE** Talk with your student about warm- and cold-blooded animals and ask him or her to describe what he or she learned about each. Have your student design a brochure about an animal that he or she found unique. Suggest that he or she include facts about the animal's habitat, life processes, and life cycle. Encourage your student to make the brochure factual but to also have a specific purpose or audience in mind. For example, the brochure might explain why the vulture is an important part of the food chain or might teach young children about the squirrels in their neighborhood.

9 **REVIEW** Review the major groups of the animal kingdom with your student. Make sure that all of the classifications have been identified and understood.

10 **DISTRIBUTE** Distribute Student Learning Pages 1.C. Guide your student to choose activities to complete. Allow time to complete all of them if your student wants to.

Branching Out

TEACHING TIPS

❑ Many young people identify strongly with animals and are passionate about protecting them and their environment. If your student is interested in the well-being of endangered species, you can encourage him or her to write to state and U.S. Congress people on behalf of their favorite animals. Their names and addresses can be found at http://www.senate.gov or http://www.house.gov.

❑ For more hands-on knowledge about animals, have your student volunteer at a local pet shelter or animal rescue organization.

ENRICH THE EXPERIENCE

Teach your student to write a first draft for his or her written projects. Talk with him or her about checking for content to be sure that the purpose is clear and that the sequence of information is logical. Encourage him or her to support important points with quotes or references from researched sources, and remind him or her to delete irrelevant information.

Most need help with walking or playing with the animals, or general feeding or other care. Be sure your student doesn't have any allergies, first.

❑ Combine hands-on animal interest with your student's entrepreneurial spirit and have him or her walk and feed dogs and/or other pets of family and friends to earn extra money.

CHECKING IN

You can assess your student's understanding of how to classify animals by having him or her make a children's magazine that includes articles with topics related to understanding the animal kingdom. Encourage your student to accurately describe the characteristics of the animals and their life processes.

FOR FURTHER READING

Animal: The Definitive Visual Guide to the World's Wildlife, by David Burnie and Don E. Wilson, eds. (DK Publishing, Inc., 2001).

Animal Diversity, 3rd Edition, by Cleveland P. Hickman, Larry S. Roberts, and Allan Larson (McGraw-Hill Higher Education, 2002).

No Bones: A Key to Bugs, Slugs, Worms and Ticks, Spiders, Centipedes, and Other Creepy Crawlies, by Elizabeth Shepard (Macmillan, 1998).

Veterinarian, by Michael Burgan (Capstone Books, 2000).

Identify the Properties of Animals

Write the major properties of each group.

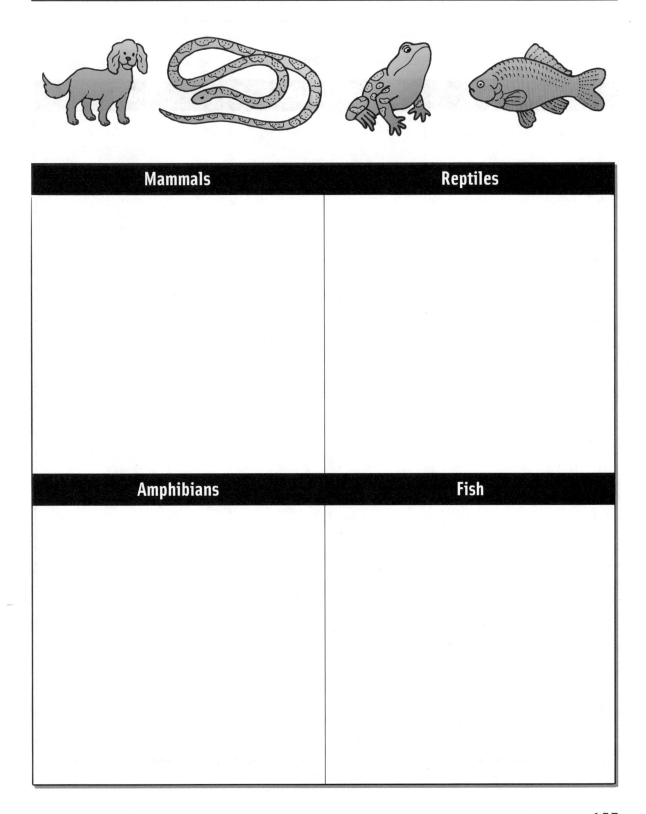

Mammals	Reptiles

Amphibians	Fish

Understand Animals

Use your research to write the names of vertebrate and invertebrate animals in the correct column of the chart. Include examples of animals that live and move in the air, on land, or in the sea. Complete the chart by writing *mammal, reptile, amphibian,* or *fish* in the Group column.

Animals

Vertebrates	Invertebrates	Group
1.		
2.		
3.		
4.		
5.		
6.		
7.		
8.		
9.		
10.		

What's Next? You Decide!

Now it's your turn to choose what to do next in the lesson. Read the activities and decide which one you want to do—you may want to try them all!

Find Careers Involving Animals

STEPS

❏ Research and identify jobs that involve animals. Research by using the Internet or going to your local library or employment office to find out what kinds of jobs are related to animals.

❏ You can try searching the U.S. Fish and Wildlife Service Web site for government jobs that involve animals at http://www.fws.gov.

Observe the Life Cycle of Fruit Flies

MATERIALS

❏ 1 small glass jar
❏ 1 piece ripe fruit
❏ 1 paper funnel
❏ 2–3 balls cotton
❏ 1 small piece paper

STEPS

❏ Before beginning this project, read the instructions with an adult.

❏ Put a small piece of ripe fruit in the bottom of a glass jar.

❏ Put a paper funnel in the top of the jar with the widest part facing up. Set the bottle out in an open area.

❏ When you see that six to eight flies have flown into the jar, take out the funnel and plug the jar with cotton.

❏ It is likely that there are males and females in the jar. The females are bigger than the males. Watch for eggs to appear. It will only take two or three days for them to hatch.

❏ Put a small piece of paper in the jar for the larvae to crawl on when they become pupae. The pupae will become young-adult fruit flies.

Investigate Endangered Species

MATERIALS

❏ desktop publishing software (optional)
❏ access to a photocopy machine

STEPS

❏ First go to the library or search the Internet for information about endangered species. Look for Web sites such as the National Wildlife Federation's at http://www.nwf.org that has conservation news, or EE-Link's (environmental education) at http://eelink.net that has fact sheets about endangered species.

(CONTINUED) ➤

❏ Design a one-page flyer that includes information about endangered species in your state or a nearby state.

❏ You can write your flyer by hand or type it.

❏ When your flyer is ready, make enough photocopies to pass out to your friends and to children in your neighborhood.

Install a Birdbath

MATERIALS

❏ 1 underdish from a large ceramic plant pot
❏ 1 medium to large plastic bottle
❏ 1 pair scissors
❏ 3–5 feet heavy string

STEPS

❏ First, dig a hole large and deep enough for the dish to fit into with a small amount of the rim sticking up.

❏ Ask a parent to help you choose a place near trees with branches hanging over.

❏ Next, poke a very small hole in the plastic bottle with the scissors (ask a parent for help with this step) and fill the bottle with water.

❏ Then use the string to hang the bottle from a tree directly over the dish.

❏ Fill the dish with no more than two inches of water. Be sure to put in fresh, clean water every few days!

❏ As the water drips from the bottle to the dish below, the birds will know their bath is ready.

❏ You can observe the birds and learn about the different species. Go to the library to find a bird-watcher's guide and see if you can list the names of all the birds that visit your bath!

Assemble a Photo Essay of Animals

MATERIALS

❏ 2–3 old magazines
❏ 1 glue stick
❏ 1 pair scissors
❏ 4 large sheets construction paper

STEPS

❏ Look through magazines and cut out photos of mammals, reptiles, amphibians, and fish.

❏ Write short, descriptive statements to go along with your photos.

❏ Using one page per group, lay out your "photos" and descriptions on the pages in a creative way and glue them onto the construction paper to make a photo essay.

❏ Hang your photo essay on the wall or put the pages together to make a book to share with your family and friends.

Exploring the Plant Kingdom

Have you thanked a green plant today?

OBJECTIVE	BACKGROUND	MATERIALS
To help your student understand the characteristics and attributes of plants	The above quotation was a slogan from the 1960s, and its purpose was to get people thinking about all the ways that plants benefit us. The plant kingdom plays a vital role in the balance of nature. Plants provide food and raw materials for animals and humans. Plants have played an essential role in the development of human civilization. With 260,000 species growing in almost all climates and environments, plants are the most abundant life form on Earth. In this lesson, your student will learn about plant characteristics, classification, and life processes.	■ Student Learning Pages 2.A–2.D ■ 1 magnifying glass ■ 1 cutting from a live green plant (e.g., philodendron) ■ 1 live weed ■ 1 glass tube or bottle ■ 1–2 sticks sugarless chewing gum ■ 1 copy Venn Diagram, page 353 ■ 1 copy Sequence Chain, page 354 ■ 1 die ■ 2 pennies

VOCABULARY

PHOTOSYNTHESIS the process by which green plants make their own food

GERMINATION the beginning growth of a seed

OSMOSIS the process whereby thin root hairs pull in water and nutrients from the soil

XYLEM small tubes in plants that conduct water through the roots and into the stems and leaves

STOMATA tiny openings in a plant part, such as a leaf, through which air and water pass

TRANSPIRATION the process by which water vapor passes out of a living thing through tiny holes or a membrane

RESPIRATION the process whereby living things break down food so its energy can be used

VASCULAR these types of plants have a system of vessels that carry water and nutrition throughout the plant

NONVASCULAR these types of plants don't have a system of vessels that carry water and nutrition throughout the plant

ANNUAL a plant that completes its life cycle in one year

BIENNIAL a plant that takes two years to complete its life cycle

PERENNIAL a plant that lives for many years

Let's Begin

1 **PREVIEW AND REVIEW** Help your student access his or her prior knowledge about plants. Have your student create a KWL Chart in his or her notebook. To make this chart have him or

her create three columns. At the top of the first column write: "What I Know"; in the second write: "What I Want to Know"; in the third column write: "What I Learned." Encourage your student to list in the left-hand column all that he or she already knows about plants. Then ask your student to write down what he or she wants to learn in the center column. You may want to adjust the focus of your lesson based on these points and questions. At the end of the lesson, allow your student time to fill in the right-hand column with new facts he or she has learned about plants.

2 **RELATE** Point out that plants produce oxygen and provide food and therefore are essential to life on Earth.

a. People eat plants (i.e., vegetables) and plant parts (i.e., fruit, cereal).

b. Many people also eat animals that live on plants.

c. Plants provide raw materials for building and writing (such as wood and paper from trees) and material for fabric (such as cotton and flax).

d. Some plants are a source of fuel: coal (from peat), wood (from trees).

3 **COMPARE AND DISCUSS** Talk with your student about how plants and animals are similar and different. You may want to glance back at Lesson 3.1. As you discuss this information with your student, have him or her organize it into a Venn Diagram copied from page 353. Ask, *Which life processes do plants and animals have in common?* [both require water, nutrients, and air; both carry out respiration; both produce young that have the characteristics of their species]

4 **CONTRAST AND DISCUSS** Next, point out ways in which plants and animals differ: Most plants do not move from the spot in which they began to grow. Animals do not make their own food. Animals inhale oxygen and exhale carbon monoxide; plants use carbon dioxide as an ingredient in **photosynthesis** and "exhale" oxygen. Some animals care for their babies; as far as we know, plants do not.

5 **DISTRIBUTE** Distribute Student Learning Page 2.A. Have your student use the Internet or a library reference source to write each label in the correct place on the worksheet. It might be helpful to have a flowering plant on hand, such as a lily. Encourage the student to find the corresponding part on the live plant.

6 **EXPLORE AND DESCRIBE** Green plants make up the majority of plant species. Identify the life processes and characteristics of green plants. The four major processes are **germination** (the sprouting of a seed), water movement, photosynthesis, and respiration. Briefly outline for your student some information about each process. Then encourage him or her to do further research on the Internet or in the library.

7 **EXPLAIN** Seeds need to experience certain conditions to begin to germinate and grow. They need warmth, moisture, and oxygen. Therefore, seeds are dormant (hibernating) during the winter. Seeds begin to grow in the spring. Ask, *How do conditions change from winter to spring so that seeds can grow?* [the air is warmer, melting ice and snow provide moisture] Ask, *What effects might moisture have on seeds to allow them to germinate?* [moisture softens the seed coat and causes the seed to swell and burst]

8 **MODEL AND OBSERVE** Water runs up into a plant through its roots. Model this process by pulling up a weed and observing how it changes when its roots are out of the soil (away from water). Tell your student that **osmosis** is the term for the process whereby thin root hairs pull in water and nutrients from the soil. Ask, *Look at the plant that has been without water for a while. What has happened?* [the leaves and stem have wilted] Now place the plant in room-temperature water and wait a few minutes. Discuss the changes. Explain that many green plants have small tubes, similar to blood vessels, that conduct water through the roots and into the stems and leaves. They are called **xylem** (ZY-lem).

9 **EXPLAIN** Ask, *What does your body do with excess water?* [it is lost through excretion or sweat] Tell him or her that plants give off excess water through tiny holes called **stomata,** which are found on the surface of leaves. This process is called **transpiration.** (Study the underside of a healthy leaf with a magnifying glass and you will probably see the stomata—they look like pinpoints.)

10 **MODEL** Your student can demonstrate transpiration by making a transpirometer. First, have your student place the stem of a cut plant into a tube of water. Then have your student chew one or two sticks of sugarless gum until it's soft and pliable. Have him or her seal the tube with the gum, being careful to work around the plant. He or she can then observe the level of the water and record the amount by which it drops. Ask, *How did the water get out of the tube?* [the only way the water could get out was by passing through the plant and leaving through the stem or the leaves]

11 **EXPLAIN** Based on what your student already knows about photosynthesis and its root word meanings, ask him or her to speculate on how photosynthesis works. Then tell your student that plants carry out a chemical process called **respiration,** through which living things break down food so they can use its energy. Explain to your student that he or she also might be familiar with the other meaning of respiration, the act of breathing. Ask, *What would the plant use energy for?* [growth, repair, reproduction] Have your student do further research on photosynthesis and respiration (and other plant life processes) on the Internet or at the library.

DID YOU KNOW?

The word *photosynthesis* is made up of two parts: *photo,* which means "light," and *synthesis,* which means "putting together." This is the process by which plants make food.

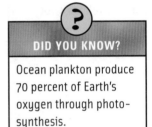

DID YOU KNOW?

Ocean plankton produce 70 percent of Earth's oxygen through photosynthesis.

DID YOU KNOW?

Earth's oldest living
things are bristlecone
pine trees, which grow
in the dry American
southwest. Groves of
ancient trees, thousands
of years old, are found
in California's White-
Inyo Mountain Range.
Scientists have dubbed
the oldest tree
Methuselah, and believe
it is more than 4,700
years old.

12 **DISCUSS** Distribute Student Learning Page 2.B. Work together
with your student and discuss which items are part of the
process of photosynthesis and why.

13 **EXPLORE AND DISCUSS** Like animals, plants are classified into
groups according to their characteristics. Plants are first classified
as **vascular** or **nonvascular.** Vascular plants have a system of
vessels that carry water and nutrition throughout the plant
(ferns, seed-bearing plants). Nonvascular plants do not have this
system of vessels (liverworts, hornworts, and mosses). Vascular
plants can be further broken down according to whether they
reproduce by spores or by seeds. Seed-bearing plants are further
broken down by whether the seed is uncovered (gymnosperm)
or covered (angiosperm). Plants that produce pine cones are
gymnosperms; plants that produce flowers are angiosperms.

14 **DISTRIBUTE AND REVIEW** Distribute Student Learning Page 2.C.
Using a plant guide, help your student find the categories for
several plants with which he or she is familiar.

15 **UNDERSTAND** Point out that plants, like all living things, have
a life cycle. With green leafy plants, *life cycle* means how long it
takes a plant to grow from seed, flower, and create new seeds.

16 **EXPLORE** Tell your student that there are three types of plant
life cycles: **annual, perennial,** and **biennial.** Annual plants
complete their life cycle in one growing season (within one
year). In that time the plants grow, flower, create seeds, and die.
Perennial plants live for three or more years, continuing to grow,
flower, make seeds, and begin all over in the spring. Biennial
plants are plants that take two growing seasons to complete a
life cycle. In the first year the plant produces leaves and rests
during the winter; the next year it grows flowers, makes seeds,
and dies. Let your student use the Internet or the library to
research examples of each kind of plant.

Branching Out

TEACHING TIP

If your lesson includes a visit to botanical gardens, focus on one aspect
of plant study, such as human uses of plants. You may wish to contact
a member of the education department before you go to find out which
exhibits suit your needs.

FOR FURTHER READING

Wacky Plant Cycles, by
Valerie Wyatt (Mondo
Publications, 2000).

What Is a Fungus? by
D. M. Souza (Franklin
Watts, Inc., 2002).

CHECKING IN

You can assess your student's understanding of this lesson on the plant
kingdom by reviewing the KWL Chart. Have your student evaluate
whether his or her questions were answered, and then have your
student list in the third column what he or she has learned.

Label Parts of a Plant

Look at the picture of the plant. Label the plant using the parts listed. Then look at the picture of the flower. Label the flower using the parts listed.

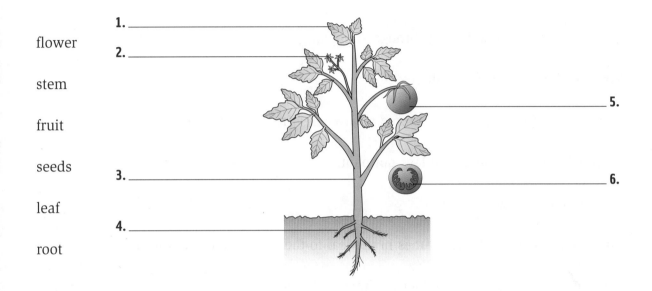

flower

stem

fruit

seeds

leaf

root

1. _____

2. _____

3. _____

4. _____

5. _____

6. _____

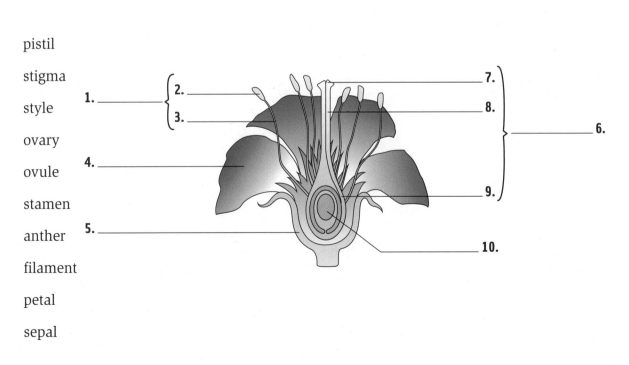

pistil

stigma

style

ovary

ovule

stamen

anther

filament

petal

sepal

1. _____

2. _____

3. _____

4. _____

5. _____

6. _____

7. _____

8. _____

9. _____

10. _____

Get a Grip on Photosynthesis

Read each phrase. Some of these steps are part of the photosynthesis process and some aren't. Make a copy of the Sequence Chain from the back of the book. Decide which are parts of the photosynthesis process and write them in the chart in the correct order. Then draw a picture illustrating the process of photosynthesis.

Carbon dioxide enters the leaf through stomata.

Water causes seed coat to soften.

Carbon dioxide combines with stored solar energy in the chloroplasts.

Seed drops to the ground and lays dormant.

Plant produces sugar (food).

Sugar is transported through tubes in the leaf to the roots, stems, and fruit.

Oxygen is formed as a by-product of photosynthesis.

Water is drawn into the plant through the roots.

Oxygen is released into the atmosphere.

Make Your Way Through the Plant Kingdom

How many different kinds of plants can you name? You and another player put your pennies, or game pieces, at Start. Player 1 rolls the die and moves that many spaces. He or she must name a plant that begins with that letter and classify it as a vascular or nonvascular plant. If Player 1 answers correctly, he or she rolls again. If he or she doesn't, Player 2 gets a try. If Player 2 answers correctly, he or she moves ahead that many places. If Player 2 doesn't, he or she takes a turn at rolling the die. The first person to reach the "garden" wins!

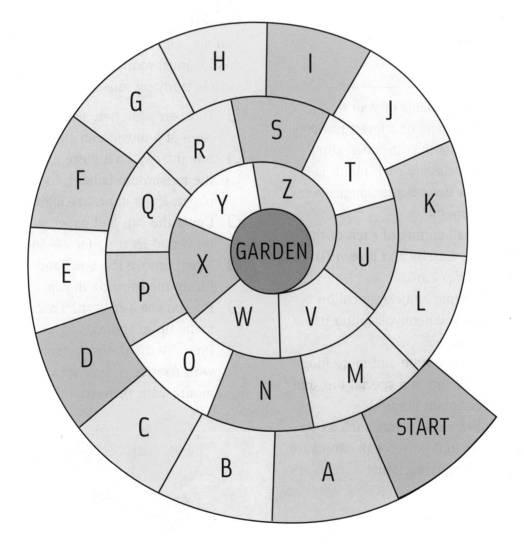

What's Next? You Decide!

Now it's your turn to choose what to do next in the lesson. Read the activities and decide which one you want to do—you may want to try them both!

Create a Plant Library

MATERIALS

❏ regional field guide for plants in your area
❏ 10–20 index cards
❏ 1 shoulder bag to carry materials
❏ 1 roll clear adhesive tape (preferably wide)
❏ 1 small clipboard

STEPS

❏ Look at some plants in your backyard, a park, or a forest preserve.
❏ Choose plants that are interesting to you and classify each plant. Is it vascular or nonvascular, angiosperm or gymnosperm?
❏ Take a small cutting of each of the plants you classify and tape it flat onto an index card.
❏ Write its name and classification information, where you found it, and the date.
❏ As you collect more and more index cards, put them in a special box and share your plant library.
❏ Remember, some plants such as poison ivy and poison oak can cause painful allergic reactions!

Make a Spore Print

MATERIALS

❏ 1 nice mushroom from supermarket
❏ 1 small bowl
❏ dark or light colored paper
❏ clear fixative (or hair spray)

STEPS

You are a mycologist (a scientist who studies mushrooms and other fungi) who is studying mushroom species.

❏ Have an adult help you cut off the stem of a mushroom close to the cap.
❏ Lay the cap on a piece of paper. If the mushroom is light, use dark paper; if it's dark, use light paper.
❏ Cover the cap and paper with the bowl and let it sit for 24–36 hours.
❏ Then remove the bowl and carefully lift up the mushroom cap.
❏ Do you see a pattern? This pattern is made up of spores.
❏ Preserve the design by spraying it with fixative or hair spray. Label and mount your picture.

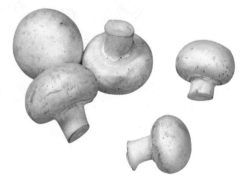

Exploring the World of Cells, Genetics, and Microscopes

If the same DNA that's in our feet is also in our fingernails and our brains, how come we don't think with our fingers and walk on our hands?

OBJECTIVE	BACKGROUND	MATERIALS
To help your student learn about cells and how they relate to genetics, and to see how we can study both using microscopes	Cells are sometimes called "the building blocks of life." In fact, each cell carries out all life functions. Animals and plants are composed of cells. Most cells are microscopic in size. Some plants and animals are only one-celled animals, but the average human body is made up of 75 trillion highly specialized cells. Inside each cell is a chemical code that describes all the traits of the entire organism and that is transmitted to future generations. In this lesson, your student will learn about cells, study genetics, and use microscopes.	■ Student Learning Pages 3.A–3.D ■ 1 microscope or magnifying glass ■ petroleum jelly ■ 1 resealable plastic bag ■ 20 1-inch pieces yarn ■ 20 colored beads ■ 20 buttons ■ 1 small resealable plastic square container

VOCABULARY

CELL the smallest unit of life that can carry out all life processes

MEMBRANE the outer covering of a cell where wastes are secreted

NUCLEUS the area of a cell that controls a cell's functions

CYTOPLASM the liquid in which a cell's life processes are carried out

ORGANELLES these are like organs in the body in that each organelle has a particular job to do

CHLOROPLASTS these are found in cytoplasm and produce chlorophyll

VACUOLE an organelle that, depending on its type, carries out different jobs

MITOSIS the process whereby cells reproduce by dividing to replace old cells, to heal wounds, and for organism growth

GENETICS the study of how genes pass traits from one generation to another

GENE a substance on a chromosome that causes a trait to be passed on

CHROMOSOMES threadlike substances that store hereditary information in cells

DNA the arrangement of proteins in a cell nucleus that tells it how to develop

TRAITS distinguishing features, such as eye color or hair texture

DOMINANT this type of trait takes precedence over a recessive trait when both are present

RECESSIVE this type of trait recedes from a dominant trait when both are present

Let's Begin

1 **REVIEW AND DISCUSS** If possible review with your student the life processes he or she learned about in Lessons 3.1 and 3.2. Ask, *How small can a plant or animal be and still carry out these processes?* Hint: The smallest plants and animals have only one **cell.** Help your student conclude that a cell is the smallest unit of life that can carry out all these processes.

2 **INTRODUCE** Tell your student that a cell is, in some ways, like a factory. It has a structure (cell wall), tasks are performed there, materials come in, waste products go out. Direct your student to these diagrams of a plant cell and an animal cell. Have these images available throughout the lesson.

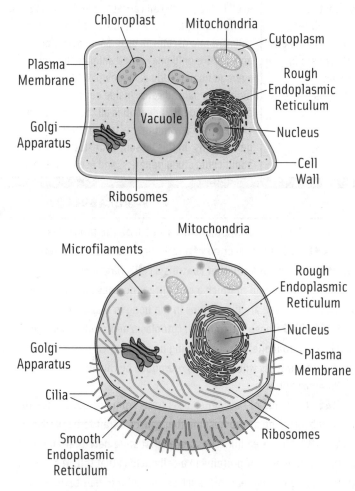

3 **MODEL AN ANIMAL CELL** Point out these parts and functions of a typical cell. Line a resealable plastic bag with clear petroleum jelly and explain that this is to model an animal cell membrane and cytoplasm. Add yarn, beads, buttons, or other objects that seem to correspond to the parts of a cell. Review:

   a. **membrane, or outer covering** semipermeable; some substances can pass through, while others are rejected; wastes are excreted through the membrane

b. nucleus a cell's command center, where cell reproduction starts, and where the chromosomes are (chromosomes are cordlike substances that store and pass along information about how the organism should be)

c. cytoplasm liquid in which the cell's life processes are carried out; in specialized cells, cytoplasm produces substances needed by the rest of the organism (such as hormones or digestive enzymes)

d. organelles like organs in the body: each organelle has a job to do (the endoplasmic reticulum, ribosomes, Golgi bodies, mitochondria, lysosomes, and vacuoles are organelles)

4   **MODEL A PLANT CELL** You can use petroleum jelly and a small square plastic container to model a plant cell. The main difference is that the organelles include **chloroplasts** and one large **vacuole** instead of several smaller ones.

5   **DISCUSS LIFE PROCESSES** Ask, *How do cells reproduce, and why?* [cells reproduce by dividing, to replace old cells, to heal wounds, and so the organism can grow] Tell your student this process of cell division is called **mitosis.**

6   **DISCUSS AND EXPLAIN** Tell your student that cell division does not always go smoothly. Sometimes, chromosomes aren't correctly distributed from a dividing cell to the two daughter cells. When this happens, one cell has twice the number of a particular chromosome and the other cell has none.

Ask, *What do you think happens when the cells incorrectly pass along information about the organism?* [the next cells would have the wrong information] The embryo might die, or physical problems such as Down syndrome may develop. Explain that all this information has begun to be available through research, and that this research is possible in part because of the invention of the microscope. Discuss.

7   **EXPLORE MICROSCOPES** Together with your student search the library or the Internet for information on microscopes. See For Further Reading too. Have your student examine a microscope and locate these parts: eyepiece, arm, revolving nosepiece (not on all microscopes), high-power objective (not on all microscopes), low-power objective (not on all microscopes), clips, fine adjustment, coarse adjustment, light source, and base. Now distribute Student Learning Page 3.A.

8   **DEFINE DNA** Read aloud to your student the definitions of **genetics, gene, chromosomes,** and **DNA** in the vocabulary list. Ask, *What is the relationship between chromosomes, genes, and DNA?* [from most general to most specific: chromosomes, genes, DNA; or, from most specific to most general, the opposite order]

9   **DISTRIBUTE** Distribute Student Learning Page 3.B. Before your student begins working on this page, explain that there are ways

---

(!)
A BRIGHT IDEA

Reasonably priced microscopes are available in department stores, toy stores, and even resale shops and discount stores. An alternative is "cell cam" at http://www.cell-salive.com/cam2.htm. This site offers continuous views of various kinds of cell division under a microscope.

DID YOU KNOW?

If you took a single cell from a single mammal, removed the DNA, and stretched it out, it would be five feet long. Are you that tall?

to predict which **traits** will be visible and which traits will not be visible, though they'll still be in the genetic code. Each parent brings 23 genes for physical traits to a forming embryo, for a total of 46 genes in all. Also review what **dominant** and **recessive** mean. A Punnett Square shows how these traits can combine.

10   **DISCUSS PEDIGREE CHARTS** Tell students that pedigree charts are another way to show the source of genetic traits. Squares stand for males, and circles stand for females. The pedigree chart can help predict what traits will show up in a person and can track traits for past generations. Show this pedigree chart to your student. Then distribute Student Learning Page 3.C.

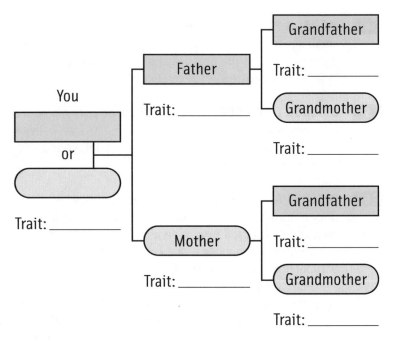

Branching Out

TEACHING TIP

Frequently on the news, the subject of genetics and DNA surfaces. Your student may want to do research on the Human Genome Project, on genetic engineering of food, or on cloning.

CHECKING IN

You can assess your student's understanding of this lesson on genetics by having him or her reteach the lesson to you. Have him or her create a microscope experiment for you to complete and/or a genetics puzzle.

FOR FURTHER READING

The Cell Works: Microexplorers: An Expedition into the Fantastic World of Cells (Microexplorers Series), by Patrick A. Baeuerle and Norbert Landa (Barron's Juveniles, 1998).

Fun with Your Microscope, by Sharon Levine and James Humphreys (Sterling Publishing, Inc., 1998).

How the Y Makes the Guy: Microexplorers: A Guided Tour Through the Marvels of Inheritance and Growth (Microexplorers Series), by Patrick A. Baeuerle and Norbert Landa (Barron's Juveniles, 1998).

Make Microscope Slides

Read the steps and conduct an experiment preparing a dry slide and a wet slide. Then record your observations. Be sure to wash your hands after handling the materials.

MATERIALS

- ❏ 1 microscope
- ❏ 2–4 flat slides
- ❏ 2–4 coverslips
- ❏ 1 eyedropper
- ❏ stain (such as food coloring)
- ❏ 2–4 toothpicks
- ❏ 1 pair flat tweezers
- ❏ 1–2 paper towels
- ❏ 1 pair scissors
- ❏ specimen (a feather, cells from inside your cheek, a piece of hair, a piece of onion skin—or anything else)

STEPS

Prepare a dry mount (slide with dry material):

1. Cut a piece of the specimen that is narrower and shorter than the slide.

2. Place a coverslip over the slide, and place the slide on the stage over the aperture.

3. Hold in position with the stage clips.

4. Record your observations:

   _____

   _____

   _____

   _____

Prepare a wet mount (slide with wet material):

1. Cut a piece of the specimen that is narrower and shorter than the slide. (If you're using cheek cells, gather them by scraping your cheek with a toothpick and then wiping it on the slide.)

2. Moisten the specimen with a drop of water. (You may want to add food coloring to the water to see the specimen better.)

3. Place a coverslip over the slide and press to make sure there are no air bubbles. Remove excess water with a paper towel.

4. Place the slide on the stage and hold in position.

5. Record your observations:

   _____

   _____

   _____

   _____

   _____

   _____

   _____

   _____

   _____

   _____

   _____

Use Punnett Squares

Punnett Squares are charts that show what traits parents could pass on to offspring. Read each example and then answer the questions.

Example 1: Eye Color

B represents brown eyes and **b** represents blue eyes. Brown is a dominant trait for eye color; blue is recessive. Parent A has brown eyes and Parent B has blue eyes.

1. What color eyes could their offspring have? _____

   Parent A could be either **BB** or **Bb.**
   Parent B must be **bb.**

   If Parent A is **BB:**   If Parent A is **Bb:**

2. If one of the offspring has blue eyes, is Parent A **BB** or **Bb**? Explain your answer.

   _____

3. If Parent A is **Bb,** what percent of the offspring could be carrying the recessive gene but might not be showing it? _____

   _____

Example 2: Right-Handed or Left-Handed?

Look at the handedness of a biological family—it could be your own or someone else's. Find out if the parents are right-handed or left-handed. **R** represents right-handedness and **r** represents left-handedness. Right-handedness is a dominant trait; left-handedness is recessive. Make a chart to help you. Then verify your answers with the traits the offspring have.

4. What percent of their offspring are right-handed? _____

5. Could any of the offspring be carrying the recessive gene and not show it? Explain your answer. _____

   _____

   _____

Tally Aunt Sally

Who resembles whom in your family? Whose nephew is left-handed? Who has Great-Uncle Ted's piercing eyes? Working with an adult, list as many family members of one biological family as you can. You could choose your own! Use the traits on this table or use your own, such as special talents or hair color. Then make a pedigree chart showing one of these traits.

Relative's Name	Eye Color	Right- or Left-Handed	Earlobes Attached?
Aunt Sally	hazel	left	no

What's Next? You Decide!

Now it's your turn to choose what to do next in the lesson.
Read the activities and decide which one you want to do—
you may want to try them both!

Use Water to Magnify

MATERIALS

- ❏ 1 glass bowl or jar
- ❏ 1 newspaper or patterned paper
- ❏ 1 water dropper
- ❏ 2 cups water

STEPS

One of the original microscopes used a tiny bead of glass as a magnifier. Can you achieve similar results by looking through different materials?

- ❏ First view your hand inside an empty glass bowl or an empty glass jar. How is it different? How is it the same?

- ❏ Fill the glass container with water and put your hand (or a finger) back in. Now how does it look?

- ❏ Place the same container on a sheet of newspaper or patterned paper. Notice any difference? Use a copy of the Comparison Chart found on page 353 to record your information.

Heat Up with Cell Cookery

MATERIALS

- ❏ 1–2 eggs
- ❏ 1 frying pan
- ❏ 1–2 cookbooks
- ❏ 1 spatula
- ❏ 1 stove
- ❏ 1 plate

STEPS

Did you know that the yolk of a chicken egg is a single cell? (So's the yolk of an ostrich egg, making it—at six inches long—the largest cell on Earth!)

- ❏ Do a little research on yummy dishes you can make with eggs. Or just go for the tried and true once-over-easy.

- ❏ Get permission from an adult before you begin.

- ❏ Sprinkle a little salt and pepper on the results of this experiment, serve it with a sprig of parsley, and remember to wash the cell remains out of the frying pan when you're done.

- ❏ Guaranteed, you will never look at an egg the same way again.

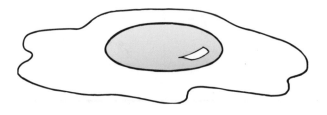

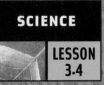

Understanding Systems of the Human Body

When we teach a child about the human body, we provide him or her with self-knowledge that can open a portal to the majesty of biological processes.

OBJECTIVE	BACKGROUND	MATERIALS
To help your student understand the major systems of the human body	The circulatory and nervous systems are crucial to our bodies. When either doesn't work properly, it puts stress on our whole body. In this lesson, your student will study the parts of the circulatory and nervous systems and conduct research to examine their functions. Your student will read up on human reproduction and understand how humans make others of their own kind.	■ Student Learning Pages 4.A–4.D ■ colored pencils

VOCABULARY

CIRCULATORY SYSTEM a system of the body that carries food and oxygen to cells and removes wastes and carbon dioxide from cells

NERVOUS SYSTEM a system of the body that carries impulses between the brain and all parts of the body

REPRODUCTIVE SYSTEM a system of the body in which plants or animals make others of their own kind

BRAIN the control center of the body that along with the spinal cord forms the central nervous system

PULMONARY CIRCULATION this is the flow of blood between the heart and lungs

HEART a muscular organ that pumps blood through the body

SYSTEMIC CIRCULATION this is the movement of oxygenated blood from the lungs to all of the body's organs except the heart and lungs

CORONARY CIRCULATION this is blood flow to the tissues of the heart

ARTERIES blood vessels that move blood away from the heart

VEINS blood vessels that move blood toward the heart

SPINAL CORD a nerve tissue in the spinal column that connects the brain to the rest of the body

NERVES these carry impulses between the brain and all other parts of the body

NEURONS these send and receive impulses within the nervous system

CEREBRUM the part of the brain that controls thought

CEREBELLUM the part of the brain that controls balance

MEDULLA OBLONGATA the part of the brain that controls involuntary functions like breathing

SPINAL NERVES these carry impulses between the spinal cord and other body parts

Let's Begin

1 **EXPLAIN** Explain that the human body is made up of several major systems that work together to sustain life. Read the names of the systems with your student:

- Nervous system
- Respiratory system
- Integumentary [in-teg-yoo-MEN-ta-ree] system
- Endocrine system
- Urinary system
- Reproductive system
- Circulatory system
- Digestive system

Post the names of the systems on a nearby wall. Tell him or her that this lesson will stress the **circulatory, nervous,** and **reproductive systems,** but that he or she can choose to study more about any system that seems interesting.

2 **DISCUSS** Talk with your student to see what he or she already knows. Ask, *What does the circulatory system do?* [moves food and oxygen to cells and removes carbon dioxide and waste from cells] *The nervous system?* [relays messages between the brain and all parts of the body] *The reproductive system?* [male and female systems that allow humans to make new humans]

3 **DISTRIBUTE AND IDENTIFY** Distribute Student Learning Page 4.A. Have your student go to the library or search the Internet for information about how the circulatory system works and for illustrations of it. Have your student identify the main parts of the circulatory system and label each one.

4 **EXPLORE AND DESCRIBE** Discuss the three sections of the circulatory system. Tell your student that it's made up of pulmonary, systemic, and coronary circulation. Explain that **pulmonary circulation** involves the flow of blood between the **heart** and lungs. Tell him or her that **systemic circulation** involves the movement of oxygenated blood from the lungs to all of the body's organs except the heart and lungs. Point out that **coronary circulation** involves blood flow to the tissues of the heart. Stress that if coronary circulation is blocked, the result is a heart attack.

5 **ILLUSTRATE AND RESEARCH** Tell your student that the human heart beats more than two and a half billion times in an average lifetime. Explain that it is a powerful pump that sustains life in a human body. Direct him or her to go to http://www.howstuffworks.com to conduct an online exploration of the heart, or to use a search engine to research other sites related to the heart. Direct him or her to find out about the parts of the heart and how blood flows through the blood vessels (**arteries** and **veins**) to and from the heart. Encourage him or her to take notes and print illustrations. Discuss.

6   **DISTRIBUTE**   Distribute Student Learning Page 4.B. Direct your student to use red and blue colored pencils to illustrate the path blood takes as blood flows between the heart and lungs. Suggest that he or she use red to represent oxygenated blood and blue to represent deoxygenated blood. Have him or her write short descriptions of the four chambers of the heart and action of the heart.

7   **REVIEW**   Review the circulatory system with your student. Make sure all of the major parts and functions have been identified and understood.

DID YOU KNOW?

The first heart transplant took place in 1967.

8   **EXPLAIN**   Tell your student that the next major body system he or she will conduct research on is the nervous system. Tell him or her that the major parts of the nervous system are the *central nervous system,* which includes the brain and **spinal cord,** and the *peripheral nervous system,* which includes the **nerves** that connect the brain and spinal cord to the rest of the body.

9   **GUIDE AND RESEARCH**   Have your student go to the library or search the Internet for information about the parts and functions of the nervous system. Encourage him or her to find diagrams and pictures. Guide your student to identify the parts of the nervous system and relate them to their functions. Ask, *How does the brain control messages between the brain and all parts of the body?* [impulses travel through nerve cells called **neurons** that make up nerve pathways in the body] *What part of the nervous system controls balance?* [cerebellum] *What part controls thought?* [cerebrum]

10   **DISTRIBUTE AND DISCUSS**   Distribute Student Learning Page 4.C. Talk with your student about these parts of the nervous system: cerebrum, cerebellum, **medulla oblongata, spinal nerves,** and spinal cord. Ask him or her to describe what he or she learned about each part during research. Have your student complete the chart by writing the nervous system part that matches each function.

DID YOU KNOW?

There are three distinct ways of learning: visually, auditorily (through hearing), and kinesthetically (through hands-on experience). Some people use one of these methods primarily and others combine more than one for best absorption. Explore different kinds of learning to see what works best for your student.

11   **REVIEW**   Review the nervous system with your student. Make sure all of the major parts and functions have been identified and understood. You can ask your student to demonstrate his or her knowledge in a way that best suits his or her style of learning. For example, a visual learner might want to draw a picture of the nervous system, or of a part of the nervous system, from memory. An auditory learner might be proud to explain how the nervous system works by giving a verbal presentation. If your student is a kinesthetic learner, you might encourage him or her to create a part of the nervous system using clay, or to create a short play where he or she acts out the different nervous system "characters."

12 **EXPLAIN** Point out that the next body system on which your student will focus is the reproductive system. Tell your student that the reproductive systems of males and females have different parts that perform different functions. Emphasize that the purpose of the reproductive system of both sexes is to produce new life. Here are diagrams of each. Caution: Sometimes discussing the reproductive system can make children nervous. Be sure to speak in a relaxed tone, which will make your student more relaxed.

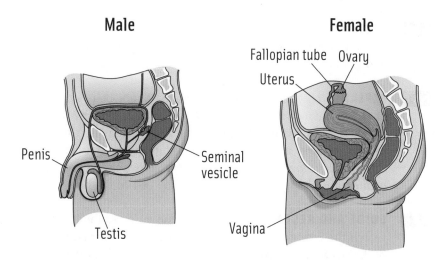

Male   Female

Fallopian tube   Ovary

Uterus

Penis

Seminal
vesicle

Vagina

Testis

13 **DISTRIBUTE** Distribute Student Learning Pages 4.D–4.F. Guide your student to choose activities to complete that appeal to his or her curiosity about different body systems.

Branching Out

TEACHING TIP

Your student's enthusiasm will guide his or her learning. Take note of the topics in the lesson that interest your student the most and find opportunities to take your "classroom" into the outside world. For example, if your student has a fascination with how the heart works, ask your doctor if you and your student could visit an office where echocardiograms are done.

CHECKING IN

You can assess your student's understanding of the parts and functions of the circulatory, nervous, and reproductive systems by having him or her create a diagram or model of a body system of his or her choice, accurately labeling the parts and describing the functions.

FOR FURTHER READING

Eyewitness: The Human Body, by Steve Parker (DK Publishing, Inc., 1999).

Heart Disease, by John Coopersmith Gold (Enslow Publishers, 2000).

The Nervous System, by Andreu Llamas (Gareth Stevens Publishers, 1998).

Identify Parts of the Circulatory System

Identify parts of the circulatory system and write them on the lines.

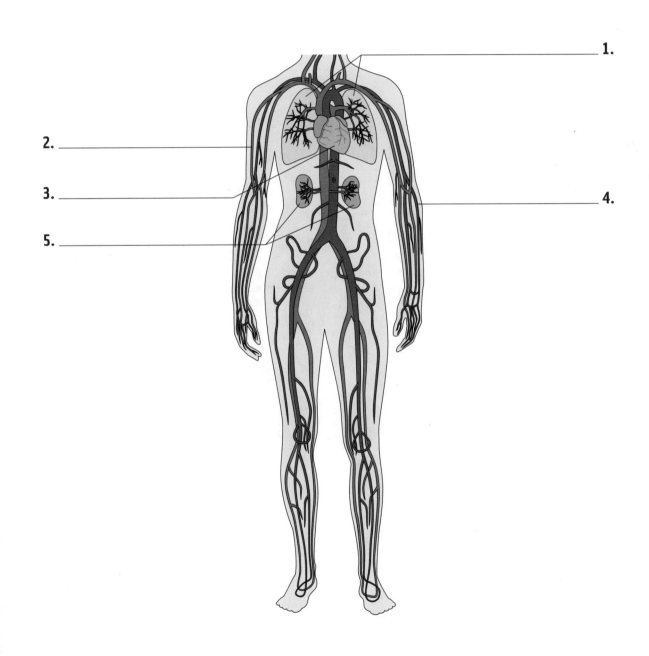

1. _____

2. _____

3. _____

4. _____

5. _____

Map Pulmonary Circulation

Go to the library or use the Internet to research pulmonary circulation. Use red and blue colored pencils. Draw arrows to illustrate how blood moves between the heart and lungs.

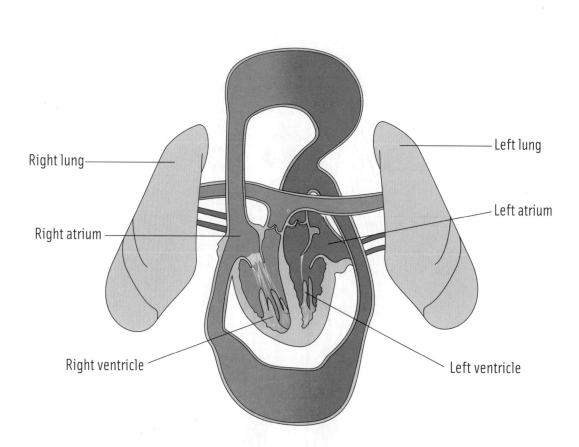

Right lung

Left lung

Right atrium

Left atrium

Right ventricle

Left ventricle

Chart the Nervous System

Search the Internet or use the library to identify the parts of the brain and their purposes. Make a list of the parts and note their jobs. Then complete the chart by writing the nervous system part that matches each job.

Nervous System

Part	Job
1.	Controls communication between the brain and other body parts
2.	Carries electrical impulses between the spinal cord and other body parts
3.	Controls breathing and the heartbeat
4.	Controls thinking, movement, and the senses
5.	Controls coordination and balance

What's Next? You Decide!

Now it's your turn to choose what to do next in the lesson. Read the activities and decide which one you want to do—you may want to try them all!

Draw the Path of an Egg

MATERIALS

❏ colored pencils

STEPS

❏ Go to the library or search the Internet to learn more about the female reproductive system.

❏ If you search on the Internet, be sure to ask an adult's permission first. He or she can help direct you to specific sites.

❏ Then create a drawing that shows the path of an egg as it makes its way from the ovary through the fallopian tube and into the uterus.

Model a Heart

MATERIALS

❏ modeling clay
❏ 1 picture of a heart

STEPS

❏ Look at the picture of a heart.

❏ Use clay to sculpt a model of a heart.

❏ If you need to, research the parts of the heart further on the Internet to make sure the parts are shaped correctly and in the correct position.

Conduct a Brain Experiment

MATERIALS

❏ modeling clay
❏ 1 jar
❏ 1 nail
❏ 1 hammer
❏ water (enough to fill jar)
❏ 1 foam block
❏ 1 yard string
❏ tape

STEPS

The foam block will represent a brain; the jar, a head; and water, brain fluid.

❏ First, use the nail to make a hole in the jar lid with the hammer.

❏ Tie the string around the foam block and thread the other end through the jar lid.

❏ Put the block into the jar and pull the extra string through the top of the lid. Hold the string and put the lid on the jar.

❏ Pull the string until the block is about 2 centimeters from the bottom of the jar, then tape the string to the jar lid.

❏ Next, fill the jar with water and tightly screw the lid on.

(CONTINUED)

❑ Put modeling clay over the hole in the jar lid. Turn the jar upside down and watch what happens to the block.

❑ Strike the side of the jar softly, then a bit harder.

❑ Write a paragraph to describe how the water in the jar is like the fluid that surrounds the brain.

Create Your Own Cookbook

MATERIALS

❑ 1–2 cookbooks
❑ 10 white sheets of paper
❑ glue
❑ colored pencils
❑ colored construction paper
❑ 1 3-hole punch
❑ 1 pair of scissors
❑ 1 empty 3-ring binder

STEPS

❑ Go to the library or search the Internet for information about how to identify heart-healthy recipes. (Look for Web sites like the American Heart Association's http://www.deliciousdecisions.org that contain recipes thought to be good for heart health.)

❑ Then find some recipes from your own cookbooks to create a cookbook that includes healthy choices for a week's worth of meals.

❑ You can type or handwrite the recipes on the white paper. Then draw pictures of what each dish will look like when it's finished.

❑ Punch holes in your paper and insert in your binder.

❑ For a final touch, use the construction paper and cut out images to glue on the front of the binder for your cookbook cover.

❑ Ask your parents to help you try out some of your recipes!

Make Carbon Dioxide

MATERIALS

❑ modeling clay
❑ $\frac{1}{2}$ tbsp. baking soda
❑ 2 flexible straws
❑ 1 cup vinegar
❑ 1 pair of scissors
❑ 1 plastic bottle
❑ 1 tall glass
❑ 1 funnel
❑ food coloring

STEPS

❑ When you breathe out, you release carbon dioxide into the air. Try this experiment to create carbon dioxide.

❑ Gently roll out a piece of clay and wrap it around the outside of one end of a straw.

❑ Cut a small slit at the other end of the straw and attach it to the second straw.

(CONTINUED)

❑ Fill the glass with water. Put a drop of food coloring in the water.

❑ Put half of a tablespoon of baking soda into the bottle. Use the funnel to fill one-fourth of the bottle with vinegar.

❑ Next, attach the end of the straw with the clay to the top of the bottle, creating a seal. Make sure there is a passageway for the air to pass from the bottle to the straw to the glass, and put the end of the second straw in the glass of colored water.

❑ Write a description of what happens in the water.

Measure Your Heart Rate

MATERIALS

❑ 1 clock with second hand

STEPS

❑ Find out how many times your heart beats per minute.

❑ Place two fingers on your wrist. Apply light pressure by pushing against the back of your wrist with your thumb until you can feel your pulse.

❑ Ask someone to time you for 10 seconds as you count the number of times your heart beats.

❑ Multiply the number of beats in 10 seconds by 6. This will tell you your resting heart rate.

❑ Try finding your heart rate after you do 10 jumping jacks.

❑ Compare your resting heart rate to your heart rate after exercise. Explain what you learned to an adult.

Research a Blood Bank

MATERIALS

❑ 1 phone book

STEPS

Consider what you know about your community blood bank.

❑ Find the phone number and with an adult's help call to arrange for an interview with a staff member.

❑ Write a list of questions about their role in your community. Find out what they do to obtain blood and to maintain their blood supply.

❑ Ask how they handle emergencies when the demand for blood is higher than usual.

❑ Take notes as your questions are answered.

❑ Then use the library or Internet to study about blood banks in other communities. Jot down any good ideas.

❑ Write a summary of your research to share with your family. You may wish to share your findings with your community blood bank as well.

Exploring Human Health and Growth

Having a strong understanding of how human beings grow and thrive helps us take better care of ourselves and our families.

OBJECTIVE	BACKGROUND	MATERIALS
To help your student understand his or her own health, growth, and development	In this lesson, your student will learn about birth, infancy, childhood, adolescence, and adulthood as developmental stages. He or she will research nutrition and various aspects of health. You will have the opportunity to guide his or her understanding of diseases and how the human body defends itself against them.	■ Student Learning Pages 5.A–5.B

VOCABULARY

INFANCY the earliest stage of life, usually from birth to one year
CHILDHOOD this begins after infancy and lasts until ages 12 to 14
ADOLESCENCE the time when one changes from a child to an adult
ADULTHOOD the life stage when physical growth is complete
NUTRIENTS substances found in our food and environment that provide energy for the body to grow, maintain, and repair itself
IMMUNE SYSTEM a group of defenses that the body has to protect itself from disease
COMMUNICABLE DISEASE a disease that can spread from one organism to another

Let's Begin

1 **EXPLAIN** Explain to your student that individual humans grow and develop at their own rates, but that their growth still occurs according to stages common to all humans. Discuss the stages of **infancy, childhood, adolescence,** and **adulthood** with your student. Ask him or her to describe what he or she already knows about the characteristics of each stage.

2 **RELATE** Mention the adolescent growth spurt that your student may notice happening to himself or herself, or to friends. Encourage your student to observe the characteristics of people at different stages of development as he or she studies human growth in this lesson.

3 **DISTRIBUTE AND IDENTIFY** Distribute Student Learning Page 5.A. Have your student go to the library or use the Internet to research the changes in physical, mental, and emotional abilities at each stage of growth.

4 **EXPLAIN** Tell your student that nutrition is important to his or her body's growth. Stress that eating foods with the right amount of **nutrients** in the correct number and size of servings is critical to his or her health. Encourage your student to research this information on the Internet, at the library, or through a public health organization, and then to evaluate his or her own eating habits.

5 **RECORD AND REVIEW** Have your student go to the library or use the Internet to research the food guide pyramid. Then have your student keep a two-day record of the foods he or she eats. In a notebook, ask him or her to write down everything he or she eats during each meal or snack and the approximate amount or serving size. Then guide your student through a review of his or her nutritional intake. Ask, *In what ways are my eating habits healthy and nutritional? What is one thing I can do to improve my eating habits?*

6 **REVEAL AND DISCUSS** Talk with your student about the environment and its relationship to world health. Invite him or her to use the Internet to study more about issues related to biodiversity and human health. He or she might try the Web site http://www.epa.gov/students. Ask, *How does the way people treat the environment affect world health?*

7 **DISTRIBUTE** Distribute Student Learning Page 5.B. Have your student choose an activity to complete. Review with your student the definitions of **immune system** and **communicable disease** if necessary.

Branching Out

FOR FURTHER READING

Good Enough to Eat: A Kid's Guide to Food, by Lizzy Rockwell (HarperCollins, 1999).

The World Health Organization, by Jillian Powell (Franklin Watts, 2001).

TEACHING TIP

Well-organized notes are a great time-saver when conducting research! Provide your student with index cards on which to take notes during research. It is helpful for your student to record sources, one per index card, and to organize notes from each source behind that card.

CHECKING IN

Have your student choose a topic related to the lesson and have him or her write a script for a public service announcement.

Identify Stages of Human Growth

Use your research information to complete this chart. Below each growth stage fill in the characteristics or changes that are common during that time. Use one box per item.

Infancy	Childhood	Adolescence	Adulthood

What's Next? You Decide!

Now it's your turn to choose what to do next in the lesson.
Read the activities and decide which one you want to do—
you may want to try them both!

Investigate the Immune System

MATERIALS

❏ 1 copy Web, page 354

❏ colored pencils

STEPS

Your body's immune system is made of cells, tissues, and systems that help your body fight bacteria and viruses.

❏ Go to the library or use the Internet to find out how your body's defense systems work to keep your body disease free.

❏ On a copy of the Web found on page 354, use your research notes to complete a Web about the immune system. Use different colors to emphasize the hierarchy of the ideas in your Web.

❏ Use your Web and notes to create an outline for writing a report of your research findings.

❏ Share your work with a friend or family member.

Understand Communicable Diseases

STEPS

Communicable diseases are spread by bacteria, viruses, protists, and fungi. They may be spread through the air, water, by food, or by animals and insects. An important organization called the Centers for Disease Control and Prevention (CDC) monitors and works to prevent the spread of diseases.

❏ Visit its Web site at http://www.cdc.gov to find out how diseases such as smallpox, anthrax, measles, mumps, and others are controlled and monitored worldwide.

❏ Find out about immunization and learn about current disease threats around the world.

❏ Create a one-page newsletter that addresses topics of current interest in world health.

❏ Share your work with a friend or family member.

Using the Scientific Method

When you teach a child the scientific method, you provide him or her with a problem-solving framework that will last a lifetime.

OBJECTIVE	BACKGROUND	MATERIALS
To help your student learn to use the scientific method	Science process skills are major tools that not only scientists can use—these skills (such as making observations and generating hypotheses) are also life skills that people use every day! This lesson introduces your student to the scientific method, a logical approach to problem solving that he or she can apply as a lifelong learner.	■ Student Learning Pages 6.A–6.B ■ 1 dandelion plant (optional) ■ 1–2 dandelion seeds (optional)

VOCABULARY

OBSERVATION the process of gathering information about a subject by using one's five senses

HYPOTHESIS a guess or idea about something based on observations

PREDICTION what you think might happen under certain conditions

EXPERIMENTAL TEST an experiment used to check if a hypothesis is correct

Let's Begin

1 **DISTRIBUTE AND EXPLAIN** Distribute Student Learning Page 6.A. Walk your student through the four main steps of the scientific method in the chart. Direct him or her to the examples given for each step. Offer the following:

Observation: When scientists observe something, they use all of their senses to notice as much as they can about it. They then carefully take notes on everything they notice. The scientist continually asks himself or herself, *Why does this do that? What might cause that to happen?*

Hypothesis: Based on the observations, the scientist forms a hypothesis, or guess, to explain what he or she noticed. For example, if someone observes that a flashlight won't light, he or she can generate several hypotheses, such as the batteries are dead, the bulb is burned out, or the switch is broken.

Prediction: The prediction is based on the hypothesis. For example, if the hypothesis is that the flashlight won't light because the batteries are dead, the prediction that the flashlight will light if new batteries are put in could be made. Your student

> **! A BRIGHT IDEA**
>
> Dandelion seeds can be found at a nursery or 4-H club.

can form predictions by filling in the blanks of this if/then thought process: *If I* _____, *then* _____ *will* _____.

Experimental test: The experimental test is used to test whether the hypothesis is correct.

2 **DIRECT** Direct your student to look at the pictures of the dandelion plant and seeds on Student Learning Page 6.A. Ask, *What do you notice about the plant and seeds?* Remind him or her of the need to look closely at every detail and thoroughly explain these details in his or her notes—just as a scientist would! Have your student record the details in his or her notebook. Discuss.

3 **ASK** Ask, *Based on what you have observed, how do you think the dandelion spreads its seeds?* Have your student record his or her hypothesis, which might be that the seeds are eaten by birds, the seeds are blown by the wind, or the seeds get stuck on the fur of animals.

4 **PREDICT** Then ask, *What prediction can you make about the seeds?* Help your student use the if/then thought process described above.

5 **ASK** Ask, *How can you test if your hypothesis is correct? What could you do with some dandelion seeds to see if you are right?* If the hypothesis is that the seeds are blown by the wind, your student could, for example, place some seeds on a tile or wood floor, place a fan close to them, and turn on the fan. If the seeds spread, then the hypothesis is correct; if they don't spread, then the hypothesis is incorrect.

6 **PRACTICE** Now have your student practice using the scientific method on his or her own. Ask him or her to choose something to observe, sketch, take notes on, and hypothesize about.

Branching Out

TEACHING TIP

Point out that the scientific method isn't only used by professional scientists. Rather, it's an approach to problem solving that can be used in many different circumstances in the real world.

CHECKING IN

Look for the following things as you attempt to assess how well your student uses the scientific method: the observations are detailed and specific; the hypothesis is based on the observations; the prediction is based on the hypothesis; and the experimental test is used to test the hypothesis only.

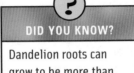

DID YOU KNOW?

Dandelion roots can grow to be more than three feet long!

FOR FURTHER READING

The Beginnings of Science, by Tom McGowan and V. A. Koeth (Millbrook Press, 1998).

Sciencing: Learning the Scientific Method, by Edward Shevick, Judy Mitchell, and Marguerite Jones (Teaching and Learning Company, 1998).

When?: Experiments for the Young Scientist, by Robert W. Wood (Chelsea House, 1998).

Learn the
Scientific Method

Read this chart, which shows how to use the scientific method.

Step	Example
Observation Use your senses to gather information.	The flashlight won't light.
Hypothesis Make a guess or form an idea based on your observations.	The batteries are dead.
Prediction Tell what you think will happen under certain conditions.	If I put in new batteries, the flashlight will light.
Experimental Test Conduct an experiment to test your hypothesis.	Replace the batteries and turn on the flashlight. If it doesn't light, make a new hypothesis.

Observe the pictures of the dandelion plant and seeds and record what you notice in your notebook. After you write your observations, write a hypothesis, a prediction, and an experimental test in your notebook. Refer to the chart above if you need help.

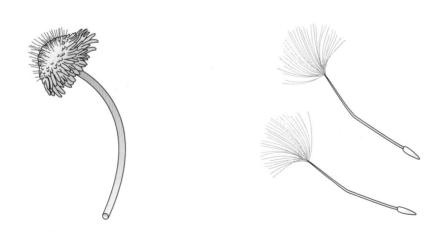

What's Next? You Decide!

Now it's your turn to choose what to do next in the lesson. Read the activities and decide which one you want to do— you may want to try them both!

Paint Nature's Details

MATERIALS

- ❏ watercolor or other paints
- ❏ 2–5 blank sheets paper

STEPS

- ❏ Go to the library and check out books by John James Audubon, the American artist and ornithologist, or someone who studies birds. Look at his careful, detailed paintings of birds.

- ❏ Then choose something found in nature, such as an animal or plant, and paint or draw your own picture. Be sure to include lots of details.

- ❏ Next, research how Audubon is connected to the National Audubon Society, the organization that helps protect birds and natural ecosystems (complex systems of interaction between living and nonliving things in the environment). What animal, plant, or ecosystem would you want to help protect?

- ❏ Think of something that you could do in your community this week to help. Be sure to ask permission from a parent or other adult first.

Brew Moldy Coffee

MATERIALS

- ❏ 1 cup caffeinated coffee
- ❏ 1 cup decaffeinated coffee
- ❏ 2 clear glass jars
- ❏ 2 blank labels
- ❏ 1 marker

STEPS

Use the scientific method to find out if caffeine in coffee stops mold from growing.

- ❏ Write C (for caffeine) on a label and attach it to one jar; write D (for decaffeinated) on a label and attach it to the second jar.

- ❏ Get help from an adult and make one cup each of caffeinated and decaffeinated coffee.

- ❏ Pour the caffeinated coffee in the first jar and pour the same amount of decaffeinated coffee in the second jar.

- ❏ Place both jars next to each other in a room.

- ❏ In a notebook write the date, your observations, and your prediction.

- ❏ Then for one week observe the jars daily and write in your notebook what you observe. At the end of the week write the results. Did your prediction come true?

Exploring Earth's Living Systems

Everything in nature is connected to each other.

OBJECTIVE	BACKGROUND	MATERIALS
To understand the interdependence of environments and life forms on Earth	All life on this planet occurs in a small zone of Earth's crust called the biosphere. All living things on Earth are interdependent within a larger system of plants and animals. Living things also interact with their climate and physical environment. Each action, natural or human made, affects the environment. In this lesson, your student will learn to think of Earth as a system and will consider the impact of variables on a larger system.	■ Student Learning Pages 7.A–7.B ■ 1 world globe ■ 1 physical map of Earth ■ 1 outdoor thermometer

VOCABULARY

ECOSYSTEM an area where living things interact with their environment and with each other

BIOME a large land area that has similar Earth cycles, climate, plants, and animals

ECOLOGISTS people who study ecosystems

HABITAT the area where a plant or animal naturally lives

COMMUNITY two or more organisms that live in an ecosystem and interact with each other

BIOSPHERE the zone at and around Earth's crust where all life is found

ECOLOGICAL SUCCESSION the process whereby the structure of an ecosystem changes over time

ECOLOGY the study of ecosystems

SPECIES a group of animals or plants that can breed to produce healthy offspring

PRODUCERS organisms that come up with, or make, their own food

CONSUMERS organisms that eat other organisms

SCAVENGERS carnivores that eat the waste that other carnivores have left behind

OMNIVORES organisms that eat both plants and animals

DECOMPOSERS organisms that eat the waste of or eat other organisms

WEATHER the way the atmosphere is behaving including temperature, wind, clouds, air pressure, and rainfall

CLIMATE the long-term weather patterns of an area

FOSSIL FUEL a nonrenewable energy resource formed underground from the remains of organisms

Let's Begin

ECOSYSTEM

1 **INTRODUCE VOCABULARY** Introduce your student to the concept of an **ecosystem** by reviewing the vocabulary words and their definitions. Write each word on a card and ask your student to sort them in an order that seems logical (excluding alphabetical order). Explain that *biome* is the name **ecologists** give to large areas of land with similar climates and plant and animal life. There are land biomes, such as forests and deserts, and water biomes, such as oceans and freshwater. Distribute Student Learning Page 7.A. Have your student list the elements within each biome.

2 **EXPLORE** Explain that all living things on Earth depend on each other. Each **habitat** within an ecosystem has a **community** of plant and animal life that interact with each other and with their environment. Ask your student to think of several examples of plants, animals, and humans interacting with their environment and with each other.

3 **EXPLAIN AND RESEARCH** Point out that the region of Earth that we live in is known as the biosphere. The **biosphere** is everything from the sky to the ocean floor and a bit beyond, including ocean trenches seven miles below the ocean floor where organisms live, the tops of mountains where lichens and mosses can be found, and everything in between. Also mention that the ecosystems of the biosphere change over time. Plants and animals also change. This is called **ecological succession.** (*Succession* means "sequence of events.") Encourage your student to do research at the library or on the Internet about ecosystems, ecological succession, climax communities, and life in extreme environments.

?

DID YOU KNOW?

The word ecology comes from the Greek word *oikos,* meaning "house," and the suffix *-ology,* meaning "study." What does this root say about the word *ecology?* It underscores the idea that Earth is the home of living things.

FOOD CHAIN

1 **DESCRIBE** In an ecosystem, the different **species** interact mainly through their need for food. Energy from our sun drives the system. Energy is transferred through an ecosystem as food. The first link in what's called the food chain are plants which use energy from sunlight in photosynthesis. Plants are called producers because they make their own food. Ask, *What would be dangerous about polluting the environment of a producer?* [all the animals above it on the food chain would eat the polluted matter]

2 **EXPLAIN AND ASK** Point out that **producers** are eaten by **consumers,** or organisms that can't produce their own food. The first consumers may be herbivores, or animals that eat only plants. These animals may become food for other animals called carnivores, or "meat eaters." Some carnivores kill their prey and others, called **scavengers,** eat the meat and carcasses left over. Vultures and buzzards are two examples of scavengers. They play an important role in the ecosystem by cleaning up after other carnivores. Ask, *What are some examples of carnivores that you can think of?* [snakes, bears, lions, sharks, birds that hunt] *What are some examples of herbivores?* [squirrels, rabbits, cows, deer]

3 **EXPAND** Explain further that besides carnivores and herbivores, there are two other types of consumers: **omnivores** and **decomposers.** *Omni-* means "all" in Latin. An omnivore eats both plants and animals. Humans that eat meat are omnivores. Other omnivores include coyotes, raccoons, and bears. After an organism dies, its remains become food for the decomposers. Decomposers break down dead plants and animals and absorb their nutrients. Decomposers such as bacteria and fungi are also essential to the health of the ecosystem. Encourage your student to do further research on the food chain and energy transfer on the Internet or at the library.

4 **DIAGRAM** Have your student diagram several food chains from different biomes such as wetland, desert, forest, or prairie. Ask him or her to label the producers and consumers as well as the herbivores, omnivores, carnivores, scavengers, or decomposers. Review and discuss.

WEATHER AND CLIMATE

1 **DISCUSS** Explain that the origin of Earth's **weather** and **climate** is our sun. Solar power causes wind, ocean currents, the water cycle, and all other weather phenomena. Weather is the day to day condition of the atmosphere—its temperature, humidity, wind speed, precipitation, and air pressure. Storms—hurricanes, typhoons, monsoons, tornadoes, blizzards, and thunderstorms— are examples of weather. Climate is the long-term weather pattern of an area. Have your student research the factors that determine an area's climate, such as solar energy and geography. Ask, *What are some of the elements that can affect climate?* [latitude, position relative to large bodies of water or land, surface features of Earth, and effect of ocean currents]

ENRICH THE EXPERIENCE

Have your student find out who in your town gives the best weather predictions. Direct him or her to collect the predictions for temperature and precipitation over a period of two weeks from several different sources: newspapers, radio, TV news, or a weather channel. Check out http://www.accuweather.com for current weather information in your area. Have your student record the actual temperature from an outdoor thermometer and whether it rained or snowed. He or she can then compare the actual data to each prediction and decide which source is more accurate.

2 **INTEGRATE** Distribute Student Learning Page 7.B. Have your student create a profile of the biome where you live. Have him or her use the Internet, the library, and personal observation to research the local plants, animals, climate, and other patterns. Ask him or her to include as many different species of plants and animals and details about weather patterns as possible. Ask him or her to write the information in a notebook. Discuss.

3 **RESEARCH AND DISCUSS** Remind your student that all living things produce wastes. Ecosystems contain natural processes that recycle wastes and clean the environment. Humans make more wastes than other animals, and the extra human waste overloads the natural recycling system, creating pollution. Natural events like volcanic eruptions and forest fires create air pollution. Point out that human use of **fossil fuel** is the biggest cause of air pollution. Coal, oil, and natural gas are fossil fuels. The buildup of air pollution over time can cause changes in the climate. Have your student research the effects of air pollution on human health, the ecosystem, and the climate. Ask him or her to find out about acid precipitation, ozone depletion, and the greenhouse effect. Talk with your student about his or her research.

Branching Out

TEACHING TIP

Help your student take his or her new awareness of ecosystems into the real world by visiting a forest preserve, ecology center, or just observing the wildlife in your own backyard or neighborhood. Dusk and dawn are times when insects and other animals are most active and easy to observe.

CHECKING IN

Ask your student to share with you the descriptions he or she wrote when completing Student Learning Page 7.A. Discuss his or her entries and help him or her gather information to complete the page if it's incomplete.

FOR FURTHER READING

Pass the Energy, Please!, by Barbara Shaw McKinney (Dawn Publications, 2000).

Complete Weather Resource: Recent Developments in World Weather, by Phillis Engelbert (U*X*L, 2000).

Biomes of the World

Use research from the library or the Internet to help you describe each biome. Include information about precipitation (rainfall, snowfall, hail, and so on), types of plants, weather, and life forms.

1. Desert

   Type of biome: _____

   Special features: _____

   Where in the world? _____

2. Grassland

   Type of biome: _____

   Special features: _____

   Where in the world? _____

3. Tropical Rain Forest

   Type of biome: _____

   Special features: _____

   Where in the world? _____

4. Temperate Forest

   Type of biome: _____

   Special features: _____

   Where in the world? _____

5. Taiga

   Type of biome: _____

   Special features: _____

   Where in the world? _____

6. Tundra

   Type of biome: _____

   Special features: _____

   Where in the world? _____

Share Information About Climate

Read the steps and conduct an experiment about climate.

MATERIALS

❑ 2–3 students in other areas who can participate in the project with you

❑ 1 world globe

STEPS

1. Have an adult help you conduct this experiment with other students in other regions.

2. Have them make a chart like the one below.

3. Find your latitude and longitude on a globe and write it below.

4. Gather weather data twice a day for two weeks and enter the data in the chart.

5. Research on the Internet to find out about the climate in your part of the world. Does the information you find agree with your experience in your climate?

6. Share your data with other students. Organize your information in a report and send the data to the people in your group.

7. Each of you can prepare a report about all the data and draw conclusions from it.

My latitude: _____

My longitude: _____

Date	Time of Day	Temperature	Precipitation	Humidity	Wind Speed	Air Pressure

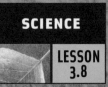

Digging into
Earth's Surface

A diamond is a piece of coal that finished what it started.

OBJECTIVE	BACKGROUND	MATERIALS
To give your student an understanding of the processes within and upon Earth's crust	Rocks are always in the process of being formed, changing their character, or wearing away. This cycle of wearing down and reforming is called the rock cycle. The land is also constantly being built up in some parts of the world and worn away in other parts of the world. Your student will gain an understanding of sequence as he or she studies the processes in this lesson.	■ Student Learning Pages 8.A–8.B ■ 1 map ocean floor

VOCABULARY

ROCKS hard substances

MINERALS the ingredients rocks are made of

ROCK CYCLE the series of events through which rocks form, erode, and reform

TOPOGRAPHY land features

EROSION the wearing down of something

DEPOSITION the process of something, such as materials, being put someplace else

VOLCANISM the activity brought about by volcanoes

VOLCANOES openings in Earth's crust through which hot, melted rock goes out

EARTHQUAKES sudden motions along breaks in Earth's crust

TSUNAMI a tidal wave

CRUST the outer layer of Earth

PLATES sections of Earth's crust

PLATE TECTONICS the theory that states that Earth's surface is made up of plates that are in constant motion

MANTLE the layer of Earth below the crust that's made up of hot, melted rock

LITHOSPHERE the layer of rock that includes the crust and part of the mantle

CORE the layer of Earth below the mantle that's made up of metal; the center of Earth

SEISMOGRAPH a device that measures the power of an earthquake

Let's Begin

1 **UNDERSTAND THE QUOTE** With your student, discuss the meaning of the opening quote. Say that **rocks** are natural substances made of **minerals,** chemical elements, and even organic matter. Show your student the diagram of the **rock cycle.** Use the Internet or the library to research the processes involved in forming coal and diamonds.

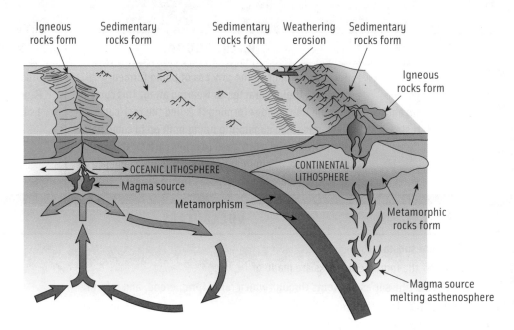

Igneous rocks form
Sedimentary rocks form
Sedimentary rocks form
Weathering erosion
Sedimentary rocks form
Igneous rocks form
OCEANIC LITHOSPHERE
Magma source
CONTINENTAL LITHOSPHERE
Metamorphism
Metamorphic rocks form
Magma source melting asthenosphere

2 **DISTRIBUTE** To help your student understand other properties of minerals, distribute Student Learning Page 8.A and have him or her complete it independently. To extend the activity, visit Mineralogy 4 Kids at http://www.minsocam.org and go to Mineral Games.

3 **EXPLAIN THE PROCESSES OF EROSION AND DEPOSITION** Explain that Earth's **topography,** or land features, is shaped by the process of **erosion,** or wearing down, and by **deposition,** where eroded materials are transported and built up someplace else. Wind, water, gravity, and **volcanism,** or the activity brought about by **volcanoes,** are the energy sources that change the shape of the land. Much erosion is due to water running downhill in rivers and streams. Natural flooding cycles also change the land. Talk with your student about places that he or she may have visited or seen where erosion or deposition may have occurred.

4 **DESCRIBE SUDDEN CHANGES** Relate that sudden, more catastrophic land changes occur during **earthquakes,** volcanic eruptions, landslides, tidal waves **(tsunami),** and floods. These major geologic events result from the motion of Earth's **crust.**

The crust is divided into about 12 sections called **plates.** Maps that show the locations of volcanoes and earthquakes show clearly that there are zones where these events occur and zones where they don't. Have your student go to the "kids" section at http://www.nasa.gov for more information on **plate tectonics,** an interactive map, and educational games.

5 **DISCUSS LANDFORMS** Look at a map of the ocean floor with your student. Ask your student to point out mountains and ridges. Examine the land surrounding the continents (continental shelf). Look for island chains that you already know, such as the Hawaiian Islands. Locate the Mid-Atlantic Ridge. Ask, *What island country rests right on the Mid-Atlantic Ridge?* [Iceland] Locate the Marianas Trench in the Pacific Ocean, and explain that it reaches a depth of seven miles below the ocean surface. Discuss why this map is important and who it might be useful to.

6 **CONSIDER THE OCEANS** Ask, *How is the ocean a natural resource?* [provides water, food, minerals] Discuss with your student ways in which the ocean is important to Earth and its inhabitants.

7 **DISCUSS HUMAN IMPACT** Encourage your student to complete the first activity on Student Learning Page 8.B. After he or she has gathered all the items, ask what the impact may have been on Earth to withdraw the petroleum, manufacture the products, and dispose of them.

ENRICH THE EXPERIENCE

Contact a university geology department or marine biology department to explore career possibilities for your student.

8 **UNDERSTAND EARTH'S LAYERS** Show your student the diagram of Earth's layers, or have your student go to http://pubs.usgs.gov/publications/text/inside.html. Explain that Earth has several layers. The crust is the outer layer of Earth, followed by the next layer, the **mantle.** The mantle is hot and dense, or very thick. Have your student look at the layers. Discuss the differences between the crust and mantle. Then ask, *What do the crust and upper layer of the mantle form?* [lithosphere] Together review what the lithosphere is.

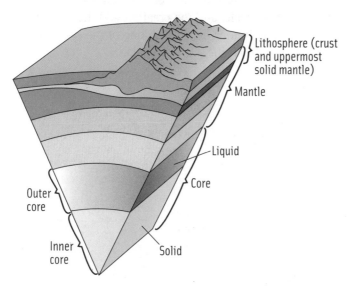

Lithosphere (crust and uppermost solid mantle)

Mantle

Liquid

Core

Outer core

Inner core

Solid

9 **DIVE INTO EARTH'S LAYERS** Reveal that the **core** is the next layer. It's made up of metal, and it's very dense—the core is at the center of Earth. Together with your student look at the drawing of the layers and discuss the depth and thickness of each layer. You may have to help him or her comprehend the depth and thickness of the layers by using everyday examples. For example, if the mantle is about 3,000 kilometers thick, that would be about equal to the distance between New York City, New York, and Phoenix, Arizona.

10 **DESCRIBE PLATE TECTONICS** Explain that the lithosphere is made up of about a dozen rigid plates of rock that are in constant motion. At the edges, or boundaries, between two plates earthquakes, volcanoes, and mountain building occur. There is much evidence for the theory of plate tectonics: the continents "fit" together like pieces of a puzzle, the location of earthquakes, and the formation of the Hawaiian Islands. Together with your student go to http://www.usgs.gov to learn more.

11 **PUT IT TOGETHER** Guide your student in seeing how it all fits together. Have him or her go to the "kids" section at http://www.usgs.gov for up-to-date information about earthquakes, interesting earthquake facts, the latest earthquakes, frequently asked questions, and activities.

DID YOU KNOW?

A **seismograph** measures the power of an earthquake. The Richter scale is used to determine the magnitude of an earthquake.

Branching Out

TEACHING TIP

As you teach your student, observe him or her and try to shape your next move to his or her needs.

CHECKING IN

Assess your student's grasp of the cycles mentioned in this lesson: the rock cycle, the water cycle, and the creation and destruction of plates through motion. Ask him or her to pick one of the cycles and explain it to you, with or without the aid of visuals.

FOR FURTHER READING

The Drop in My Drink: The Story of Water on Our Planet, by Meredith Hooper (Viking Children's Books, 2000).

Earthquakes and Volcanoes, by Lin Sutherland (Reader's Digest Children's Publishing, Inc., 2000).

Eyewitness: Volcano and Earthquake, by Susanna VanRose and James Stevenson, photographer (DK Publishing, Inc., 2000).

Volcanoes: Earth's Fiery Fury, by Sandra Downs (Millbrook Press, 2000).

Discover the Mystery Minerals

Can you tell a Poodle from a Great Dane? Everyone knows that different breeds of dogs have different features. It's the same with minerals. We identify minerals by crystal shape, hardness, sometimes by color, and by chemical reactions. Read the steps and conduct an experiment on minerals.

MATERIALS

❑ mineral samples: quartz crystal, gypsum, calcite, pyrite, hematite, and mica, plus whatever other minerals you can find (ask a local gem or mineral club, a university geology department, a crystal healing shop or health food store, or a museum if they have samples that you can use)

❑ 1 glass jar or jelly jar

❑ 1 light-colored brick

❑ 1 paper lunch bag

STEPS

1. Do this activity with a partner. Put the minerals into the paper bag.

2. On a sheet of paper make a chart with your partner. Make four columns and label them "Mineral," "Color," "Scratch Test," and "Results and Observations." In the column under Mineral list the minerals you'll be using.

3. Tell your partner to pick out two clear minerals. Explain that the soft mineral is gypsum, used to make sheetrock, and the hard mineral is quartz.

4. Have your partner test to see which mineral he or she can scratch with his or her finger. (That's gypsum.)

5. Record your information for each mineral, noting the color of the mineral, the type of scratch test performed, and, in the final column, the results of the scratch test and your observations.

6. If you have hematite and pyrite, scrape them both on the brick. The one that makes the rust-colored streak is hematite. What color streak does the pyrite make? (grayish black)

7. Record your information on your chart.

8. Continue with other minerals: If you have mica, tell your partner to find a mineral that will split easily into thin sheets. If you have talc, ask your partner to find a mineral that feels soapy and soft. If you have galena, ask your partner to find a mineral that is very heavy and makes a dark gray-black streak on the brick.

9. Record your information in your chart.

10. Then review your chart. What similarities and differences do you see between the minerals?

What's Next? You Decide!

Now it's your turn to choose what to do next in the lesson.
Read the activities and decide which one you want to do—
you may want to try them both!

Live with Petroleum

MATERIALS

- ❏ 1 balloon
- ❏ 1 candle
- ❏ 1 cassette tape
- ❏ 1 crayon
- ❏ 1 credit card
- ❏ dishwashing liquid
- ❏ 1 pair eyeglasses
- ❏ floor wax
- ❏ 1 garden hose
- ❏ 1 guitar string
- ❏ 1 hair curler
- ❏ house paint
- ❏ 1 ice cube tray
- ❏ 1 lipstick
- ❏ 1 milk jug
- ❏ 4 roller-skate wheels
- ❏ 1 shoe
- ❏ 1 shower curtain
- ❏ 1 soft contact lens
- ❏ 1 sweater
- ❏ 1 tube toothpaste
- ❏ 1 trash bag
- ❏ 1 skein yarn

STEPS

- ❏ Read the items on the list. Gather as many of these products as you can.

- ❏ These products are made from oil. How many are recyclable?

- ❏ Read the ingredients of the products and see if you can determine what the containers are made of.

- ❏ Why do you think certain items are recyclable and certain items aren't?

Discover a Topographic Map

STEPS

- ❏ Go to the U.S. Geological Survey Web site at http://www.usgs.gov for a topographic map.

- ❏ Look at the map and answer these questions:

  - Where the lines are tightly bunched together, what does that show?

  - What features are labeled?

  - What numbers do you see, and what do you think they mean?

  - What would be the difference between a hill and a mountain on a topographic map?

  - What other differences do you notice between a topographic map and your other map?

- ❏ If possible, go orienteering with an adult. Orienteering involves using a detailed map and a compass to find your way around a course. It's fun! To learn more, visit www.orienteering.org.

Exploring the Universe

Our exploration of the universe is limited only by our imagination.

OBJECTIVE	BACKGROUND	MATERIALS
To provide your student with an overview of the solar system and human exploration of the universe	The system of planets and other bodies (comets, asteroids, and moons) that rotate around our sun is called the solar system. We live on Earth, the third of the nine planets. The solar system is part of a larger conglomeration of billions of stars. In this lesson, your student will pay special attention to cause-and-effect relationships found in space, and throughout will be called upon to draw conclusions based on the evidence he or she uncovers about Earth and the solar system.	■ Student Learning Pages 9.A–9.B ■ 1 copy Comparison Chart, page 353

VOCABULARY

SOLAR SYSTEM the sun and all bodies that orbit around it

ORBIT one body's repeated circular motion around a larger body

ASTEROIDS a group of small, planetlike objects orbiting the sun between Mars and Jupiter

COMETS objects made mostly of ice and dust that orbit the sun

MOONS planetlike satellites that revolve around planets

FUSION the atomic process that produces a star's energy in the form of heat and light

UNIVERSE space and all the natural things in it

BIG BANG THEORY a scientific theory about how the universe began

Let's Begin

1 **GET ORIENTED** To gain perspective on where we are in the universe, tell your student to write his or her address. After she or he writes the street or apartment, continue with the country, the continent, and the hemisphere. Then continue this way: third planet, solar system, Milky Way Galaxy, universe. Review with your student these terms and any other terms he or she doesn't know.

2 **MODEL AND EXPLAIN** Refer to a diagram of the solar system as you work together. These are available in most atlases and encyclopedias. You also can go to http://www.nasa.gov and

check out NASA for Kids where you'll find information about the solar system and the universe.

Then explain that the **solar system** is made up of the sun and the celestial bodies that **orbit** it. Ask, *What are the names of the planets?* [Mercury, Venus, Earth, Mars, Jupiter, Saturn, Uranus, Neptune, Pluto] Tell your student that Mercury, Venus, Earth, and Mars are classified as inner planets. Jupiter, Saturn, Uranus, Neptune, and Pluto are classified as outer planets. Then distribute Student Learning Page 9.A.

3 **REVIEW AND DISTRIBUTE** Explain that, besides planets, the solar system includes **asteroids, comets,** and **moons** that orbit around each planet. Have your student do further research at the library or on the Internet to find out about these many elements that are found in the solar system. Distribute a copy of the Comparison Chart found on page 353 to compare these various orbiting bodies.

4 **INTRODUCE THE SUN AND OTHER STARS** At the center of the solar system is our sun, an average yellow star. Explain that stars are made mostly of hydrogen and helium gases, which go through a process called **fusion.** During fusion, two hydrogen atoms fuse to form a helium atom. Huge amounts of energy are released in the form of light and heat. Then have your student research the life cycle of stars, including each stage of a star.

5 **INVESTIGATE THE ORIGINS OF THE UNIVERSE** Explain that there are many theories about the origins of the **universe.** Share that although there are many theories, remember that none of them have proven to be 100 percent accurate. One scientific theory is called the big bang theory. Ask, *What do you know about this theory?* [about 15 billion years ago all the matter and energy that now exist over trillions of light-years were packed together in one tiny point; this point exploded outward at great speed, and all bodies in space—stars, planets, gases—formed as this mass of matter cooled]

FOR FURTHER READING

Eyewitness: Space Exploration, by Carole Stott (DK Publishing, 2000).

The Reader's Digest Children's Atlas of the Universe, by Robert Burnham (Reader's Digest Children's Publishing, Inc., 2000).

The Solar System: An A-Z Guide (Watts Reference), by Christina Wilsdon (Franklin Watts, Inc., 2000).

Branching Out

TEACHING TIP

Keep a list of questions as you proceed through the lesson and schedule time to write to experts at Web sites such as *Scientific American* magazine: http://www.sciam.com.

CHECKING IN

Assess your student's understanding of the material by having him or her create a web showing the elements of the solar system and their relationship to each other. The student should then make a larger web showing the relationship between the elements of the universe.

Are You 248 Years Old?

Every time Earth completes one orbit around the sun, a year passes—that's how we measure birthdays. However, each planet has its own orbit times. Read the directions to complete the chart to find your age on the planets. Then find an adult and calculate his or her age.

1. Figure your age in Earth days. (years × 365)

2. For Mercury, Venus, and Mars, divide your age in Earth days by the number of Earth days in that planet's year. The answer is your new age.

   Example:

   If you are 11:

   11 × 365 = 4,015 Earth days old

   4,015 ÷ 88 (days in Mercury's year) = 45.625

   Your age on Mercury is 45.625 Mercury years.

3. For Jupiter, Saturn, Uranus, and Pluto, find the number of Earth days in that planet's year.

   Example:

   If you are 11 on Earth but want to find your age on Jupiter:

   11 × 365 = 4,015 Earth days old

12	Earth years (the length of one year on Jupiter—see chart)
× 365	Earth days/year
4,380	Earth days in one Jovian (Jupiter) year

   4,015 ÷ 4,380 = 0.91666

   You haven't had your first birthday yet!

Planet	Inner or Outer Planet	Length of Year	Your Age
Mercury	inner	88 Earth days	
Venus		225 Earth days	
Earth			
Mars		687 Earth days	
Jupiter		12 Earth years	
Saturn		29.5 Earth years	
Uranus		84 Earth years	
Neptune		165 Earth years	
Pluto		248 Earth years	

What's Next? You Decide!

Now it's your turn to choose what to do next in the lesson.
Read the activities and decide which one you want to do—
you may want to try them both!

Turn Your Home into a Space Museum

MATERIALS

❑ self-stick notes

STEPS

What do cellular phones and freeze-dried coffee have in common? They're just a sample of the technology that was developed for space programs but has been put to practical, everyday use on Earth.

❑ Go to NASA's Web site at http://www.nasa.gov and learn about the technology developed. Then list as many developments as you can.

❑ Find out what they were first used for.

❑ Then hunt around and see how many you can find at home and label them with self-stick notes that tell a little about what you learned.

❑ Make your home into a science museum! Then give your family a tour of your "museum."

"Make" Gravity with a Tennis Ball

MATERIALS

❑ 1 old tennis ball or old rubber eraser

❑ 2 yards strong string or fishing line

❑ 1 long nail or short pencil

❑ white glue

❑ 1 knife (check with an adult first)

❑ 1 piece chalk

STEPS

❑ Have an adult cut a one-inch slit in the tennis ball. Meanwhile, tie the string securely to a long nail and glue the knot so it stays put. Slip the nail through the slit in the tennis ball.

❑ Now go outside with an observer. Twirl the tennis ball so that it orbits around you. Do you feel a pull?

❑ Have your partner use chalk to draw the shape and size of the orbit. Then let the tennis ball go—watch out for others!

❑ Have your observer draw the direction in which it flew and where it landed. This demonstrates the forces that cause planets to orbit.

❑ To find out more, look up Isaac Newton's first law of motion in the library or on the Internet.

Understanding Energy

It's energy that breathes life into all that surrounds us.

OBJECTIVE	BACKGROUND	MATERIALS
To teach your student about the different kinds of energy on Earth	Energy is plentiful on Earth in such forms as light, heat, electricity, wind, and organic matter, such as fossil fuels. Energy moves and works. Light, heat, sound, and electromagnetic energy travels in waves. In this lesson, your student will get an overview of energy on Earth. He or she also will develop operational definitions for these forms of energy.	■ Student Learning Pages 10.A–10.B

VOCABULARY

ENERGY the ability to do work

THERMAL having to do with heat

FOSSIL FUELS fuels found underground that formed millions of years ago from the remains of plants and animals

HYDROELECTRIC having to do with electricity produced by flowing water

GEOTHERMAL having to do with heat created by molten rock below the surface of Earth

CONDUCTION the process of heat moving that doesn't involve the flow of matter

CONVECTION the process of heat moving that does involve the flow of matter

Let's Begin

1 **INTRODUCE SOLAR POWER** Explain that the sun is a major energy source. A fraction of its light and heat reaches Earth's surface. That tiny percent of solar energy that reaches Earth powers a number of systems on the planet. Solar energy comes to Earth mainly as light. Ask your student what he or she knows about solar energy, for example, solar panels on houses and buildings. Have him or her tell you why he or she thinks solar energy is important. Then have him or her research on the Internet and confirm his or her responses.

2 **DISTRIBUTE** Distribute Student Learning Page 10.A. Have your student learn more about solar power.

3 **INTRODUCE ENERGY, MATTER, WAVES** Reveal that in physical science, **energy** is the ability to do work. Share that matter is anything that has mass and takes up space. Then tell your

student that energy travels in waves. There are two kinds of waves: mechanical and electromagnetic. Mechanical waves travel through matter. Electromagnetic waves can travel without matter. Ask, *What kind of waves are those at the beach?* [mechanical] *What kind of waves are radio waves?* [electromagnetic] *What kind of waves are sound waves?* [mechanical] Then ask, *How do you know?* [sound doesn't travel through a vacuum] Go to the library with your student and review how energy travels in waves. Ask him or her to explain it back to you for a quick check on comprehension.

4   **MEASURE WAVES** Explain that we can measure the size and shape of waves. The highest point of a wave is the crest. The lowest point is the trough. The distance from one trough to another is the wavelength. Different kinds of waves have different wavelengths. Electromagnetic energy moves at the speed of light, 186,000 miles per second. Walk through this diagram with your student highlighting each point.

Gamma rays   X rays   Ultraviolet   Visible   Infrared   Microwave (radar)   FM (TV)   AM

(Trough)   (Trough)

(Crest)

Wavelength

5   **EXPLAIN THE SUN'S ENERGY** Mention that energy from the sun travels 93,000,000 miles (150 million kilometers) through empty space to Earth. Some of the incoming energy reflects back into space, some is absorbed by the atmosphere, oceans, and land, and some is used to power photosynthesis. The radiant energy that is absorbed changes to **thermal** energy. Have your student research what thermal energy is on the Internet. Then have him or her give you its definition in his or her own words.

6   **EXPLORE ENERGY USED ON EARTH** Reveal that we use **fossil fuels,** such as oil, coal, and natural gas, for many human energy needs. To a lesser extent, we use **hydroelectric** power, **geothermal** energy, and wind energy. Have your student use the Internet or the library to find some examples of each of these kinds of power. Walk through each type of energy with him or her.

7   **INVESTIGATE HEAT** Explain that heat energy has certain properties: It flows from warmer objects to cooler ones until both reach the same temperature. It moves through solids by **conduction,** which doesn't involve any flow of matter, and through liquids and gases by conduction and **convection.** In convection, the liquid or gas always moves. Have your student go to http://songsforteaching.homestead.com/ getmoleculesmovin.html for lyrics to a song that describes in simple terms the processes of conduction and convection.

8   **MEASURE HEAT** Ask, *What is the measurement used for heat?* [temperature] Then see if your student can tell you the three different temperature systems used. Reveal that the three major systems of temperature measurement are Celsius (C), also known as Centigrade; Fahrenheit (F); and Kelvin (K). Ask him or her if he or she knows the temperature at which water freezes and boils. Share that water freezes at 0°C and 32°F and boils at 100°C and 212°F. Now have your student research the Kelvin measuring system. Ask him or her to find what Kelvin is typically used to measure and why it's important. Then have him or her find out who it's named after. Encourage him or her to "teach" this information back to you.

9   **LOOK INTO FOSSIL FUELS** Explain that fossil fuels include coal, petroleum, and natural gas. Have your student research on the Internet why these are called "fossil" fuels. Then discuss. Then mention that coal and petroleum are nonrenewable resources: once they're gone, they're gone! Have your student research to find out when coal and petroleum became widely used and how many years' supply remains. Also have him or her research how critical the use of fossil fuels was to the Industrial Revolution and to the rise of modern society. Point out that entire industries, such as the automotive industry, rely on oil. Ask your student to find on a map the places where coal is mined in the world and the location of oil resources. Then have him or her list the countries that are members of OPEC (Organization of the Petroleum Exporting Countries) and find those places on a map. Have your student consider what it means economically and politically to be a producer of oil or a country that produces no oil. Discuss.

10   **DISCUSS POLLUTION** Explain that although fossil fuels are useful as an energy source in that they're abundant right now and are very inexpensive, they do produce some negative by-products. Burning them produces smoke and gases that pollute the air. Burning fossil fuels produces "acid rain" (sulfur and nitrogen oxide combined with water), which is rain that acts like acid when it falls on forests and lakes. Have your student find out what happens to these forests and lakes and what is being done to remedy the problem. You may want to have your student complete the activity Grow with an Acid Thumb? on Student Learning Page 10.B.

11   **REVEAL OTHER POLLUTION** Point out that another form of pollution is connected with our dependence on oil: When oil's transported from the well to the refinery by large ships called tankers, these tankers sometimes get caught in storms or are damaged by rocks. When this happens, millions of gallons of crude oil can spill into the open sea. This causes much environmental damage. Have your student research a recent large oil spill by looking at past magazine and newspaper

SCIENCE

LESSON 3.10

articles on the Internet. Have him or her then tell you how an oil spill affects the environment, the air, animals, humans, and the company that spilled the oil. Suggest that he or she think of ways that this could be prevented.

Mining coal also causes serious environmental problems. Ask your student to find out what strip mining is and then research the problems caused by it. Have him or her find out why it's harmful and what its effects are. Then have him or her brainstorm to find ways to prevent the pollution.

12 **MOVE FORWARD** Have your student use the Internet or library to research both the problems caused by fossil fuels and the benefits of fossil fuels. Also have your student research new technologies that are making fossil fuels cleaner than they have been. Ask your student to think about the pros and cons of fossil fuels and ways he or she can help keep the environment clean.

Branching Out

TEACHING TIP

Encourage your student to think about energy and fossil fuels used in his or her community. Then have him or her think about how they're used in your state, country, North America, and the world.

CHECKING IN

The concepts and ideas in this lesson are often hard to grasp. Have your student give definitions based on his or her own knowledge and experience for the terms used in this lesson.

FOR FURTHER READING

Eyewitness: Energy, by Jack Challoner and Clive Streeter, photographer (DK Publishing, 2000).

Fossil Fuels (Energy Forever), by Ian S. Graham (Raintree/Steck Vaughn, 1999).

Heat Fundamentals: Funtastic Science Activities for Kids, by Robert W. Wood, Rick Brown, ill., and Stever Hoeft, ill. (Chelsea House Publications, 1998).

Cook Solar

Read the steps and conduct an experiment cooking with solar energy. Then record your observations. Before beginning, review this experiment with an adult and get permission.

MATERIALS

- ❑ 1 long, narrow cardboard box
- ❑ 1 piece heavy-duty aluminum foil
- ❑ 1 posterboard
- ❑ glue
- ❑ 1 pair scissors

- ❑ 1 wire hanger
- ❑ 1 hot dog
- ❑ 1 bun
- ❑ condiments
- ❑ tape

STEPS

1. Have an adult cut the box so it looks like this.

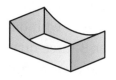

2. Cover the entire cutout area with a piece of posterboard. Attach it with tape.

3. Cover the curve with glue and place a piece of aluminum foil over it.

4. Hold the box in the sun or under a bright light to find the point where the light is most concentrated.

5. Paste two cardboard strips on the sides, like this. The wire hanger you are using for a skewer will go through these strips.

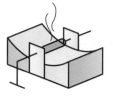

6. Cook the hot dog and enjoy.

What's Next? You Decide!

Now it's your turn to choose what to do next in the lesson.
Read the activities and decide which one you want to do—
you may want to try them both!

Hunt for Resources

MATERIALS

- ❏ 300 white beans
- ❏ 1 stopwatch or clock with a second hand

STEPS

- ❏ Work with a partner and have him or her sprinkle beans around the room. Don't peek.

- ❏ Your partner times you for 30 seconds as you gather as many beans as you can.

- ❏ At the end of 30 seconds, count the beans. Continue this until you can't find any more beans.

- ❏ Graph the results of how many beans you found each time.

- ❏ You have just taken part in a search for nonrenewable resources. What have you learned about the search for nonrenewable resources over time? What would happen if many people were looking for beans at the same time?

Grow with an Acid Thumb?

MATERIALS

- ❏ 2 plastic containers of the same size
- ❏ 2 potted plants (same kind and size)
- ❏ 2 cups vinegar

STEPS

- ❏ Label one container A and the other B.

- ❏ Then label one plant A and the other B. Fill container A with only water. Fill container B three-quarters full of water and one-quarter full of vinegar.

- ❏ For two weeks, water plant A from container A and plant B from container B.

- ❏ Observe any changes in your plants' appearance and growth. How do you think acid in the water affected the plants? How do you think acid rain affects plants?

Discovering Sound and Light

Sound and light are always around us, even though we can't always see and hear them.

OBJECTIVE	BACKGROUND	MATERIALS
To help your student understand characteristics of sound and light	When we teach a child about the properties of energy forms such as sound and light, we enable him or her to develop an awareness of how these natural energies profoundly impact the planet and all living things that inhabit it. In this lesson, your student will study the properties of light and sound, conduct experiments, and research about the properties, movement, and uses of each.	■ Student Learning Pages 11.A–11.B

VOCABULARY

VIBRATION the rapid back-and-forth motion of an object that produces sound

FREQUENCIES the numbers of sound wave crests that pass on a place each second

REFRACTION the bending of light waves caused by a change in their speed

REFLECTION when a light wave strikes a surface and bounces off

Let's Begin

1 **EXPLAIN** Explain that sound is energy caused by the movement of molecules through matter, and that this is known as **vibration.** Point out that sound energy can be thought of as vibrations that move through matter in a pattern of back-and-forth motion similar to ripples in water.

2 **RELATE** Mention that we hear many different kinds of sounds every day. Discuss the different uses of sound with your student. [music, communication] Point out that different sounds have unique properties. Tell your student that how you hear a sound depends on the properties of its sound wave. With your student, record a list of examples of how sounds are used in the real world.

3 **DISTRIBUTE AND ILLUSTRATE** Distribute Student Learning Page 11.A. Have your student complete the activity described. Then have your student draw and label two diagrams. Ask, *How are high-pitched sound waves and low-pitched sound waves different?* [high-pitched sounds have short wavelengths and high frequencies; low-pitched sounds have long wavelengths and low frequencies]

Light moves fast. It travels at about 186,000 miles per second. Sound, on the other hand, moves more slowly. It travels at about 1,100 feet per second.

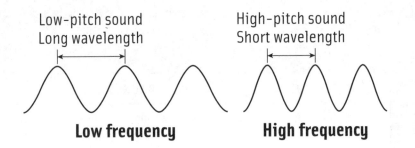

Low-pitch sound
Long wavelength

High-pitch sound
Short wavelength

Low frequency   **High frequency**

4 **EXPLAIN AND RESEARCH** Tell your student that light is energy that, like sound, also travels in waves. Point out that unlike sound, light is energy that we can see. Explain that light also travels in waves of different lengths and **frequencies.** Point out that we usually think of light as being white, but that when it is bent in different ways it appears as different colors to our eyes.

Then have your student go to the library or use the Internet to research the properties of light rays. Tell him or her to study light waves and find out how and why we see the colors that we see. Explain that when light passes through a transparent object, such as glass, it bends. This is called **refraction.** Sometimes light bends when it touches an object with a smooth surface. Objects with smooth surfaces don't absorb as much light as objects with uneven surfaces. When light bounces off an object with a smooth surface, this is called **reflection.**

FOR FURTHER READING

Awesome Experiments with Light and Sound, by Michael A. Dispezio (Sterling Publishing Company, 1999).

The Optics Book: Fun Experiments with Light, Vision, and Color, by Shar Levine and Leslie Johnstone; Jason Coons, ill. (Sterling Publications, 1999).

Sound Fundamentals: Funtastic Science Activities for Kids, by Robert Wood and Rick Brown, ill. (Chelsea House Publications, 1998).

Branching Out

TEACHING TIP

Have your student keep a journal in which to record his or her observations of sound and light in the natural world. Examples of what he or she might record are how light looks different (refracts) when going through water or that noises might sound like they have an echo in a large room.

CHECKING IN

Have your student create a short booklet to explain key properties of sound or light to assess his or her knowledge.

Model Sound Waves

Remember that air and water are both forms of matter. Different forms of matter act as conductors for sound. Conduct an experiment to represent a sound wave.

1. Set a glass bowl full of water on a table.
2. Drop a small rock into the bowl and observe the movement on the surface of the water.
3. Notice that the water is moving in waves.
4. Consider that sound waves travel in a similar way to the waves in your model.
5. Draw a picture of your model below and write a paragraph explaining the direction, shape, and movement patterns of the waves. Tell why you think this model might accurately depict the movement of sound waves.

What's Next? You Decide!

Now it's your turn to choose what to do next in the lesson. Read the activities and decide which one you want to do— you may want to try them both!

Explore Refraction and Reflection

MATERIALS

- ❏ 1 handful salt
- ❏ 1 pencil
- ❏ 1 glass pan filled with water
- ❏ 1 flashlight

STEPS

Explore refraction by modeling it with salt and a pencil.

- ❏ Put a handful of salt on your table.
- ❏ Roll a pencil toward the salt so that the point hits the salt.
- ❏ Observe the movement of the pencil.
- ❏ Note that the pencil doesn't roll in a straight line. The pencil moves around the salt in a sort of semicircle. The path of the pencil is bent toward the salt the same way that light is bent when it moves through transparent objects!

Now model reflection.

- ❏ Fill a glass pan with water.
- ❏ Turn off the lights in your room.
- ❏ Shine a flashlight beam through one side of the pan to the other.
- ❏ Jot down what you observe.

- ❏ Then shine the light through a different side of the pan to test another angle.
- ❏ Record what you see happen to the light beam as it hits the transparent object at different angles.

Investigate Mirrors and Lenses

STEPS

Mirrors are found in most homes. However, a mirror can be any smooth surface that reflects light, such as aluminum foil or a window. In a mirror, it's easy to see your own image since light is reflected off of you onto the mirror where it's reflected back to your eyes. A curved transparent substance is called a lens. Lenses focus light rays and cause them to converge into a point. Examples of lenses are telescopes, magnifying glasses, and eyeglasses.

- ❏ Go to the library or use the Internet to find out about the effect of mirrors and lenses on light rays.
- ❏ Think of an experiment you can conduct to investigate each.
- ❏ Record your findings and share them with your family and friends.

Understanding Matter

Atoms are everywhere, yet rarely do we take the time to consider them.

SCIENCE

LESSON
3.12

OBJECTIVE	BACKGROUND	MATERIALS
To help your student understand the properties of matter	Matter is anything that physically takes up space. It may be solid, liquid, or gas. Understanding the physical and chemical properties of matter helps us better interact with our environment and live safely in the world. In this lesson, your student will learn about physical and chemical reactions, identifying elements, and chemical formulas. He or she will also perform experiments and observe the properties of matter and their interactions.	■ Student Learning Pages 12.A–12.B ■ access to a freezer ■ 1 glass water ■ 1 straw ■ 1 small lump clay ■ 2 one-liter glass bottles or jars ■ 1 liter water ■ 1 liter vinegar ■ 1 tablespoon lemon juice ■ 3–5 galvanized nails ■ 5 heaping teaspoons washing soda ■ 2 cups distilled water ■ 1 teaspoon epsom salts ■ 2 two-liter plastic bottles, with screw caps ■ several drops of liquid dish detergent

VOCABULARY

MATTER   the substance of anything that takes up space

ATOMS   the units that make up matter

NUCLEUS   the positive-charged center of an atom containing protons and neutrons

ELECTRONS   particles with a negative charge that surround the center of an atom

PROTONS   particles with a positive charge that are part of the nucleus of an atom

NEUTRONS   particles with no charge that are part of the nucleus of an atom

PHYSICAL PROPERTIES   characteristics of substances that can be seen without changing the substance itself

CHEMICAL REACTIONS   when one or more substances are changed into a new substance

COMPOUNDS   substances containing a mixture of two or more elements

ELEMENTS   substances in which all the atoms are alike

PERIODIC TABLE   a table of the elements arranged by each element's tendency toward change

CHEMICAL FORMULA   a set of elements that make a compound

ACIDS   materials that make hydrogen ions when mixed with a solution

BASES   materials that make hydroxide ions when mixed with a solution

Let's Begin

1 **EXPLAIN** Reveal that all **matter** is composed of small particles called **atoms.** Explain that atoms are made of a **nucleus,** or center, with a positive charge that is surrounded by particles with a negative charge called **electrons.** The nucleus is made up of **protons,** which have a positive charge, and **neutrons,** which are neutral. Scientists consider the atom to be the smallest part of matter. Have your student use the Internet to explore atomic structure further. Then ask him or her to draw or build a model based on his or her research. Discuss.

Nucleus

Electron Cloud Model

2 **EXPLAIN** Tell your student that matter can be described as everything that takes up space. Explain that it can be a solid, such as a chair; a liquid, such as water; or a gas, such as carbon dioxide. Point out that matter has physical as well as chemical properties. **Physical properties** of matter include its boiling and melting points, color, shape, size, and density.

3 **REVEAL AND DISCUSS** Invite your student to describe the physical properties of an object, such as a red crayon. [pointed red cylinder made from a waxy red solid] Have your student choose other objects and describe their physical properties. Ask your student to picture the objects in the different states. [solid, liquid, and gas] Discuss what might cause that object to change its physical state.

4 **RELATE** Mention that it's easy to observe a liquid changing to a solid when you make ice cubes from water. Changes in the state of matter, such as when water freezes, demonstrate how matter can change when its temperature changes. The freezing temperature for water is 0°C or 32°F. Have your student check his or her resources to find the boiling point of water (when water turns to gas).

5 **DISTRIBUTE AND EXPERIMENT** Distribute Student Learning Page 12.A. Suggest that your student check the Miami Science Museum's Web site at http://www.miamisci.org to observe simulations that show how temperature changes affect a solid, a liquid, and a gas.

6 **REVEAL AND DISCUSS** Tell your student that **chemical reactions** take place around us every day. Explain that chemical properties of matter relate to how forms of matter react when combined with other matter. There are thousands of forms of matter, or substances, that can be combined to make mixtures, or **compounds,** that produce different chemical reactions. Point out that these reactions can be used to further identify chemical properties of matter.

7   **REVIEW** Review with your student what he or she has just learned. Explain that a physical change doesn't change the identity of a thing, but it does change its physical state. For example, when you freeze water it becomes ice. It still has the same make-up, it's just in a different state—frozen. Now explain that a chemical change alters the identity of something so that it becomes something else, for example, when you light a match and the match burns. The make-up of the match changes when it gets on fire. If you'd like, review with your student other examples of these types of changes.

8   **EXPLAIN** Explain to your student that chemists use a system for naming substances called **elements.** Elements are substances that can't be changed by chemical means. Some examples include: gold, silver, carbon, oxygen, and iron. The elements were organized into a system by a Russian chemist named Dmitri Mendeleev. The system was called the **periodic table.** It shows the chemical symbols for elements grouped according to atomic mass.

    The periodic table has been changed to include the use of chemical properties to help organize it. Have your student look in the library or on the Internet to find examples of the periodic table and information about the elements and their chemical symbols. A fun Web site that relates elements in the table to comics can be found at http://www.uky.edu/projects/chemcomics.

9   **INVESTIGATE** Explain that water, carbon dioxide, and table salt are all compounds. Table salt is a compound made of two elements, sodium and chlorine. The symbol for sodium is Na and the symbol for chlorine is Cl. The **chemical formula** for table salt is written NaCl. Have your student use library books or the Internet to find other common chemical formulas—such as for water, iron, and carbon dioxide—and what each symbol in the formulas represents. If it interests your student, encourage him or her to take the research one step further by finding out how chemists use formulas to write equations for combining common acids, such as sulfuric acid with other compounds. Your student can also try finding equations for combining bases such as ammonia with other compounds to make new chemicals.

10   **DISTRIBUTE AND EXPERIMENT** Distribute Student Learning Page 12.B. Have your student complete the experiments and record his or her observations.

11   **EXPLAIN** Explain to your student that all liquids, except for distilled water, are grouped into classes called **acids** or **bases,** which are both compounds. Acids are generally a class of substances that taste sour, such as vinegar. Explain that some common products made with acids are aspirin, citrus fruits, and carbonated drinks. Point out that bases, or alkaline substances, are characterized by their bitter taste and slippery feel. They are used in dishwashing liquid, most soaps, and ammonia. Have

SCIENCE

LESSON 3.12

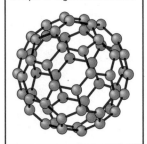

DID YOU KNOW?

The "buckyball" was discovered in 1985. It has 60 atoms arranged in the shape of a geodesic dome.

FOR FURTHER READING

Elements and Compounds (Chemicals in Action), by Chris Oxlade (Heinemann Library, 2002).

Eyewitness: Matter, by Christopher Cooper (DK Publishing, Inc., 1999).

Solids, Liquids, and Gases, by Jacqueline Barber, Lincoln Bergman and Kay Fairwell, eds.; Carol Bevilacqua, Rose Craig, and Lisa Klofkorn, ills.; Cary I. Sneider, Saxon Donnelly, Marion E. Buegler, Jim Chapman, and Karen Preuss, photos (University of California, Berkeley, Lawrence Hall of Science, 2000).

your student look for information about the pH scale used by scientists to measure acidity and alkalinity. Have him or her draw a model of the scale.

12 EXPLORE AND MODEL Mention that many things you use every day are salts. Most salts are made of a metal and a nonmetal. Salts can be used in many different ways. One way is to soften water. Try this experiment with your student. You will need 2 two-liter plastic bottles with screw caps. Pour 1 cup of distilled water into each of the bottles. Add 1 teaspoon epsom salts to one of the bottles. Shake the bottle until the salts dissolve. Add 3–4 drops of liquid detergent to each bottle. Put the caps on and shake the bottles. Have your student observe and compare the amount of suds in the bottles. Ask, *Why do you think soap and salt work together so well?* [soaps are organic salts] Encourage your student to research the structural formula of detergents and compare it to the structural formula of salt.

Branching Out

TEACHING TIP

Have your student keep a notebook in which to record his or her observations during this lesson.

CHECKING IN

Have your student create an oral presentation about the properties of matter. Encourage him or her to support the presentation with photos or illustrations. Discuss.

Explore Changing States of Matter

SCIENCE

12.A

Read the steps and conduct an experiment to observe the changes in liquid matter. Remember that matter has physical and chemical properties. Different forms of matter expand or shrink when their temperature changes.

MATERIALS

- ❏ access to a freezer
- ❏ 1 glass water
- ❏ 1 straw
- ❏ 1 small lump modeling clay

STEPS

1. Set a glass full of water on a table.

2. Put one end of the straw in the water and one end in your mouth.

3. Suck water into the straw and plug the end with your tongue. This will create a vacuum.

4. Gently remove the straw from the glass with your tongue still on it.

5. Use your fingertips to keep the water in the straw while you plug each end with clay so that it's watertight.

6. Put the straw full of water into the freezer.

7. Check the straw in 1–2 hours.

8. Record your observations. What has happened to the water? Did it expand or contract?

_____

_____

_____

_____

_____

Investigate Chemical Reactions

Read the steps and conduct the experiments to observe the changes that take place as a chemical reaction occurs. New chemicals are created in a chemical reaction. The new chemicals may have different properties.

MATERIALS

- ❏ 2 one-liter glass bottles or jars
- ❏ 1 liter white vinegar
- ❏ 1 liter water
- ❏ 5 heaping teaspoons washing soda
- ❏ 1 tablespoon lemon juice
- ❏ 3–5 galvanized nails

STEPS: EXPERIMENT 1

1. Fill one bottle with 1 liter of vinegar.
2. Place galvanized nails in vinegar.
3. Observe reaction and record.

_____

_____

_____

_____

_____

_____

_____

_____

_____

_____

_____

_____

_____

_____

STEPS: EXPERIMENT 2

1. Fill one bottle with 1 liter of water.
2. Add 5 heaping teaspoons of washing soda.
3. Shake until washing soda is dissolved.
4. Add 1 tablespoon lemon juice.
5. Observe reaction and record.

_____

_____

_____

_____

_____

_____

_____

_____

_____

_____

_____

In Your Community

To reinforce the skills and concepts taught in this section,
try one or more of these activities!

Your Local Weather Station

Find out where the closest weather station is to your home. Contact the weather bureau to arrange a visit or tour. Before you go, ask your student to learn about the different kinds of weather measurement tools and devices that are used. Also have your student find out why that site was chosen for a weather station. Encourage him or her to ask specific questions about measuring weather as he or she gets the opportunity to see the process firsthand.

Museum Exploration

Ask your student what he or she is interested in learning more about in the realm of science. Astronomy and the planets? The steam engine? Historic inventions? Plan a trip to a local planetarium or museum of science and industry. Before you go, have your student research the current special exhibit and make a list of specific things he or she would like to see and learn. Arrange to talk with someone at the museum.

Sound Experiences

Is there a symphony hall in or near your town? These halls are specially constructed to channel, amplify, absorb, and refine sound. Plan a trip to one of these buildings. Contact the building manager and find out about tours or sound demonstrations they might have there. Have your student research the date of construction and style of architecture before your visit. You may choose to be there during the performance of a favorite group or composer, or you might want to visit while the hall is unoccupied so you can experiment with your own voices.

Solar Energy Firsthand

Have your student find out about buildings in your community that use solar power. These buildings usually have a solar panel installed on the roof. Look in your phone book to find the name of a company that installs solar panels. It should be able to help you find local buildings that use solar power. Arrange for a visit to one of these places and for your student to talk with the owner about how the solar power provides energy for the house or building.

Environment Volunteer

Visit a nature center or contact the local chamber of commerce, city hall, or forest service to find out about environmental cleanup or restoration projects going on in your community. Find out about volunteer opportunities and have your student choose an event or project to participate in. If it is a restoration project, have your student write a list of things he or she would like to learn about the native plants or waterways in your area.

Community Health

Locate the office of the Department of Health in your community. Arrange an interview with a public health official. Have your student prepare a list of questions about current health concerns in your community and their causes, prevention, and treatment. Have your student find out what he or she should be doing now for optimum health and growth. Then talk about how today's public health has changed since the Middle Ages (see Lesson 4.5).

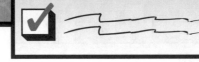

We Have Learned

Use this checklist to summarize what you and your student
have accomplished in the Science section.

❏ **Classification of Animals**
❏ characteristics of animals, life
processes of animals
❏ classifying invertebrates, vertebrates,
carnivores, herbivores

❏ **Classification of Plants**
❏ characteristics of plants, life processes of plants
❏ classifying the kingdoms Monera,
Protista, Fungi

❏ **Cells and Genetics**
❏ cell structure, function, division
❏ growth patterns of plants, animals,
humans
❏ chromosomes, genes, DNA

❏ **Human Body and Human Health**
❏ nervous system, circulatory system,
human reproduction system
❏ stages of growth, individual
development
❏ defense systems, diseases
❏ nutrition, environment, world health

❏ **Scientific Process**

❏ **Ecosystem**
❏ biomes, habitat, environmental
changes
❏ transfer of energy between living
things, food chain
❏ climate, weather

❏ **Earth's Surface**
❏ rocks, minerals, land, water
❏ natural resources, conservation
❏ Earth's history, surface activity,
changing life forms

❏ **Solar System**
❏ sun, moon, Earth, inner planets,
outer planets
❏ stars, eclipses, comets, meteors

❏ **Physical Energy**
❏ solar energy, waves
❏ properties, measurement of heat
❏ energy consumption, fossil fuels,
pollution

❏ **Light and Sound**
❏ light rays, refraction, color
❏ sound waves, sound properties

❏ **Chemical Properties of Matter**
❏ atoms, elements, compounds
❏ chemical formulas, equations
❏ acids, bases, salts

We have also learned:

_____

_____

_____

_____

_____

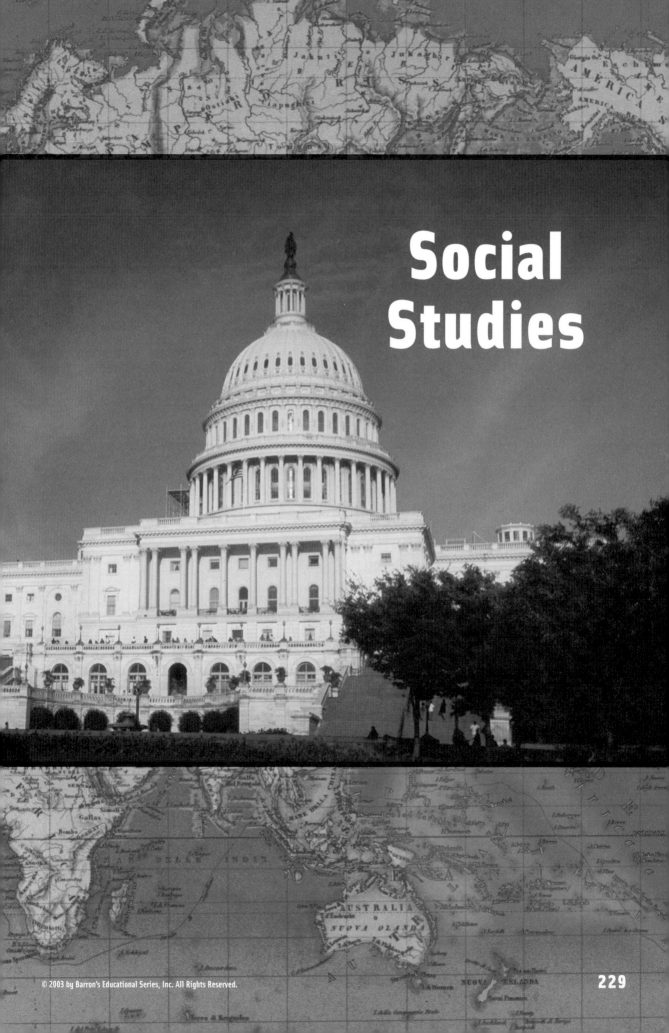

Social Studies

Social Studies

Key Topics

Mesopotamia and Egypt
Pages 231–242

Asian and African Cultures
Pages 243–248

Ancient Greece and Rome
Pages 249–254

Feudal Europe
Pages 255–260

The Crusades
Pages 261–264

Renaissance and Reformation
Pages 265–274

Scientific Revolution and Enlightenment
Pages 275–280

Industrial Revolution
Pages 281–286

"Contemporary" Conflicts
Pages 287–292

Exploring the Contributions of Ancient Civilizations

Understanding the past gives clues about the present.

OBJECTIVE	BACKGROUND	MATERIALS
To help your student understand the important contributions of ancient civilizations	Today the Middle East is most often known for being an important oil-producing area. The ancient civilizations that sprang up in and around the Fertile Crescent, in present-day Middle East, made invaluable contributions in the areas of language, laws, religion, and culture even before oil was discovered. In this lesson, your student will learn how the contributions of the ancient civilizations of this region affect us today.	■ Student Learning Pages 1.A–1.B ■ colored pencils ■ 1 copy Comparison Chart, page 353

VOCABULARY

FERTILE able to produce or develop; good for growing crops

ARCHAEOLOGY the study of remains humans have left behind, such as goods and materials

CUNEIFORM an ancient system of writing using symbols to describe things

ZIGGURATS ancient buildings, often called temples, that are pyramid-shaped

PROPHET one who is believed by followers to speak for God

Let's Begin

1 **EXPLAIN** Explain that the Fertile Crescent is a crescent-shaped area located in present-day Middle East. It spans from the Mediterranean Sea to the Persian Gulf. The Tigris and Euphrates Rivers made parts of the land **fertile,** or good for growing crops and raising animals. The rivers, as well as nearby bodies of water, provided water for crops, drinking, washing, and transporting people and goods. Mesopotamia, which in Greek means "land between the rivers," was a region in the Fertile Crescent situated between the Tigris and Euphrates and was the site of early great civilizations of people beginning 7,000 years ago. Ask, *Why do you think ancient civilizations settled along water?* [water can be used for many things, such as for drinking, transportation, crops, washing, and cooking]

2 **RELATE** Mention that most of what we know about the peoples of the Fertile Crescent comes from **archaeology,** or the study of remains humans have left behind. Archaeologists study ancient civilizations by looking at the things people have used and left behind, such as clothing, houses, cookware, and tools, to learn how a group of people lived and survived. By examining these items, archaeologists can tell what the civilization ate, what clothing they wore, and so on. Ask, *If you found fishing hooks at a site, what might that tell you about the people?* [they went fishing, they ate fish] Ask, *What might a bow and arrow tell you?* [they hunted animals]

3 **DISTRIBUTE AND IDENTIFY** Distribute Student Learning Page 1.A. Have your student go to the library or search the Internet for a map showing the Fertile Crescent, Mesopotamia, and the ancient civilizations that once occupied the Middle East. Then find another map identifying the region's present-day countries. Have your student identify the water of the area and color it in blue pencil on the map on Student Learning Page 1.A. Then in green pencil have him or her draw the areas of the Fertile Crescent and Mesopotamia. In yellow have your student identify and draw the boundaries of present-day countries. [Mesopotamia occupied present-day Turkey, Syria, Iraq, Kuwait] Throughout the lesson you will ask your student to add to the map.

4 **ILLUSTRATE AND RESEARCH** Explain that by around 3000 B.C., in the area of Mesopotamia known as Sumer, the Sumerians developed one of the first great civilizations known. The Sumerians settled near rivers and grew crops, constructed buildings, and created a government. The Sumerians also invented **cuneiform,** an ancient system of writing using symbols to describe things. It consisted of 550 symbols. Here is a photo of Sumerian cuneiform written on an ancient clay tablet.

Sumerian cuneiform

Now have your student go to the library and research life in Sumer. Ask, *What did their homes look like?* [mud-brick houses] *What was the importance of* **ziggurats,** *or temples?* [they were places of worship; there were many in Sumer] Then ask, *What is "The Epic of Gilgamesh"?* [an epic, or long narrative poem, that contains stories of Gilgamesh, which reveals how the Sumerians lived] Then have your student research the cuneiform symbols they used. Direct him or her to write things that he or she might encounter during a typical Sumerian day using these symbols. Also have your student locate Sumer on his or her map in green pencil.

5 **EXPLAIN AND CHART** Explain that the Sumerians eventually turned to fighting each other over land and usage of water. Sumer's downfall occurred around 2000 B.C. only to have another empire, Babylonia, rise to power. Have your student locate Babylonia on his or her map in green pencil. Ask, *In what present-day country was it located?* [Iraq]

6 **COMPARE** Relate that King Hammurabi was a powerful Babylonian king who had a strong army. He built a wall around the city of Babylon for protection—the wall was believed to be 11 miles long and about 80 feet thick! Hammurabi is best known for putting together one of the first sets of laws for his people, called Hammurabi's Code, in about 1800 B.C. Many of these rules form the basis of our laws today.

Have your student use the Internet or go to the library and research Hammurabi's Code. Have him or her select a handful of today's laws and compare them to Hammurabi's. Ask how the laws are different and similar. Have your student use a copy of the Comparison Chart found on page 353 to take notes. Discuss.

DID YOU KNOW?

Some believe that the Tower of Babel was the ziggurat built by Babylonian king Nebuchadnezzar for another "god." God wasn't pleased. He then made the people's speech confusing so that they couldn't understand each other. People traveled to other regions to communicate, which explains how different languages developed.

7 **EXPLAIN AND IDENTIFY** Explain that at the north end of the Fertile Crescent, around 1100 B.C., the Phoenicians lived in Canaan, an area with many cedar trees. They took advantage of the trees and built ships. Their location on the Mediterranean Sea, along with the wood, helped them become important sea traders. Have your student locate Canaan and Phoenicia on his or her map using green pencil.

8 **REVEAL AND DISCUSS** Reveal that the Phoenicians traveled to various parts of the world, such as present-day Africa and Europe, farther than anyone had at that point! They were the first sailors to navigate using the North Star. Through their trading and communication with various lands, they spread the culture and goods of the area to other regions and brought back many products and ideas to Phoenicia. This helped begin the spread of ideas around the world. Direct your student to use the Internet or go to the library to research what items and ideas the Phoenicians traded and spread. Ask, *Why was the spread of ideas important?* [it opened up people's minds to different things and shared knowledge and culture] Discuss.

9 **DIRECT AND WRITE** Point out that in addition to spreading ideas, the Phoenicians are best known for creating an alphabet of 22 letters. Have your student search the Internet for the Phoenician alphabet and print it out if possible. Have him or her write his or her name using the Phoenician alphabet. Ask, *How is the alphabet different from ours?* [ours has 26 letters, the letters look different] *How is it different from cuneiform?* [rather than using symbols to indicate something, the letters are put together to name that item] *Why do you think they created a different, smaller alphabet?* [easier to work with and remember] Discuss.

10 **EXPLAIN AND IDENTIFY** Explain that, near Phoenicia along the Mediterranean Sea, were the Israelites. They were located in Israel, which itself was in Canaan. Have your student identify their location in green pencil on his or her map.

11 **RELATE** Explain that the story of the Israelites is written in the Bible. The Israelites traveled around the Fertile Crescent, came

into contact with other peoples, and developed their own traditions and beliefs. The Israelites recorded events, their history, and their beliefs in the Torah, which is also the first five books of the Old Testament of the Christian Bible. This belief system is called Judaism.

Point out that Israel, although in a different form, exists today. Discuss with your student what he or she has learned about today's Israel from other people and from the news. Go to http://www.CNN.com or your favorite news Web site and see what news there is about Israel and its capital city, Jerusalem, from the past month. Discuss.

12 **EXPLAIN AND RESEARCH** Explain that the Assyrians were another important Mesopotamian civilization. By around 800 B.C. they had come to power because of their fearsome skills as warriors. They learned how to work with iron to make weapons and other tools. Have your student research the Assyrian Empire and learn about the importance of the Assyrians' use of iron. Ask, *How did they work with iron?* [three-step process] *What did they use the iron for?* [weapons, tools]

13 **REVEAL AND IDENTIFY** Explain that traders criss-crossed the Fertile Crescent for years, moving into various regions that included Persia, Syria, and Arabia. In the town of Mecca, in Arabia, the Islam religion began with Muhammad, a man born in the late 500s. He is believed to have been chosen by Allah, or God, to receive God's teachings. He became known as a **prophet,** or one who is believed by followers to speak for God. Islam's followers are Muslims, and the Quran contains these teachings. Have your student locate Arabia on his or her map and color the region in green. Then have him or her identify the present-day countries that make up Arabia and color those in yellow. [Arabia was largely Saudi Arabia and also the United Arab Emirates, Qatar, Yemen, and Oman; Persia was largely present-day Iran]

Branching Out

TEACHING TIP

Periodically refer to the map and review how the ancient civilizations have evolved into the present-day countries that we hear about on the news.

CHECKING IN

You can assess your student's understanding of the importance of the peoples of this area and time period by having him or her create a time line. Based on this lesson and the research he or she completed, have him or her identify the years when certain groups flourished, accurately naming the groups and their important contributions.

Identify Ancient Civilizations

Use this map to locate and identify regions and water in the Fertile Crescent and surrounding areas.

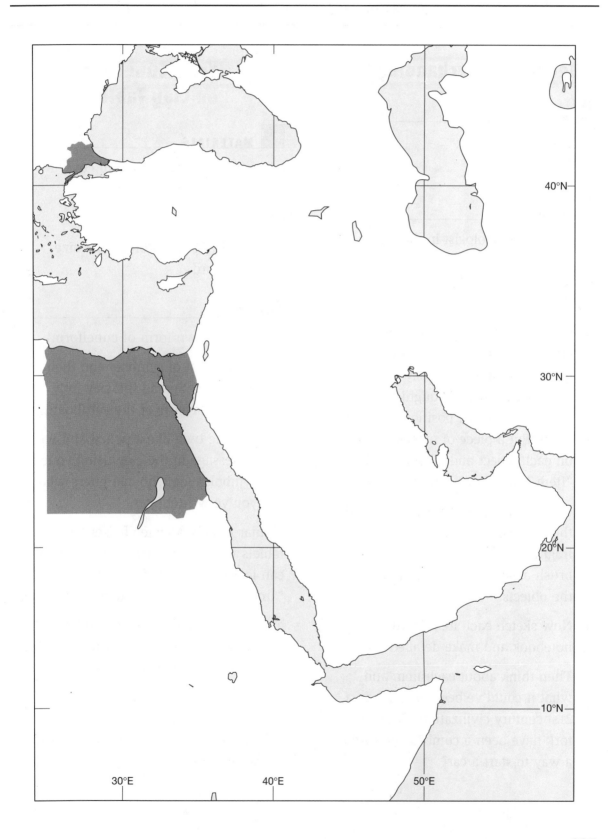

What's Next? You Decide!

Now it's your turn to choose what to do next in the lesson. Read the activities and decide which one you want to do—you may want to try them both!

Become an Archaeologist

MATERIALS

❑ masking tape

❑ 1 paint brush

STEPS

You are an archaeologist in the future, and you've been assigned to identify how certain objects from the 21st century were used.

❑ Search around your home for a stapler, hair dryer, fork, piece of jewelry, or other everyday objects. Don't move them, though! Leave the items in the exact positions you find them. Put a piece of masking tape on each object and label it, such as "Item No. 1," or however you want.

❑ Use a paint brush to scatter dirt off the objects. Archaeologists often find fragile objects and have to gently brush away dirt so as not to disturb the objects.

❑ Now sketch each item in your notebook and make detailed notes.

❑ Then think about each item and what it could've been used for in a 21st century civilization. Could a fork have been a comb? A hair dryer a way to start a car?

Write Cuneiform on Clay Tablets

MATERIALS

❑ molding clay, enough to cover a 10-by-10-inch area

❑ 1 twig

❑ 1 10-by-10-inch (or similar size) cardboard

STEPS

Create your own form of cuneiform!

❑ Make a list of symbols and their meanings. Spread the clay in a smooth layer over the cardboard.

❑ Use the twig like a pencil and write a message in the clay using your symbols. See who can guess what you've written!

Similar to how archaeologists found clay tablets with ancient cuneiform, you also can leave a message for some "archaeologist" in your home to uncover.

❑ Make your clay writing tablet smooth again. Then write a friendly message that you want someone to find.

❑ Let the clay dry and place your tablet in a place for another person to uncover.

Discovering Ancient Egypt

Studying historical cultures can help us understand the cultures of today.

OBJECTIVE	BACKGROUND	MATERIALS
To explore the geography, culture, people, and traditions of ancient Egypt	Studying ancient Egypt is a fascinating and mystical experience. Many of the agricultural techniques and infrastructure of our modern world began in ancient Egypt. This lesson uses history, maps, and ancient artifacts to explore the geography, culture, people, and traditions of ancient Egypt.	■ Student Learning Pages 2.A–2.B ■ colored pencils ■ 1 copy Venn Diagram, page 353

VOCABULARY

NILE RIVER the longest river in the world (4,000 miles long); flows north from central Africa to the Mediterranean Sea

PAPYRUS a type of plant called a reed that grows in the Nile

PHARAOH a ruler or "god-king" of ancient Egypt

PYRAMIDS large stone structures built as tombs for ancient Egyptian pharaohs

ROSETTA STONE a famous rock carved with hieroglyphics, hieratic writing, and Greek that helped people decipher the language and picture symbols of ancient Egypt

HIEROGLYPHICS a picture-symbol language used by ancient Egyptians

Let's Begin

1 **DISTRIBUTE** Distribute Student Learning Page 2.A. Explore the map of ancient Egypt. Walk through the map and identify everything, including regions of Upper and Lower Egypt. Highlight the importance of the **Nile River** in ancient Egypt; explain that the Nile is the longest river in the world and that it provides water for farming, irrigation, and drinking in a land surrounded by desert. The Nile also united people in Upper and Lower Egypt.

2 **EXPLORE** Explain to your student that the Nile River made it possible for people to thrive in this ancient civilization. The area where the river meets the sea is called the delta. Ask your student to find the delta on the map. The delta flooded each year, making the soil very fertile for farming. The annual flooding also made it possible for farmers to provide water for their crops through irrigation. Farmers built huge basins so that when the Nile flooded the basins filled up with water. This

method was known as basin irrigation, which is still used today. The crops were abundant and the Egyptians traded with other people for things that they needed. Ask, *Why was the annual flooding of the Nile so important?* [it made the land and soil fertile for farming and irrigation, enabling the Egyptians to produce their own food and be self-sufficient] Have your student think of a local river and discuss its importance.

3 **IDENTIFY** Point out that a special reed called **papyrus** grew in the Nile. Papyrus was used to make boats and paper. Have your student research ancient Egypt and the goods that came from there. Then discuss and ask, *Why was Egypt called "the gift of the Nile"?* [the Nile made it possible for Egypt to thrive during ancient times by providing abundant food and materials for clothing, paper, and boats; it enabled trading and travel to occur between Upper and Lower Egypt]

4 **CONNECT** Invite your student to make connections between ancient Egypt and present-day Egypt. Have him or her go to the library or search the Internet to find different types of maps, looking at the boundaries of the country, major cities, natural resources, and population distribution. Encourage him or her to examine political, topographical, natural resource, and historical maps too. Discuss with your student how the Nile has changed since ancient times.

5 **DESCRIBE AND PREDICT** Explain to your student that there were three different classes in ancient Egyptian society: the ruling class, the middle class, and the peasants and slaves. Explain that the ruling class was led by the **pharaoh,** or "god-king," and included his governors, advisors, and priests. The middle class included people with specific skills who worked as craftspeople, musicians, soldiers, or physicians. The third class represented the majority of the population and included peasants and farmers. Have your student predict what daily life for children in each class would be like. Then talk about his or her predictions.

6 **RESEARCH AND RELATE** Have your student research the daily lives of the three different social classes. Encourage him or her to find out how they dressed, what their homes were like, how they ate and celebrated, the type of work they did, and how many hours they worked each day. Invite your student to compare and contrast the three classes and decide which class he or she would have wanted to be in. Ask, *Why would you want to be in that social class?* Discuss.

7 **CONNECT** Help your student relate to the experience of ancient Egyptians. Ask him or her to copy the following questions into a notebook and write a short paragraph to answer each one: *If you were an ancient Egyptian and you needed a drink of water,* *what would you do? If you needed new clothes, where would you get them? What would they be made of and how would you pay for them?* Then discuss the answers. Have your student search the Internet to verify his or her answers.

8 **DISTRIBUTE AND COMPARE** Now focus on the pharaohs in ancient Egypt. The word *pharaoh* means "great house," and the people believed pharaohs were gods in human form. Explain that the pharaohs were powerful rulers and were responsible for the economy and government of ancient Egypt. The people believed pharaohs were descendents of the sun god, Ra. They worshiped Ra and credited Ra with all of life on Earth. Likewise, they worshiped pharaohs and credited them with life in Egypt. Have your student research the responsibilities, powers, and length of rule of the pharaohs. Then, make a copy of the Venn Diagram on page 353 and distribute it. Have your student use the diagram to compare what he or she knows about the pharaohs to modern-day U.S. presidents. Ask, *Why do you think these leaders are so different?* [in the United States, leaders are elected and not born into office; industrialized society versus agricultural; separation of religion and state]

9 **EXPLAIN AND DISCUSS** Explore the importance of **pyramids** in ancient Egyptian civilization. Explain that the pyramids were built as tombs for the pharaohs after they died. A pharaoh was placed inside a pyramid and surrounded by luxurious clothing, art, and jewelry. Have your student research ancient Egyptian pyramids. Have him or her find out why they were built, what they were made of, and why so much emphasis was placed on them. Then have your student present this to you and others in an oral presentation. Encourage him or her to incorporate images, artifacts, and anything else.

10 **EXPLORE AND DESCRIBE** Explain that most of our information and knowledge about ancient Egypt comes from the discovery of artifacts. One of these important artifacts is the **Rosetta stone,** which was discovered by French soldiers in 1799. The Rosetta stone is a rock carved with **hieroglyphics,** which is picture-symbol language. It provided clues to understanding the language, writing, and picture symbols used in ancient Egypt. Have your student research hieroglyphics at the library or on the Internet. Then ask, *How did French soldier Jean Champollian use the Greek writing to help him decode the meaning of the ancient Egyptian writing?* [he used his knowledge of Greek, compared the Greek meaning to the Egyptian symbols, and realized that the Greek and Egyptian writing on the stone meant the same thing] Ask, *Why was the understanding of this hieroglyphic writing important to uncovering the mystery of ancient Egypt?* [after the meaning of the hieroglyphics was understood, archaeologists could understand the many hieroglyphic writings they had discovered]

?
DID YOU KNOW?

King Tutankhamen was only eight years old when he became a pharaoh. When he died, he was buried in the Valley of the Kings. For thousands of years, his tomb remained undiscovered. Many of the ancient Egyptian tombs had been destroyed by grave robbers seeking treasure, but Tutankhamen's tomb was never found. In 1922, an archaeologist discovered the tomb of "King Tut." His tomb was filled with beautiful furniture, pictures, statues, and a golden funeral mask.

?
DID YOU KNOW?

The word *hieroglyphics* comes from the Greek words meaning "sacred carving." Hieroglyphic writing is picture-symbol language used by the ancient Egyptians. Many ancient artifacts are carved with hieroglyphics. Thanks to the discovery of the Rosetta stone, we can now translate the meaning of this ancient language.

Branching Out

TEACHING TIP

It's important to appeal to many different learning styles throughout the lesson on ancient Egypt. Use pictures, magazines, and maps as well as discussions, notetaking, role-playing, research, and any other visual or auditory clues to impart information.

CHECKING IN

Assess your student's understanding of ancient Egypt by having him or her research the lives of two important pharaohs, Amenhotep IV and King Tutankhamen. Have your student compare both rulers and everyday life in Egypt under both rulers. Then work with your student to write a skit sharing this information with others.

FOR FURTHER READING

Ancient Egypt, by Ruth Akamine Wassynger (Scholastic Trade, 1999).

Eyewitness: Ancient Egypt, by George Hart and Peter Hayman, photo. (DK Publishing, 2000).

Mummies of the Pharaohs: Exploring the Valley of the Kings, by Melvin Berger and Gilda Berger (National Geographic Society, 2001).

The Land of Ancient Egypt

SOCIAL
STUDIES

2.A

Use this map to identify and locate important ancient cities, regions, rivers, and deserts in ancient Egypt. Use colored pencils to color in each area as you learn about it. Use a different colored pencil to identify the delta area of the Nile River.

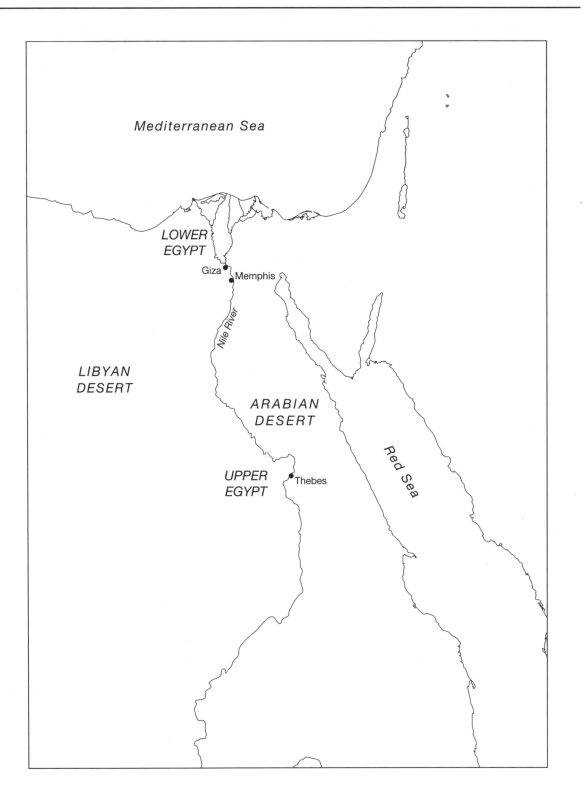

What's Next? You Decide!

Now it's your turn to choose what to do next in the lesson.
Read the activities and decide which one you want to do—
you may want to try them both!

Build a Pyramid

▮ MATERIALS

- ❑ 1 piece heavy duty cardboard
- ❑ 1 package modeling clay
- ❑ nontoxic craft paint in Earth-tone colors
- ❑ 1 paintbrush

▮ STEPS

Suppose you are a pharaoh in ancient Egypt. Design your own pyramid using modeling clay.

- ❑ Look at a magazine or book picture of a pyramid to help create your design.
- ❑ When you have finished building your pyramid, leave it on the cardboard in a warm place to dry.
- ❑ Then share your work with a friend or family member.
- ❑ If you would like to challenge yourself further, try to create a sphinx or a statue of a pharaoh using modeling clay.

Create Your Own Hieroglyphic Language

▮ MATERIALS

- ❑ construction paper
- ❑ markers

▮ STEPS

The ancient Egyptians used hieroglyphic symbols and pictures as their written language.

- ❑ Create your own hieroglyphic language using creative pictures and symbols to represent words.
- ❑ Create a key giving each symbol or picture a corresponding English word.
- ❑ Write a short message to a friend or family member using this new language.
- ❑ Ask a friend or family member to try to decipher your message using the key. If he or she wants to, he or she can write you a reply message for you to decipher.
- ❑ Remember that we found out how to read Egyptian hieroglyphics though the discovery of the Rosetta stone!

Exploring Asian and African Cultures

Studying other cultures can give us a new perspective on our own.

OBJECTIVE	BACKGROUND	MATERIALS
To reveal to your student the historical influence of Asian and African cultures	Early Asian and African civilizations made many contributions to the development of modern society. The people of these cultures were often well educated and invented many things that are used today, such as printing, gunpowder, the clock, the magnetic compass, and the abacus. In this lesson, your student will learn about the leaders, religion, and societies of early Asian and African civilizations.	■ Student Learning Pages 3.A–3.B ■ 1 present-day world map ■ 1 copy Venn Diagram, page 353 ■ 1 copy Sequence Chain, page 354

VOCABULARY

MONSOON the seasonal wind in India that causes heavy rains

REINCARNATION the belief that people have many lives

CASTE SYSTEM a social system where people cannot move out of their birth class

DYNASTY a powerful family who rules for a long period of time

ABACUS a frame of wires with beads that slide across, used for calculating

SAMURAI the noble class of soldiers and landowners in feudal Japan

SHOGUN the governor of the samurai

CALLIGRAPHY the art of precise, decorative handwriting

ARTIFACTS things from past cultures that we use today to understand those cultures

Let's Begin

1 **LOCATE** On a world map, ask your student to identify the continents of Asia and Africa. Locate the main focus areas for this lesson: India, China, Japan, West Africa, and Zimbabwe. Keep this map on hand for reference throughout the lesson.

2 **EXPLAIN** Explain that Indian civilization is one of the oldest in the world, dating back about 4,500 years. The two major rivers in India are the Ganges River and the Indus River. Indian civilization depends on these rivers because the land is very dry. Most of the rain in India falls during the **monsoon** season. Have your student research the climate and farming practices in India.

SOCIAL STUDIES

LESSON 4.3

Ask, *What are the main reasons that civilizations usually develop near water?* [to provide fertile soil and water for farming, for trade and transportation]

3 **COMPARE** Explain that two different religions originated in India. The first was Hinduism. Hinduism teaches that everything is God. The belief in **reincarnation,** or that people have many lives, is also part of Hinduism. Hindus don't kill animals. They also believe in the **caste system,** which says that people are born into castes, or hierarchical classes, that they must remain in for the length of their life. Explain that Buddhism began later in India. Buddhism teaches that in order to stop suffering, a person must overcome desire, jealousy, greed, and selfishness. Buddhism teaches that all living things should be treated with equal respect. Ask your student to research the origins of Hinduism and Buddhism. Have him or her use a copy of the Venn Diagram found on page 353 to compare the two. Discuss.

4 **DISCUSS** Explain that while India was growing, civilizations in China were developing as well, especially along the Huang River. This area was ruled by one family for a long time and became known as the Shang dynasty. It was the first dynasty in China. A **dynasty** is a line of rulers from the same family where control is passed from generation to generation. Talk with your student about the way we choose leaders in our society. Ask, *How is the way leaders are chosen in our society different from the Chinese dynasties?* [our leaders are elected, the dynasty rulers were born into power]

5 **EXPLAIN** Explain to your student that the government, religion, and writing developed in the Shang dynasty influenced Chinese society for hundreds of years. Shang society was organized like a pyramid, with a few ruling people at the top and many lower-ranking people at the bottom. Ask your student to research Shang society and its social and political structure. Have him or her list the different ranks of social classes in a notebook, and then have a conversation about his or her thoughts on what he or she wrote.

6 **REVEAL AND DISCUSS** Reveal to the student that after the Shang dynasty lost power, the region of Qin began to grow. Its ruler was a general who won many battles and called himself Shihuangdi, or first grand emperor. Shihuangdi was so proud of his empire that he ordered a tomb to be built for himself. The tomb included more than 8,000 life-sized clay soldiers and horses to protect it. Farmers digging a well discovered this "clay army" in 1974. Have your student read about Shihuangdi and the people of Qin. Ask, *How would you feel if Shihuangdi was the ruler of our country today?* Discuss.

7 **DESCRIBE** Tell your student about a famous Chinese thinker, Confucius, who was born in 551 B.C. His thoughts about how people should behave and treat one another became the foundation of Chinese society and government. One of his quotes was "Do not do unto others what you would not want others to do to you." A positive version of this ("do unto others . . .") is found in the Bible. This is now referred to as the Golden Rule by Western people. Together with your student research the life and philosophies of Confucius.

8   **EXPLAIN** Explain to your student that between A.D. 618 and 1279 two very prosperous dynasties ruled China. In the T'ang dynasty, the ruling class was well educated. During this time Chinese painting and sculpture developed and printing was invented. The Sung dynasty was a very clean society that even had a fire department! During this time, clocks, gunpowder, the magnetic compass, and the **abacus** were invented. Discuss the importance of these inventions. Encourage your student to think about what life was like before people had these things.

9   **REVEAL AND DISCUSS** Explain that in 1279 a warrior named Kublai Khan conquered China. This was the beginning of the Mongol dynasty. Transportation was improved and Chinese inventions spread to Europe. The Chinese people who Kublai Khan had removed from government began writing plays and operas, and Chinese theater grew. Marco Polo was a European traveler who served as a court official for Kublai Khan and wrote about the wealth and culture in China. When the Mongols fell from power in 1368, the Ming dynasty began. There was a big change. The Ming rulers thought other countries were uncivilized, and they restricted trade and travel.

10   **DESCRIBE** Explain that another important power at this time was the Ottoman Empire, which was centered in Asia Minor. Before 1300, it was known as the Turkish Empire. The Ottomans first invaded Europe in 1345, eventually capturing Constantinople and making it their capital. It became the largest empire in the world. Have your student research the Ottoman empire, its social and religious beliefs, art, and political structure. Ask him or her to give a brief presentation about this empire.

11   **DISCUSS AND CHART** Distribute Student Learning Page 3.A. Locate Japan on the world map. Explain that, as in many other places, ancient Japan had a feudal system of government. At the top of society was an emperor. The noble class of landowners and soldiers were called **samurai.** The actual ruler of the samurai was the **shogun.** These samurai were honorable people who believed in bravery, self-discipline, and obedience. In addition to fighting, the samurai developed his strength through martial arts such as judo, karate, and sumo wrestling. Art, especially **calligraphy,** was also popular. Below this samurai class were the peasants and artisans who provided food and weapons for the samurai, and the merchants were at the bottom. Have your student complete Student Learning Page 3.A. Then discuss.

     Exploring Asian and African Cultures   **245**

12 **EXPLORE** Have your student find West Africa on a world map. Explain to the student that in A.D. 400 large trading kingdoms formed in West Africa. The basis of these kingdoms was knowledge of iron smelting. The first, Ghana, gained land and control using their iron weapons. They traded their salt in the south and bought gold. Ghana became weak after a war with Muslim people from North Africa and was overtaken by Mali. Mali rulers continued the salt and gold trade, organized a permanent army, and appointed generals in each province who kept the peace and made sure there was food for the people. Mali became a great center of learning.

Then, in the late 1400s, a new kingdom called Songhai conquered Mali and became the largest kingdom in West Africa until the North Africans invaded, this time with guns, and easily defeated Songhai's soldiers, who had only swords and spears. Ask your student to research Ghana, Mali, and Songhai further. Have him or her use a copy of the Sequence Chain found on page 354 to organize the chain of events that took place. Discuss.

13 **DESCRIBE** Have your student locate East Africa on a world map. Explain that Zimbabwe was a successful trading kingdom in East Africa. People came to Zimbabwe from present-day Nigeria around A.D. 700. There had been a large growth in population and they were looking for a new place to live. The chief of Zimbabwe was viewed as a god-king and the people were skilled at creating stone buildings without using mortar. Zimbabwe remained strong for many years due to its gold, copper, and ivory trade. Have your student research the development and society of Zimbabwe. Ask, *Do you think the people made a good decision by moving to Zimbabwe? What might have happened if they remained in Nigeria?* [they might have starved to death or started a war for land]

Branching Out

TEACHING TIP

There is a large amount of information in this lesson. Try not to focus on dates and details as much as on main ideas. Encourage your student to focus on similarities and differences between countries, as well as on contributions to today's society.

CHECKING IN

To assess your student's understanding of this lesson, ask him or her to give an oral summary of a few major events that happened in the countries that were discussed. Prompt your student with key questions from the lessons.

FOR FURTHER READING

Confucious: The Golden Rule, by Russell Freedman and Frederic Clement, ill. (Arthur A. Levine, 2002).

Marco Polo: A Journey Through China, by Fiona McDonald (Franklin Watts, 1998).

The Samurai, by Anthony J. Bryant (Osprey, 1999).

Samurai: The Weapons and Spirit of the Japanese Warrior, by Clive Sinclaire (Lyons Press, 2001).

Compare Social Organization

Complete the diagrams with class levels from the Chinese Shang dynasty and the Japanese feudal system using the information and research from this lesson. Then write a paragraph about the similarities and differences of these two class systems.

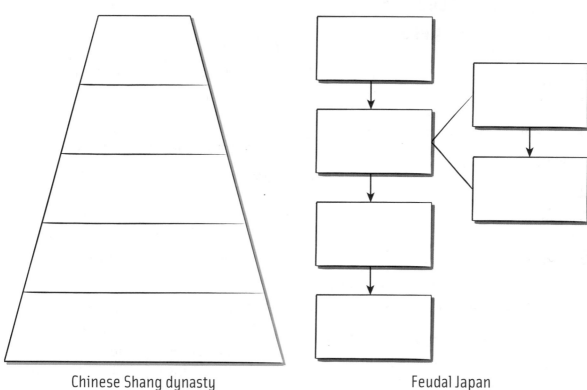

Chinese Shang dynasty   Feudal Japan

_____

_____

_____

_____

_____

_____

_____

_____

_____

_____

_____

What's Next? You Decide!

Now it's your turn to choose what to do next in the lesson.
Read the activities and decide which one you want to do—
you may want to try them both!

Create a Tomb Fit for an Emperor

MATERIALS

- ❑ 1 shoe box
- ❑ assortment of paper, beads, buttons
- ❑ glitter
- ❑ glue
- ❑ 1 pair scissors

STEPS

- ❑ Design a tomb like the Chinese ruler Shihuangdi built for himself.
- ❑ Use a shoe box to create a model for an elaborate tomb using the materials listed above and any others you find.
- ❑ Be creative! If Shihuangdi had 8,000 soldiers protecting his tomb, you can do whatever you want with yours!
- ❑ Share your creation with a friend.

Construct a Time Capsule

MATERIALS

- ❑ 1 plastic box or container that can be sealed tightly
- ❑ several miscellaneous items that represent our society and culture

STEPS

Much of our information about civilizations from the past comes from burial sites, **artifacts,** or writings that are discovered accidentally.

- ❑ Imagine that it's the year 3500. You are digging in your garden and you come across an ancient box that contains artifacts from 2003. What would the box contain to represent our current civilization?
- ❑ Find inexpensive items in or around your home that represent our culture and would help someone in 3500 understand your life.
- ❑ Place these items in the box with a short description of each.
- ❑ Share your time capsule with your family. Ask them if they would like to add any items to the box and why.
- ❑ If you want, bury the box. You never know who will find it!

Discovering Ancient Greece and Rome

By discovering ancient Greece and Rome, we can discover roots of the West.

OBJECTIVE	BACKGROUND	MATERIALS
To have your student explore the geography, culture, traditions, and influences of ancient Greece and Rome	Many of the defining characteristics of Western society can be traced to ancient Greece and Rome. These include political organization, philosophical thought, art, architecture, and more. This lesson includes historical information and exploring of maps to examine and understand ancient Greece and Rome.	■ Student Learning Pages 4.A–4.B ■ 1 map ancient Greece with topography ■ 1 map the growth of the Roman Empire

VOCABULARY

CITY-STATES self-governing cities in ancient Greece

DEMOCRACY a government where citizens participate in every decision

PHILOSOPHY the study of reality, ethics, government, and justice

PHILOSOPHER one who questions and searches for wisdom and truth

REPUBLIC a government where people choose representatives to make laws

VETO POWER the power of a political leader to say no to a decision or law

DICTATORSHIP a government where all the power belongs to one leader

PATRICIANS the wealthy class of ancient Rome

PLEBIANS the working class of ancient Rome

AQUEDUCTS structures for carrying water

MESSIAH the leader of a cause

Let's Begin

1   **EXPLORE** Explore a map of ancient Greece. Point out the large amount of coastline, peninsulas, and islands. The Greeks were very good sailors. Also point out that Greece is very mountainous. Because mountains divide the land, the ancient Greeks lived in separated settlements called **city-states.** Travel was difficult because of the mountainous terrain of the land, so people traveled and traded by sea. Ask your student to find the city-state Athens on the map.

2 **EXPLORE** Explain that the city-states were the centers of government. The Greek word for city-state is *polis,* which is the origin of the English word *politics.* We can also see *polis* in the name of such cities as Annapolis. The early city-states, beginning around 800 B.C., were governed first by kings, then by families, and eventually by one single ruler or tyrant. The Greeks wanted to create a fair and just government, and in 500 B.C. the first democratic city-state began in Athens. The Greek word for **democracy** is *demos,* which means "rule by the people." Have your student research the political organization in Athens. Ask, *Why do you think democracy is considered the most important Greek contribution to the modern world?* [because it was the first time in recorded history that people participated in their own government] Discuss.

DID YOU KNOW?

Even though Athens was considered a democracy, women, slaves, and people from other city-states did not have the right to vote in Athens.

3 **DESCRIBE** Describe what's called the Golden Age of Athens. Explain that ancient Athenians had democratic freedom and choice, which enriched culture and attracted artists, writers, and teachers to the city. Athenians valued truth and beauty. The Athenians were so dedicated to achieving excellence that the ancient ruins of a gigantic temple called the Parthenon remain standing in Athens today. Have your student research the details of the Golden Age of Athens. Have him or her list the values of Athenian society and compare them to our society today.

4 **EXPLAIN** Explain that theater became an important part of Greek culture. The first known theatrical performances were in Greece. The Greeks performed two types of plays: comedies and tragedies. *Oedipus,* written by the playwright Sophocles, is the most famous Greek tragedy. Invite your student to research the names and topics of famous Greek comedies and tragedies and look for pictures of the theaters where they were performed.

DID YOU KNOW?

Socrates didn't actually write anything. All we know of his teachings comes from Plato's writings.

5 **DESCRIBE** The Greeks also valued education and **philosophy.** **Philosophers** spent their lives asking questions to find the truth. Their questions focused on human behavior, society, government, and justice. Socrates, Plato, and Aristotle were three famous philosophers who lived in Athens during the Golden Age. Have your student research one of these famous Greek philosophers. Then ask your student what information about this person would be beneficial to include in a biography.

6 **EXPLORE** Explain that the modern-day Olympic Games began in 1896. The games were modeled after the traditional games of ancient Greece. These games were held in the city of Olympia during a festival to honor gods beginning as early as 776 B.C. Ask how he or she thinks the modern Olympic Games benefit us and our world relationships.

7 **EXPLAIN** Explain that Alexander was a famous conqueror from Macedonia. His father, Phillip II, the king of Macedonia, conquered Greece in 338 B.C. Alexander was well educated in reading, writing, science, and philosophy. Aristotle was one of his teachers. Alexander and his army conquered Persia, Egypt, and Babylon. He became known as Alexander the Great. He is known today as one of the most powerful leaders of ancient times. The growth of his empire was responsible for the spread of Greek culture throughout the ancient world. Ask, *Why was King Alexander known as Alexander the Great in ancient times?* [he conquered all of the land from Greece to Persia and spread Greek culture throughout the ancient world]

8   **TRANSITION AND RESEARCH**   Explain that the Greeks were conquered by the Romans in 146 B.C. The Roman Empire grew and was considered the greatest empire in ancient history. Review a map of the growth of the Roman Empire with your student. Ask your student to research the history of ancient Rome and make a time line showing the important events in the history of the Roman Empire, beginning with the founding of Rome in 753 B.C. and ending with the fall of Rome in A.D. 476.

9   **DISTRIBUTE AND COMPARE**   Distribute Student Learning Page 4.A. Explain that, like the Greeks, the Romans wanted to create better government. In 509 B.C., the leaders of Rome created a **republic.** In a republic, the right to rule is not inherited. There are laws and **veto power** to prevent any one person from becoming too powerful. People elect the leaders they want to represent their interests in government. Rome's republic was led by two officials called consuls who served one-year terms. There was also a 300-member elected senate. Ask, *What are the main differences between a **dictatorship**, a republic, and a democracy?* [in a dictatorship one person has all the power and there are no elections and no vetos; in a democracy decisions are made by a vote from all the people; in a republic leaders are elected to carry out the responsibilities of government]

10   **REVEAL AND DISCUSS**   Explain that there were two classes in Rome, the **patricians** and the **plebeians.** The patricians made up 10 percent of the population and were wealthy, powerful, and controlled the government. The plebeians were the working class of soldiers, farmers, craftsmen, and tradesmen and were not allowed to participate in government. As time went on the Roman republic evolved into more of a democracy and the plebeians were allowed more control and power in the government, but there was always conflict between the two classes. Ask, *Is the government of the United States more like the republic of the Roman Empire or the democracy of ancient Greece?* [it is more like a republic but maintains democratic values] Discuss.

11   **RESEARCH AND DISCUSS**   Explain that Hannibal, the warrior leader from Carthage, and Julius Caesar, the military leader and dictator in Rome, were important leaders during the Roman Empire. Ask your student to research these two important historical figures. Encourage your student to write brief biographies of both Hannibal and Caesar.

12 **EXPLORE AND ILLUSTRATE** Explain that the Romans were highly skilled builders. Many of our modern ideas about building and engineering come from the Romans. They built roads, bridges, **aqueducts,** temples, and stadiums much like the ones we build today. Beauty and balance were emphasized in Roman architecture. Ask your student to research Roman architecture and find pictures of famous Roman buildings and structures such as the Pantheon, the Forum, the Colosseum, the Via Appia Roads, and the Baths of Caracalla. Encourage your student to make drawings of the examples of the domes, arches, and other structural advancements of the Romans.

13 **EXPLAIN AND DISCUSS** Explain that Christianity began during the time of the Roman Empire and is based on the teachings of Jesus and the belief that he rose from the dead. Jesus lived in Palestine, which was then part of the Roman Empire. Jesus' message of hope and his ability to heal the sick made him well loved and popular with the poor people of Palestine. They called him "the Christ," the Greek word for **messiah.** The leaders were afraid that Jesus had too much influence among the people, and he was arrested and killed. His followers believed he was resurrected and continued to spread his teachings. They were called Christians. Christianity became a widely practiced religion in the Roman Empire. Christians refused to worship the emperors as gods, so many suffered. Even so, Christianity continued to grow and in A.D. 395 became the official religion of the Roman Empire. Ask, *Why do you think the Christians were made to suffer before Christianity became accepted?* [because challenging new ideas are not always accepted at first] Discuss.

Branching Out

TEACHING TIP

Help your student absorb the complex content of this lesson by using pictures, books, videos, museum visits, and other visual and experiencial aids. Also, if you wish to challenge your student, have him or her read the dialogue "Euthyphro" by Plato. It is within the grasp of sixth graders, especially when read aloud.

CHECKING IN

To make sure that your student understands specific facts and events, have him or her create a time line to record specific events in ancient Greek and Roman history. Have him or her include dates, locations, and a brief description of the events in chronological order.

FOR FURTHER READING

Alexander the Great and Ancient Greece (Rulers and Their Times), by Miriam Greenblatt (Benchmark Books, 2000).

Classical Athens (Journey to the Past), by Mario Denti and Aldo Ripamonti, ill. (Raintree/Steck Vaughn, 2001).

Eyewitness: Ancient Greece (Eyewitness Books), by Anne Pearson (DK Publishing, 2000).

Eyewitness: Ancient Rome (Eyewitness Books), by Simon James; Nick Nichols and Christi Graham, photographers (DK Publishing, 2000).

Julius Caesar and Ancient Rome in World History, by James Barter (Enslow Publishers, 2001).

Identify Roman Influences

Complete the chart of the political and social organization in ancient Greece, the Roman Empire, and present-day United States using information from the lesson and your research. Once your chart is complete, consider the similarities and differences of these three societies. Write a short paragraph of your thoughts. Share your paragraph with an adult.

	Type of Government	Who Makes Laws	Citizen Responsibilities	Primary Values
Ancient Greece				
Roman Empire				
United States				

_____

_____

_____

_____

_____

_____

What's Next? You Decide!

Now it's your turn to choose what to do next in the lesson.
Read the activities and decide which one you want to do—
you may want to try them both!

Perform Greek Theater

STEPS

Practice the art of playwriting by creating your own Greek comedy or tragedy!

❑ Create a setting, a theme, and characters based on what you know about Greek society.

❑ Write a script for your play.

❑ Invite friends and family members to play roles.

❑ Then act out the play together.

❑ Don't forget to think of costumes. What types of clothing would you wear?

❑ Remember to include props or any other visual elements in your play.

Use Roman Numerals

STEPS

The numbers we write with today are called Arabic numerals. The Romans used letters to represent numbers in their system. There are seven letters in the Roman numeral system. The number 1 is shown by the letter *I* (1 = I). The numbers 2 and 3 are shown by repeating the letter *I* (3 = III). The numbers 4 and 9 are shown by putting the letter *I* before the letter *V* or *X* (4 = IV and 9 = IX). The numbers 40 and 90 are shown by putting the letter *X* before the letters *L* or *C* (40 = XL and 90 = XC). The numbers 400 and 900 are shown by putting the letter *C* before the letter *D* or *M* (400 = CD and 900 = CM).

❑ Use the chart and write the Roman numerals for the numbers 1 to 10, 50, 100, and 1,000 on a separate sheet of paper.

❑ Then try the numbers 25, 54, 110, and 1,050.

❑ See if you can write the year in which you were born in Roman numerals!

Arabic	1	5	10	50	100	500	1,000
Roman	I	V	X	L	C	D	M

Investigating Feudal Europe in the Middle Ages

*Social studies is best enjoyed as a series of interesting
stories about real people and events!*

OBJECTIVE	BACKGROUND	MATERIALS
To help your student understand life and cultural growth in the Middle Ages	Although the Middle Ages isn't usually considered a time of growth for civilization, in reality much progress was made in education, architecture, literature, and law. Because the political system of the time was so different from the one we know today, we can learn from studying its structure. In this lesson, your student will learn about the cultural and political history of the Middle Ages and explore the influence of the Middle Ages in our society today.	▪ Student Learning Pages 5.A–5.B ▪ 1 copy Venn Diagram, page 353

VOCABULARY

FEUDALISM, OR FEUDAL SYSTEM a political and social system based on land ownership

NOBLES people who helped protect and govern a kingdom

VASSAL a person who was given land to govern but was under the rule of a higher nobleman or lord

KNIGHT the son of a noble who went through special training in riding and weaponry

MAIL a protective body covering made of metal links and worn in battle

MANOR a piece of land that was farmed by peasants to support the manor lord

SERFS people who were bound to the land they worked on and subject to the rule of the landowner

GOTHIC ARCHITECTURE a style of architecture that began in Europe in the 1200s

MAGNA CARTA an important government agreement signed by King John of England that secured the rights of the noblemen and church leaders

Let's Begin

1   **INTRODUCE** Explain to the student that **feudalism** was a political and social system that formed in the Middle Ages after the end of Roman rule. The Middle Ages generally are thought to have occurred between the years 500–1500. Feudalism was based on the idea that all land belonged to a king. The king gave land to **nobles** who helped to protect and govern the kingdom. These nobles then gave land to soldiers. Someone who gave out land was called a lord, and a person who was

given land was called a **vassal.** A person could be both a lord and a vassal. The lowest type of vassal, whose land was too small to divide, was a **knight.** Refer to the chart below to learn about the expectations and training for knights. Compare the life of a knight-in-training to the life of a young person today.

Stage of Training	Expectations
1. Page	Learn religion, manners, and obedience; serve as a messenger on the manor
2. Squire	Learn to ride a horse and use weapons
3. Knight	Obey code of chivalry: be loyal to lords, defend the church, protect the weak, be polite to women

2 **DESCRIBE** Explain to your student that knights, lords, and kings in the Middle Ages wore armor when they went into battle. In 1055, knights wore simple cone-shaped helmets or hats. Their shirts were made of **mail,** which was composed of many overlapping small metal links. Under the mail, knights wore padded coats and caps. Over time, armor, weapons, and fighting methods changed. By the 1200s, the small cone-shaped helmet was replaced by a large iron one that covered the knight's head and face. A breastplate was added to protect the chest, and coverings for the shoulders (called pauldrons), the hands (gauntlets), and the legs (greaves) were added as well. A knight carried weapons into battle, including a sword, a dagger, and a battle ax. A knight might carry as much as 100 pounds of armor and weapons!

3 **DISTRIBUTE** Distribute Student Learning Page 5.A. Point out that later in the Middle Ages each knight painted a coat of arms on his clothes to show everyone who he was.

4 **EXPLAIN** Explain to your student that in the Middle Ages in Europe the governing control of the Roman Empire was gone. Tribes of people from the north, such as the Franks, the Anglo-Saxons, and the Vikings, began invading the land to the south. However, during the early Middle Ages there was much destruction, theft, and violence from invasions and civil wars. Government was not centralized but was organized into many small kingdoms. Ask, *How do you think the nobles protected and defended their kingdoms?* [built castles]

5 **RELATE AND ILLUSTRATE** Explain that most castles had high walls and were surrounded by a moat, or a ditch filled with water. A drawbridge was lowered to allow visitors to cross the moat. Castles were often built on hilltops or bends in rivers so they could be easily defended. The houses of the noble and all his household helpers were within the castle walls, while the homes of serfs were outside the walls. Inside the castle walls was a large, open area called a courtyard. The windows were small, and the floor of the dining room was often dirty and covered with straw. Food was cooked in another building and was cold when it reached the table. Invite your student to draw a picture of a castle that includes each element listed above. Then ask your student to imagine the inside of a castle and discuss. He or she might be surprised to find out that castles were dark and damp and had rather unpleasant living conditions.

6 **EXPLAIN AND DISCUSS** Explain that in the feudal system the land was divided into manors. A **manor** was a piece of land that was farmed by peasants to support the lord and his family. Almost everything needed by the family was either made or grown on the manor grounds. Most peasants lived on manors as **serfs.** Serfs were people who were not free to move from the manor on which they were born, but they weren't bought and sold like slaves. They did all the farmwork as well as other work that needed to be done on the manor. Encourage your student to research the life of the serfs. Discuss.

7 **COMPARE AND CONTRAST** Explain to your student that one area of progress in the Middle Ages was architecture. With your student, look at some pictures of Romanesque architecture, which was used until about 1100. Point out that the windows are small, the walls are thick, and there are large rounded arches. This type of architecture made the castles and churches of this time dark and gloomy. Now look at some examples of **Gothic architecture.** This style began being used around 1200. In this style, the arches are pointed up and the windows are larger. Narrow, heavy ribs of stone support the roof. The walls are thinner and supported by outside braces called flying buttresses. Ask, *What do you think was a main reason for the change in architecture?* [civilizations became more stable and there was less need to make buildings into fortresses]

8 **EXPLAIN AND COMPARE** Tell your student that in the Middle Ages schools were opened in monasteries to prepare boys to become monks or priests. The towns where these schools were located became important learning centers. The students studied seven subjects in these schools: Latin grammar, rhetoric (the art of speaking and writing), logic (figuring things out), arithmetic, geometry, astronomy, and music. As the years passed, the number of subjects increased until universities were founded in the 1200s. Ask, *How does this compare to what you have studied? Do you learn about some of the same subjects?*

DID YOU KNOW?

Life was hard for students in the Middle Ages. Classes lasted 10 hours a day, and lazy or poor students weren't treated fairly.

DID YOU KNOW?

Throughout English history there has only been one King John, who signed the Magna Carta. They called John an unlucky king, and people's opinion of King John has been so low that no other English king has ever been named John!

FOR FURTHER READING

A Knight and His Armor, by R. Ewart Oakeshott (Dufour Editions, 1999).

Life in a Medieval Castle, by Gary L. Blackwood (Lucent Books, 2001).

The Middle Ages, by Jane Shuter (Heinemann Library, 1999).

The Middle Ages: A Watts Guide for Children, William C. Jordan, ed. (F. Watts, 1999).

9   **REVEAL**   Reveal to your student that literature also blossomed during the Middle Ages. There were two main types of literature. One type was written in Latin and mostly consisted of essays on religion. The other type of literature was written in the language of the common people. One example of this type of literature is Geoffrey Chaucer's *Canterbury Tales.* Ask, *What might people of the future learn about us from today's literature?* Discuss.

10   **ASK AND COMPARE**   Ask your student to think about the judicial system in our country. Talk about the main components of our system. [judge, jury, witnesses, lawyers] List these components in a notebook. Explain to your student that many parts of our legal system today began in the Middle Ages. King Henry II, who ruled from 1154 to 1189, introduced the use of a jury in English courts.

11   **RELATE AND DISCUSS**   Relate the story of King John and the **Magna Carta** to your student. John became king of England in the early 1200s when his brother, a great king, died. The nobles and church leaders did not respect King John and believed he was not a strong enough leader to have so much power.

    In 1215, the nobles decided to join together. They told King John that if he didn't grant them certain rights they would declare war on him. King John agreed to the terms of the nobles and signed a document called the Magna Carta. This document gave rights to the nobles and church leaders that would never be taken away. This was the beginning of the modern-day principle that no one, even the highest ruler, is above the law. For this reason, the Magna Carta is considered one of the most important documents of English history. Ask why it is important that political leaders follow the law.

Branching Out

TEACHING TIP

If possible, visit a museum exhibit about the Middle Ages or a theater reenactment from the Middle Ages. After studying this lesson, your student will better appreciate and understand the material. Take time to discuss his or her experience and reference the information in the lesson.

CHECKING IN

You can assess your student's progress by asking him or her to give you a verbal overview of what it was like to live in feudal society. You can prompt him or her with questions from the lessons. Then ask your student to tell you about one or two important areas of growth or new ideas that were part of the Middle Ages.

Design a Coat of Arms

Suppose you live in the Middle Ages. Design your own coat of arms to represent yourself and let other people know who you are. Then, on a separate sheet of paper, describe what you drew and why. Share your coat of arms with an adult and, if you like, display it somewhere in your room for other people to see.

What's Next? You Decide!

Now it's your turn to choose what to do next in the lesson.
Read the activities and decide which one you want to do—
you may want to try them both!

Study Representations of Knights

MATERIALS

❑ 3–4 magazines or books

STEPS

❑ Look in magazines or books for pictures of knights.

❑ Compare them to the description of knights and armor that you learned about. Are the pictures realistic? Why or why not?

❑ Then examine what the uniform is for the armed forces today.

❑ Choose your favorite uniform and draw a picture of it.

❑ Then identify each component of the uniform, giving its importance and history.

❑ Give an oral presentation sharing your information.

Look Closely at Gothic Architecture

MATERIALS

❑ 1 pair scissors

❑ glue

❑ 20–30 craft sticks

❑ 2–3 brown paper grocery bags

STEPS

The cathedral of Notre Dame in Paris, France, is a famous example of Gothic architecture that we can still see and visit today. It's large enough to hold 9,000 people!

❑ Look in the library for books or on the Internet for pictures and descriptions of Notre Dame.

❑ Compare the information to what you have learned about Gothic architecture. Do you agree that it's a good example? Why or why not?

❑ Now make a list of significant details about Notre Dame.

❑ Then build the cathedral using the sticks for support and the brown paper cut into the shapes you want. Remember to include examples of Gothic architecture.

Investigating the Church and the Rise of Monarchies

One can never foresee the extent of the effects he or she will have on others, and a country may never anticipate the full effects of its actions on its own or other countries.

OBJECTIVE	BACKGROUND	MATERIALS
To help your student understand how events in history are interrelated	Throughout history, politics and government have often been closely tied to religion. In this lesson, your student will learn about the influence of the Christian Church in these changing times and the rise and fall of monarchies.	■ Student Learning Pages 6.A–6.B

VOCABULARY
PILGRIMAGES long trips to places that have religious importance to the travelers
CRUSADES a series of wars fought by the Christian Church to win the Holy Land
NATIONALISM a sense of loyalty to and feelings of superiority for one's own nation

Let's Begin

1 **DESCRIBE THE SETTING** Explain to your student that after the fall of the Roman Empire the church became the only strong and united force in Europe. Religious orders of monks and nuns took care of the sick and homeless, taught farming methods to local farmers, and supplied teachers to new towns. The church also worked to preserve the knowledge and writings from the history of Greece and Rome. Monks and nuns spent many hours in libraries copying classical works. Since printing was not yet invented, each book had to be copied by hand. Ask your student to think about who is responsible for taking care of such tasks in modern society. Share with your student one example of a modern-day project: the production of an illustrated, handwritten Bible. (Go to http://www.saintjohn'sbible.org for more information about this.) Discuss.

2 **EXPLAIN THE CRUSADES** Reveal that during the Middle Ages many Christians began to go on **pilgrimages.** Mostly they visited Palestine, which was considered the Holy Land because it was where Jesus lived. Many Christian pilgrims visited

Palestine until 1071, when a new group took Palestine and became violent against the Christians. In 1095, Pope Urban II called for a holy war to claim Palestine. Have your student research the **Crusades**. Invite your student to make a chart of the positive and negative effects of the Crusades. Discuss.

3 DISTRIBUTE AND DISCUSS Distribute Student Learning Page 6.A. Take time to discuss your student's answers to the questions.

4 REVEAL AND DISCUSS Reveal that for many years the land around the eastern Mediterranean Sea was controlled by a civilization called the Byzantine Empire. Its capital, Constantinople, was founded by Rome's first Christian emperor, Constantine. Constantinople was unique. It was a Christian city but people from many different religions and backgrounds also lived there. Have your student research the Byzantine Empire. Ask him or her to find out about the goals of Constantine and why the empire eventually ended. Discuss.

5 ELABORATE Explain that in 862, during the growth of Constantinople, Russia was founded. Its capital city was Kiev, which was an important trading link between Europe and Asia. It was also located at the center of another trade route between Scandinavia and the Middle East. Have a conversation with your student about the role Kiev played in the growth of trade in Europe and the Middle East.

6 EXAMINE Remind your student that it wasn't until the end of the Middle Ages that nations began to form and people became more aware of common languages, cultures, and geography. Feelings of **nationalism** began to grow and countries sought to be more powerful than others. Ask your student to consider how nationalism affected people's attitudes toward their government, other countries, and the wars they fought.

Branching Out

FOR FURTHER READING

Joan of Arc, by Diane Stanley (Morrow Junior Books, 1998).

Crusades: The Struggle for the Holy Lands, by Chris Rice, Peter Dennis, Melanie Rice, Christopher Gravett, and Richard Platt (DK Publishing, 2001).

TEACHING TIP

As you progress through this lesson, periodically refer to a modern-day map of Europe and discuss with your student the different changes that have taken place.

CHECKING IN

To assess your student's learning, have him or her create a time line of the Middle Ages. This will also help organize the wide range of information in this lesson.

Study and Compare Maps

Study the map and then answer the questions.

1. Name three present-day countries whose land was part of the Holy Roman Empire.

   _____

2. Name the bodies of water that bordered the Holy Roman Empire.

   _____

3. Based on this map, what are the differences and similarities among the three Crusades?

   _____

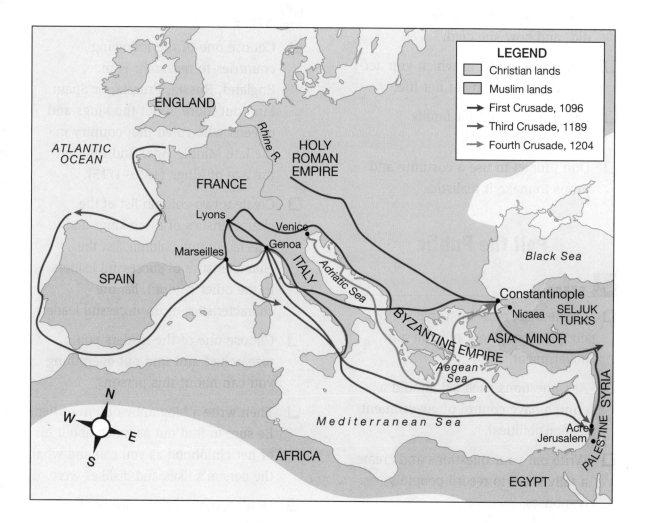

What's Next? You Decide!

Now it's your turn to choose what to do next in the lesson.
Read the activities and decide which one you want to do—
you may want to try them all!

Reenact the Story of Joan of Arc

STEPS

❑ Research the life of Joan of Arc, a young French woman who led the French army in a war against England.

❑ Find out how she became a leader, what motivated her to do what she did, and how she died.

❑ Write a short skit in which you act out important parts of her life.

❑ Perform your skit for family members or friends.

❑ Don't forget to use a costume and props to make it realistic.

Poll the Public

STEPS

❑ Create a list of at least five *yes* or *no* questions about religion and government.

❑ Ask questions such as: Should a church have control of government responsibilities?

❑ Write out your questions and create a tally sheet to record people's responses.

❑ Ask your family members, friends, and people in your community or at church. Try to poll at least 10 people.

❑ Then add up the totals and create a graph or chart to show the outcome.

❑ Share your work with an adult.

Write a Biography

STEPS

❑ Choose one of the following countries to research: France, England, Russia, Prussia, or Spain. Find out more about the kings and queens who ruled that country in the late Middle Ages and through the age of kings (1519–1715).

❑ Create a two-column list of the characteristics of these kings and queens. In one column, list the characteristics of successful leaders. In the other column, list the characteristics of unsuccessful leaders.

❑ Choose one of the leaders you researched and find out everything you can about this person.

❑ Then write a biography of him or her. Be sure to find out as much about his or her childhood as you can and what the person's likes and dislikes were.

❑ Don't forget to give your book a title!

Exploring the Beginnings of Modern Society

Rediscovering the past can help create a path to the future.

OBJECTIVE	BACKGROUND	MATERIALS
To help your student understand the origins and growth of the European Renaissance	The Renaissance began after the Middle Ages, around 1350. It was a gradual change, as centers of learning began to spring up in the city-states of Italy. The new learning led to advances in art, literature, science, and philosophy. We can trace the origins of much of modern society back to this period. In this lesson, your student will learn about the origins, geography, art, and daily life of the European Renaissance.	■ Student Learning Pages 7.A–7.B ■ 1 copy Comparison Chart, page 353

VOCABULARY

RENAISSANCE a "rebirth" of learning, art, and culture that occurred in Europe from 1350 to 1600

CITY-STATES cities and the areas around them, with their own government

PLAGUE a disease that makes a lot of people sick and often kills them

HUMANISM a way of thinking that puts importance on having a happy life

MIDDLE AGES the period of European history from the fall of the Roman Empire in 476 to the beginning of the Renaissance (1350–1500, depending on the country)

REPUBLIC a type of government consisting of elected officials that represent the people

SONNET a 14-line poem that uses a set rhyming and verse pattern and focuses on a single idea

Let's Begin

1 **EXPLAIN** Explain that ***Renaissance*** (ren-uh-SAHNTS) is a French word that means "rebirth." We use this term to describe the series of changes in life in southern and western Europe from about 1350 to 1600. These changes generally began in the **city-states** of Italy and spread west and north to Spain, France, the Low Countries, the German states, and England. Ask, *What do you know about the Renaissance?*

2 **RESEARCH AND COMPARE** Mention that the Black Death, a **plague** that killed millions of people in Europe, began in 1348 and lasted until around 1400. It caused major economic and social changes. People didn't know what caused the plague.

Until about 150 years ago, people had various ideas about what caused illness and plagues such as the Black Death. Have your student research the Black Death. Then ask, *What did people think caused it then, and what do they think caused it now?*

Introduce your student to three modern "plagues": the flu (influenza) epidemic at the end of World War I; polio, which was widely feared until the 1950s; and AIDS. Have your student research one of them. Then ask, *Which do you think was worse, the Black Death or the modern plague you researched? Why?*

3 **EXAMINE** Have your student look over the map of Italy from 1490. Help him or her pronounce the names of the various city-states. Then have him or her find a map of Italy in a contemporary atlas. Ask, *What kind of map will you look for: geographical, topographical, or political?* [political] Have your student compare the borders of 1490 with Italy today. Ask, *Is Italy larger or smaller today?* Discuss other similarities and differences between the maps.

4 **DISTRIBUTE** Distribute Student Learning Page 7.A. Tell your student that the clues in the crossword puzzle test his or her knowledge of the Renaissance. All the answers can be found in the material covered in the lesson. He or she can fill in the answers while going through the lesson or wait until the end to work on it.

DID YOU KNOW?

Even today, someone who knows a lot about many different things is called a Renaissance man or woman. In the Renaissance, a well-educated person—usually a man—was skilled in more than one area. He had a knowledge of what we call "the classics," especially ancient Greek and Roman writings as well as art, science, philosophy, and government.

5 **EXPLAIN AND COMPARE** Explain that the arrival of the Renaissance was marked by a new way of thinking called **humanism.** Humanists looked toward Rome and also Greece for inspiration and discovered a common point of view: the importance of living life for its own sake and enjoying the pleasures it has to offer. Distribute a copy of the Comparison Chart found on page 353. Then have your student research and compare attitudes in ancient Greece and Rome and during the Renaissance with those of the **Middle Ages.** Ask him or her to compare at least three things, such as the role of religion, the importance of learning, and the place of art and literature.

6 **DESCRIBE AND DISCUSS** Describe the city of Florence at the height of the Renaissance. It was a rich city because of its role

in the cloth industry and was a leading center of art. Tell your student that Florence was also one of the few places in its time with a government that was a **republic;** that is, its leaders were elected. Have your student search the Internet for information on Florence's government. Ask, *In what ways did the government of Florence during the Renaissance differ from that of the United States, which we also call a republic?* Then ask, *Who controlled the elections in Florence and who could vote?* Discuss.

7 **REVEAL AND WRITE** Michelangelo—one of the most important artists of the Renaissance—was born in 1475 near Florence. He had a strong desire to become a sculptor, but his father was bitterly against it. The ruler of Florence, Lorenzo de Medici, convinced Michelangelo's father to let him study. Have your student read a biographical article of Michelangelo. Discuss the book when your student has finished reading it.

8 **PREDICT** Have your student look at a geographical/topographical map of Europe. Ask, *Predict to where the Renaissance first spread from Italy.* [France] *Why?* [because it shared a coastline] *How do you think ideas and goods were most likely spread during this time?* [by water and primitive roads] *What physical features might slow down the spread of culture?* [mountains, forests, other rough land]

9 **DISCUSS AND COMPARE** Explain that art became very important during the Renaissance. Artists made their art lifelike and chose subjects of classical interest. Renaissance art was different from the art of the Middle Ages, which mostly involved religion and wasn't "realistic." Have your student look through an art book from the library that has paintings from the Middle Ages and the Renaissance. Have him or her compare a Madonna painting by Raphael with a painting from the Middle Ages. Then examine works by Michelangelo, Donatello, and Leonardo da Vinci.

10 **DIRECT AND WRITE** Explain that writing also changed a lot during the Renaissance. An important form of poetry was the **sonnet,** a 14-line poem that expresses one idea. Have your student find sonnets by Petrarch, an Italian Renaissance poet, and choose one or more to read. Then read sonnets together by William Shakespeare, who wrote in England in the late 1500s and early 1600s. Reveal to your student the differences between the Italian and English sonnet: the Italian sonnet is broken down into a group of eight lines followed by a group of six lines with the rhyming *abbaabba cdecde.* The Shakespearean sonnet is three groups of four lines each, followed by one grouping of two lines. The rhyme scheme here is *abab cdcd efef gg.* Discuss at least one sonnet. Ask, *What is the sonnet about? Who is the speaker? To whom is it addressed? What images does the poet use to make observations or express feelings?* Then have your student try writing a sonnet by following the list of questions above to get started.

DID YOU KNOW?

A popular cartoon action-figure series of the late 1980s and early 1990s was *Teenage Mutant Ninja Turtles.* The turtle heroes had the names Donatello, Leonardo, Michelangelo, and Raphael—after four important artists of the Italian Renaissance.

11 **OBSERVE AND DISCUSS** For more exploration, go to Lesson 1.6 to read *Romeo and Juliet* by Shakespeare. You also can borrow or rent a video or DVD of one of Shakespeare's plays. You may want to preview the video before watching it with your student to be sure the content is appropriate. Remind your student that in Shakespeare's time all theater was experienced live. After you have seen the play, discuss the plot, setting, characters, and theme as you would with a story or novel.

Branching Out

TEACHING TIP

Whenever possible, use photos of paintings (especially ones that show clothing people wore and daily activities), sculptures, buildings, and everyday objects to provide a strong visual context for Renaissance life. You may also want to visit a museum Renaissance exhibit with your student.

CHECKING IN

You can assess your student's understanding of the origins and growth of the Renaissance by having him or her create a time line. Based on this lesson and the research he or she completed, have him or her identify the major events of the time period and the years when and places where important artists and writers lived.

FOR FURTHER READING

The Art of the Renaissance, by Lucia Corrain; L. R. Galante and Simone Boni, ills. (Peter Bedrick Books, 2001).

Eyewitness: Renaissance, by Alison Cole (DK Publishing, 2000).

Leonardo da Vinci, by Diane Stanley (HarperCollins, 2000).

Michelangelo, by Diane Stanley (HarperCollins, 2000).

Explore the Beginnings of Modern Society

Read the clues and complete the crossword puzzle about life in the Renaissance.

Across

1. Famous ceiling painter
6. Artist-inventor, ideal Renaissance man
9. Meaning of *renaissance*
10. Great English writer of plays and sonnets
11. Plague in the 1300s

Down

1. Period before the Renaissance
2. Renaissance movement of ideas
3. Important city in Renaissance Italy
4. Last name of ruler of Florence
5. One of a number of areas in Renaissance Italy
7. Renaissance ideas came from Greeks and _____
8. Sonnet writer in Renaissance Italy

What's Next? You Decide!

Now it's your turn to choose what to do next in the lesson. Read the activities and decide which one you want to do— you may want to try them all!

You're a Sculptor, Too

MATERIALS

- ❑ modeling clay
- ❑ several "sculpting" tools, such as a plastic knife or spoon
- ❑ 1 small bowl water

STEPS

- ❑ Choose a subject for your sculpture, such as famous statue or your pet. Work from a picture or real life.
- ❑ Follow the directions on the package of modeling clay.
- ❑ Use your hands and tools to shape your sculpture.
- ❑ Smooth its surface by wetting it with water and going over it lightly with the plastic knife.
- ❑ When you are finished, sign your sculpture with your name.
- ❑ Display it so that others will see it.

What I Did During the Plague

STEPS

You're living in Florence during the Black Death. Your best friend's family has decided to leave the city to avoid getting sick, but your family is staying.

Your father is an important person who feels he can't leave his duties.

- ❑ Get a friend or a family member to play the part of your Renaissance friend.
- ❑ Write at least three pairs of letters or e-mails telling what your daily lives are like during this dreadful period.
- ❑ Describe the sights, sounds, smells, and so on.
- ❑ Tell how you and the people you know feel about what's going on.

Become an Art Critic

MATERIALS

- ❑ 1 photo of a favorite Renaissance drawing, painting, or sculpture
- ❑ colored pencils

STEPS

Select a piece of art by a Renaissance artist. Why do you like it? How does it make you feel?

- ❑ Decide what you would like to tell a person about the artwork.
- ❑ Write a paragraph telling about this piece of art.
- ❑ Then draw a sketch of the artwork you selected, using the style of the Renaissance.

Investigating the Causes and Effects of the Reformation

The events of today will impact history forever.

OBJECTIVE	BACKGROUND	MATERIALS
To help your student understand the events that led up to and followed the Reformation	The revolution in the 1500s within the Christian Church is referred to as the Reformation. During this time period, which followed the Renaissance, reformers such as Martin Luther and John Calvin promoted change. Some of these changes still exist today, and have also affected how religion is studied and discussed today. The outcomes consisted of much more than church reform. Many European regions gained political and/or religious independence, and the world became more open to modern capitalism and democracy. In this lesson, your student will learn the true impact of the Reformation.	■ Student Learning Pages 8.A–8.B

VOCABULARY

DEMOCRACY a political system in which the people rule

CAPITALISM an economic system in which private businesses make and exchange goods and services

INDEPENDENCE freedom from unwanted authority

REFORM to change

Let's Begin

1 **DISCUSS** Discuss with your student the impact one person or a group of people can have on history. Ask, *How could one person make a difference?* Ask him or her if he or she knows what democracy, capitalism, and independence are. Ask, *Are these good things? Why? When and where did these things begin?* Does he or she think one person came up with these ideas, or was it a group of people? Discuss. While discussing, remind your student that **democracy, capitalism,** and **independence** are why the United States fought against Great Britain years ago.

2 **EXPLAIN** Explain to your student that Reformation was a change in the structure of the Christian Church. Before the Reformation, the church and the political rulers shared power. After the Reformation, the power was distributed more evenly and many branches of the Christian religion, such as Protestantism and one

of its own branches, Lutheranism, were developed. The Council of Trent was the official committee that reformed the church. Mention that Martin Luther, John Calvin, and others promoted this change, which led to major **reform** outside the church as well.

Talk about how the connection between the church and government meant that if one had to change, so did the other. This meant changes in many areas of life for the people in Europe. Ask, *What kinds of changes do you think would have to happen?* Have your student make a list of changes. Then have him or her search the library or Internet for information on the Reformation and see if the changes he or she wrote happened.

3 **CONNECT AND COMPARE** Review the prior knowledge your student has of the events leading to the Reformation. Discuss the Renaissance and the changes that occurred during this time period. Ask, *Who and what does he or she believe was responsible for this?* Connect and compare the Renaissance to the Reformation. Ask, *What do they have in common?* [change, new ideas] *Why might the Reformation have followed the Renaissance?* [people were beginning to think about things in a new way, including religion] If you haven't completed Lesson 4.7 on the Renaissance, discuss how the United States won its independence from Great Britain. Then connect and compare the Reformation to the U.S. quest for independence.

4 **RESEARCH** Have your student then research information about the causes and the effects of the Reformation. Also, highlight or note important information about Martin Luther and John Calvin.

5 **DISTRIBUTE AND CHART** Distribute Student Learning Page 8.A. Using the research notes from Step 4, have your student complete the questions. Then discuss.

6 **VISUALIZE** Have your student locate a map from the time period. Photocopy the map so that your student can write on it. Have your student mark the places where the Reformation took place. Then discuss.

Branching Out

TEACHING TIP

Note that much of the reading material on this topic may be difficult for your child to read and understand independently. You might need to read along with him or her.

CHECKING IN

You can check for your student's understanding by having him or her create a time line of events relating to the Reformation.

FOR FURTHER READING

The Adventures of Martin Luther, by Carolyn Bergt (Concordia Publishing House, 1999).

Martin Luther: The Great Reformer, by Edwin P. Booth and Dan Harmon (Chelsea House, 1998).

The River of Grace: The Story of John Calvin, by Joyce B. McPherson and Jennifer B. Robinson, ill. (Greenleaf Press, 1999).

Identify the Causes and Effects of the Reformation

Read and answer the questions.

1. Name two causes of the Reformation and explain how they led to changes.

_____

_____

_____

_____

2. Name two important outcomes (effects) of the Reformation and explain how they affect modern life.

_____

_____

_____

_____

Now read your local newspaper and find a reform, or change, that someone or group would like made in your community and find its causes and effects. An example would be lowered speed limits. The causes, or reasons, for the reform could be because people have gotten hurt from speeding cars. The effects could be less injuries. You might have to read the Letters to the Editor section or Opinions page. Then write a newspaper article outlining your opinions about the reform. Do you think the reform is a good idea? Write the causes and effects here before beginning your article.

Reform: _____

Causes:

_____

_____

Effects:

_____

_____

What's Next? You Decide!

Now it's your turn to choose what to do next in the lesson.
Read the activities and decide which one you want to do—
you may want to try them all!

Become a Reformer/Activist

MATERIALS

❑ 1 posterboard
❑ markers or paints

STEPS

❑ Think of something you would like to change around you.

❑ Make a list of all the things that need to change about it and why they need to change. Be sure you have good reasons to support your ideas.

❑ Next, create a plan for how you would go about getting this change to take place. Think about the people in charge. Try using posters, flyers, petitions, and written persuasion like that of Martin Luther.

❑ Finally, follow through on your plan and see what happens.

Hold a Friendly Debate

MATERIALS

❑ 1 copy Venn Diagram, page 353

STEPS

❑ Read about two important people from the Reformation, Martin Luther and John Calvin.

❑ Make a copy of the Venn Diagram found on page 353. Compare and contrast the two people and their ideas.

❑ Then choose which reformer you'd like to be and, with a friend as the other person, hold a debate.

❑ Have another friend be the moderator and go through the points on the Venn Diagram. Remember to be courteous in this friendly debate.

Make a Wall-to-Wall Time Line

MATERIALS

❑ 10 feet rope or string
❑ 20 clothespins
❑ 20 index cards
❑ 1 timer

STEPS

❑ Research the history of democracy or capitalism and create a time line showing how it came about and changed over time.

❑ Write each event on an index card.

❑ Then tie the rope to two pieces of furniture. (Get permission first!)

❑ Put the cards in order and attach them to the rope with the clothespins.

❑ Be a tour guide and walk through the time line with an adult.

❑ Then take the cards down and shuffle them. See how fast you can hang the cards in order.

Exploring the Seas, the Skies, and the Mind

Expanding your awareness expands your world.

OBJECTIVE	BACKGROUND	MATERIALS
To help your student understand the scientific revolution, the Age of Exploration, and the Enlightenment in Europe	From the 1500s to the 1700s, the European view of the world changed on many levels. Explorers journeyed to the Americas for the first time, scientists proved that Earth revolved around the sun, and new ideas about government and people's rights were introduced. In this lesson, your student will develop an understanding of the historical events of this period and how they helped shape the world today.	■ Student Learning Pages 9.A–9.B ■ colored pencils ■ 1 copy Web, page 354

VOCABULARY

LOGIC a system of reasoning

GEOMETRY a type of math that studies the relationship between lines, angles, and shapes

THEORY an educated guess, or hypothesis, about how something works

HERETIC a person whose opinions are different or opposite than those of official religious beliefs

CONQUISTADORES the name given to Spanish explorers who conquered new lands and people

ENCOMIENDA the system in which Native Americans were forced to work for the Spanish

ABSOLUTE POWER a system of rule where people do not have the opportunity to question or challenge authority

ENLIGHTENMENT the historical time during the late 1600s and 1700s called the Age of Reason

Let's Begin

1 **EXPLAIN** Explain to your student that the scientific method was created in the 1620s by English scientist Francis Bacon. For more information on the scientific method, see Lesson 3.6. Remind him or her that the scientific method outlines a series of steps to follow to investigate the truth of a theory or an idea. The steps are hypothesis, experiment, observation, and conclusion. This new way of testing old and new ideas and using logic created an important shift in the nature of scientific discovery. Before the scientific method, much of what people believed to be true about the world came from accepted ideas that were passed down from previous generations.

2 **COMPARE** Have your student search the library or Internet for a drawing of the universe according to Ptolemy (TAHL-uh-mee) and one according to Nicolaus Copernicus and Johannes (yo-HAHN-iss) Kepler. The universe according to Ptolemy, an Egyptian astronomer in A.D. 150, shows Earth as the center of the universe. The other illustration shows the universe according to a Polish churchman named Copernicus. Explain to your student that his theory that Earth revolved around the sun started a long debate between scientists and the Catholic Church, which said that Earth was the center of the universe. Have your student research the work of Ptolemy, Copernicus, and the German scientist Kepler and compare the theories of each. Ask, *Which of these scientists' theories were in agreement?* [Copernicus and Kepler] *How did they develop their theories?* [Copernicus used logic and geometry, Kepler used theory and observation] Discuss.

3 **DESCRIBE AND RESEARCH** Tell your student about the life of Galileo Galilei (gal-luh-LAY-oh gal-luh-LAY), an Italian mathematician, astronomer, and physicist who is considered to be the father of experimental science. He was a very important supporter of Copernicus's theory. He set out to understand nature by performing experiments and taking careful measurements. He was the first person to see the surface of the moon and observe the moons of the planet Jupiter through a telescope. Many of his discoveries contradicted the long-accepted beliefs of his time. Have your student find a biography of Galileo on the Internet. Ask, *What happened to Galileo because of his ideas and discoveries?* [he was put on trial by the church, condemned as a heretic, and sentenced to house arrest]

4 **EXPLAIN AND RESEARCH** Tell your student that Isaac Newton was born in 1642, the year Galileo died. Living in England, he didn't have to worry that his scientific findings would land him in prison. Explain to your student that by the time he was grown most scientists agreed with Copernicus, Kepler, and Galileo that the sun was at the center of the solar system. Newton made many new scientific discoveries. The two that he is best known for are the theory of the gravitational pull of the universe and the discovery that sunlight is made up of all the colors of the rainbow. Have your student look up Newton's laws of motion. Read them together and discuss what they mean.

5 **COMPARE** Have your student research and find a map of the world as imagined by Christopher Columbus before his first voyage in 1492 and then compare it to a current world map. Ask, *What are the differences between what Columbus believed and what we know now?* [the size and shape of Earth, that North and South America existed] *How did that affect his voyages?* [he thought he had a shorter distance to travel from Spain to Asia]

6 **DISTRIBUTE AND EXPLAIN** Distribute Student Learning Page 9.A. Explain that during the 1500s and 1600s many European explorers traveled to parts of the world that were previously unknown to them. They usually were looking for better trade opportunities and new land to claim for their country. Have him or her complete the page. Then ask, *What was each explorer searching for? Which explorers went first and which built on knowledge of earlier explorers?* Discuss.

7 **RESEARCH AND COMPARE** Tell your student that people had created advanced civilizations in Central and South America before important explorers such as Francisco Pizarro and Hernando Cortés arrived in the 1500s. The Olmec, the Maya, and the Aztec lived in what we now call Mexico. A group of people called the Incas lived in the areas of Peru, Ecuador, and northern Chile. Have your student search the Internet or at the library for information about each of these four civilizations. Have him or her copy the Web found on page 354 four times in his or her notebook. He or she will use this to organize the research. The name of each civilization goes in the center rectangles. The characteristics of each civilization can be listed and organized in the outside ovals. Have your student include information about the time period, geographical location, type of architecture, religious practices, occupations, diet, and other aspects of daily life. Ask, *What are the similarities and differences among the four civilizations?* Discuss.

?
DID YOU KNOW?

The Olmec, the Maya, the Aztec, and the Inca all built temple pyramids. They differ from one another and from the pyramids that the Egyptians built.

8 **REVEAL AND DISCUSS** Tell your student that Cortés and Pizarro were Spanish explorers who landed in what we now know as Mexico and Peru. Have him or her review the routes of their voyages. Explain to him or her that the desire of the Spanish **conquistadores** for wealth, and their mission to spread Christianity, led to many hardships for the native people they encountered. Have your student research what happened when they met the native people of the Americas. Ask him or her to find out about the **encomienda.** Ask, *Why did so many natives die after the Europeans landed?* [lack of immunity to European dieases, forced labor in dangerous conditions] Discuss.

+
ENRICH THE EXPERIENCE

Help your student investigate the European artists and composers of the early to mid-1700s. Collect CDs or cassette tapes from the library with music by Bach, Handel, or Scarlatti, who all wrote during this period, and play them at home during your lesson or leisure time. Find art books with works by Chardin, Hogarth, Tiepolo, or Watteau. Encourage your student to identify any connections between the art and music and the thoughts and beliefs of the Enlightenment.

9 **EXPLAIN** Tell your student that in 1651 a man named Thomas Hobbes published a book called *Leviathan*. In his book he argued that the best kind of government was a government where the ruler had **absolute power,** like a king. Soon after that, another new wave of thought began in Europe called the **Enlightenment,** or the Age of Reason. Explain to your student that the themes of the Enlightenment centered around better government and political, religious, and economic freedom. The famous thinkers of this time disagreed with Hobbes. They were John Locke and three Frenchmen: Baron de Montesquieu, Jean-Jacques Rousseau, and François Arouet, who called himself Voltaire.

10 **RESEARCH AND CONNECT** Have your student gather information about the ideas of Locke, Montesquieu, Rousseau, and Voltaire. Ask him or her to create a Comparison Chart like

the one found on page 353 to list the main ideas of these thinkers. Ask, *Can you find the ideas and beliefs from the Enlightenment that have become a part of today's democratic societies?* Discuss.

Branching Out

TEACHING TIP

Maps are important for giving your student a knowledge of where—and sometimes why—things take place. Use them as often as possible to find the location of events that your student is researching and that you are discussing.

CHECKING IN

You can assess your student's understanding of the importance of the discoveries of science and exploration during the period 1492–1720 by having him or her keep a "where and when chart." Based on this lesson and the research he or she has completed, have him or her identify the year and the country of origin of an important scientific discovery or a new exploration. Your student can organize the information on a time line, a map of Europe, or as a list by country.

FOR FURTHER READING

The Age of Exploration, by Sarah Flowers (Lucent Books, 1999).

Around the World in a Hundred Years: From Henry the Navigator to Magellan, by Jean Fritz (Paper Star, 1998).

Christopher Columbus and the Age of Exploration in World History, by Al Sundel (Enslow Publishers, Inc., 2002).

The Enlightenment (World History Series), by John M. Dunn (Lucent Books, 1999).

Eyewitness: Aztec, Inca, and Maya, by Elizabeth Baquedano (DK Publishing, 2000).

Galileo Galilei: Inventor, Astronomer, and Rebel, by Michael White (Blackbirch Marketing, 1999).

Isaac Newton: Discovering Laws That Govern the Universe, by Michael White (Blackbirch Marketing, 1999).

Trace the Routes of Important Explorers

Use this map to draw the routes of at least four prominent early explorers, such as Christopher Columbus, Vasco da Gama, Ferdinand Magellan, Hernando Cortés, Francisco Pizarro, Amerigo Vespucci, or Sir Frances Drake. Research their voyages and use different colored pencils to trace their routes. Label the routes with the name of the explorer, country of origin, and the approximate date of each journey. Then share your map with another person.

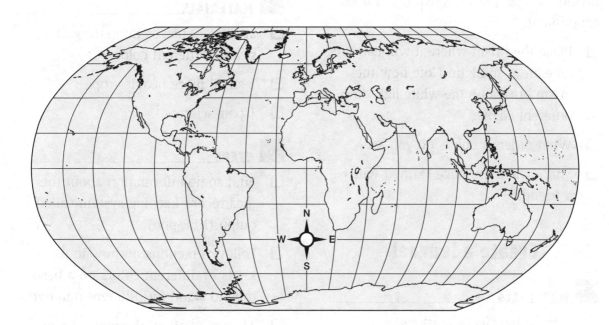

What's Next? You Decide!

Now it's your turn to choose what to do next in the lesson. Read the activities and decide which one you want to do—you may want to try them all!

Let in the Light

MATERIALS
- ❑ 1 glass prism or faceted crystal piece

STEPS

Follow the directions that come with a prism or those on an Internet site about prisms to repeat Isaac Newton's famous experiment.

- ❑ Place the prism where it will capture a beam of sunlight. Note how the prism breaks up the white light into different colors.

- ❑ What order of colors do you see?

- ❑ Share what you have learned with a friend.

Create a Journal

MATERIALS
- ❑ colored pencils or markers

STEPS
- ❑ Choose one of the Native American civilizations from the lesson and suppose you're growing up in that civilization.

- ❑ Create a journal of a period of at least a week.

- ❑ Tell about your daily life. Describe your family, friends, what you do

each day, and so on. Write about a special celebration, too.

- ❑ Illustrate your journal with pictures of people, places, and things. Then share your journal with a friend.

Learn the Ropes

MATERIALS
- ❑ at least 10 pieces thin string of several different colors

- ❑ 1 small piece heavier rope

- ❑ 1 pair scissors

STEPS
- ❑ Find some information about the Inca record-keeping system called quipu (KEE-poo).

- ❑ Follow directions on how to use knots of different colors on a base rope to stand for different numbers.

- ❑ Then read about the ways the Incas used quipu.

- ❑ Decide on something you would like to record. For example, it can be how many books you read during the week.

- ❑ Make a duplicate record with pencil and paper. When your recording period is done, compare your two records. Do they agree?

Tuning In to the Industrial Revolution

Not all revolutions overthrow governments.

OBJECTIVE	BACKGROUND	MATERIALS
To help your student understand how the Industrial Revolution brought western Europe and the United States into the modern era	During the Industrial Revolution, science, industry, and trade worked together to transform the farming and "cottage-trade" economies of nations to industry-driven economies. The modern countries we know today are a product of this revolution. This lesson will introduce the history of industrialization and capitalism and tell how it affected national economies and personal lifestyles.	■ Student Learning Pages 10.A–10.B ■ 1 copy Comparison Chart, page 353 ■ 1 set colored pencils ■ 1 pair scissors ■ 1 roll tape

VOCABULARY

NATURAL RESOURCES the materials from nature that can be used in the production of energy and goods

CAPITAL money that is invested to make more money

CAPITALISM an economic system in which individuals and companies own and control most of a country's means of production and wealth

ECONOMIC SYSTEM the way a country conducts its business and financial affairs

TEXTILE cloth

EXPORT a product that is shipped out of a country for trade

INTERCHANGEABLE PARTS manufactured parts that are made so exactly that they fit into all similar products the same way

LABOR UNION a group of workers who unite to make company owners improve working conditions

CANAL a human-made waterway built for transporting goods and travelers

Let's Begin

1 **EXPLAIN AND DISCUSS** Explain that England was the first nation to industrialize, beginning in the 1750s. In the 1800s, France industrialized followed by Germany. After the Civil War, in the 1870s the United States joined the strong industrial nations. Point out that for a country to develop an industrial economy, it needs three things: (1) **natural resources** such as steam power, water power from rivers, iron ore, wool from sheep, and cotton; (2) a workforce such as immigrant workers

or former farmers; and (3) **capital** (or money) from people who have already made money and are willing to risk investing in new businesses. Have your student research the industrialization of the United States. Ask, *What resources, workers, and capital was the United States able to draw on to industrialize in the 1800s?* [resources: lots of land, water, forests, mineral deposits, etc.; workers: immigrants; capital: the wealth of men such as Vanderbilt, Morgan, Rockefeller, Carnegie] Discuss.

2 **COMPARE** Tell your student that the Industrial Revolution led to the growth of **capitalism.** Capitalism is an **economic system** in which individuals and companies own and control most of a country's means of production and wealth. Before the Industrial Revolution in the 1800s, the church, nobles, and rulers controlled wealth. An important Scottish economist, Adam Smith, is known as the Father of Capitalism. He believed that if a country allowed its people to follow their own interests, they would work to better themselves. He said that competition without government interference would make products better and cheaper.

Have your student research this economic change and use a copy of the Comparison Chart found on page 353 to list the differences between the economic system before capitalism and during capitalism. Suggest categories to your student such as who controlled the means of production and wealth, who were the workers, and the locations and types of workplaces.

3 **RESEARCH AND WRITE** Distribute Student Learning Page 10.A. Tell your student that machines made large-scale industry possible. One of the first industries to be influenced by machines was the British **textile** industry. Between 1733 and 1800, machines led to the faster production of cloth. Have your student research how cloth was made previous to the invention of spinning machines. Have him or her write a sentence or two on how each of the following machines improved the process. Ask your student which of the machines he or she thinks was the most useful and why.

- John Kay's flying shuttle (1733)
- James Hargreaves's spinning jenny (1769)
- Richard Arkwright's water frame (1769)
- Samuel Crompton's spinning mule (1778)
- Eli Whitney's cotton gin (1793)

4 **RELATE AND DISCUSS** Explain that the nature and conditions of work changed after industrialization. Before industrialization, people worked at home at their own pace, work was slow and costly, products differed from one to another, and wood provided most of the power. After industrialization, people worked in a central factory with set hours and expectations about their productivity, all parts were the same, products were mass-produced on assembly lines, and coal was used for power more often. Have your student think of a type of product that he or she uses. Discuss how it's made and how industrialization benefits or doesn't benefit the manufacture of the product.

5 **EXPLAIN** Explain that although the factory system created more jobs for people and saved time and money, the working conditions were often poor and unhealthy. People moved into the cities and whole families worked long hours. Even young children worked long hours. Workers were not able to vote or form a **labor union** to protect themselves. Ask, *How many of these conditions still exist in some parts of the world today?* [all; although there are strict rules governing child labor, they're often ignored] Discuss.

6 **RELATE AND RESEARCH** Tell your student that when England began to industrialize it needed an efficient way to move supplies and goods around the country. In 1760, the first modern **canal** was dug in England. Coal could be shipped from the mines to the cities at less cost. By 1825, England had an excellent system of canals. That was the year that the Erie Canal opened in New York, connecting the Hudson River and New York City with Lake Erie. Ask, *Why was building a canal system in the United States harder than building one in England?* [the United States is larger; there are more mountains and forests] Ask your student to research the Suez or Panama Canals or the Chinese canal system, which was begun in ancient times. Have him or her write a short paragraph about the canal, and then talk about it together.

DID YOU KNOW?

Although for many years the Erie Canal hasn't been used for shipping, the canal still exists in many places across New York State. There are parks and historic areas you can visit along the canal. Tell your student that horses and mules on shore used to slowly pull barges through the canal!

7 **EXPLAIN AND INTERPRET** Explain that industrialized countries needed cost-efficient and reliable ways to transport materials. Canals were costly to dig and needed a water source. At that time roads were largely unpaved, so they often became impassable in wet weather. As steam engines became more powerful in the early 1800s, railroads provided the solution. Railroads grew quickly and became the most important form of transportation in England and the United States. In 1869, the United States completed the transcontinental railroad that ran from the east coast to the west coast of the country. By 1870, there were 53,000 miles of railroad in the United States. Have your student look up U.S. railroad mileage in an almanac or on the Internet. Ask him or her if the United States has more or less railroads today than in 1870.

8 **EXPLORE** Have your student consider what methods of commercial transportation are more popular today and why. Ask, *How can we determine the best way to transport materials within a country? By boat, truck, train, or plane?* [by considering the distance, geography, condition of roads, fuel costs, travel time, and so on] Discuss.

9 **REVEAL AND RESEARCH** During the 1800s, electricity became an important power source and led to new forms of communication. In 1844, the first message by Samuel F. B. Morse's electric telegraph was sent from Washington, D.C., to Baltimore, Maryland. Other important advances in communication through electricity came in

SOCIAL STUDIES

LESSON 4.10

the 1870s, including the telephone from Alexander Graham Bell and Thomas Edison's phonograph. Have your student research one of these inventions. Then have him or her write an outline of the story of the invention, including any earlier inventions upon which the inventor drew.

Branching Out

TEACHING TIP

In order to understand how an inventor or a scientist made a breakthrough, it's often important to be familiar with what he or she already knew from previous experiments. Stress the scientific and technological importance of innovators building on what has come before.

CHECKING IN

You can assess your student's understanding by having him or her suppose himself or herself to be a typical worker in the textile industry or the shipping industry at a certain time during the Industrial Revolution. Have your student tell what a typical workday and living conditions were like. He or she can answer questions or create a monologue to read or act out.

FOR FURTHER READING

Alexander Graham Bell: An Inventive Life, by Elizabeth MacLeod (Kid's Can Press, 1999).

Building the Transcontinental Railroad, by James Barter (Lucent Books, 2001).

Erie Canal (Building America Series), by Craig A. Doherty and Katherine M. Doherty (Blackbirch, 2001).

Thomas Alva Edison (Groundbreakers), by Brian Williams (Heinemann Library, 2000).

The Industrial Revolution (Cornerstones of Freedom), by Mary Collins (Children's Press, 2000).

Trace the Time Line of Invention

Turn this page so that the time line reads left to right. Complete the time line with important machine inventions from the 1760s to the 1870s. Include those that helped industrialization, transportation, and communication.

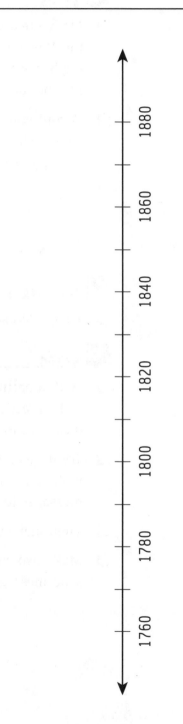

What's Next? You Decide!

Now it's your turn to choose what to do next in the lesson. Read the activities and decide which one you want to do— you may want to try them all!

Call All Workers

MATERIALS

- ❏ 1 posterboard
- ❏ colored pencils or markers
- ❏ glue
- ❏ 1 pair scissors

STEPS

- ❏ Choose an industry, a date between 1760 and 1880, and an industrialized country of the time.
- ❏ Design an ad for workers in the industry. Talk up the benefits of the job. Make the ad colorful and snappy. Use whatever pictures or illustrations you can to help you make your point.
- ❏ Share your poster with an adult.

Sing a Song

MATERIALS

- ❏ 1 cassette recorder
- ❏ 1 blank cassette tape
- ❏ sheet music or recordings of 1800s work songs
- ❏ instruments, background music, sound effects (optional)

STEPS

- ❏ Many great work songs came out of the 1800s. Look up some that you might have at home, or check the Internet or your library.
- ❏ Record your own versions of the songs. Think of fun ways to add music and sound effects.
- ❏ Play your recording for your family.

Use Morse Code

MATERIALS

- ❏ 1 copy Morse code letter symbols

STEPS

- ❏ With a partner, study the Morse code. Practice writing simple messages to each other.
- ❏ Try to read the messages without looking at the symbols. Tap out messages to each other on a table.
- ❏ Then make up your own code.
- ❏ Make two copies of the code and send messages to each other.

Understanding Contemporary Conflicts

*Neither a king nor a tyrant holds any power
if consent from the people isn't granted.*

OBJECTIVE	BACKGROUND	MATERIALS
To help your student understand nationalist movements and revolutions and their results	The United States was the first example of a European colony winning its independence. It would become the inspiration for other colonial revolutions and nationalist movements. In this lesson, your student will become familiar with the wars and revolutions of contemporary society and their effects.	■ Student Learning Pages 11.A–11.B ■ 1 present-day map of Europe ■ maps of Europe, Asia, and the Pacific during World War I and World War II

VOCABULARY

REVOLUTIONS   actions in which a government is overthrown and replaced by a new government

COLONIST   a person who lives in an area of the world controlled by another country

BOYCOTT   to refuse to trade or associate

NATIONALISM   the desire to support the interests of one's country, especially for self-rule

CZAR   a Russian king

PARLIAMENT   an elected group of people who make laws for a country

SOCIALIST   a person who believes in a system in which the government of a country controls or regulates most of the means of production

COMMUNIST   a person who believes in a system in which the government of a country has complete control of the economy

DICTATORSHIP   a government with an absolute ruler who is often cruel

AXIS   an imaginary line around which a planet or moon revolves

Let's Begin

1 **DISTRIBUTE** Distribute Student Learning Page 11.A. Tell your student that as you work your way through the lesson he or she will be using the chart to record and compare information about three very different **revolutions:** the American, the French, and the Russian. As you walk through each step, review the vocabulary words.

2 **EXPLAIN AND DISCUSS** Explain that a series of events led up to the American Revolution. The British were heavily taxing the

SOCIAL STUDIES

LESSON 4.11

American colonists without allowing them a representative in the body that levied the taxes, and the **colonists** protested. They dumped tea in Boston Harbor, and the British responded by closing the port of Boston and sending its army to Massachusetts. The First Continental Congress met in Philadelphia in 1774 and voted to **boycott** British goods. When the British came to seize the colonists' weapons, the colonists resisted and the American Revolutionary War started. In the beginning, few colonists wanted independence from Great Britain. As the fight grew, independence seemed to be the only solution to the problems between the colonists and their rulers. Have a conversation with your student about what he or she knows about the colonists and their struggle for independence from Great Britain. Then have him or her fill in a portion of the chart.

3 **RELATE AND RESEARCH** Explain that other nations also experienced revolutions. Reveal that in France there were many enlightened French thinkers who had new ideas about government and thought that the right to govern was derived from the people, but the French king was an absolute ruler. The French people lived under a system that was much like those of the Middle Ages. The people were divided into three "estates." Rich churchmen (first estate) and nobles (second estate) had most of the wealth but paid no taxes. The third estate, which included business and professional people but was mostly peasant farmers, paid huge taxes to the government. Have your student research the events that led up to the French Revolution of 1789. Have him or her write the appropriate information in the chart.

4 **PREDICT AND DISCUSS** Have your student read an article on the life of Napoléon Bonaparte up to the point when he became ruler of France in November 1799. Then ask your student to draw on what he or she knows of history and predict the kind of ruler he or she thinks Napoleon will become. Then have your student read on and find out if his or her predictions are correct. Then have your student read about Napoléon's campaign in Russia, the Code of Napoléon, and also what finally happened to Napoléon. Discuss.

?

DID YOU KNOW?

An **axis** is an imaginary line around which a planet or moon revolves. Germany, Italy, and Japan tried to create a military axis around which the rest of the world would revolve. That is how they became known as the Axis Powers in World War II.

5 **EXPLAIN AND COMPARE** Explain that after being conquered by Napoléon some of the people who had been living under the rule of foreign governments for years wanted their own countries. This is known as **nationalism.** Nationalist movements would play an important role in the history of Europe for the next hundred years. Explain also that the separate states in both Germany and Italy finally united in the late 1800s. A united Germany and a united Italy would play key roles in the first half of the next century. Next, have your student compare the map of Europe from just before World War I with a present-day map. Ask your student to name the new countries that now exist and discuss.

6 **RELATE AND DISCUSS** Explain that when Russia joined World War I the Central Powers had to fight on two fronts. Have your

288 Making the Grade: Everything Your 6th Grader Needs to Know © 2003 by Barron's Educational Series, Inc. All Rights Reserved.

student find and review a map of World War I battle sites. Tell your student that the United States tried to stay out of the war. Have him or her look on the Internet or go to the library and find out how the war started, what countries did to protect themselves, and which countries got involved in the war first. Then have him or her research why and how the United States finally entered the war. Ask, *Do you think the Central Powers would have won if the Allied Powers hadn't had U.S. help?* Discuss.

7   **EXPLAIN AND WRITE** Explain that millions of people starved and were killed in Russia during World War I. The country blamed **Czar** Nicholas II for its losses. Workers rioted. Peasants burned the estates of nobles. Nicholas agreed to more freedom, including an elected **parliament,** but he quickly changed his mind. On February 25, 1917, there was a riot and Nicholas's soldiers turned against him. Nicholas had to step down from his throne. The Bolsheviks, a **socialist** party led by a man who called himself Lenin, seized control. They renamed their party the **Communist** Party. Russia became the Union of Soviet Socialist Republics (U.S.S.R), or the Soviet Union. There was a civil war but the Communist **dictatorship** won. The nation had exchanged one absolute ruler for another. Have your student research additional information about the Russian Revolution to add to his or her chart. Discuss.

8   **EXPLORE** Explain that 20 years after World War I ended, World War II began. Nationalism, greed over colonial control, and the buildup of weapons had led to World War I. Have your student explore how Adolf Hitler in Germany, Benito Mussolini in Italy, Joseph Stalin in the U.S.S.R., and the military leaders of Japan followed these same paths in the 1930s until the world was again at war. Ask, *Why do you think countries such as Germany, Italy, and Japan didn't respect the rights of other countries and other peoples?*

Adolf Hitler and Benito Mussolini are shown here before World War II.

9   **REVIEW** Have your student find a map that shows the countries that Germany and Italy overtook before and during World War II. Ask your student what the phrase "geography is destiny" means. Then ask how it can explain why Germany and Italy lost the war. Discuss.

10   **READ BIOGRAPHIES** Have your student choose a biography to read on one of the following leaders of World War II: Hitler, Mussolini, Franklin D. Roosevelt, Winston Churchill, or Stalin. Then have him or her write a paragraph that tells how the leader helped or hurt his people.

11   **EXPLAIN AND EXPLORE** Until the Japanese attacked Pearl Harbor in Hawaii on December 7, 1941, the United States had not entered the war. Japan believed that the United States was the only country that could stop its military expansion in Asia and the Pacific. Have your student look at a map of Japanese

Joseph Stalin was the leader of the Soviet Union during World War II.

FOR FURTHER READING

The Age of Napoleon (World History Series), Harry Henderson, ed. (Lucent Books, 1999).

Air Raid—Pearl Harbor!: The Story of December 7, 1941, by Theodore Taylor (Harcourt, 2001).

American Revolution: Almanac, by Barbara C. Bigelow, Stacy A. McConnell, and Linda Schmittroth (U*X*L, 2000).

Angel on the Square (Russian Revolution), by Gloria Whelan (HarperCollins, 2001).

The Children We Remember: Photographs from the Archives of Yad Vashem, by Chana Byers Abells (HarperCollins Children's Books, 2002).

The Cold War, by Britta Bjornlund (Lucent Books, 2002).

Good-Bye Marianne: A Story of Growing Up in Nazi Germany, by Irene N. Watts (Tundra Books, 1998).

Where Poppies Grow: A World War I Companion, by Linda Granfield (Stoddard, 2002).

expansion in the 1930s and early 1940s. Ask, *What would suggest that the war in Asia and the Pacific needed to be fought differently from the war in Europe?* [warmer lands, larger area, much more water]

12 **RELATE** U.S. President Harry Truman ended the war with Japan by using atomic weapons. In August 1945, atomic bombs were dropped on the cities of Hiroshima and Nagasaki. Many people died, many more were seriously hurt, and large parts of the cities were entirely destroyed. Have your student research the effects of the bombs on the land and people of Japan. Ask your student why he or she thinks Truman decided to drop the bombs. Discuss.

13 **EXPLAIN AND IDENTIFY** After World War II, political and economic power shifted. The strongest countries were the United States and the Soviet Union. An "iron curtain" divided the democratic countries of western Europe and the communist countries in the east. The division of Europe led to a "cold war" between the United States and the Soviet Union. Have your student research the iron curtain and cold war, exploring what they were, the causes and effects of the nations involved, the political leaders, and how everyday life was affected. Discuss your student's findings with him or her.

14 **RESEARCH AND DISCUSS** Have your student research the breakup of the Soviet Union. Have him or her find a map that shows the countries that used to be part of the U.S.S.R. Discuss with him or her how life is different for the people and the government in those nations.

Branching Out

TEACHING TIP

It may be more beneficial to a student's understanding of history to be able to explain cause and effect, reasons for actions, and how leaders and people interact.

CHECKING IN

You can assess your student's understanding of the shifts in world power by choosing a time period and asking him or her to name the major events happening at that time and the strongest countries.

Compare Revolutions

Complete the chart of the American, French, and Russian Revolutions using what you've learned in the lesson and from your research.

	American	French	Russian
Date			
Opposed Ruler			
Reason			
Result			
New Government			

What's Next? You Decide!

Now it's your turn to choose what to do next in the lesson. Read the activities and decide which one you want to do— you may want to try them all!

Can We Talk?

MATERIALS

- ❑ 2 old socks
- ❑ buttons, fabric scraps, needle, thread
- ❑ drawings or photos of world leaders
- ❑ glue
- ❑ 1 pair scissors

STEPS

- ❑ Choose two world leaders from different times. Imagine them getting together for a "chat."

- ❑ Write a short script in which they discuss their points of view, their plans, their successes, their failures.

- ❑ Then make two sock puppets that look like your leaders.

- ❑ Have them act out the script you've written. Put on a show for your family or friends.

Ready, Aim, Sing!

MATERIALS

- ❑ 1–3 songbooks
- ❑ 1 or more musical instruments (optional)

STEPS

- ❑ Every war has had its popular songs. Look in songbooks for war songs from the American Revolution, World War I, and World War II.

- ❑ Learn a song from each of the wars.

- ❑ Sing and/or play them for a family member or a friend.

Make a Famous-Name Acrostic

MATERIALS

- ❑ 1 copy Grid, page 355
- ❑ 1 dark-colored marker

STEPS

- ❑ Choose a famous political or military leader from the period beginning with the American Revolution to present times.

- ❑ Read about him or her. Write out the letters of his or her name vertically down a copy of the Grid found on page 355. Use each letter to start a line of a poem about the person.

- ❑ Revise your work to make your acrostic poem read as well as you can.

- ❑ Share it with a family member. Tell him or her why you picked the person as the subject for your poem.

- ❑ Then make an acrostic for someone you know! Think about his or her hobbies, likes and dislikes, and any other good things about him or her.

In Your Community

To reinforce the skills and concepts taught in this section,
try one or more of these activities!

Democracy in Your Community

The ancient Greeks believed that citizen partic-
ipation was very important to the success of
society. Encourage your student to be an active
citizen. The first step is being informed about
the issues, current decisions, and events in
your community. Check your local newspaper
or call your city hall to find out about local
meetings and events. Have your student
choose one or more events to participate in.
Have your student invite family and friends to
participate, too!

Original Art at Your Museum

Have your student pick a favorite topic, culture, or period of art and arrange for a trip to a
local museum to see original examples of what
he or she has been studying. Find out about
special presentations for young people or the
possibility of a guided tour with a museum
expert on the subject. If you do not have any
museums near you, consider taking a trip to
the nearest city and visiting several museums
while you're there.

People Who Came Before

Just like the Mayans and Aztecs before the
Spanish came, every community in the
Americas once had native inhabitants. Visit
your local historical society with your student.
Ask to speak with a local historian and have
your student interview him or her. Have your
student write a summary about the culture of
the native people and what happened to them.
He or she might want to submit the summary
to a local newspaper.

Government Elections

Government elections occur every two years,
and campaigning goes on for much of the time
in between. Have your student discover the
names of the local candidates and some information about their political positions. Arrange
an interview with your student's favorite can-
didate. Have your student prepare some questions about citizen and representative responsibility and government. On election day, invite
your student to visit the polling place with you
and observe the voting procedures. He or she
also may want to interview an election official.
There also are other elections, about referenda,
tax levies, and other issues, too, that can occur
annually. You can help your student learn
more about them, too.

Local Veterans

Contact your local veterans association and
arrange for your student to speak with a war
veteran about his or her experiences in war. Be
sure to prepare your student with some background information about the suffering of war.
Have him or her think of several specific questions to ask.

Your Community's Railroad

Have your student research the history of the
railroad in your community. Ask him or her to
find out when the railroad first came to your
town and where the first station was located.
If the first station still exists, visit that place
and/or another large station. Show your student
the locomotives and, together, find out how the
railroad is being used in your town today.

We Have Learned

Use this checklist to summarize what you and your student
have accomplished in the Social Studies section.

❏ **Fertile Crescent and Mesopotamia**
❏ geography, importance of waterways, Babylon, Persia
❏ Phoenicians, Hebrews, beginnings of Judaism, beginnings of Islam

❏ **Egypt**
❏ geography, agriculture, Nile River, hieroglyphics
❏ pharaohs, pyramids, Rosetta stone

❏ **Ancient Greece and Ancient Rome**
❏ government, responsibilities of citizens
❏ Julius Caesar, Alexander the Great
❏ Roman architecture, beginning of Christianity in Rome
❏ Greek philosophers, Greek theater, Olympic Games

❏ **Asian and African Cultures**
❏ India's caste system
❏ society of ancient China, dynasties of ancient China
❏ beginnings of Buddhism, beginnings of Hinduism
❏ Japanese feudal structure, Mongol Empire, Ottoman Empire
❏ history of West Africa, history of Zimbabwe

❏ **Feudal Europe**
❏ Medieval society, law, art, architecture, knights
❏ Franks, Anglo-Saxons, Vikings

❏ **Power of Church and Reformation**
❏ church influence in government, church influence in economics
❏ Charlemagne, Constantinople, Byzantine Empire
❏ Crusades
❏ decline of Catholic Church, indulgences, inquisition
❏ Martin Luther, Protestantism

❏ **Renaissance**
❏ Italian Renaissance, Florence
❏ rebirth of art, rebirth of literature, humanism, plague

❏ **Scientific Revolution, Enlightenment, and Industrial Revolution**
❏ scientific discoveries
❏ European world exploration, expansion of trade, early American civilizations
❏ industrialization, capitalism, factories
❏ transportation, communication

❏ **Contemporary Conflicts**
❏ American, French, Russian Revolutions
❏ World War I, World War II, rise of communism, decline of communism

We have also learned:

_____

_____

_____

Read each question and answer choices that follow. Circle the letter of the correct answer.

1. *MLA Style Manual* is useful for documenting _____ in research.

   A sources

   B antonyms

   C the five Ws

   D characters in a play

2. _____ are timeless tales that usually are passed down through generations.

   A Persuasive speeches

   B Folktales

   C Symbols

   D Biographies

3. Which step of the writing process occurs first?

   A Add Details

   B Choose a Topic

   C Organize and Plan

   D Evaluate

4. Checking for misspellings occurs during which stage of the writing process?

   A Add Details

   B Evaluate

   C Publish and Present

   D Edit and Revise

5. Making a time line of events can occur during which stage of the writing process?

   A Add Details

   B Choose a Topic

   C Organize and Plan

   D Evaluate

6. A true story of a person's life as told by another person is called what?

   A persuasive writing

   B autobiography

   C biography

   D drama

7. Stage directions are important when reading what?

   A poetry

   B folktales

   C explanatory writing

   D drama

Read the sentences in the box. Decide the best way to write the underlined sentences. Circle the letter of the correct answer.

8.

> Bimal took a trip to Italy last year. He visited many museums and studied Italian art he also saw several plays.

  A He visited many museums. And studied Italian art. He also saw several plays.

  B He visited many museums. And studied Italian art he also saw several plays.

  C He visited many museums and studied Italian art. He also saw several plays.

  D Correct as written

9.

> Beverly is a doctor. She specializes in treating children. With serious illnesses. Beverly likes being a doctor because she enjoys helping people.

  A She specializes in treating children: with serious illnesses.

  B She specializes in treating children with serious illnesses.

  C She specializes in treating children with serious illnesses?

  D Correct as written

10.

> Steven went to the sporting goods store yesterday. He bought. A brand-new red bicycle. And matching helmet. With his own money. He rode the bicycle home.

  A He bought a brand-new red bicycle and matching helmet with his own money.

  B He bought a brand-new red bicycle. And matching helmet with his own money.

  C He bought a brand-new red bicycle and matching. Helmet with his own money.

  D Correct as written

Read each passage. Decide which type of writing it is. Circle the letter of the correct answer.

11. This soap contains no chemicals, no perfumes, and no dyes. You should use this soap because it is perfect for the entire family.

    A persuasive

    B narrative

    C explanatory

    D biography

12. The small, brown mouse just sat there looking at me. His tiny black eyes shone like two marbles, while he held his diminutive paws as if he were holding handfuls of delicate pearls.

    A explanatory

    B descriptive

    C folktale

    D persuasive

13. After our soccer game was over, we all headed to the pool for a swim. Swimming seemed to last forever, but then we changed our clothes, ate dinner, and saw a movie.

    A persuasive

    B narrative

    C drama

    D folktale

Read each selection. Read the questions and answer choices that go with each selection. Circle the letter of the correct answer.

Use for 14.

Sandra is trying out for a part in the school play. She memorized the lines for the audition and has been practicing them for two weeks. Sandra practiced for an hour the night before the audition. On her way to the audition, she is excited and is confident she can get the part.

14. Which word best describes Sandra before the audition?

   A   nervous

   B   prepared

   C   uneasy

   D   bored

Use for 15–17.

There are seven species of sea turtles that live in the ocean. All species of sea turtles are **endangered.** There are many obstacles to their survival. Beaches are part of the turtles' habitat, but they are being crowded out by humans. Another danger faced by sea turtles is garbage dumped in the ocean. If they swallow this trash, they can die. Many turtles also die from getting tangled in fishing nets.

15. How many species of turtles are endangered?

   A   five   C   seven

   B   six   D   eight

16. Which is NOT a reason sea turtles face extinction?

   A   garbage in the ocean

   B   humans on the beach

   C   water that is too cold

   D   fishing nets

17. Which word best describes **endangered**?

   A   at risk

   B   at sea

   C   deformed

   D   cold-blooded

Use for 18–21.

Sometimes my mom and Aunt Tanya argue a lot. She lives with us along with Reggie. He's Aunt Tanya's three-year-old son. Everyone thinks he's cute with his curly brown hair and chubby cheeks and the way he says cheethbugah for cheeseburger. But they don't have to watch him when my mom and Aunt Tanya are arguing.

   "Lisa, play with Reggie for a while, will ya?" says Mom.

I just **detest** having to play with Reggie sometimes. It used to be Mom and me until Aunt Tanya—who is Mom's older sister—moved in for a while. Then Reggie was born and look who became the babysitter. It's not that I don't like babies, but sometimes I have some very important things to get done. And Mom and Aunt Tanya argue a lot. Most of the time I can't really tell what they're arguing about, but it seems to be about the same things. At the end of every argument, though, they always make up and give each other a hug. Their arguments are their way of discussing important things.

18. Why does everyone think Reggie's cute?

A He's three years old.

B He's Aunt Tanya's son.

C He has curly hair and chubby cheeks.

D He eats cheeseburgers.

19. Based on the passage, the definition that best describes **detest** is—

A admire

B like a lot

C enjoy

D don't like

20. What is Lisa's opinion of the arguments at the end?

A The arguments are about Lisa's babysitting.

B The arguments are because of Reggie.

C The arguments get worse.

D The arguments are discussions.

21. Why doesn't Lisa like to babysit Reggie?

A Lisa doesn't like babies.

B Lisa has important things to do.

C Lisa wants to argue too.

D Lisa wants to do her homework.

Use for 22–24.

Pandas are rare animals. You won't see many of them living in zoos. Only seven live in the United States: two in Atlanta, three in San Diego, and two in Washington, D.C.

The two pandas in Washington, D.C., Tian Tian [tea YEN tea YEN] and Mei Xiang [may SHONG], were born in China, where pandas live in the wild, and were loaned to Washington, D.C.'s National Zoo for 10 years. In return, the National Zoo will donate $1 million each year for protection and safety of animals and plants in China.

Zoogoers enjoy seeing the pandas and are fascinated by their unique features. One unique feature is their "thumbs." They're not exactly like human thumbs—for one reason, they don't move—but they can help pandas hold things. Another reason is their looks. With their large head, chubby cheeks, and black and white fur, they **captivate** everyone's attention.

However, entertaining zoogoers isn't the only reason the pandas were brought to the zoo. Scientists and others want people to know that pandas need help protecting them in order for them to continue surviving.

22. What do scientists hope will happen when people see Mei Xiang and Tian Tian?

  A They will do things to help pandas survive.

  B They will keep pandas as pets.

  C They will travel to China.

  D They will name their children after the pandas.

23. According to this article, what is special about China?

  A It has the greatest number of zoos.

  B It has great weather.

  C Pandas live wild there.

  D It contributes a large amount of money to the National Zoo.

24. What does the word **captivate** mean in the fourth paragraph?

  A dislike

  B hide from

  C attract

  D are scared of

Use for 25–26.

A clock has hands.
Why doesn't it tap me
on the shoulder to wake me?
A clock has a face
Why doesn't it smile
when I come through the door?
If a clock keeps time,
Why can't I have some of it
so that I'm not always late?

25. "Why doesn't it tap me on the shoulder to wake me?" is an example of—

  A alliteration

  B onomatopoeia

  C personification

  D simile

26. What is the poet saying about himself or herself in the poem?

  A He or she is always on time.

  B He or she is always late.

  C He or she likes to smile.

  D He or she wears a watch.

> Read each selection and the questions that follow.
> Answer the questions in complete sentences.

Use for 27–30.

This morning I woke up and said to myself, "Today is the day." I wondered if anyone would even remember. I got dressed and went downstairs for breakfast. Mom, Dad, and Lili were all there, but no one said a word.

"That just figures," I said to myself. Ever since my baby sister was born I feel like I have been invisible. This is the day I came into the world, but she is more important now.

All day at school I thought about the fact that my own parents had forgotten this important day. To make things worse, none of my friends said a word about it either! After school I hurried home. I wanted to go straight to bed so this horrible day would finally be over.

Everything changed when I walked through the door at home. My whole family and all of my friends yelled, "Surprise!" Mom gave me a big hug. I said, "I thought you forgot." She said "Don't be silly! I could never forget this day."

27. What event is the narrator describing?

_____

28. What is the narrator's tone at the beginning of the passage?

_____

29. Who, in the selection, is probably the narrator's little sister?

_____

_____

30. How do you think the narrator feels at the end of the selection?

_____

_____

_____

Use for 31–33.

Leaves fall, winds chill, days shorten.
This is the time I enjoy.
No more flowers to make me sneeze.
No more grass to mow.
Pinks and greens turn to oranges and
    brown.
These are my favorite days.

31. What time of year is the speaker describing?

_____

_____

32. How does the speaker feel about the change that is occurring?

_____

_____

33. What is the poet describing in the sentence, "Pinks and greens turn to oranges and brown"?

_____

_____

Use for 34–35.

Melissa: Why do you look so sad?
Enrique: I think I have the winter
  doldrums.
Melissa: Cheer up! It will be spring soon.
Enrique: That's true; I do love spring.
Melissa: See, just a few more weeks and
  it will be your favorite time of year.

34. What is the meaning of **doldrums** in the selection?

_____

_____

35. What is Melissa's tone?

_____

_____

Use for 36–38.

Angelina loves to ride horses. She ride for the first time when she visited her grandparents ranch in wyoming. When angelina returned home she asked her parents for a horse At first her parents were reluctant. Angelina's family lives in the City where there is no place to keep a horse. However, they found a **stable**

that was close to home, so they got Angelina a horse. Now Angelina rides her horse everryday

36. Rewrite the paragraph in the space below using correct grammar, spelling, capitalization, and punctuation.

_____

_____

_____

_____

_____

_____

_____

_____

_____

_____

_____

_____

_____

_____

_____

_____

_____

_____

37. What is another meaning of the word **stable** in the paragraph?

_____

_____

_____

38. Sequence the following events. Number them 1–3.

____ Angelina got a horse.

____ Angelina rode a horse at her grandparents' ranch.

____ Angelina's parents found a stable for a horse

Use for 39–41.

Hamad the squirrel was busy collecting food for the long winter months ahead. It was only summer, but he knew that if he didn't save the food now, he wouldn't have anything to eat in the winter. Jordan was a squirrel who lived in a tree near Hamad. He spent his summer playing by the river and taking long naps. He kept telling himself that he'd go collecting for food tomorrow. But then each day came and he'd be too busy playing. "It'll just have to wait until tomorrow," he'd say to himself. Soon the cold, snowy winter came. Jordan had no food. Jordan felt bad and asked Hamad for food. Hamad said, "Tomorrow." The next day Hamad did give some food to Jordan. Jordan was very thankful and said he wouldn't wait until tomorrow again.

39. How would you classify this story?

_____

_____

_____

_____

40. What lesson does this story teach?

_____

_____

_____

_____

41. Why did Hamad wait until the next day to give Jordan food?

_____

_____

_____

_____

42. Choose one of the following types of writing and construct a well-organized essay using one of the ideas. Write an introduction, several paragraphs, and a conclusion. You have 15 minutes to complete your essay.

- **Persuasive**

  Idea A: Persuade someone to buy a particular brand of toothpaste

  Idea B: Persuade someone to take a trip to a particular island

- **Descriptive**

  Idea A: Describe your favorite sweater

  Idea B: Describe your favorite food

- **Explanatory**

  Idea A: Explain how to ride a bicycle

  Idea B: Explain how to tie shoes

- **Narrative**

  Idea A: Tell about a time when you were really scared

  Idea B: Tell about a time when you were really nervous

_____

_____

_____

_____

_____

_____

_____

_____

_____

_____

_____

_____

_____

_____

_____

_____

_____
_____
_____
_____
_____
_____
_____
_____
_____
_____
_____
_____
_____
_____
_____
_____
_____
_____
_____
_____
_____
_____
_____
_____
_____
_____
_____
_____
_____
_____
_____
_____

Read each question and answer choices that follow. Circle the letter of the correct answer.

1. What is the place value of 8 in 4.589?

   A tenths

   B hundredths

   C thousandths

   D ten thousandths

2. Which is 14.067985 rounded to the nearest thousandth?

   A 14.1

   B 14.07

   C 14.067

   D 14.068

3. $12 - 3.046 =$

   A 8.364

   B 8.954

   C 9.364

   D 9.954

4. $7.45 + 25.203 =$

   A 32.068

   B 32.498

   C 32.523

   D 32.653

5. $13.92 \div 4 =$

   A 3.48

   B 3.52

   C 3.68

   D 3.72

6. $15.06 \times 2.5 =$

   A 30.65

   B 35

   C 37.65

   D 39

7. $23 \times 0.32 =$

   A 7.16

   B 7.26

   C 7.36

   D 7.46

8. $31 \div 6.2 =$

   A 4

   B 5

   C 6

   D 7

9. $11.04 \div 4.8 =$

   A 2.3

   B 2.6

   C 3.1

   D 3.2

10. The circle graph shows how the U.S. government spends its money. What percentage is spent on Social Security and the military combined?

U.S. Government Spending

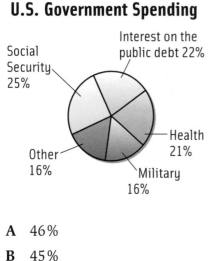

A 46%

B 45%

C 42%

D 41%

11. The bar graph shows how many sit-ups each student did in soccer practice on Wednesday. How many more sit-ups did Becky do than Robert?

Sit-Ups in Soccer Practice

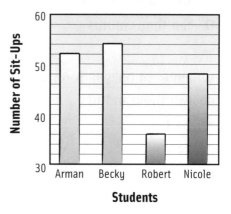

A 12

B 14

C 16

D 18

12. What is the greatest common factor of 36 and 48?

A 2

B 4

C 6

D 12

13. Which is a prime number?

A 8

B 29

C 34

D 49

14. $\frac{7}{10} =$

   A 7.0

   B 0.7

   C 0.07

   D 0.007

15. Which is correct?

   A $\frac{1}{4} < \frac{3}{8} < \frac{1}{2} < \frac{3}{4}$

   B $\frac{1}{2} < \frac{1}{4} < \frac{3}{4} < \frac{3}{8}$

   C $\frac{3}{4} < \frac{1}{2} < \frac{3}{8} < \frac{1}{4}$

   D $\frac{3}{8} < \frac{3}{4} < \frac{1}{4} < \frac{1}{2}$

16. What is the least common multiple of 6 and 9?

   A 12

   B 18

   C 24

   D 27

17. $-18 + 4 =$

   A -22

   B -20

   C -16

   D -14

18. $-16 - (-9) =$

   A -7

   B -11

   C -19

   D -25

19. $3\frac{2}{5} =$

   A $\frac{13}{5}$

   B $\frac{15}{5}$

   C $\frac{17}{5}$

   D $\frac{19}{5}$

20. $\frac{7}{8} + \frac{1}{4} =$

   A $1\frac{1}{8}$

   B $1\frac{1}{4}$

   C $1\frac{3}{8}$

   D $1\frac{3}{4}$

21. $\frac{5}{6} - \frac{2}{3} =$

   A $\frac{1}{12}$

   B $\frac{1}{6}$

   C $\frac{1}{4}$

   D $\frac{1}{3}$

22. $2\frac{3}{7} + \frac{5}{7} =$

    A $2\frac{5}{7}$

    B $2\frac{6}{7}$

    C $3\frac{1}{7}$

    D $3\frac{2}{7}$

23. $4\frac{2}{5} - \frac{4}{5} =$

    A $3\frac{1}{5}$

    B $3\frac{2}{5}$

    C $3\frac{3}{5}$

    D $3\frac{4}{5}$

24. $\frac{3}{8} + 2\frac{1}{4} =$

    A $2\frac{1}{12}$

    B $2\frac{1}{2}$

    C $2\frac{5}{8}$

    D $2\frac{3}{4}$

25. $1\frac{3}{5} - \frac{9}{10} =$

    A $\frac{2}{5}$

    B $\frac{1}{2}$

    C $\frac{3}{5}$

    D $\frac{7}{10}$

26. $2\frac{1}{2} \times \frac{3}{4} =$

    A $1\frac{1}{2}$

    B $1\frac{7}{8}$

    C $2\frac{1}{4}$

    D $2\frac{3}{8}$

27. $\frac{5}{8} \div \frac{3}{4} =$

    A $\frac{1}{2}$

    B $\frac{3}{4}$

    C $\frac{5}{6}$

    D $\frac{3}{8}$

28. $3\frac{1}{2} \div \frac{4}{21} =$

    A $18\frac{1}{4}$

    B $18\frac{3}{8}$

    C $18\frac{5}{8}$

    D $18\frac{3}{4}$

29. 180 inches = _____ feet

    A   10

    B   12

    C   15

    D   18

30. Which unit would be most appropriate to measure the length of a swimming pool?

    A millimeter

    B centimeter

    C meter

    D kilometer

31. 32 ounces = _____ pounds

    A 1

    B 2

    C 3

    D 4

32. 3 liters = _____ milliliters

    A 30

    B 300

    C 3,000

    D 30,000

33. Classify the angle.

    A acute angle

    B right angle

    C obtuse angle

    D straight angle

34. Classify the triangle.

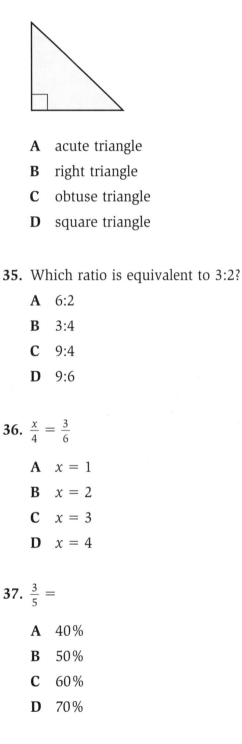

    A acute triangle

    B right triangle

    C obtuse triangle

    D square triangle

35. Which ratio is equivalent to 3:2?

    A 6:2

    B 3:4

    C 9:4

    D 9:6

36. $\frac{x}{4} = \frac{3}{6}$

    A $x = 1$

    B $x = 2$

    C $x = 3$

    D $x = 4$

37. $\frac{3}{5} =$

    A 40%

    B 50%

    C 60%

    D 70%

38. 85% =

   A 8.5

   B 0.85

   C 0.085

   D 0.0085

39. What is 60% of 15?

   A 6

   B 7

   C 8

   D 9

40. A pair of shoes costs $30.00 plus 5% sales tax. What is the total cost?

   A $30.00

   B $31.50

   C $32.50

   D $33.00

41. What is the perimeter?

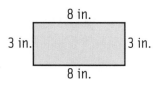

   A 11 inches

   B 16 inches

   C 22 inches

   D 24 inches

Use for 42–43.

Height of Students

Name	Height (in inches)
Alice	59
Rory	48
Bimal	54
Chandra	52

42. Read the information in the chart Height of Students. Draw a bar graph showing the information in a different way from the chart.

43. What is the mean height? _____

MATH

Graph each set of integers on a number line. Then order the integers from least to greatest.

44. 6, −8, 3, −4

_____

45. −10, 1, −5, 5

_____

Use for 46–49. Give the coordinates for each point.

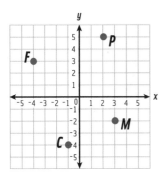

46. *M* _____

47. *C* _____

48. *P* _____

49. *F* _____

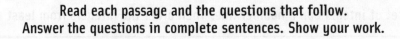

Read each passage and the questions that follow.
Answer the questions in complete sentences. Show your work.

---

50. During Gustavo's bike ride, he drank a liter-sized bottle of water. After the bike ride, he drank a 300-milliliter cup of water. How many milliliters of water did he drink in all?

_____

_____

_____

_____

51. The mass of 4 apples is about 1 kilogram. Estimate the mass of 1 apple in grams.

_____

_____

_____

_____

52. There are about 5 milliliters in a teaspoon. There are 3 teaspoons in a tablespoon. About how many milliliters are there in a tablespoon?

_____

_____

_____

_____

53. Name all points, segments, lines, and rays.

_____

_____

_____

_____

_____

54. Name three different figures in the flag.

_____

_____

_____

55. What percent of 4 is 9?

_____

_____

_____

_____

56. What is the area of the triangle and rectangle combined?

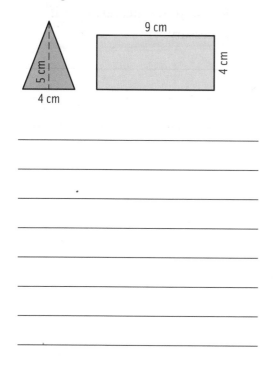

_____

_____

_____

_____

_____

_____

_____

57. What is the volume of the triangular prism?

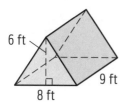

_____

_____

_____

_____

_____

_____

_____

Use for 58–60.

Supply Store

Item	Price
Pencils	$2.09 per box
Pens	$0.78 each
Markers	$3.98 per box
Erasers	$0.53 each

58. Ben has $10. He wants to buy 3 boxes of pencils, 1 pen, 1 box of markers, and 2 erasers. Estimate to decide if he has enough money. Explain your answer.

_____

_____

_____

_____

_____

_____

_____

_____

_____

_____

_____

_____

_____

_____

_____

_____

_____

59. What is the cost of 1 box of pencils and 4 pens?

_____

_____

_____

_____

_____

60. If there are 5 markers in each box, how much does each marker cost? Round to the nearest cent if necessary.

_____

_____

_____

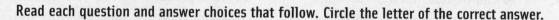

Read each question and answer choices that follow. Circle the letter of the correct answer.

1. Using a microscope, Sarah observed a cell. She made a list of some of the structures and organelles of the cell she observed. What can you infer from Sarah's list?

nucleus
ribosomes
cell membrane
vacuole

   A   Sarah is looking at a plant cell.

   B   Sarah is looking at an animal cell.

   C   It is not possible to determine if Sarah is looking at a plant cell or an animal cell.

   D   The cell Sarah is looking at could not have come from either a plant or an animal.

2. Which statement about the water cycle is true?

   A   Deposition is part of the water cycle.

   B   Refraction is part of the water cycle.

   C   Plants play no part in the water cycle.

   D   Human activity can affect the water cycle.

3. Which statement best summarizes all of the information in the table?

Planets' Years in Earth Days

Planet	Length of Year (in Earth Days)
Mercury	87.969
Venus	224.7
Earth	365.26
Mars	686.98
Jupiter	4,330.6
Saturn	10,747
Uranus	30,588
Neptune	59,800
Pluto	90,591

   A   The inner planets have a year that is longer than Earth's year.

   B   The outer planets have a year that is longer than Earth's year, and the inner planets have a year that is shorter than Earth's year.

   C   The inner planets have a year that is shorter than Earth's year.

   D   The inner planets have a year that is longer than Earth's year, and the outer planets have a year that is shorter than Earth's year.

4. Waves can be described by several characteristics. Which characteristic of the wave is measured by line *B*?

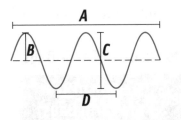

A amplitude

B frequency

C wavelength

D intensity

5. Which of the properties of light is shown in this picture?

A reflection

B refraction

C absorption

D magnification

6. Your blood, a part of your circulatory system, carries substances to and from the cells in your body. Which answer correctly identifies two substances that are carried to your cells by your blood?

A carbon dioxide and oxygen

B wastes and glucose

C glucose and oxygen

D oxygen and wastes

7. This diagram is a model of one stage of cell division. What is the correct label for *A* in the diagram?

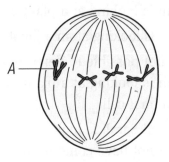

A chromosomes

B cell membrane

C cytoplasm

D nucleus

8. Which definition best describes **matter**?

   A   the substance of anything that takes up space

   B   the process by which mechanical energy is converted to electrical energy

   C   the process by which chemical energy is converted to mechanical energy

   D   a table of elements

9. Which definition best describes a **compound**?

   A   the nucleus of an atom

   B   a chemical reaction

   C   a chemical formula

   D   a substance whose molecules are made up of two or more elements

10. Which is an example of a compound?

   A   sodium

   B   gold

   C   oxygen

   D   carbon dioxide

11. What do you call someone who studies plants?

   A   geologist

   B   botanist

   C   anthropologist

   D   astrologist

12. Which definition best describes **photosynthesis**?

   A   the process by which green plants make their own food

   B   the process by which plant seeds are germinated

   C   the process by which water evaporates

   D   the process by which water condenses

13. Which of these are parts of an animal cell?

   A   nucleus, cytoplasm, membrane

   B   atom, cytoplasm, membrane

   C   nucleus, sodium, cytoplasm

   D   nucleus, membrane, energy

14. Punnett Squares are useful in studying what?

   A   photosynthesis

   B   compounds

   C   genetics

   D   food groups

15. Which is NOT a part of the nervous system?

   A   spinal cord

   B   heart

   C   brain

   D   nerve

16. Which definition best describes **dendrites**?

    A carry nutrients between the brain and all other parts of the body

    B carry impulses between the brain and all other parts of the body

    C conduct impulses to the main part of a nerve cell

    D send and receive impulses within the nervous system

17. Why is the circulatory system important?

    A It carries food and oxygen to cells and removes wastes and carbon dioxide from cells.

    B It decides what traits offspring will have.

    C It carries food through the body for proper digestion of food and removal of waste matter.

    D It assists cells in reproduction.

18. Which best describes the stages of human life in order?

    A infancy, childhood, adolescence, adulthood

    B puberty, infancy, adolescence, adulthood

    C infancy, childhood, adulthood, senior

    D infancy, puberty, adulthood, adolescence

19. Which are parts of the scientific method?

    A hypothesis, observation, precipitation

    B hypothesis, prediction, transmission

    C hypothesis, observation, prediction

    D hypothesis, prediction, deposition

20. The scientific method would be useful for—

    A swimming in cold water

    B problem solving

    C reading directions

    D drawing sketches

21. Which of these are NOT found in the solar system?

    A inner planets

    B middle planets

    C outer planets

    D moon

22. Which definition best describes **ecosystem**?

    A   an area where the planets orbit around the sun

    B   an area where living things interact with their environment and with each other

    C   an area where living things do not interact with their environment and with each other

    D   an area where parts of cells reproduce

23. A **habitat** is an area—

    A   where a plant or animal naturally lives

    B   where a plant or animal will only find its kind

    C   where a plant or animal can only go for food

    D   where a plant or animal cannot live

24. Which of these animals are NOT carnivores?

    A   lion

    B   snake

    C   squirrel

    D   bear

25. Heat energy moves through liquids and gases by—

    A   conduction and reduction

    B   conduction and convection

    C   precipitation and convection

    D   precipitation and evaporation

26. Which definition best describes **reflection**?

    A   when a light wave strikes a surface and bounces off

    B   the bending of light waves caused by a change in their speed

    C   the process of light becoming solar energy

    D   the changing of light energy into thermal energy

27. Which definition best describes the **producers** in a food web?

    A   organisms that eat the waste of other organisms

    B   organisms that make their own food

    C   organisms that eat only plants

    D   organisms that eat only animals

28. What is the difference between high-pitched and low-pitched sound waves?

   A High-pitched sounds have short wavelengths, and low-pitched sounds have long wavelengths.

   B High-pitched sounds have long wavelengths, and low-pitched sounds have short wavelengths.

   C High-pitched sounds have low frequencies.

   D Low-pitched sounds have high frequencies.

29. How does sound travel?

   A in light

   B in frequencies

   C in waves

   D in pitches

Read each selection and the questions that follow. Answer the questions in complete sentences.

Use for 30–31.

Wind turbines can be used to produce electricity. The blades of the turbines are turned by the wind. The turning blades are connected to a generator, which produces electricity. Electricity is only produced when enough wind is present to turn the turbines.

30. Natural resources can be classified as renewable, nonrenewable, or inexhaustible. Which of these terms best describes wind? Why?

_____

_____

_____

_____

_____

31. What is the difference between renewable and nonrenewable resources?

_____

_____

_____

_____

_____

_____

_____

_____

_____

_____

_____

_____

SCIENCE

32. Erosion and deposition are related processes that change Earth's surface. Write a sentence that explains the relationship between erosion and deposition.

_____

_____

_____

_____

_____

33. An ecosystem consists of both abiotic (nonliving) and biotic (living) parts. List two abiotic and two biotic parts of a stream ecosystem. Explain how these four parts of the ecosystem would be affected by a severe drought.

_____

_____

_____

_____

_____

_____

_____

_____

_____

_____

_____

34. Not all animals are alike. An animal can be either a vertebrate or an invertebrate. Some are carnivores, while some are herbivores, and some are even both. Similarly, animals can be either warm-blooded or cold-blooded. Write a paragraph explaining the differences between each of these characteristics of animals.

_____

_____

_____

_____

_____

_____

_____

_____

_____

_____

_____

_____

_____

_____

_____

_____

_____

_____

Use for 35–36.

35. Punnett Squares can be helpful for determining what traits offspring will have. If an offspring has the recessive trait of blue eyes, explain what genes for eye color the parents could have and why.

_____

_____

_____

_____

_____

_____

_____

36. If one offspring has blue eyes and one offspring has brown eyes, explain what genes the parents could have and why.

_____

_____

_____

_____

_____

_____

37. Jorge left a glass of water on the kitchen table for two weeks. At the end of two weeks, water was missing from the glass. Jorge has some ideas about why the water is missing. Use the scientific method to set up a way to test why the water might be missing.

Observations:

_____

_____

_____

_____

Hypothesis:

_____

_____

_____

Prediction:

_____

_____

_____

Description of Experimental Test:

_____

_____

_____

_____

38. Describe how Earth, the sun, and the moon are connected. Include in your explanation the words **orbit**, **gravity**, and **rotation**.

_____

_____

_____

_____

_____

_____

_____

_____

_____

_____

_____

_____

_____

_____

_____

_____

_____

_____

_____

_____

_____

_____

_____

_____

Use for 39–40.

Food Pyramid

39. Identify the food groups in the food pyramid.

A. _____

_____

B. _____

_____

C. _____

_____

D. _____

_____

E. _____

_____

F. _____

_____

40. Explain what the food pyramid means.

_____

_____

_____

_____

Use for 41–43.

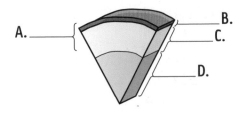

41. Identify the crust, mantle, core, and lithosphere.

A. _____

B. _____

C. _____

D. _____

42. Explain the theory of plate tectonics.

_____

_____

_____

_____

_____

_____

_____

_____

_____

_____

_____

_____

43. Explain how earthquakes and volcanoes are related.

_____

_____

_____

_____

_____

_____

_____

_____

_____

_____

_____

_____

_____

_____

_____

_____

_____

_____

_____

_____

_____

_____

_____

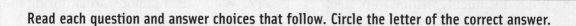

> **Read each question and answer choices that follow. Circle the letter of the correct answer.**

1. What was the name of the system of laws developed by the Babylonians?

   A Zoroastrianism

   B Code of Hammurabi

   C Constitution

   D Justinian Code

2. What architectural achievement are the ancient Egyptians known for?

   A Colosseum

   B cathedrals

   C high-rise buildings

   D pyramids

3. The Romans established a _____ form of government.

   A republican

   B oligarchical

   C communist

   D tyrannical

4. The Roman Empire was the site of the rise and spread of _____.

   A Buddhism

   B Islam

   C Hinduism

   D Christianity

5. Two famous ancient Greek philosophers were _____.

   A Plato and Alexander the Great

   B Justinian and Aristotle

   C Plato and Aristotle

   D Alexander the Great and Justinian

6. The ancient Greeks are known for creating the _____.

   A Olympics

   B Championships

   C Super Bowl

   D Playoffs

7. What influential Chinese philosopher taught that emphasis on family and the choice of virtuous rulers led to a healthy society?

   A Hannibal

   B Gilgamesh

   C Confucius

   D King Tutankhamen

8. What document, written to protect the liberties of the nobles in medieval Europe, became the cornerstone of constitutional government and representative democracy?

   A   Declaration of Independence

   B   Magna Carta

   C   Bill of Rights

   D   Crusades

9. Which was NOT a class of person under feudalism and manorialism in the Middle Ages?

   A   lord

   B   vassal

   C   president

   D   serf

10. The European expeditions to take back the Holy Land in the Middle Ages were called the _____.

    A   Crusades

    B   Punic Wars

    C   Escapades

    D   War of the Roses

11. The renewed interest in Greek and Roman literature and life beginning in the 1300s was called the _____.

    A   Scientific Revolution

    B   Pax Romana

    C   Renaissance

    D   Industrial Revolution

12. Who was a famous artist during the Renaissance?

    A   Homer

    B   Michelangelo

    C   Joan of Arc

    D   Plato

13. Francis Bacon, Nicolaus Copernicus, Galileo Galilei, and Isaac Newton were all important thinkers during the

    _____.

    A   Industrial Revolution

    B   Scientific Revolution

    C   War of 1812

    D   Spanish Civil War

14. The introduction of power-driven machinery that significantly changed manufacturing began the _____.

    A   Scientific Revolution

    B   Renaissance

    C   Reformation

    D   Industrial Revolution

15. Which definition best describes **hieroglyphics**?

    A   a method of turning papyrus into paper

    B   a picture-symbol language used by ancient Egyptians

    C   tools used to construct pyramids

    D   a letter language used by ancient Egyptians

SOCIAL
STUDIES

16. Which definition best describes **city-state**?

  A   a self-governing city in ancient Greece

  B   a castle constructed by a lord to keep out serfs

  C   a self-governing city in Mesopotamia

  D   a city set up by Buddhists

17. Which words describe people during the Middle Ages?

  A   Pharaoh, lord, serf

  B   noble, vassal, serf

  C   knight, soldier, freedom fighter

  D   lord, saint, serf

18. Which definition best describes **monarchy**?

  A   republic

  B   democracy

  C   rule by the people

  D   undivided power held by a single ruler

19. A Spanish explorer who conquered new lands and people was called a(n) _____.

  A   serf

  B   conquistador

  C   encomienda

  D   enlightener

20. The Industrial Revolution led to the growth of _____.

  A   totalitarianism

  B   capitalism

  C   city-states

  D   feudalism

21. Which of the following is NOT associated with the Industrial Revolution?

  A   British textile industry

  B   increase in transportation methods

  C   Eli Whitney's cotton gin

  D   Crusades

© 2003 by Barron's Educational Series, Inc. All Rights Reserved.

Assessment   **329**

Answer the questions in complete sentences.	

Use for 22–25.

Roman Government

Senate	Popular Assemblies	Magistrates
• Controlled public funds • Determined public policy • Could appoint a dictator for a maximum of six months	• Voted on laws • Elected officials • Voted to make war or peace	• Consuls: — Chief Executives — Military commanders — Veto power • Praetors: — Assisted consuls in times of war — Oversaw the legal system • Censors: — Oversaw the moral conduct of citizens

22. The division of power between the Roman Senate, popular assemblies, and magistrates is similar to what feature of the U.S. government?

_____

_____

_____

23. What important power did the Roman Senate have that the U.S. Senate does not have?

_____

_____

_____

24. What power did the Roman consuls have that is similar to a power that the U.S. president has today?

_____

_____

_____

_____

_____

_____

_____

_____

_____

_____

_____

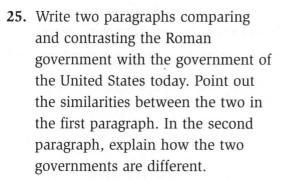

25. Write two paragraphs comparing
and contrasting the Roman
government with the government of
the United States today. Point out
the similarities between the two in
the first paragraph. In the second
paragraph, explain how the two
governments are different.

_____

_____

_____

_____

_____

_____

_____

_____

_____

_____

_____

_____

_____

_____

_____

_____

_____

_____

_____

_____

_____

_____

_____

_____

_____

_____

_____

_____

_____

_____

_____

_____

_____

_____

_____

_____

_____

_____

_____

_____

_____

_____

_____

_____

Read each selection and the questions that follow. Answer the questions in complete sentences.

Use for 26–27.

Together Spain and Portugal controlled the southern seaways, forcing other nations to search for an alternate route to reach the Pacific Ocean and the fabled riches of China and southeast Asia. Two possibilities emerged: the Northeast Passage, traversing the northern coasts of Russia, and the Northwest Passage, passing around the northern coasts of North America. [Sir Francis] Drake himself tried unsuccessfully to locate the Northwest Passage, from the Pacific side, in 1578. Having completed his mission to attack Spanish ports on the west coast of South America, he headed north to find a way home, but was forced back across the Pacific and so sailed home around the world, though that was never his original intention.

While few Europeans suspected the existence of North and South America in the 16th century (China was believed to lie due west across the Atlantic Ocean), legends abounded of a vast "Southern Continent" somewhere in the South Atlantic, which many presumed to be the fabled lost continent of Atlantis. Several attempts at discovery were made, including by Drake on the return voyage of his circumnavigation. Explorers hoped to discover an inhabited and highly civilized land, where they could trade, but it remained elusive. At the same time, the merchant adventurers were also looking to forge trading links with southeast Asia.

26. Why was there a need to find either the Northeast or the Northwest Passage?

_____

_____

_____

_____

_____

_____

_____

_____

27. What motivated the explorers' search for the Southern Continent?

_____

_____

_____

_____

_____

_____

_____

_____

Use for 28–30.

Francis Drake was only the second commander (and the first Englishman) to successfully circumnavigate the world. The main reason for Drake's epic journey, however, was not in the interests of scientific discovery, but of trade and plunder, motivated by greed. At the time, Spain was the most powerful nation in Europe and jealously guarded the seaways to her lucrative new colonies. Elizabeth I commissioned Drake to sail across the southern Atlantic, through the Straits of Magellan, and attack Spanish treasure ships and settlements on South America's unprotected west coast. He then went on to cross the Pacific Ocean and reach the Spice Islands of the East Indies. Drake returned home a rich man, his successful circumnavigation being little more than a bonus to his reputation.

The idea of establishing new colonies around the world came slowly to the Elizabethans. The original motivation for exploring new countries was born first out of trade and the need to establish new markets, and later by greed. [When England did begin to build an empire, it established colonies] around trading posts, with the result that the British Empire was scattered right across the globe along trade routes, rather than radiating out from a coherent center.

The need to discover new trade routes during Elizabeth's reign grew directly out of England's on-going war with Spain. Spain was then the richest and most powerful country in Europe and had already extended her empire to much of the West Indies and Central America, jealously guarding the southern and western seaways. International trade was as important to the Elizabethan economy and society as it is to us today and so it became essential to open up new trade routes.

28. What was the primary motivation for Drake's journey?

_____

_____

_____

_____

29. What determined where the English established colonies?

_____

_____

_____

_____

30. Why was it important for England to discover new trade routes?

_____

_____

_____

_____

Use for 31–32.

Sir Francis Drake, Explorer

1541	1566	1576	1577	1580	1585	1595	1596
Birth	First voyage to the Caribbean	Sails to the coast of Panama	Begins voyage around the world	Circum-navigation	First command as admiral	Last voyage	Death

31. How long did Drake's career as an explorer last?

_____

_____

_____

_____

_____

_____

_____

_____

_____

_____

_____

_____

_____

_____

_____

_____

_____

32. What voyages led up to Drake becoming admiral?

_____

_____

_____

_____

_____

_____

_____

_____

_____

_____

_____

_____

_____

_____

_____

_____

_____

Assessment Answers

1. A
2. B
3. B
4. D
5. C
6. C
7. D
8. C
9. B
10. A
11. A
12. B
13. B
14. B
15. C
16. C
17. A
18. C
19. D
20. D
21. B
22. A
23. C
24. C
25. C
26. B
27. The narrator is describing his or her birthday.
28. The narrator's tone at the beginning of the passage is sad.
29. The narrator's sister is probably Lili.
30. Answers will vary. Possible answer: The narrator feels surprised and excited.
31. The speaker is describing autumn.
32. Answers will vary. Possible answer: The speaker is happy because he or she enjoys autumn.
33. The speaker is describing leaves changing colors and other vegetation dying.

34. Answers will vary. Possible answer: In the passage, doldrums means that Enrique is sad or is down.
35. Answers will vary. Possible answer: Melissa's tone is upbeat and cheerful.
36. Angelina loves to ride horses. She rode for the first time when she visited her grandparents' ranch in Wyoming. When Angelina returned home, she asked her parents for a horse. At first her parents were reluctant. Angelina's family lives in the city where there is no place to keep a horse. However, they found a stable that was close to home, so they got Angelina a horse. Now Angelina rides her horse every day.

Scoring Rubric for Question 36:

4 POINTS
The student demonstrates excellent understanding of grammar, spelling, punctuation, and capitalization. There are no errors or omissions.

3 POINTS
The student demonstrates good understanding of grammar, spelling, punctuation, and capitalization. There are a few minor errors.

2 POINTS
The student demonstrates some understanding of grammar, spelling, punctuation, and capitalization. There are significant errors.

1 POINT
The student demonstrates little understanding of grammar, spelling, punctuation, and capitalization. There are only a few correct changes.

0 POINTS
The student demonstrates no understanding of grammar, spelling, punctuation, and capitalization. There are many errors.

37. Answers will vary. Possible answer: *Stable* also means "steady or firm."
38. 1. Angelina rode a horse at her grandparents' ranch. 2. Angelina's parents found a stable for a horse. 3. Angelina got a horse.
39. The story is a folktale, or fable.
40. Answers will vary. Possible answer: This story teaches us that we shouldn't put things off. Tomorrow never comes.

Assessment Answers

41. Answers will vary. Possible answer: Hamad waited until tomorrow to teach Jordan a lesson.

Scoring Rubric for Question 42:

4 POINTS
Essay is clearly written, easy to understand, and free of grammar mistakes. Essay follows the type of writing he or she chose.

3 POINTS
Most of the essay is easy to understand. There are a few grammar mistakes. Most of the essay follows the type of writing he or she chose.

2 POINTS
Parts of the essay are easy to understand but other parts are confusing. There are many grammar mistakes. Parts of the essay follow the type of writing he or she chose.

1 POINT
Most of the essay is difficult to understand. There is no evidence of an attempt to use correct grammar. Most of the essay does not follow the type of writing he or she chose.

0 POINTS
Overall, the essay is difficult to understand, is filled with incorrect grammar, and does not follow the type of writing he or she chose.

MATH

1. B
2. D
3. B
4. D
5. A
6. C
7. C
8. B
9. A
10. D
11. D
12. D
13. B
14. B
15. A
16. B
17. D
18. A
19. C
20. A
21. B
22. C
23. C
24. C
25. D
26. B
27. C
28. B
29. C
30. C
31. B
32. C
33. A
34. B
35. D

Assessment Answers

36. B

37. C

38. B

39. D

40. B

41. C

42. Possible graph:

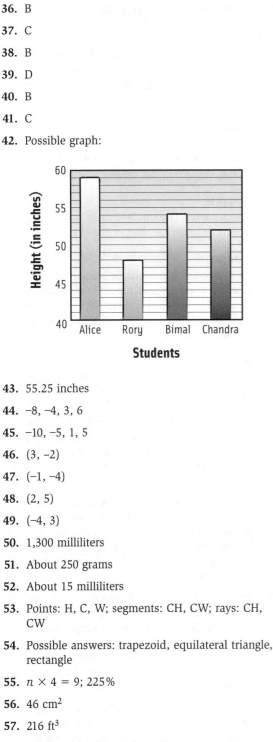

43. 55.25 inches

44. −8, −4, 3, 6

45. −10, −5, 1, 5

46. (3, −2)

47. (−1, −4)

48. (2, 5)

49. (−4, 3)

50. 1,300 milliliters

51. About 250 grams

52. About 15 milliliters

53. Points: H, C, W; segments: CH, CW; rays: CH, CW

54. Possible answers: trapezoid, equilateral triangle, rectangle

55. $n \times 4 = 9$; 225%

56. 46 cm²

57. 216 ft³

58. No, he would need about $12.

59. $5.21

60. $0.80

SCIENCE

1. C

2. D

3. B

4. A

5. B

6. C

7. A

8. A

9. D

10. D

11. B

12. A

13. A

14. C

15. B

16. C

17. A

18. A

19. C

20. B

21. B

22. B

23. A

24. C

25. B

26. A

27. B

28. A

29. C

30. Wind is an inexhaustible resource. It is classified this way because the supply of wind never runs out.

31. The difference is that renewable resources can be depleted, but natural processes will replenish them. Nonrenewable resources, if used up, will never be replenished.

Assessment Answers

32. Erosion wears away earth materials, and deposition is the process of depositing earth materials.

33. Answers will vary. Possible answer: Two abiotic parts of a stream ecosystem are the rainfall and the temperature. Two biotic parts of a stream ecosystem are fish and the underwater plants. If there were a severe drought, the stream would dry up and the fish and plants would die. There would have to be enough rainfall to make the stream again, and the temperature would have to be not too cold (so that the water would freeze) and not too hot, which could result in not enough stream water.

Scoring Rubric for Question 33:

4 POINTS
The answer indicates an understanding of abiotic and biotic factors, correctly identifies two of each, and correctly identifies their response to a drought. The concept of ecosystem is clearly understood.

3 POINTS
The answer indicates some understanding of abiotic and biotic factors. The answer may correctly identify three of the four items asked for. The answer shows some understanding of the response to a drought.

2 POINTS
The answer indicates some understanding of abiotic and biotic factors. One or two factors may be correctly identified. The answer shows some understanding of the response to a drought.

1 POINT
The answer indicates little understanding of abiotic and biotic factors. One or two factors may be correctly identified. The answer shows little understanding of the response to a drought.

0 POINTS
The answer indicates no understanding of abiotic and biotic factors. No factors are correctly identified. The answer shows no understanding of the response to a drought.

Scoring Rubric for Question 34:

4 POINTS
The response is correct and effectively demonstrates the student's understanding of animal characteristics. There are no errors or omissions.

3 POINTS
The response is adequate and demonstrates the student's understanding of animal characteristics. It may contain minor omissions and errors.

2 POINTS
The response is partially correct but lacks adequate understanding of the characteristics.

1 POINT
The response demonstrates some evidence of relevant knowledge of the differences and similarities between animals; however, there is little evidence that the student knows why his or her response is incorrect.

0 POINTS
The response demonstrates a lack of scientific knowledge related to the content.

35. If an offspring has the recessive trait of blue eyes, the parents could either be Bb or bb. Blue eyes are recessive and therefore for an offspring to have this color both parents must provide the gene.

36. If one offspring has blue eyes and one offspring has brown eyes, both of the parents must carry the gene for blue eyes. Each parent would have to have the gene combination Bb because each parent gave a gene for blue eyes and a gene for brown eyes.

37. Observations: After two weeks, water in the glass is missing; hypothesis: Since no one removed the water, the water evaporated; prediction: The water will evaporate; description of test: Put another glass of water on the table for two weeks and daily measure how much of the water remains in the glass.

38. Earth orbits around the sun and the moon orbits around Earth. Earth and the moon are in constant rotation. Gravity keeps the moon and Earth in orbit.

Assessment Answers

39. **A.** This section is the fats, sweets, and oil group; **B.** This section is the milk, cheese, and yogurt group; **C.** This section is the meat, chicken, fish, eggs, and nuts group; **D.** This section is the vegetable group; **E.** This section is the fruit group; **F.** This section is the bread, rice, cereal, and pasta group.

40. The food pyramid tells us what amount and what types of foods we should be eating to be healthy.

41. **A.** lithosphere, **B.** crust, **C.** mantle, **D.** core

42. This is the theory that Earth's surface is made up of plates that are in constant motion.

43. Earthquakes and volcanoes are related in that they are both breaks or openings in Earth's crust.

SOCIAL STUDIES

1. B
2. D
3. A
4. D
5. C
6. A
7. C
8. B
9. C
10. A
11. C
12. B
13. B
14. D
15. B
16. A
17. B
18. D
19. B
20. B
21. D

22. The division of Roman power is similar to the U.S. system of checks and balances.

23. The Roman Senate had the power to appoint a dictator for up to six months.

24. The consuls had veto power, similar to the U.S. president.

Scoring Rubric for Question 25:

4 POINTS

The paragraphs demonstrate clear understanding of the organization of both the Roman and U.S. governments. The first paragraph recognizes similarities such as the system of checks and balances, veto power, and the lawmaking roles of the Senate and popular assemblies. The second paragraph points out differences such as the ability of the Senate to appoint a dictator, the differences in the way officials are elected, and the role of the censors in overseeing the moral conduct of citizens.

Assessment Answers

3 POINTS
The paragraphs demonstrate good understanding of both systems of government. There are minor omissions of similarities and differences.

2 POINTS
The paragraphs demonstrate adequate understanding of both systems of government, but there are major omissions of similarities and differences.

1 POINT
The paragraphs demonstrate some understanding of both systems of government, but they fail to point out significant similarities and differences.

0 POINTS
The paragraphs demonstrate little understanding of either system of government. There are no comparisons made.

26. Spain and Portugal controlled the southern seaways and the route to the Pacific Ocean.

27. The explorers hoped they could establish trade there.

28. Francis Drake sought trade and plunder.

29. The location of where the English established colonies was determined by trade routes.

30. Spain controlled many of the trade routes, and trade was essential to England's economy.

31. Drake's career lasted for 29 years.

32. The voyages that led up to Drake becoming admiral were his voyages to the Caribbean, coast of Panama, and around the world.

PROMOTING LITERACY

Lesson 1.1

Student Learning Page 1.B

1. Answer will vary depending on the character chosen.
2. Elizabeth George Speare
3. *The Sign of the Beaver*
4. Facts will vary depending on which character was chosen.
5. Opinions will vary depending on which character was chosen.
6. Answers will vary. Predictions should be well thought out.

Lesson 1.2

Student Learning Page 2.B

Possible answers:

Story Structure:

Setting: Ancient Persia, in the shah's palace, in a fort outside the city; takes place over many days

Characters: shah, queen, false holy man, chief bandit, bandits

Problem: people were disappearing from the city

Resolution: shah followed the people and sent word back to the palace that he needed help

One Character:

Student should choose one of the main characters from the story and give accurate adjectives describing him or her, with examples from the story to support the adjectives.

Lesson 1.4

Student Learning Page 4.B

Answers will vary but should accurately represent book.

Lesson 1.5

Student Learning Page 5.C

Answers will vary. Poetry log should include student's own thoughts and feelings.

Lesson 1.6

Student Learning Page 6.B

The excerpt fits into rising action. Accept all reasonable responses for the other parts of the story structure.

Lesson 1.7

Student Learning Page 7.B

Answers will vary. Household items should be selected with players finding various numbers of items.

Lesson 1.8

Student Learning Page 8.A

Answers will vary but should accurately list who, what, where, when, why, and how.

Lesson 1.9

Student Learning Page 9.B

All items on checklist should be checked.

Student Learning Page 9.C

1. Answers will vary depending on what areas the student needs to work.
2. Answers will vary depending on the areas that need improvement.

Answers

MATH

Lesson 2.1

Student Learning Page 1.A

1. 2×23
2. $2^2 \times 3 \times 5$
3. 3^3
4. $2^3 \times 3^2$
5. 67 is prime
6. 2^5
7. GCF: 2; LCM: 210
8. GCF: 5; LCM: 1,050
9. GCF: 3; LCM: 693
10. GCF: 3; LCM: 90

Lesson 2.2

Student Learning Page 2.A

1. $\frac{3}{4}$
2. $\frac{4}{6}$
3. $\frac{2}{10}$
4. $\frac{3}{15}$
5. $\frac{4}{20}$
6. $\frac{12}{30}, \frac{16}{40}, \frac{20}{50}$; pattern is times 5
7. $\frac{5}{8}$
8. $\frac{10}{12} = \frac{5}{6}$
9. $6\frac{7}{8}$
10. $4\frac{1}{4}$
11. $3\frac{1}{2}$
12. $8\frac{4}{7}$

Student Learning Page 2.B

1. $\frac{6}{15}$
2. $4\frac{2}{5}$
3. $8\frac{8}{9}$
4. $1\frac{55}{56}$
5. $\frac{3}{8}$
6. $5\frac{1}{2}$
7. $2\frac{21}{60}$
8. $\frac{3}{8}$
9. $\frac{1}{20}$ cup rolled oats
10. 5 cups rolled oats
11. $\frac{1}{2}$ and $\frac{1}{4}$

Lesson 2.3

Student Learning Page 3.A

1. 6.88
2. 29.5
3. 36.5
4. 20.229
5. 77.511
6. 9.635
7. 96.46
8. 31.05
9. 74.931

Student Learning Page 3.B

1. 5.848
2. 2.2714
3. 27.204
4. 21.1
5. 127.765
6. 10
7. 4.444
8. 11,000
9. 2,038.608

Answers

Lesson 2.4

Student Learning Page 4.A

	No. of Squares out of 100	Percent	Decimal	Fraction
Lettuce	6	6%	.06	$\frac{3}{50}$
Bell peppers	7	7%	.07	$\frac{7}{100}$
Hot peppers	2	2%	.02	$\frac{1}{50}$
Tomatoes	16	16%	.16	$\frac{4}{25}$
Heirloom tomatoes	15	15%	.15	$\frac{3}{20}$
Green beans	9	9%	.09	$\frac{9}{100}$
Radishes	1	1%	.01	$\frac{1}{100}$
Walking paths	44	44%	.44	$\frac{11}{25}$

Lesson 2.5

Student Learning Page 5.A

1. $\frac{7}{10}$, 7:10, 7 to 10

2. $\frac{9}{4}$, 9:4, 9 to 4

3. $\frac{20}{5}$ or $\frac{4}{1}$, 4:1, 4 to 1

4. possible answers: $\frac{1}{2}$, $\frac{14}{28}$

5. possible answers: $\frac{4}{5}$, $\frac{24}{30}$

6. possible answers: $\frac{2}{10}$, $\frac{4}{20}$

7. 275 miles

8. 2 miles an hour

9. $15 an hour

10. Answers will vary. The problem and solution should be accurate.

Lesson 2.6

Student Learning Page 6.A

A. range: 6, mean: 6.6, median: 6.5, mode: 5, 7

B. range: 49, mean: 37, median: 50, no mode

1. the top five dog breeds

2. Labrador retriever; beagle

3. about 173,548

4. Possible answer: Calculate the percents to find the actual numbers of the breeds and use those numbers to make a bar graph.

Answers

Intervals	Tally Marks	Frequency
45–49	II	2
50–54	I	1
55–59	IIII	4
60–64	HHT I	6
65–69	HHT I	6
70–74	HHT II	7
75–79	IIII	4
80–84	III	3
85–89	II	2
90–94	II	2

1. age 70–74
2. age 50–54
3. age 60–64, 65–69, 70–74

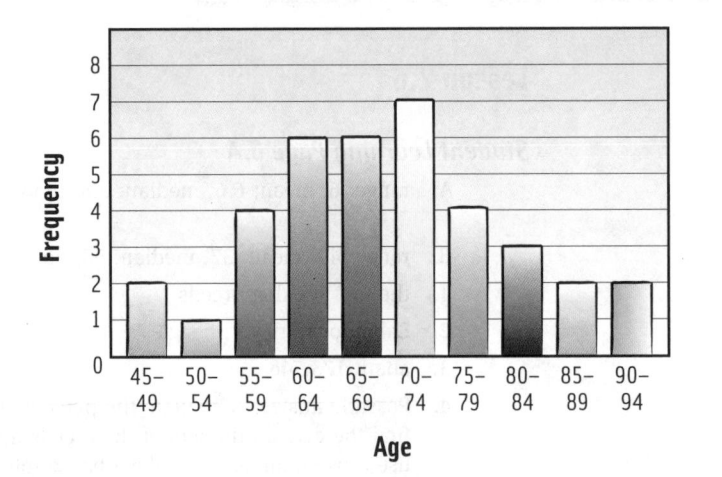

4. both show the same ages for average allowances
5. graph A; because it shows a better representation of allowances for children ages 7–12
6. Answers will vary. Possible answer: Round the allowances to whole numbers, and cents to quarters, fifty, and seventy-five cents.

Student Learning Page 6.C

All answer lines should be completed. A graph on a separate paper should be completed.

Answers

Lesson 2.7

Student Learning Page 7.A

1. +5
2. 0
3. −3
4. +2
5. −5
6. +4
7. 16°F
8. 3°F
9. −12°F
10. 2°F
11. −7, −5, −3, 0, +2, +4, +6
12. F
13. F
14. F

Student Learning Page 7.B

1. library
2. school
3. market
4. pharmacy
5. Answers will vary. Check student's work.
6. Check student's ordered pairs on graph.

Lesson 2.8

Student Learning Page 8.A

1. 2 ft 6 in.
2. 216 in.
3. 10,560 ft
4. 5,280 yd
5. 1 mi 490 yd
6. 1,152 in.
7. 300 cm
8. 500 mm
9. 6,000 mm
10. 200,000 cm
11. 3,000,000 mm
12. 0.096 m
13. 3 lb 2 oz
14. 100,000 lb
15. 144 oz
16. 46,000 lb
17. 0.75 lb
18. 32,000 oz
19. 50,000 g
20. 23,000 kg
21. 2,370,000 mg
22. 1,000,000 mg
23. 3.1 kg
24. 3,100,000 mg

Student Learning Page 8.B

1. 32 fl oz
2. 8 pt
3. 4 qt
4. 1 gal
5. 112 pt
6. 7.5 qt
7. 4,000 ml
8. 0.09 l
9. 0.016 kl
10. 14,000,000 ml
11. 0.033 kl
12. 0.24 l

Charts should be filled in accurately.

Student Learning Page 8.C

1. 7:00 A.M.
2. 9:25 A.M.
3. 11:20 P.M. the day before
4. 12:36 P.M.
5. 4:50 P.M.
6. 6:00 P.M.
7. 5:09 A.M.
8. 4 hours
9. 3 hours
10. 1 hour

Lesson 2.9

Student Learning Page 9.A

1. 58.5 ft
2. 59 in.
3. 40 ft
4. 48 in.
5. 172.5 ft
6. 1,728 ft

Answers

7. 270 ft

8. 252 in.

9. 198 in.

10. 184 ft

11. 1.125 m

12. 143 cm

Student Learning Page 9.B

1. 21.98 in.

2. 219.8 in.

3. 15.7 m

4. 91.06 m

5. 125.6 cm

6. 37.68 ft

7. 38.465 in.^{2}

8. 3,846.5 in.^{2}

9. 19.625 m^2

10. 660.185 m^2

11. 1,256 cm^2

12. 113.04 ft^2

13. 8,004 in.^{3}

14. 2,160 cm^3

15. 952 m^3

16. 1,870 ft^3

17. 160,000 ft^3

18. 140,000 ft^3

19. 8,664 m^3

20. 90,000 ft^3

Lesson 2.10

Student Learning Page 10.A

Answers will vary.

Student Learning Page 10.B

Angles:
∠LMO, 45°, acute;
∠LMP, 90°, right;
∠LMQ, 120°, obtuse;
∠LMN, 180°, straight;
∠OMP, 45°, acute;
∠OMQ, 75°, acute;
∠OMN 135°, obtuse;
∠PMQ, 30°, acute;
∠PMN, 90°, right;
∠QMN, 60°, acute.

Drawings should be accurate.

Student Learning Page 10.C

1. 90°, rectangle

2. 90°, trapezoid

3. 20°, trapezoid

4. 60°, parallelogram

5. 7 in., square

6. 7 in., parallelogram

7. 16 ft, rectangle

8. 110°, trapezoid

9. 8 in., parallelogram

Student Learning Page 10.E

Drawings should be accurate.

Student Learning Page 10.F

Drawings should be accurate.

SCIENCE

Lesson 3.1

Student Learning Page 1.A

Sample properties: mammals: vertebrate, warm-blooded, nurse their young, have hair; reptiles: vertebrate, cold-blooded, most don't nurse their young, have scales; amphibians: vertebrate, cold-blooded, metamorphosis occurs during growth of most amphibians, have scaleless skin; fish: vertebrate, cold-blooded, have fins, live in water, must have scales.

Student Learning Page 1.B

The examples of vertebrates and invertebrates should be correct and their groups should be accurately reflected.

Lesson 3.2

Student Learning Page 2.A

Flower

1. stamen

2. filament

3. anther

4. petal

5. sepal

6. pistil
7. stigma
8. style
9. ovary
10. ovule

Plant

1. leaf
2. flower
3. stem
4. root
5. fruit
6. seeds

Student Learning Page 2.B

1. Carbon dioxide enters the leaf through stomata.
2. Carbon dioxide combines with stored solar energy in the chloroplasts.
3. Plant produces sugar (food).
4. Oxygen is formed as a by-product of photosynthesis.
5. Oxygen is released into the atmosphere.

Lesson 3.3

Student Learning Page 3.B

1. brown or blue
2. Bb; since blue eyes are recessive, the gene must be present in both parents
3. 50%
4. Answers will vary.
5. Answers will vary.

Lesson 3.4

Student Learning Page 4.A

1. lungs
2. artery
3. heart
4. vein
5. kidneys

Student Learning Page 4.B

The red and blue arrows should indicate the path of the blood correctly.

Student Learning Page 4.C

1. spinal cord
2. spinal nerves
3. medulla oblongata
4. cerebrum
5. cerebellum

Lesson 3.5

Student Learning Page 5.A

Suggested characteristics:

Infancy:

period of rapid growth for mental and physical skills; begins to smile; can laugh; can sit when propped; can recognize mother; can say a few words; may be able to stand unsupported

Childhood:

develops muscular coordination and mental abilities; can walk without help; can control bladder and bowel; speaks in simple sentences; can read; develops abilities to read, write, speak, and reason; develops emotionally and socially

Adolescence:

develops the ability to reproduce; changes in hormones and physical appearance of both males and females; may experience feelings of sexual attraction; increase in growth known as growth spurt; better coordination; improved reasoning abilities; usually spends more time with peers

Adulthood:

muscular and skeletal system stops growing; individual takes on responsibility as a provider and caretaker for himself or herself, family, and community; continues to mature mentally and emotionally; after midlife signs of aging begin to appear, wisdom increases

Lesson 3.6

Student Learning Page 6.A

Possible answer: observation: the seeds look like little parachutes; hypothesis: the wind carries the seeds in the air; prediction: if I blow on the seeds, they'll lift into the air and move away from the dandelion plant; experimental test: hold up a dandelion plant and blow on the seeds.

Answers

Lesson 3.7

Student Learning Page 7.A

1. land biome:
   Special features: less than 25 cm rainfall; plants, shrubs, and animals that don't require regular rainfall and can adapt to extreme temperatures; humans compete for water supply; deserts grow

   Where in the world? western North America, western South America, northern Africa, southwestern Africa, central Australia, central Asia

2. land biome:
   Special features: nearly 75 cm precipitation; mostly grasses; wide temperature range; irregular rainfall

   Where in the world? central North America, central South America, much of Africa, much of Asia, Australia

3. land biome:
   Special features: nearly 250 cm precipitation; always hot and humid; widest variety of life forms; fast growth

   Where in the world? around equator in South America, Asia, Central America, Africa

4. land biome:
   Special features: nearly 100 cm precipitation; varied forests; leaves fall off in fall; regrow in spring; four seasons; climate lends itself to human development

   Where in the world? middle latitudes, North America, Europe, Asia; less: South America, Australia, Africa

5. land biome:
   Special features: nearly 50 cm precipitation; coniferous forests; forests are a natural resource; warmer than tundra; rain and fog

   Where in the world? North America, Europe, Asia, south of tundra

6. land biome:
   Special features: nearly 20 cm precipitation; mosses and lichens grow there; most precipitation is snow; permafrost—frozen ground; short growing season; fragile ecosystems

   Where in the world? North America, Europe, Asia, around Arctic Circle

Lesson 3.8

Student Learning Page 8.A

Answers will vary. The color of the minerals should be recorded accurately, and a scratch test should be performed and results recorded for each mineral.

Lesson 3.9

Student Learning Page 9.A

Mercury: inner; answer will vary.

Venus: inner; answer will vary.

Earth: inner; 365 Earth days; answer will vary.

Mars: inner; answer will vary.

Jupiter: outer; answer will vary.

Saturn: outer; answer will vary.

Uranus: outer; answer will vary.

Neptune: outer; answer will vary.

Pluto: outer; answer will vary.

Lesson 3.10

Student Learning Page 10.A

Materials should be constructed accurately so that hot dog is cooked.

Lesson 3.11

Student Learning Page 11.A

Check to be sure both diagrams are drawn and labeled accurately.

Student Learning Page 11.B

Check to be sure that your student accurately completes the activities he or she chooses.

Answers

Lesson 3.12

Student Learning Page 12.A
Check your student's written observations.

Student Learning Page 12.B
Check your student's written observations.

Lesson 4.1

Student Learning Page 1.A
The map should be filled in accurately.

Lesson 4.2

Student Learning Page 2.A
Map should be colored and the delta should be identified accurately.

Lesson 4.3

Student Learning Page 3.A
Diagram 1: Top row: King and family; Row 2: Nobles; Row 3: Craftworkers; Row 4: Farmers; Row 5: Prisoners of war

Diagram 2: Top row: Emperor; Row 2: Samurai class (shogun, landowners, and soldiers); Row 3: Peasants and artisans; Row 4: Merchants

Lesson 4.4

Student Learning Page 4.A
Ancient Greece

Government: democracy

Who made laws: the citizens

Citizen responsibilities: to participate in all meetings, votes, and decisions

Primary values: truth, beauty, balance, moderation, harmony, political responsibility

Roman Empire

Government: republic

Who made laws: elected representatives

Citizen responsibilities: to vote for representatives

Primary values: order, practicality, family, education

United States

Government: federal republic

Who makes laws: elected representatives

Citizen responsibilities: to vote for congressional, executive, and judiciary representatives

Primary values: equal opportunity, checks and balances, justice, freedom, pursuit of happiness (other answers also apply)

Lesson 4.5

Student Learning Page 5.A
Coat of arms should be completed.

Lesson 4.6

Student Learning Page 6.A
1. Possible answers: Germany, Austria, Poland, Czech Republic, Slovakia, Hungary
2. Black Sea, Mediterranean Sea, Adriatic Sea
3. Possible answers: The Fourth Crusade seemed to cover the shortest distance. The Third Crusade seemed to cover the largest distance. The Third Crusade travelers went over much water. The First Crusade was mostly on land. The Fourth Crusade didn't go to present-day Africa.

Lesson 4.7

Student Learning Page 7.A

Across	Down
1. Michelangelo	1. Middle Ages
6. Leonardo	2. humanism
9. rebirth	3. Florence
10. Shakespeare	4. Medici
11. Black Death	5. city-state
	7. Romans
	8. Petrarch

Answers

Lesson 4.8

Student Learning Page 8.A

Possible answers:

1. Causes: Decline in the power of the pope and the Holy Roman Emperor due to their preoccupation with threats from Turks; Invention of printing in the 1400s; Growth of secular learning; Rise of nationalism; Resentment of the pope's power by rulers and common people.

2. Effects: Religious literature no longer only written in Latin; Religious restrictions on trade and banking removed; Power and wealth redistributed from the nobility and Roman Catholic hierarchy to middle class and monarchical rulers; Various European regions gained political, religious, or cultural freedoms; Further development of democratic government; Opened avenues to modern capitalism.

Lesson 4.9

Student Learning Page 9.A

The map should be filled in accurately.

Lesson 4.10

Student Learning Page 10.A

Time lines may vary, but dates should be accurate and entries should include the various machines used in the textile industry, canal and railroad advancements, and communications tools.

Lesson 4.11

Student Learning Page 11.A

Answers will vary.

	American	French	Russian
Date	1775	1789	1917
Opposed Ruler	King George II of Great Britain	King Louis XVI	Czar Nicholas II
Reason	Taxation without representation	People heavily taxed to support clergy and nobles; poverty	Absolute rule; terrible losses in World War I; supply shortages
Result	Independence from Britain	Overthrow of king	Abdication of czar
New Government	Federal republic	Military dictatorship with Napoleon as its head	Communist dictatorship

GLOSSARY

Like any other specialty area, teaching and homeschooling have their own unique vocabulary. We've included some terms we thought might be helpful.

accelerated learning

when a student completes a certain set of lessons faster than normal; this can happen due to a student's natural motivation or in a more structured manner, such as continuing lessons throughout the year versus taking the summer off

assessment

a review of a student's learning progress and comprehension; traditionally done through tests or grades, assessments in progressive learning environments such as homeschooling take on many different forms, including summary discussions, demonstrative projects, and oral questions and answers; formalized assessment is included in this book, beginning on page 295

auditory learner

an individual who absorbs new information most effectively by listening; an auditory learner will remember information that is spoken or related through sound such as musical lyrics, reading aloud, or audio-cassettes

child-centered learning

a type of learning in which the teaching style places the child at the center of his or her learning, meaning that a child begins and proceeds with new subjects, such as reading, as he or she is ready; this style of teaching requires intimate awareness of the student by the teacher

correlated to state standards

a phrase that means that something meets or exceeds a particular state's mandatory educational requirements for the intended grade level

critical thinking skill

the ability to assess information, make independent judgments, and draw conclusions; this skill is independent of and goes beyond the memorized information that a student has learned

curriculum

an ordered list of specific topics of study that is used as a teaching map

distance learning

a type of instruction in which classes are completed at a different physical location than at the school that offers them; formerly known as correspondence classes, this term now includes video and Internet classes

graphic organizer

a way to visually organize information for the purpose of learning enhancement; usually referring to charts and graphs, these can be useful for visual learners; several graphic organizers are included in this book: Venn Diagram, Comparison Chart, Web, and Sequence Chain

inclusive

a homeschool group that is inclusive and welcomes anyone who homeschools regardless of religious or educational beliefs or practices; as homeschooling becomes more popular, more inclusive groups have been formed

kinesthetic learner

an individual who absorbs new information most effectively through experience; a kinesthetic learner will understand information by completing hands-on exercises, doing, and moving

learning style
> the singular manner and rate that each child naturally pursues his or her education; educators have identified three primary ways of describing learning styles: audio, kinesthetic, and visual

lesson plan
> a detailed description of the part of the curriculum one is planning to teach on a certain day

multicultural
> adapted to relate to diverse cultures; some homeschool teachers incorporate multicultural learning materials into their lessons to encourage exposure to different traditions

real books
> books you get at the library or the bookstore that aren't textbooks; some homeschoolers work almost exclusively from real books and don't use textbooks at all; this book provides a curriculum that's based on reading and research with real books

scoring rubric
> a measurement tool used to assess student work that includes a system of scoring levels of performance; scoring rubrics are used with some lessons in this book and with the formalized assessment section in the back of this book

self-directed learner
> an individual who is free to pursue education by his or her own means and guidance versus through traditional classes or schools; a term used in homeschool literature

self-teaching
> when an individual naturally learns about a topic of particular interest on his or her own, without formal instruction and usually as a result of natural attraction to or talent in the subject matter

standardized test
> a test is considered standardized when it is given in the same manner, with same directions to children of the same grade level across the country; the test shows how your student is doing compared to the national average; the assessment section beginning on page 295 offers examples of standardized test questions

teaching strategy
> a creative way to motivate and inspire students, such as using a visual aid, entertaining or humorous delivery, interactive activity, or theme-based lessons; if your student is bored, he or she might benefit from a change in teaching strategies

unschooling
> a teaching philosophy first identified by educator John Holt that's based on the idea that, as a homeschool parent, you may proceed however you see fit as long as there is confidence that your child is learning; works under the assertion that textbook-type teaching can dull a child's natural zest for learning and the belief that a student will comprehend more when he or she is engaged, uninterrupted, and enjoying what he or she is learning

visual learner
> an individual who absorbs new information most effectively through the sense of sight; a visual learner will comprehend information by reading, watching a video, using a visual computer program, and looking at pictures in books

Waldorf
> a method of education that was developed by Rudolph Steiner and attempts to teach the whole child: physical, emotional, and academic; Waldorf schools are located throughout the country, and there is also a network of Waldorf homeschoolers

Venn Diagram

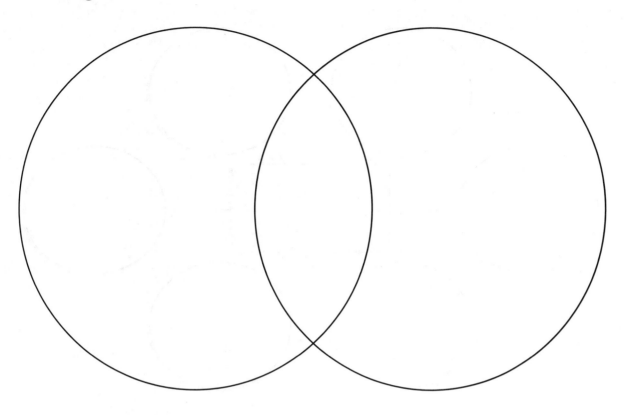

Comparison Chart

Issue:_____	A: _____	B: _____
I.	1.	2.
II.	3.	4.
III.	5.	6.

Web

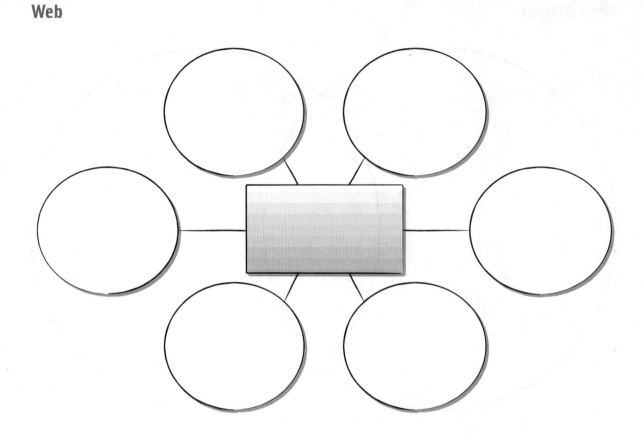

Sequence Chain

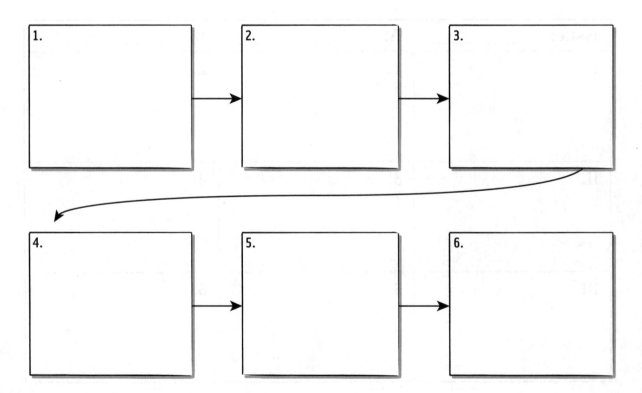

Grid

Index

Note: Page numbers in bold indicate the definition of a term.

A

Abacus, **243**, 245
Abbreviations, units of measure, 125–128
Absolute power, **275**, 277
Acids, **221**, 223–224
  acid rain, 213
  plant growth and, 216
Acrostic, 292
Acting
  directing activity, 54
  dramatic scene, 46
  fictional scene, 11
Activism activity, 274
Acute angle, **139**
Acute triangle, **141**
Addition
  of decimals, 91–92, 95
  of fractions, 83–84, 87
  of integers, 120
Adolescence, **187**, 189
Adulthood, **187**, 189
Advertisements, writing, 74, 286
African civilizations, 246
Age, calculating, 209
Age of Reason, **275**, 277–278
Alexander the Great, 250–251
Alphabet, 233, 234
Amenhotep IV, 240
American Revolution, 271, 272, 287–288, 291
Amphibians, 154, 157, 158
Ancient Egypt, 237–242
  culture, 237–239
  map exercise, 241
  Nile River, 237–238
  optional activities, 242
Ancient Greece, 249–251, 253
Ancient Rome, 251–253
Angles, **140**
  measuring and labeling, 144–145
  quadrilateral, 142, 145
  triangle, 141
  types, 141, 143
Animals, 153–160
  cell structure, 170–171
  characteristics, 154, 157
  classifying, 153, 154–155, 158
  optional activities, 159–160
Annual plants, **161**, 164
Aqueducts, **249**, 252
Arabic numerals, 254
Arc, **147**
Archaeology, **232**
  Rosetta Stone, 239
  21st Century activity, 236
Architecture
  Gothic, 257, 260
  Roman, 252, 257
Area, **133**
  circle, 135, 138
  polygon, 134–135, 137
Armor, 256

Art and artists
  criticism activity, 270
  Enlightenment, 277
  Renaissance, 267
Arteries, **177**, 179
Asian cultures
  China, 244–245, 247
  India, 243–244
  Japan, 245, 274, 289–290
  optional activities, 248
  Ottoman, 245
Assessment
  literacy, 295–306, 335–336
  mathematics, 307–316, 336–337
  science, 317–326, 337–339
  social studies, 327–334, 339–340
Assyrian civilization, 234
Asteroids, **207**, 208
Athens, Golden Age of, 250
Atom(s)
  in buckyball, 224
  components, 222
  fusion, 208
Atomic bombs, 290
Audubon, John James, 194
Autobiography, **31**
Average (mathematical), **111**, 112
Axis, **287**
  Axis Powers, 288
  coordinate grid, 121–122
Aztec civilization, 277

B

Babel, Tower of, 233
Babylonian civilization, 232–233
Bar graphs, **112**, 113–114
Bases, **221**, 223–224
Bibliographies, 64
Biennial plants, **161**, 164
Big bang theory, **208**
Biography, **31**
  concepts and analysis, 31–32
  on monarchs, writing, 264
  optional activities, 38
  reading selection, 33–36
  reading strategies, 37
Biomes, **196**, 198, 199
Biosphere, **196**
Birdbath activity, 160
Black Death, 265–266, 270
Blood bank, researching, 186
Board game, designing, 98
Body systems. *See* Human body
Bonaparte, Napoléon, 288
Boycott, **287**, 288
Brain, **177**
  function and structure, 179, 183
  modeling experiment, 184–185

Brochure, designing, 155
Buckyball, 224
Buddhism, 244
Business card, designing, 38
Byzantine Empire, 262, 263

C

Caesar, Julius, 251
Calendar, 238
Calligraphy, **243**, 245
Calvin, John, 272, 274
Canaan, 233
Canals, **281**, 283
Capacity units, **127**–128, 130
Capital, **282**
Capitalism, **271**, **281**
  origins and growth, 281
  time line activity, 274
Carbon dioxide experiment, 185–186
Career search, 159
Carnivores, **155**, **196**–197
Cartoon. *See* Comic strip
Caste system, **244**
Castles, 257
Catholic Church, 261–263.
  See also Christianity
Cause and effect, literary, 16, 24–25, 48
CDC (Centers for Disease Control and Prevention), 190
Cell division, 171
Cell membrane/wall, **170**
Cells, **170**–173
  genetic material, 171–172, 174–175
  microscopic analysis, 173
  optional activities, 176
  structure and reproduction, 171–172
Centers for Disease Control and Prevention (CDC), 190
Cerebellum, **177**, 179, 183
Cerebrum, **177**, 179, 183
Character traits, 21, 47
Chemical formula, **221**, 223
Chemical reactions, **221**, 222, 223, 226
Childhood, **187**, 189
Chinese civilization, 244–245, 247
Chloroplasts, **169**, 170, 171
Christianity, 252
  pilgrimages and Crusades, 261–262, 263
  Reformation, 271–273
Chromosomes, **169**, 171
Church. *See* Christianity
Circle, **133**, 135, 138
Circle graph, **112**, 115
Circulatory system, **177**
  concepts, 178–179
  organs and vessels, 181
  pulmonary blood flow, 182
Circumference, **135**, 138
Citing sources, MLA style, 63–64

City-states
  Greek, 249–250
  Italian, 265, 266–267
Classics, 266
Classification
  animal, 153–155, 158
  element, 221, 223
  plant, 164
Climate, **197**–198
  of biomes, 199
  experiment about, 200
  monsoon season, 243
Coat of arms, 256, 259
Coffee experiment, 194
Cold-blooded animals, **153**, 154, 155
Cold War, 290
Colonists, **287**, 288
Color, light waves and, 218
Columbus, Christopher, 276
Comets, **207**, 208
Comic strip, designing
  folktale illustration, 22
  humorous, 62
  personal experience, 74
Common denominator, 84
Communicable disease, **187**, 188
  plague, 265–266
  spread of, 190
Communists, **287**, 289
Community, **195**, 196
Community outreach activities
  literary, 75
  mathematics, 149
  science, 227
  social studies, 293
Comparison Chart graphic organizer, 353
Composite numbers, **79**–81
Compounds, **221**, 223
Conclusions, drawing literary, 25, 32, 37
Conduction, **212**–213
Conflict, literary, 21, 47.
  See also Revolutions;
  World War *entries*
Confucius, 244–245
Congruent, **139**
  angles, 141
  lines, 147
Conquistadores, **275**, 277
Constantine, 262
Constantinople, 262
Consumers (food chain), **196**–197
Context clues, 3, 16, 47–48
Convection, **212**–213
Converting, **99**
  metric conversion table, 130
  percentages, 99–103
  units of measure, 126–130
Cookbook, creating, 185
Cooking. *See also* Recipes
  coffee experiment, 194
  eggs, 176
  with solar energy, 215

Coordinate grids, 121–122, 124
Coordinates, **119**, 122, 124
Copernicus, Nicolaus, 276
Core (Earth's), 203, **204**
Coronary circulation, **178**
Cortés, Hernando, 277
Crossword puzzle test, 269
Crusades, **261**, 262, 263
Crust (Earth's), **201**, 202–203
Cube, volume, 138
Cuneiform, **232**
Cuneiform tablets, 232, 236
Currency exchange rate
  activity, 98
Customary measuring system,
  125
    abbreviations, 125, 126,
      127
    conversion exercises,
      129–130
    units, 125–127
Cylinder, volume, 136
Cytoplasm, 170, **171**
Czar, **287**, 289

D

Dandelions, 192, 193
Data, interpreting and
  presenting, **111**–118.
  See also Graphs
Debate activity, 275
Decimal derby, 97
Decimals
    adding and subtracting,
      91–92, 95
    converting percents to,
      99, 101, 103
    decimal derby game, 97
    multiplying and dividing,
      93–94, 96
    optional activities, 98
Decomposers, **197**
Democracy, **249**, **271**
    etymology, 250
    time line, 274
Denominator, **83**
Deposition, **202**
Descriptive writing, 68
Details
    interpreting, 48
    personal narrative, 69
    predicting and inferring
      from, 15
    supporting main idea,
      55, 56
Developmental stages,
  human, **187**–188, 189
Diameter, **135**, 138
Dictatorship, **249**, 251, **287**, 289
Dinner out activity, 104
Directing a play, 54
Directions, giving and
  following, 62
Direct quote, punctuation, 56
Discounts, calculating, 100–101
Disease. *See* Communicable
  disease

Division
    converting units of
      measure, 126
    of decimals, 93–94, 96
    to determine percents,
      100, 101, 103–104
    of fractions, 84–86, 88
DNA (deoxyribonucleic acid),
  169, 171
Dominant traits, **169**, 172,
  174–175
Double bar graph, **112**
Drama
    concepts and analysis,
      45–48, 53
    Greek, 250, 254
    optional activities, 54
    reading selection, 49–52
Drawing conclusions (literary),
  25, 32, 37
Dynasties, **244**, 245

E

Earlobe traits, 175
Earth, living systems,
  195–200. *See also* Geology
    ecosystem, 196, 199
    food chain, 196–197
    weather, 197–198.
      See also Climate
Earthquakes, **201**, 202–203, 204
East Africa, 246
Eating habits, 188
Ecological succession, **196**
Ecologists, **195**, 196
Ecology, **195**, 196
Economic system, **281**
    capitalist, 282
    communist, 287
    socialist, 287
Ecosystem, **195**
    concepts, 196, 199
    food chain, 196–197
    pollution, 196, 198
    weather and climate,
      197–198, 200
Editing and publishing process,
  69–74
Education, Middle Ages, 257
Eggs
    cooking, 176
    reproductive path activity,
      184
Egypt, ancient *versus* modern,
  238. *See also* Ancient Egypt
Electricity, 283–284
Electronic publications, 64, 66
Electrons, **222**
Elements, **221**, 223
Encomienda, **275**, 277
Endangered species, 159–160
Energy, **211**
    consumption, 212,
      213–214
    in food chain, 196–197
    light energy, 218, 220

    optional activities, 216,
      220
    pollution effects, 198,
      213–214
    solar cooking, 215
    sound energy, 217–218,
      219
    sources, 211–213
Engineering methods, 252
England
    American Revolution,
      271, 272, 287–288,
      291
    Industrial Revolution,
      281, 282, 283
Enlightenment, **275**, 277–278
Environment, 188. *See also*
  Ecosystem; Pollution
Equations, **119**, **121**, 123
Equilateral triangle, **141**
Equivalent fractions, **83**–84,
  87, 90, 100
Erie Canal, 283
Erosion, **202**
Escher drawings, 148
Estimating
    fractions, 86
    percents, 100–101
Europe
    Christian Church,
      261–263
    Middle Ages, 255–260
    Reformation, 271–273
    Renaissance, 265–270
    revolutions and world
      wars, 287–291
Evaluating
    biographical selection,
      32, 37
    folktale selection, 24, 25
    personal narrative,
      69–70, 73
Exchange rates activity, 98
Experimental test, **192**, 193
Explanatory writing, 68
Explorers, 276–277, 279
Eye color traits, 174–175

F

Factorization, prime, 79–81
Factory system, 282–283
Fact *versus* opinion, 14
Fertile, **231**
Fertile Crescent
    civilizations, 232–234
    location, 231, 232, 235
    optional activities, 236
Feudalism, **255**
Feudal systems, **255**
    European, 255–260
    Japanese, 245
Fiction. *See also specific type
  of fiction*
    analysis, 3–4
    optional activities, 11–12
    reading excerpt, 5–9
    story cube, 10

Fish, 154, 157, 158
Flipping motion, 142, 146
Florence, Italy, 266–267
Flower, elements, 165
Flyer, designing, 160
Folktales, **23**
    concepts and analysis,
      13–16, 23–26
    optional activities, 22
    reading selections,
      17–20, 27–30
    structure and character
      traits, 21
Food, nutrition, 188.
  See also Cooking
Food chain, 196–197
Fossil fuels, **195**, **211**
    consumption, 213
    pollution effects, 198,
      213–214
    types, 198, 212, 213
Fractions
    adding and subtracting,
      83–84, 87
    converting percents to,
      99–100, 103
    equivalent, 83–84, 87,
      90, 100
    estimating, 86
    improper, 83, 84, 85, 86
    multiplying and dividing,
      84–86, 88
    optional activities, 90
    roll-them game, 89
Free verse, 40
French Revolution, 288, 291
Frequencies, sound wave,
  217, 218
Frequency table, 113, 114,
  116
Fruit fly activity, 159
Fusion, **207**, 208

G

Galilei, Galileo, 276
GCF (Greatest common factor),
  79–81
Generalization
    by author, 14, 47
    by reader, 25, 37, 56
Genes, **169**, 171–172
Genetics, **169**
    concepts, 171–172
    traits, 172, 174–175
Geology
    catastrophic events,
      202–203
    Earth's layers, 203–204
    erosion and deposition,
      202
    landforms and oceans,
      203
    minerals, 201, 202, 205
    optional activities, 206
    plate tectonics, 201,
      203, 204

Index

Note: Page numbers in bold indicate the definition of a term.

Geometry, **139, 275.** *See also*
  specific shape
    angles, 140, 141
    area, 133, 134–135, 137,
      138
    line concepts, 140, 143
    motion, 142, 146, 148
    optional activities, 148
    perimeter, 133–134, 137
    volume, 136, 138
Geothermal power, **211,** 212
Germany, 288, 289
Germination, **161,** 162–163
Ghana, 246
Gifted students, xvii–xviii
Globe Theater activity, 54
Golden Age of Athens, 250
Gothic architecture, **257,** 260
Government
    ancient Greece, 250
    ancient Rome, 251
    Enlightenment, 277–278
    Middle Ages, 256
    poll activity, 264
    Reformation and,
      271–273
    Renaissance Florence, 267
Graph book activity, 118
Graphs
    analyzing and creating,
      113–118
    coordinate grid, 124
    optional activities, 118
    types, 112–114
Gravity exercise, 210
Greatest common factor
  (GCF), **79–**81
Greece, ancient, 249–251, 253
Grid, 355
Growth, human stages,
  187–188, 189

H

Habitat, **195,** 196
Hammurabi, 233
Handedness traits, 174–175
Hannibal, 251
Health
    communicable disease,
      187, 188, 190
    immune system, 187,
      188, 190
    nutrition, 188
Heart, **177**
    function and structure,
      178–179, 181–182
    measuring rate of, 186
    modeling activity, 184
Heat energy, 212–213
Herbivores, **155, 196**
Heretic, **275**
Hieroglyphics, **239,** 242
Hinduism, 244
Histogram, **113–**114, 116
Hitler, Adolf, 289
Hobbes, Thomas, 277
Holy Roman Empire, 261–263

Homeschooling, xi, xiv
    military families, xiii
    regulations, xi–xiii
    resources, xiv–xvi
Human body
    circulatory system,
      178–179, 181–182
    developmental stages,
      187–188, 189
    immune system, 187,
      188, 190
    nervous system, 179, 183
    optional activities,
      184–186, 190
    reproductive system, 180
Humanism, **265,** 266
Hydroelectric power, **211,** 212
Hypothesis, **191,** 192, 193

I

Imagery, **3,** 4, 25
Immune system, **187,** 188, 190
Improper fraction, **83,** 84, 85,
  86
Incan civilization, 277, 280
Independence, **271,** 272
Indian civilization, 243–244
Industrial Revolution
    elements and conditions,
      281–284
    invention time line, 285
    optional activities, 286
Infancy, **187,** 189
Inferrence (literary), 3, 15,
  24, 37
Integers, **119**
    adding and subtracting,
      120–121
    coordinate grids,
      121–122, 124
    number lines, 120, 123
Interest rate, **101–**102
Intersecting lines, **140,** 143
Intervals, **113**
Inventions, 282, 283–284, 285
Invertebrates, **154,** 158
Islam, 234
Isosceles triangle, **141**
Israel, 234
Israelite civilization, 233–234
Italy
    nationalism and world
      war, 288, 289
    Renaissance, 265,
      266–267

J

Japan
    feudalism, 245, 247
    World War II, 289–290
Jesus, 252
Joan of Arc skit, 264
John, King of England, 258
Journal activity, 280
Judaism, 234

K

Kennedy, John F., 113
Kepler, Johannes, 276
Kiev, Russia, 262
Kingdom Animalia, **153.**
  See also Animals
Knights, **255,** 256, 260
Kublai Khan, 245

L

Labor union, **281,** 283
Landforms, 203
Languages, origin, 233.
  See also Writing systems
Laws
    Hammurabi's Code, 233
    Magna Carta and, 258
LCM (least common multiple),
  80
Learning styles, 179
Least common multiple
  (LCM), 80
Legal system. *See* Laws
Length, units of, 125–126, 129
Lenses, light reflection, 220
Leviathan, 277
Library
    plant library activity, 168
    reference materials, 63–64
Life cycle
    animal, 154
    fruit fly activity, 159
    plant, 164
Light energy, 218, 220, 280
Line(s)
    geometric, **140,** 143
    number, 120, 123
    time line, 69, 274, 285
Line graph, **112,** 115, 116
Line segment, **140**
Linnaeus, Carolus, 154
Liquid state, changing to/from,
  222, 223, 225
Listening
    modeling and practicing,
      55
    optional activities, 61–62
    reading selection, 57–60
Literary concepts
    evaluating, 25, 32, 37
Literacy skills. *See also*
  specific skill
    assessment, 295–306
    assessment answers,
      335–336
Literature
    biography, 33–36
    classics, 266
    drama, 49–52, 250
    fiction excerpt, 5–9
    folktales, 17–20, 27–30
    Middle Ages, 258
    poetry, 41–42, 267
Lithosphere, **203,** 204
Locke, John, 277
Logic, **275**

Lords, 255–256
Luther, Martin, 272, 274

M

Machines, Industrial
    Revolution and, 282,
      283–285
Magazines reader poll, 104
Magna Carta, **258**
Magnification activity, 176.
  See also Microscopes
Mail (armor), **256**
Main idea, 55, 56, 68
Mali, 246
Mammals, 154, 157, 158
Manor, **257**
Mantle, **203**
Maps/mapping
    coordinate grids, 122, 124
    Crusades, 263
    Egypt, 238, 241
    Fertile Crescent, 232, 235
    Holy Roman Empire, 263
    Italy, 266
    map scale, 106
    Reformation sites, 272
    Renaissance Europe, 267
    topographic map, 206
    Web sites and electronic
      publications, 66
Marco Polo, 245
Mass, **125**
    conversion exercises,
      129–130
    metric units, 127
    versus weight, 127
Mathematics
    assessment, 307–316
    assessment answers,
      336–337
    data, statistics, and
      graphs, 111–118
    decimals, 91–98
    fractions, 83–90
    geometry, 139–148
    integers, 119–124
    motion geometry, 142,
      146, 148
    number theory, 79–82
    percents, 99–104
    perimeter, area, and
      volume, 133–138
    ratios, proportions, and
      probability, 105–110
Matter, 211, **221**
    acids and bases, 223–224
    elements and chemical
      symbols, 223
    energy waves and, 212,
      217
    properties and reactions,
      222–223, 225
    salts, 224
Mayan civilization, 277
Mean, **111,** 112, 115

Measurement(s). *See also*
  Customary measuring
  system; Metric measuring
  system
    capacity units, 127–128
    common factors activity,
      82
    conversion exercises,
      129–130
    heart rate, 186
    heat units, 213
    length units, 125–126
    mass units, 127
    optional activities, 132
    speed of light and sound,
      218
    time zones, 128, 132
    waves of energy, 212
    weight units, 126–127
Median, **111,** 112, 115
Medulla oblongata, **177,** 179,
  183
Membrane of cell, **170**
Mesopotamia, 231. *See also*
  Fertile Crescent
Messiah, **249,** 252
Metaphor, **3,** 4, 40, 46
Metric conversion table, 130
Metric measuring system, **125**
    abbreviations, 126, 127,
      128
    capacity units, 127–128
    conversion exercises,
      129–130
    length units, 126
    mass units, 127
Michelangelo, 267
Microscopes
    components, 171
    slide preparation and
      analysis, 173
Middle Ages
    arts and education,
      257–258
    coat of arms, 256, 259
    feudal system, 255–258
    legal system, 258
    optional activities, 260
    Renaissance and, 266
Middle East. *See* Fertile
  Crescent
Military families,
  homeschooling, xiii
Minerals, **201,** 202, 205
Mining, 214
Mirrors, light reflection, 220
Mitosis, **169,** 171
Mixed number, **83,** 84, 85, 86
MLA style, 63, 64, 66
Mobile project, 11–12
Mode, **111,** 112, 115
Modern Language Association
  of America (MLA) style, 63,
  64, 66
Modern society, origins.
  See Renaissance
Mold growth experiment, 194
Monarchs activity, 264
Monsoon, **243**

Montesquieu, Baron de, 277
Moons, **207,** 208
Morse code activity, 286
Motion geometry, 142, 146,
  148
Muhammad, 234
Multiplication
    converting units of
      measure by, 126
    of decimals, 93–94, 96
    of fractions, 84–86, 88
    in percent calculations,
      100, 101–104
    in probability calculations,
      107
Mushroom spore print activity,
  168
Music
    Enlightenment, 277
    19th century songs
      activity, 286
    war songs activity, 292
Muslims, 234
Mussolini, Benito, 289

N

Napoléon, 288
Narrative writing, 68
National Audubon Society, 194
Nationalism, **261,** 262, **287,** 288
Natural resources, **281**
    energy sources, 212, 213
    industrialism and, 281
    nonrenewable, 213, 216
    oceans, 203
Nebuchadnezzar, 233
Negative integers, **119**
Nerves, **177,** 179, 183
Nervous system, **177,** 179, 183
Neurons, **177,** 179, 183
Neutrons, **222**
Newscast, writing, 66
Newspaper articles
    family newspaper project,
      66
    identifying 5 Ws and H in,
      65
Newton, Isaac, 276
Nile River, **237**–238
Nobles, **255**
Nonfiction reading selection,
  57–60
Nonrenewable resources, 213,
  216. *See also* Natural
  resources
Nonvascular plants, **161,** 164
Notetaking, 56
Notre Dame cathedral activity,
  260
Novel, **13**
Nucleus
    atom, 169, 222
    cell, 170, 171
Number line, 120, 123
Number theory, 79–82
Numerals, Arabic and Roman,
  254

Numerator, **83**
Nutrients/nutrition, **187,** 188

O

Observation, **191,** 192, 193
Obtuse angle, **139**
Obtuse triangle, **141**
Oceans, 203
Oil spills, 213–214
Olmec civilization, 277
Olympic Games, 250
Omnivores, **197**
Onomatopoeia, **13,** 14, 22
Opinion, 14, 47
Oral folktale, 23–24. *See also*
  Folktales
Orbit, **207,** 209
Ordered pair, **119,** 122
Organelles, **171**
Orienteering, 206
Osmosis, **161,** 163
Ottoman Empire, 245

P

Palestine, 261–262, 263
Papyrus, **238**
Parallel lines, **140,** 143
Parallelogram, area, **134**–135
Paraphrasing, **3**
    as notes, 56
    reading selection, 3–4, 16
Parliament, **287,** 289
Patricians, **251**
Pedigree charts, 172
Percents, **99**
    converting fractions and
      decimals to, 99–103
    optional activities, 104
Perennial plants, **161,** 164
Perimeter, **133**–134, 137
Periodic table, **221,** 223
Perpendicular lines, **140,** 143
Personal knowledge, 15
Personal narrative, 68
    reading selection, 71
    writing process, 68–70
Personification, 40
Persuasive writing, 67
Petroleum-based products, 206
Pharaoh, **238,** 239
Philosophers, **249,** 250
Philosophy, **249,** 250
Phoenician civilization, 233
Photo essay, 160
Photosynthesis, **161**
    etymology of
      photosynthesis, 163
    process, 162, 166
Physical properties of matter,
  221, 222
Pictograph, **111,** 118
Pie slicing activity, 148
Pilgrimages, **261**–262
Pizarro, Francisco, 277
Plague, **265**–266, 270

Planets, 208, 209
Plant library activity, 168
Plants, 161–168
    acid effects exercise, 216
    cell structure, 170–172
    characteristics and
      processes, 162–164, 165
    classifying, 164
    dandelion research, 192,
      193
    in food chain, 196
    oldest living forms, 164
    optional activities, 168
Plates, **203**
Plate tectonics, **201,** 203, 204
Play. *See* Drama
Plebeian, **251**
Poetry
    concepts and analysis,
      39–40, 43
    free verse, 40
    optional activities, 44
    reading selections, 41–42
    Renaissance and, 267
Poetry log, 43
Point, geometric, **140**
Polling activities
    magazine readers, 104
    religion and government,
      264
Pollution, 198
    food chain, 196
    fossil fuel, 198, 213–214
Polygon, **133**
    perimeter and area,
      134–135
    types, 142
Positive integers, **119**
Prediction
    and inference, literary,
      3, 15, 24, 37
    of probable outcomes,
      110
    in scientific method,
      191, 192, 193
Preview, reading selection, 37
Prime factorization, 79–81
Prime numbers, **79**–81
Principal, interest on, **101**–102
Prism experiment, 280
Probability, **105,** 106–108, 110
Problem resolution, literary,
  21, 47
Producers (food chain), **196**
Proofreading
    checklist, 72
    nature and purpose, 69
Prophet, **234**
Proportions, **105,** 106, 109, 110
Protons, **222**
Protractor, **139**
Ptolemy, 276
Publishing, 70
Pulmonary circulation, **178,** 182
Punctuation
    abbreviation for *inches,*
      125
    direct quote, 56
    proofing, 69, 73

Index

Note: Page numbers in bold indicate the definition of a term.

Punnett Squares, 174
Pyramid(s)
 Ancient Egyptian, 239
 modeling activity, 242
 temple pyramids, 277
 volume, calculating, 136

Q

Quadrilaterals, **133**
 area, 134, 137
 length of side or angle in, 145
 sum of angles in, 142
 types, 141, 145
Questions, five Ws and H, 64, 65
Quilt, creating, 38
Quipu, 280
Quote, punctuation, 56

R

Radius, **135**
Railroads, 283
Range (mathematical), **111**, 112, 115
Rate (ratio), **109**
Rate of interest, **101**–102
Ratios, **105**–106, 109, 110
Ray, geometric, **140**, 143
Reading. *See* Literature
Reagan, Ronald, 113
Recessive traits, **169**, 172, 174–175
Recipes
 calculating costs, 90
 cookbook activity, 185
Record-keeping activity, 280
Rectangle, perimeter and area, **134**–135
Rectangular prism, volume, **136**, 138
Recycling, 206
Reference materials, 63–64
Reflection
 geometric, 142, 146
 light, 218, 220
Reform, **271**, 272, 274
Reformation
 causes and effects, 271–273
 optional activities, 274
Refraction of light, **217**, 218, 220
Reincarnation, **244**
Religion
 ancient Egyptian, 239
 Buddhism, 244
 Christianity, 252, 261–263, 271–273
 Hinduism, 244
 Islam, 234
 Judaism, 234
 polling activity, 264
 Reformation and, 271–273

Renaissance, **265**
 crossword puzzle, 269
 elements, 266–268
 optional activities, 270
Reporter activity, 62
Reproduction
 cell division, 171
 male and female systems, 180
 path of egg activity, 184
Reptiles, 154, 157, 158
Republic, **249**
 Florence, 267
 Rome, 251
Research sources, selecting and citing MLA style, 63–64
Resources, nonrenewable, 213, 216. *See also* Natural resources
Respiration, **161**
 carbon dioxide experiment, 185–186
 plant, 163
Revising, personal narrative, 69, 70
Revolutions, **287**
 American, 271, 287–288
 comparing, 291
 French, 288
 optional activities, 292
 Russian, 289
Rhythm, poetic, 39
Richter scale, 204
Right angle, **139**
Right triangle, **141**
Rock cycle, **201**, 202. *See also* Geology
Rocks, **202**
 geologic principles, 202–204
 mineral identification, 205
Role-playing. *See* Acting
Roll-them fractions, 89
Roman architecture, 252, 257
Roman Empire. *See* Rome
Roman numerals, 254
Rome
 ancient era, 251–253
 Holy Roman Empire, 261–263
Romeo and Juliet, 268
 analyzing, 45–48, 53
 reading selection, 49–52
Rope activity (quipu), 280
Rosetta Stone, **239**
Rotation, geometric, 142, 146
Rounding
 mixed numbers, 86
 percents, 100–101
Rousseau, Jean-Jacques, 277
Russia
 Cold War, 290
 founding and growth, 262
 Russian Revolution, 289, 291
 World War I, 288–289
Russian Revolution, 289, 291

S

Sales tax, 101
Salts, 224
Samurai, **245**
Scale
 map scale, 106
 scale drawing, 110
Scalene triangle, **141**
Scavenger hunt, 61
Scavengers (food chain), **197**
School, communicating with, xvii–xviii
Science
 animal kingdom, 153–160
 assessment, 317–326
 assessment answers, 337–339
 cells, genetics, and microscopes, 169–176
 classification, 153–155, 158, 164
 Earth's living systems, 195–200
 Earth's surface, 201–206
 energy, 211–216
 human body systems, 177–186
 human health and growth, 187–190
 matter, 221–226
 plant kingdom, 161–168
 scientific method, 191–194
 sound and light, 217–220
 universe, 207–210
Scientific method, 191–194
Scoring rubric, personal narrative, 69–70, 73
Script writing
 fictional scene, 11
 newscast, 66
 world leaders' chat, 292
Sculpting activity, 270
Seeds
 experimenting with, 192, 193
 germination, 162–163
Seismograph, 204
Sequence chain graphic organizer, 354
Sequence of events
 comic strip, 22
 personal narrative, 69
 photosynthesis, 166
 reading selection, 24
Serfs, **257**
Shakespeare, William, 267–268
Shang dynasty, 244, 247
Shihuangdi, 244
Shogun, **243**, 245
Shopping activities
 comparison shopping, 104
 exchange rate, calculating, 98
 sales tax, calculating, 101, 104

Short story, **13**. *See also* Drama; Folktales
Simile, 40, 46
Simple interest, **101**–102
Singing. *See* Songs/singing activity
Sixth graders, xix–xxii
Skew lines, **140**
Skit, Joan of Arc, 264
Slide motion, 142, 146
Slides, microscope, 173
Smith, Adam, 282
Social classes
 ancient Egyptian, 238
 caste system, 244
 feudal, 247, 256
 French estates, 288
 Roman, 251
 Shang dynasty, 247
Socialists, **287**, 289
Social studies
 ancient civilizations, 231–236
 ancient Egypt, 237–242
 ancient Greece and Rome, 249–254
 Asian and African cultures, 243–248
 assessment, 327–334
 assessment answers, 339–340
 beginnings of modern society, 265–270
 Christian Church and monarchies, 261–264
 European Middle Ages, 255–260
 Reformation, 271–274
Solar power, 211, 215
Solar system, **207**–208
Solid state, changing to/from, 222, 223, 225
Songhai, 246
Songs/singing activity
 19th century songs, 286
 war songs, 292
Sonnet, **267**
Sound energy, 217–218, 219
Sources, citing MLA style, 63–64
Soviet Union, 290. *See also* Russia
Space museum, 210
Special needs students, xvii
Species, **195**, 196
Speed of light and sound, 218
Spelling, proofing, 69, 73
Spinal cord and nerves, **177**, 179, 183
Spore print, 168
Square, area, **134**
Stalin, Joseph, 289
Stars, **208**
Statistics, interpreting and presenting, 111–118. *See also* Graphs
Stomata, **161**, 163
Story cube, 10
Story quilt, creating, 38

Note: Page numbers in bold indicate the definition of a term.

Story structure, 21, 47, 53
Storytelling activity, 22
Straight angle, **139**
Subtraction
  of decimals, 91–92, 95
  of fractions, 83–84, 87
  of integers, 120
Succession, ecological, **196**
Sumerian civilization, 232
Sun, 208, 211, 212
Supporting details, 55, 56
Symbolism, **3**, 4, 25
Symbols
  chemical, 223
  cuneiform, 232
  geometric, 140, 143
  hieroglyphics, 239
Systemic circulation, **178**

T

Tally Aunt Sally, 175
Taxonomy categories, 153–154
Technology
  cleaner fuels, 214
  space program, 210
Teenage Mutant Ninja Turtles, 267
Temperature
  changing states of matter, 222
  measurement scales, 213
Temples
  temple pyramids, 277
  ziggurats, 231, 232
Textile, **281**
Textile industry, 282
Theater. *See* Drama
Theories, **275**
  number theory, 79–82
  origin of language, 233
  origins and processes of universe, 208, 276
Thermal energy, **211**, 212
Time capsule activity, 248
Time line
  history of democracy/ capitalism, 274
  machine inventions, 285
  personal narrative, 69
Time zones, 128
  time comparisons across, 131
  travel activity, 132
Tombs
  Egyptian pyramids, 239
  Shang dynasty, 244, 248
Topographic map, 206, 267
Topography, **202**
Tower of Babel, 233
Traits, genetic, **169**, 172, 174–175. *See also* Character traits
Translation, geometric, 142, 146
Transpiration, **161**, 163
Transportation, commercial, 283
Travel

ancient era, 233
New World explorers, 276–277, 277
time zone activity, 132
Triangles, **133**
  area, 134, 137
  sum of angles, 141
  types, 141
Triangular prism, volume, 136
Truman, Harry, 290
Tsunami, **201**, 202
Turkish Empire, 245
Turning motion, 142, 146
Tutankhamen, King "Tut," 239, 240

U

United States
  American Revolution, 271, 272, 287–288, 291
  ancient influences, 250, 251, 252, 253
  presidential histogram, 113–114
  time zones, 128, 131
  world wars, 288–290
Units of measure. *See* Measurement(s)
Universe, **207**
  components, 207–208
  optional activities, 210
  planet orbit activity, 209
  theories, 208, 276

V

Vacuole, **169**, 170, 171
Vascular plants, **161**, 164
Vassals, **255**, 256
Veins, **177**, 179
Venn Diagram graphic organizer, 353
Vertebrates, **154**, 158
Vertex, **140**, 143
Veto power, **249**, 251
Vibration, **217**
Vikings, 276
Volcanism, **202**
Volcanoes, **201**, 202–203, 204
Voltaire, 277
Volume, **136**, 138
Voting rights, ancient Athens, 250

W

War. *See* Revolutions; World War *entries*
Warm-blooded animals, **153**, 154, 155
Water, geologic cycles, 202
Waves, energy, 212. *See also* Light energy; Sound energy
Weapons, Middle Ages, 256
Weather, **197**–198

Web. *See* World Wide Web sites
Web graphic organizer, 354
Weight, **125**
  conversion exercises, 129–130
  customary units, 126–127
  versus mass, 127
West African civilizations, 246
Workforce and work conditions
  advertisement activity, 286
  industrial era, 281–283
  Middle Ages, 257
World health, 188
World War I, 288–289
World War II, 289–290
World Wide Web sites
  citing, MLA style, 64
  navigating, 66
Writing process, 155
  editing and publishing, 68–73
  researching and referencing sources, 63–65
Writing styles, 67–68
Writing systems
  alphabet, 233
  creating your own, 236, 242
  cuneiform, 232, 236
  hieroglyphics, 239, 242

X

Xylem, **161**, 163

Z

Ziggurats, **231**, 232
Zimbabwe, 246

Credits

Art & Photo Credits

Promoting Literacy
Background/Icon: Creatas LLC
Opener (page 1): © PhotoDisc; Amy DeVoogd/Artville, LLC
Page 7: © PhotoDisc; 9: Carol Stutz Illustration; 10: Precision Graphics;
12: Carol Stutz Illustration; 15: Precision Graphics; 21: PP/FA, Inc.;
29: © Getty Images; 34: © Lance Lekander/Getty Images;
36: © PhotoDisc; 43: PP/FA, Inc.; 51: © Jonnie Miles/Getty Images;
53: PP/FA, Inc.; 59, 64: © PhotoDisc; 68: © Stockbyte; 73: PP/FA, Inc.

Math
Background/Icon: © Royalty-Free/CORBIS
Opener (page 77): © PhotoDisc
Page 79, 80, 83: Precision Graphics; 85: © EyeWire Collection/
Getty Images; 89 (top): Precision Graphics; 89 (bottom): PP/FA, Inc.;
90: Precision Graphics; 92: © EyeWire Collection/Getty Images;
97: Precision Graphics; 99: © Chet Phillips/Getty Images;
103 (top): Precision Graphics; 103 (bottom): PP/FA, Inc.; 106, 107,
110, 112, 113, 114: Precision Graphics; 115 (top): PP/FA, Inc.;
115 (bottom), 116, 118, 120, 121, 123, 124, 130: Precision Graphics;
130: PP/FA, Inc.; 134, 135, 136, 137, 138, 140, 141, 142, 143, 144,
145, 146, 147: Precision Graphics

Science
Background/Icon: © Royalty-Free/CORBIS
Opener (page 151): © Royalty-Free/CORBIS
Page 157: Carol Stutz Illustration; 157, 158: PP/FA, Inc.; 165,
167: Precision Graphics; 168: © Royalty-Free/CORBIS; 170, 172,
174: Precision Graphics; 175: PP/FA, Inc.; 176: Carol Stutz
Illustration; 180, 181, 182: Precision Graphics; 183: PP/FA, Inc.;
188: Precision Graphics; 189: PP/FA, Inc.; 193: Precision Graphics;
197: © Don Farrall/Getty Images; 200: PP/FA, Inc.; 202,
203: Precision Graphics; 208: © PhotoDisc; 209: PP/FA, Inc.;
212, 215, 218: Precision Graphics; 219: PP/FA, Inc.; 222,
224: Precision Graphics

Social Studies
Background/Icon: © PhotoDisc
Opener (page 229): © PhotoDisc
Page 232: © Gianni Dagli Orti/CORBIS; 235, 241: Mapping
Specialists, Ltd.; 245: Dynamic Graphics; 247, 253: PP/FA, Inc.;
254, 256: Precision Graphics; 259: © PhotoDisc; 263, 266: Mapping
Specialists, Ltd.; 269: Precision Graphics; 279: Mapping Specialists,
Ltd.; 285: Precision Graphics; 289: © CORBIS; 289: © Bettmann/
CORBIS; 291: PP/FA, Inc.

Page 308, 311, 312, 313, 314 (top): Precision Graphics;
314 (bottom): Carol Stutz Illustration; 315 (top left): PP/FA, Inc.;
315 (top right, bottom), 317, 318: Precision Graphics; 324: PP/FA,
Inc.; 325, 326, 330, 334, 337, 343, 344, 350: Precision Graphics;
353, 354, 355: PP/FA, Inc.

Literature Credits

5–9, Chapter One from THE SIGN OF THE BEAVER by Elizabeth George
Speare. Copyright © 1983 by Elizabeth George Speare. Reproduced
by permission of Houghton Mifflin Company. All rights reserved.

17–20, From THE ELEPHANT'S BATHTUB by Frances Carpenter,
copyright © 1962 by Frances Carpenter Huntington. Used by
permission of Doubleday, a division of Random House, Inc.

27–30, "A Frog's Gift", from MYSTERIOUS TALES OF JAPAN by
Rafe Martin, copyright © 1996 by Rafe Martin, text. Used by
permission of G.P. Putnam's Sons, an imprint of Penguin Putnam
Books for Young Readers, a division of Penguin Putnam Inc. All
rights reserved.

33–36, From *Albert Einstein and the Theory of Relativity* by Robert
Cwiklik. Copyright © 1987 by Eisen, Durwood & Co., Inc. Reprinted
by arrangement with Barron's Educational Series, Inc.

41, Bobbi Katz for "October Saturday." Copyright © 1990 by
Bobbi Katz. Reprinted with permission of the author.

42, Permission of Felice Holman. Copyright 1985. From *The Song in
My Head* published by Charles Scribner's Sons.

49–52, From *Romeo and Juliet* by William Shakespeare. Copyright ©
2002 by Barron's Educational Series, Inc. Reprinted by arrangement
with Barron's Educational Series, Inc.

57–60, From *Winning Women in Soccer* by Marlene Targ Brill.
Copyright © 1999 by Marlene Targ Brill. Reprinted by arrangement
with Barron's Educational Series, Inc.

332–333, Reproduced by kind permission of ticktock Media Ltd,
a division of ticktock Entertainment Ltd. Copyright ticktock
Entertainment Ltd 2002.